LIFE OF A PIONEER

JAMES S. BROWN

AMS PRESS
NEW YORK

James S Brown

LIFE OF A

PIONEER

BEING THE

AUTOBIOGRAPHY

OF

JAMES S. BROWN.

SALT LAKE CITY, UTAH:

GEO. Q. CANNON & SONS CO., PRINTERS.

1900.

Reprinted from the edition of 1900, Salt Lake City

First AMS edition published in 1971
Manufactured in the United States of America

International Standard Book Number: 0-404-08432-X

Library of Congress Catalog Card Number: 78-134389

AMS PRESS INC.
NEW YORK, N.Y. 10003

PREFACE.

THE life of a pioneer in Western America always is full of peril and hardship; often it has a large share of startling episodes and thrilling adventures; not infrequently it is associated with notable historic events; and the experiences met with develop independence of character, firmness of purpose, and, in those whose spiritual nature is not dwarfed by unworthy conduct, a sublime faith in God that when man puts forth his highest endeavor all things beyond the scope of his efforts are ordered for the best by the Great Ruler of the universe. When to the pioneer's experiences are added those that come from travel in foreign lands, perils of the sea, and the hostility of warlike foes, the narrative of such a life cannot fail to be alike profitable and interesting reading to both young and old.

The subject of the autobiographical sketch in this volume feels that he is not presumptuous in saying that each class of experience named in relation to the pioneer and the traveler has been his. The perils and hardships of the pioneers in whose work he commingled have been the theme of song and story for half a century; the thrilling and adventurous character of his experiences as frontiersman and Indian interpreter were of a kind notable even in those avocations; his association with historic events of moment includes the period when the territorial area of the great Republic was almost doubled by the acquisition of the Pacific slope and the Rocky Mountain region, and when the great gold discovery in California was made, since he was a member of the famous Mormon Battalion and also was present at the finding of gold in California, being the first man to declare—on tests made by himself—that the little yellow flakes were the precious metal; and his reliance on Deity is portrayed in his missionary work at home and in foreign lands, with civilized people and among savages, often in circumstances when life itself apparently was forfeit to duty conscientiously performed.

In the following pages there is no claim to transcendent literary merit. Yet the writer feels that the narrative is presented in the plain and simple language of the people, with a clearness and force of expression that will be pleasing and impressive to every reader possessed of ordinary or of superior educational attainments; while the very simplicity and directness of the language used, far from embellishing the events described, prove an invaluable guide in securing accuracy, that not an incident shall be overdrawn or given undue importance.

The purpose of the writer has been to relate the story of his life, for the benefit and entertainment of his children and friends, and of all others who may read it, and to do so with a strict regard for veracity; for he feels that the numerous thrilling and sensational incidents in his life were sufficiently exciting to bear a toning down that comes from calm contemplation when the agitation of the immediate occurrence has passed, rather than to need the coloring of a graphic pen. In such a presentation, too, he feels that the result of his labors in this respect will be a further step in carrying out that which has been the leading purpose of his life, namely, to do good to all mankind, to the glory of God.

With a fervent desire and firm confidence that every worthy aim in presenting this autobiography shall be achieved, and shall find a vigorous and ennobling response in the hearts of those who read it, the leading events of his life, and the narration thereof, are respectfully submitted to his family and friends by

THE AUTHOR.

CONTENTS.

CHAPTER I.

CHAPTER II.

CHAPTER III.

CHAPTER IV.

CHAPTER V.

CONTENTS.

CONTENTS.

CHAPTER XXXIX.

CHAPTER XL.

CHAPTER XLI.

CHAPTER XLII.

CHAPTER LX.

CHAPTER LXI.

CHAPTER LXII.

CHAPTER LXIII.

CHAPTER LXIV.

CHAPTER LXV.

CHAPTER LXVI.

CHAPTER LXVII.

CHAPTER LXVIII.

ILLUSTRATIONS.

LIFE OF A PIONEER.

BEING

THE AUTOBIOGRAPHY

OF

JAMES S. BROWN.

CHAPTER I.

HOME OF THE AUTHOR—A CAREER OF THRILLING EXPERIENCES—HIS
BIRTH AND PARENTAGE—EARLY AVOCATIONS—MIGRATION FROM
NORTH CAROLINA TO ILLINOIS—LIFE ON THE FRONTIER—DAN-
GERS TO EARLY SETTLERS—A FRONTIERSMAN—FATHER'S ADVICE
—MORE SETTLERS COME—CHURCHES AND SCHOOLS—LIMITED
OPPORTUNITIES—FROZEN FEET—UNIMPRESSIONABLE TO THE
PREACHING OF THE TIME—TALK OF A NEW RELIGION, PROPHETS,
MIRACLES, ETC. —PERSECUTION OF THE NEW CHURCH—"SHOWERS
OF STARS"—POPULAR ADVERSE VIEWS OF THE MORMONS—THE
MORMONS DRIVEN FROM MISSOURI INTO ILLINOIS—MORMON
ELDER COMES TO PREACH—CONVERTS UNCLE JAMES BROWN—
PREACHES AGAIN—PREPARATIONS TO MOB THE ELDER—HIS
SCRIPTURAL DOCTRINE DISCONCERTS ENEMIES AND SECURES
HIM FRIENDS—HIS DISCOURSE—EFFECT ON YOUNG JAMES S.
BROWN OF THIS FIRST GOSPEL SERMON TO HIM—HIS TESTIMONY
TO THE SPIRIT AND TRUTH OF THE ELDER'S MESSAGE.

THE subject and author of this Life-Sketch of a Pioneer
is James Stephens Brown, now (1900) in his seventy-
second year, a resident of Salt Lake City, Utah, his home
less than a quarter of a mile from and within the summer
morning's shadow of the majestic Temple of the Lord
erected on that spot which he beheld a barren and desolate

wilderness, on his entrance into the valley of the Great Salt Lake, over half a century ago. His life has been one of thrilling experiences—more than ordinarily falls to the lot even of a pioneer settler in the Great West—a life in which hardship and perils by sea and land, among dusky savages and with white men, have contributed largely to the events of his career; withal one in which he has had abundant occasion to recognize and acknowledge the power and protecting care of an Almighty Providence.

It is at the urgent request and advice of valued friends, familiar to a considerable extent with my life and labors, that I place this autobiography in form to be easily accessible to those desirous of perusing it; and I am not unmindful of the fact that this simple recital of events is not only of intense interest in numerous episodes which it records, but is of historic value in being a plain and truthful narrative of the personal experiences of a western pioneer.

I was born on Independence Day, July 4, 1828, in Davidson County, North Carolina, U. S. A. My father was Daniel Brown; he was the youngest son of his father's family, and was born in Rowan County, North Carolina, June 30, 1804. My father's father was James Brown, a native of Rowan County, North Carolina, 1757 being the year of his birth. His wife was the widow of a Revolutionary War soldier named Emerson, who was killed in the war for American independence, leaving his wife and two children, Margaret and John Emerson. My grandfather James Brown married the widow Emerson, who bore him nine children—three sons and six daughters—Jane, Polly, Nancy, Susan, Patsy, William, Obedience, James (captain of Company C, Mormon Battalion), and Daniel (my father); her maiden name was Mary Williams. All the family had an excellent reputation, being upright, thrifty, and good and industrious citizens.

With these introductory remarks, I will proceed to an

account of my boyhood's days. I was reared at the farming and stock business, also at getting out saw timber and wood for cooperware.   My parents had moved from North Carolina to Brown County, Illinois, in the autumn of 1831, and had purchased an extensive tract of land.   We were a large family; the country was then wild and with very few inhabitants, and the climate was unhealthy; so it was with great effort that father and mother succeeded in making a home and gathering about them the comforts of life.

We were frontier settlers, and while father had his pick of land, he also had the hardships and privations of a new country to endure.   There were no churches or schoolhouses nearer than ten miles from our home, and grist mills and blacksmith shops were equally distant.   Thus the family was reared without the advantage of schools, or of church-going religious training.   But we were thoroughly acquainted with border life, with hunting, fishing, and all the sports indulged in by hardy pioneers, and even learned to shake terribly from the ague, and burn with fever spells, while we were well dosed with quinine and calomel, and had enormous doctor's bills to pay.

In our operations we trained horses and cattle to work, stocked our own plows, made our own harrows, rakes and forks, braided our own whips from the pelts of wild beasts which we ourselves dressed, raised our own honey, and made our own sugar, with some to sell.   We had a good sugar orchard, and plenty of wild fruits and nuts for the gathering.   As the first settlers of new countries are more or less subject to dangers from outlaws, wild beasts, and savage men, we found it important to be well armed, and on the alert day and night to defend life and liberty.

Thus we learned the use of firearms and the tomahawk.   My father was an expert with the old Kentucky rifle, and some of his boys were not far behind him; he trained them always to shoot with a rising sight, to keep cool, and always to have their powder dry and plenty of it. He also taught us to tell the truth, and used to say: "Be honest, stand up for your rights, and fight for your country and friends."

In the year 1835, people began to settle in around us, and then the circuit riders, as they were called—the ministers—commenced to call around and hold meetings in private houses. There were Baptists, Freewill Baptists, Methodists, Campbellites, and others. From 1836 to 1838 some small churches and schoolhouses were built, so that we began to get spiritual food, such as it was; and also some schooling, with the benefit of the hickory rod that always was kept "in soak," so to speak, and woe to the unruly student when it was called into service!

So far as the author is concerned, he managed to get along without the rod the short time he was permitted to attend school. He was kept close at work on the farm in summer, and in the winter months was engaged getting out timber and hauling to market the farm products. Once his feet were frozen so that he lost every nail from his toes. As to the religious teachings of the time, there was a great deal of thundering and thundering, but it failed to indicate any lightening of the author's path, for he fished and hunted on the Sabbath day, just the same.

Some time in the '30s we began to hear a little about false prophets, a new religion, miracles, money-diggers, thieves, liars, miracle-workers, deceivers, witches, speaking in tongues and interpretation of the same, walking on the water, and visits from angels. As time went on, all these things were combined to form a grand excuse for raising mobs to expel the new Church from the borders of civilization. Then came news of murder, rapine, house-burning, and destruction of towns and cities in Missouri. There were great "showers" of stars in the firmament about this

time.   On popular rumor, and from hearing only one side
of the story, almost everybody decided that such a previously unheard-of people as the Mormons ought to be
shot or burned at the stake.   This was the sentiment to
be found on every hand.

As a culmination of these things came the tidings that
the Missourians had driven the Mormons from the state of
Missouri into Illinois.   A little later, and a Latter-day
Saint Elder named Jacob Pfoutz entered the neighborhood
of my Uncle James Brown's home, converted him, his wife,
and several of the neighbors.   This Elder was brought
down by my uncle to see his two sisters, Aunts Polly and
Nancy Brown.

Elder Pfoutz was given permission to preach in the
schoolhouse about three miles from my father's house.
The news spread like a prairie fire that the Mormons had
come and would preach on Friday.   I think this was in the
autumn of 1840.   I was at my aunt's at the time, and
decided to go and hear the strange preacher.   Like most
of the people, I went out of curiosity, more than anything
else.   I had just turned my twelfth year, and had begun to
take some interest in religion, going to every meeting
for which I could obtain permission from my parents, yet
not thinking for a moment but that all religions were right.

At the first meeting held by the Mormon, the house
was pretty well filled.   Some who attended did so with the
thought that after the services were over they would tar
and feather the Elder and ride him on a rail, as such things
had been indulged in in Missouri, and threats had been
made freely.   Others were going to confound him, and still
others wanted to see the fun, as they said.

The preacher was a plain-spoken man of thirty-five to
forty years old, of German descent.   He was plainly
dressed, and without that urbane polish which ministers
usually have.   When he began his discourse, he raised up

very calmly and deliberately,and read from Matthew,seventh chapter, verses fifteen to twenty. He spoke from that text and corroborating passages, supporting his argument throughout by scripture. At the conclusion of his address, some of the people said they did not want to mob a man who preached like that, while others "sniffed" their noses and tried to get up a sneering laugh, but failed. The Elder was invited to my aunt's house and was granted permission to preach on Sunday in their oak-grove, while several of the religiously inclined followed him to his stopping place and plied him with questions.

As to myself, it seemed that I had not only heard it thunder, but I had seen the lightning and felt it through every fibre of my system, from the crown of my head to the soles of my feet. I was revived as the showers of heaven revive the parched earth and impart life to the languishing vegetation. Notwithstanding the fact that I knew the Latter-day Saints, or Mormons, were looked upon as filth, in fact as even worse than rubbish, that they had been called the very off-scourings of the earth, that they were regarded as deserving to be put to death, yet from that very day I received their doctrine in or by the spirit.

Now that sixty years have rolled by since the events here narrated; that I have passed through mobbings, robbings, fines and penalties; have been banished and once sentenced to death; Paul-like have fought with wild beasts, have been shipwrecked and almost starved; have famished on thirsty deserts; have had the scalping-knife wielded over my head while the Indian warwhoop saluted my ears and the savage warrior danced with tomahawk in hand, exulting over the victim intended to be slain and scalped in trophy of victory; have laid in dungeons for my religion's sake—thanks be to God that I yet live and bear a faithful testimony of the truth and spirit that possessed my soul from that first Gospel sermon I ever heard. I have listened to ministers of various Christian denominations advocate good and virtuous principles, but I never knew any of them to preach the fullness of the Gospel of the Lord Jesus as did that humble Mormon Elder.

CHAPTER II.

PERSECUTED BY PLAYMATES—GIVE THEM AN EFFECTIVE CHECK—FIGHT WITH WILD BEASTS—PARENTS JOIN THE MORMONS—THE AUTHOR HOLDS BACK—ASSASSINATION OF JOSEPH AND HYRUM SMITH— MORMONS LEAVE ILLINOIS FOR THE WEST—EXCITING TIMES- MY WINTER'S WORK—FATHER DECIDES TO WAIT A WHILE BEFORE LEAVING ILLINOIS—MY DETERMINATION TO GO WITH THE MOR- MONS -CONFIDE A SECRET TO MY MOTHER—A NEW CONSULTA- TION—CHANGE IN THE FAMILY PLANS—FATHER PREPARES TO START—GIVES ME PERMISSION TO GO—THINKS OF LEAVING ME BECAUSE OF MY ILLNESS—I FEEL TO PREFER DEATH TO BEING LEFT BEHIND.

FROM the very day my parents entertained the Latter- day Saint Elders in their house my former playmates in the neighborhood commenced a crusade on me, calling me a Mormon, and many hard names, whenever they met me. When we gathered at the mill pond, our usual place of bathing, they would baptize me, as they called it, in the name of Beelzebub; but I called it drowning, for it seemed to me that when three or four of them got me under the water they never knew when to let me up. Then when I got out of the water they would mockingly "lay hands" on me in the name of Beelzebub, going through a ceremony and at short intervals calling "Pluck," when they would pull my hair with a severe twitch, and would spit on me and laugh. Once my clothes were taken and thrown into a bed of itching nettles, and when I tried to get them out with a pole I was pushed in among the nettles. At the gristmill, also, they would punish me in a shameful manner. At last I became so provoked that I went after them with a strong jack-knife. Though some of them were eighteen or nineteen years old, they ran off, fully convinced that I would have hurt them if I could have caught them. The miller interposed and gave them a severe reprimand. From that time they never tried to punish me. My medicine had worked well, and thereafter I was looked on as a leading boy among them.

During this period I had some perilous experiences with wild animals. My father had a pet deer, and a bull-dog owned by the family caught it by the nose; I tried to get the dog off, when the frightened deer kicked and tore my clothes almost off, lacerating my flesh considerably. Soon after this the deer was followed, in the woods near the house, by a large buck, which my father shot. The animal's shoulder was broken, and I followed it to the mill-pond and sprang into the water to hold it. As I seized its horn the buck, which had a footing, threw me around, lacer-ating my left hand considerably. For a time my life was in peril from the wild animal, but I struggled and finally used my pocket knife on its throat. Some time after this episode a man named John Bos shot and wounded a big buck near our home. It being night, he came to the house for assistance, and father and I went out. The dogs reached the buck, which charged on them, and as it was seized by the nose by one of them father and I caught the buck's hind feet. It kicked us free, and I had a close call from being severely if not fatally hurt; but we returned to the attack, and finally secured the game.

As time went on the older people in our neighborhood took interest in the Mormon Elders, and some of them joined the new Church, while others became very intoler-ant and hostile. My parents and my eldest brother and sister united with the Mormons; yet I held back, for though fully in sympathy with what my relatives had done I did not consider myself worthy to join, for I thought that to be a church member I must have some great experience and see great lights, such as I had heard people testify of. Thus I stayed out and watched developments.

Finally, in July, 1844, the news reached us that the Prophet Joseph Smith and his brother Hyrum, the Patriarch, had been assassinated in Carthage jail by a mob; also, that the Mormons had been ordered to leave the state, and were going either to the Rocky Mountains, California, or Vancouver Island. In fact, there were many kinds of rumors afloat, and there was great excitement.

In the fall of 1845 permission was given me to go to a river town five miles from home, to work at a slaughter and packing house, where my cousin, Homer Jackson, and I got employment that season. We heard that the Mormons were going to start west the next spring—in fact, their purpose was a topic of frequent conversation. We returned home in the latter part of January, 1846, and soon learned that the Church leaders were leaving Nauvoo for a new home in the unknown western wilds, and that every true Mormon was expected to join them as soon as possible.

Shortly after this, father called a family meeting to consider what to do. It was a great venture to start out with a large family on a journey of a thousand miles or more into an unknown wilderness, among savage tribes; so after long discussion of the matter, it was decided to be too great an undertaking at that particular time. It was regarded as inadvisable to take the chances of starving to death in the wilderness. Besides, property was very low, and it was folly to sell out a good home at so great a sacrifice as seemed necessary.

When this decision was reached, father turned to me and said: "Well, Jimmy, what do you think about it?" I answered that where the Mormons went I would go, and where

they died I would die.   This was the first time I had been
asked a question, and as I was not a member of the Church
my reply surprised the others.   Being inquired of as to how
I would go, I suggested that perhaps someone wanted a
teamster, or maybe there was some widow who would take
a boy for his labor in return for food and clothing.   Father
asked if I would leave the family and go out west and starve;
and he suggested that as I did not belong to the Mormons
they would not have me.   To this I said I would join them,
and that my mind was made up to go with the Mormons at
all hazards.   Then father ordered me to keep quiet, saying
he would thrash me if I talked of leaving home.   This
closed the discussion, for in those days thrashing was the
great panacea for disobedience, whether at home or in the
school room.   But that threat clinched my resolve to go
with the Mormons even at the risk of life, for I was
thoroughly satisfied of the justice of their cause.

I said no more then, but at the first opportunity told my
mother that soon I would come up missing, as I was going
with the Mormons, and should hide if searched for, if I had
to go among the Indians.   Mother said I would starve, but
my reply was that I could live on what others did.   My
mother was convinced that I would go, and her mother's
heart was so touched that she could not withold my secret
from my father, who believed, too, that I would do as I had
said.

One evening, soon afterward, I overheard them talking
of the matter.   Father said it would break up the family if
they did not move west, for Jim certainly would go; they
were satisfied that the Mormon doctrines were true, and
thought that perhaps they had better make an effort to sell
out and move.   My heart was filled with joy at these
words.

When morning came, father set out to buy oxen, and
was successful.   He also sold his farm but reserved the

crop, as he had to wait till after harvest for part of his pay for the land.   He thought that by fitting out two good teams, and providing wagons and tools, he and Alexander Stephens (mother's brother) and two of his sisters (old maids), and myself could go out into Iowa, where we could put in some corn and build a cabin or two.   Then my uncle and I could do the rest while father returned, took care of the harvest, and brought up the family, when we would follow the Church as best we could until a resting place was found.

The way now seemed open.   My father felt encouraged, and all went well until a few days before the time for starting, when I was stricken down with fever and ague, and shook or chilled every other day till the first of May, at which time all was ready for moving.   Efforts were made to persuade me that I could not stand the journey, but should allow one of the other boys to go in my stead.   But I could not see it in that light.   While father was talking of the matter to mother I overheard him say, "We will have to let James go, for he will not be satisfied without, but he will get enough of it when he has had a few days, and has camped out and shaken a few times with the ague."   I thought to myself, "You are mistaken, father, for I would rather die than be left behind."

CHAPTER III.

MAY 1st, 1846, was a pleasant day, and we made our
start for Nauvoo, passing through Versailles to a
point some ten miles from home to the first night's camp.
I was encouraged to think I had kept so well, but about
ten o'clock the second day I began to shake, and my teeth
fairly to crack. I prayed earnestly to the Lord to heal me.
I was quite weak, and all thought me very sick. But that
was the last "shake" I had, for I began to get well from
that time.

It was on May 4th, I believe, that we reached Nauvoo,
having passed through Mount Sterling, the county seat of
Brown County, also through Carthage, where the Prophet
Joseph Smith and his brother the Patriarch Hyrum Smith
had been assassinated. We found the roads so muddy and
such hard traveling that we did not make more than fifteen
miles a day. When we came in sight of the Temple at
Nauvoo our hearts were filled with mingled joy and sorrow—joy that we had seen the Temple of the Lord, and
sorrow that the Saints had been so cruelly driven from it.

As we passed through the city we 'saw many houses which had been abandoned—indeed, the city itself seemed almost deserted. At some of the houses stood covered wagons, into which people were packing goods preparatory to their flight into the wilderness, they knew not where.

Looking westward across the great Mississippi River, we saw long trains of wagons strung out over the high rolling prairie. The country was new, and the roads muddy, so we rested three or four days, visiting the Temple and viewing the city that was beautiful for situation, but now was left with few inhabitants. Everything in and about the city that formerly hummed with industry and life was now lonely, saddened, and forlorn, and silent but for the preparations for flight by the remnant therein.

About the 8th of May we crossed the great "father of waters" and joined the "rolling kingdom" on its westward journey. We found friends and acquaintances, made up a company of our own, and passed and were repassed on the trip. Climbing an eminence from which we looked east and west, covered wagons could be seen as far as the eye could reach. The teams were made up of oxen, milch cows, two-year-old steers and heifers, and very few horses and mules. The teamsters were of both sexes, and comprised young and old. The people who could walk did so, and many were engaged in driving loose stock.

Hundreds of teams stuck in the mud, and we had to double-up and help one another out. Many times we had to wade in mud half to our knees and lift our wagons out of the mire. In this the women not infrequently would join their husbands and sons, and the old adage came true in numerous instances—women for a dead lift; when they plunged into the mud and put their shoulders to the wheels the men were urged to do double effort, and the wagon always rolled out and onward, at the rate of twelve to fifteen miles per day.

At every creek we found campers, some repairing wagons, yokes, chains, etc., doctoring sick cattle, washing clothes, or helping forward friends whose teams were weak. In all this there was excellent order, for the camps were organized in a general way by tens, fifties and hundreds. Peace and harmony prevailed all along the line. Evening prayers were attended to in each camp. There was much singing, mostly of sacred hymns or sentimental songs; and from no quarter could coarse songs be heard. Sometimes the camp would meet in a sociable dance in the evenings, to drive dull care away; and then there always was good order and the most perfect friendship and peace.

The camps were instructed not to kill game of any kind to waste its flesh; they were not even to kill a snake on the road, for it was their calling to establish peace on earth, and good will toward man and beast. Thus all went on in peace and order.

At one of the headwaters of the Grand River, Iowa, we found some hundreds of people putting in gardens and field crops (corn and potatoes). A few cabins had been built, so father and our party decided to stop there. We put in a few acres of corn and garden stuff, then father returned to Illinois to bring up the rest of the family, leaving my Uncle Alexander Stephens and myself to look after the crop and stock, which we did faithfully.

About the 6th of July we heard that President Young and several of the Twelve Apostles had returned from the most advanced companies, and that there would be a meeting held at the white oak grove—the usual place of meeting—the next day. There was also a rumor in camp that a government recruiting offcer had come to enlist volunteers, for the United States had declared war against Mexico.

Of course this latter tidings was a great surprise, as the Mormons had been denied protection against mob vio-

lence and had been forced beyond the borders of civilization in the United States, and our camps were stretched out
in an Indian country, from the Mississippi River to the
Missouri. Surprised as we were at the government's demand, we were still more so to think that our leaders would
entertain for a moment the idea of encouraging compliance
therewith. Yet rumor said that President Young and the
prominent men with him had come as recruiting officers
as well.

All who could be spared from the tents went eagerly
to the White Oak grove, and there learned that the rumors
were true. The United States government demanded that
a battalion of five hundred men be raised by the Mormon
Church, then fleeing from mob violence for the want of
protection by that government whose right and duty it was
to protect them. The men of the moving camp were required to leave their families in the wilderness, almost
unprotected, and go to a foreign land to fight their country's
battles.

But wonders never cease. The leading men among
the Mormons—Brigham Young, Heber C. Kimball, Wilford Woodruff, and others of the Twelve Apostles—stood
before the people and called for volunteers to engage in the
Mexican war, saying that the five hundred men must be
raised if it took the whole strength of the camp to do it. If
the young men would not enlist, the middle-aged and old
men would, said President Young; the demand of our
country should be met if it took the Twelve Apostles and
the High Priests.

At the close of the meeting there were many who
were enthused, while others appeared confused and did not
seem to catch the spirit of the matter. I was not yet a
member of the Church, but all the old stories of the war of
the Revolution and that of 1812, with the later Black Hawk
Indian wars, brightened in my memory so that the spirit of

the patriots awoke within me, and although I was averse
to war and bloodshed, I had a desire to serve my country
in any legitimate way.   Yet I felt that, as I was under age,
and, as my Uncle Alexander Stephens had decided to
enlist, the responsibility of my father's affairs now rested
on me.

My uncle and I were standing by the roadside talking
over the situation, when along came Ezra T. Benson, who
had been recently selected as one of the Twelve Apostles;
there also came Richmond Louder, one of my associates
from boyhood, and Matthew Caldwell.   Richmond Louder
and I had talked previously of being baptized together. He
said they were going down to attend to that sacred ordinance, and invited me to accompany them, which I did
gladly.   We went to the south fork of the Grand River, and
with Uncle A. Stephens as a witness were baptized.   This
was on the 7th of July, 1846.   Then we went to the house
of General Charles C. Rich, where we were confirmed, I think
under the hands of Elders Willard Richards and Ezra T.
Benson, in the presence of President Brigham Young and
others of the Twelve Apostles.

This done, the happiest feeling of my life came over
me.   I thought I would to God that all the inhabitants of
the earth could experience what I had done as a witness of
the Gospel.   It seemed to me that, if they could see and
feel as I did, the whole of humankind would join with us
in one grand brotherhood, and the universe would be
prepared for the great Millennial morn.

When we returned to camp, my aunts partook of the
same feeling that had filled me.   Then I got the spirit to
enlist, and after a short consultation with those most concerned they advised me to lay the matter before Ezra T.
Benson.   Accordingly, the next morning Uncle A. Stephens and I went over to the grove.   I told the Elder my
feelings, and the responsibilities left upon me by my father.

Elder Benson said the Spirit's promptings to me were right, and I had started right. He told me to go on, saying I I would be blessed, my father would find no fault with me, his business would not suffer, and I would never be sorry for the action I had taken or for my enlistment. Every word he said to me has been fulfilled to the very letter.

Uncle Alexander Stephens and I then went to a tent where men were giving in their names as volunteers. We handed in our names, and were enrolled as members of the historic Mormon Battalion.

CHAPTER IV.

START FOR THE BATTALION RENDEZVOUS—A JOURNEY OF HARDSHIP—
IN THE MORMONS' CAMP ON MISSOURI RIVER—FIRST EXPERI-
ENCES IN THE ARMY—BLESSED BY APOSTLES—PROPHETIC AD-
DRESS BY PRESIDENT BRIGHAM YOUNG—THE BATTALION STARTS
ON ITS LONG JOURNEY—DOING CAMP DUTY—HEAVY STORMS AND
INSUFFICIENT RATIONS—HARD EXPERIENCES—AT FORT LEAVEN-
WORTH—MEXICAN MULES AS A CURE FOR EGOTISM—COLONEL
ALLEN TAKEN ILL—ON THE SANTA FE ROAD—SUFFERING FROM
THIRST—SICKNESS AMONG THE TROOPS—DR. G. B. SANDERSON, A
TYRANNICAL QUACK—ARMY MERCHANTS—ORDER OF MARCHING.

IT was about one o'clock in the afternoon of July 9 when we bade our friends an affectionate farewell, and started on what we understood to be a journey of one hundred and thirty-eight miles, to join the army of the United States at our country's call. We had provisions enough put up to last us on our trip. The night previous our old clothes had received the necessary repairs. Our preparations were hasty and incomplete, for we had been told (by an unauthorized person, as we afterwards learned) that when we got to Sarpy's Point, on the Missouri River, we would draw uni-

forms, clothing, blankets, and rations, and would have to
cast aside our old clothes.

Our initial trip was begun without a blanket to wrap
ourselves in, as we thought we could find shelter in the
camps along the line of march. But in this we were mistaken, for everybody seemed to have all they could do to
shelter their own. The first night we camped on the bank
of a small stream, where we fell in with twelve or fifteen
other volunteers who had not so much as a bit of bread,
but plenty of assurance in asking for what others had. We
divided with them, then scraped what leaves we could and
laid down thereon, with a chunk of wood for our pillow.
Next morning we divided our last morsel of food with
what we learned later were the very roughest element of
the battalion.

For five days we journeyed, much of the time in heavy
rain and deep mud, sleeping on the wet ground without
blankets or other kind of bedding, and living on elm bark
and occasionally a very small ration of buttermilk handed
to us by humane sisters as we passed their tents. We
thought our experience was pretty rough, but I do not
remember that I heard murmuring from the lips of anyone,
for we felt that we were in the service of God and our
country.

When we reached the Missouri River we found that
some four hundred men had rendezvoused there. In the
camps of the Latter-day Saints, close by, there were some
thousands of men, women and children; a brush bowery
had been erected, where the people met for religious worship. We soon found friends who welcomed us to camp,
and we were invited to a social dance and farewell party.
We had excellent music, the best dinner that the country
could afford, and, above all, a spirit of brotherly love and
union that I have never seen surpassed. With all on the
altar of sacrifice for God and His kingdom and for our

country, it seemed that everything and everybody looked to the accomplishment of one grand, common cause, not a dissenting voice being heard from anyone.

July 16, 1846, we were mustered into the service of the United States, and, under command of Col. James Allen, marched down the bluffs to the Missouri bottoms, where we camped in a cottonwood grove. Some flour and other provisions were issued to us, and we peeled the bark off a tree for a bread tray or kneading trough. Some rolled their dough around sticks and stuck or held it before the fire, and others baked their bread in the ashes; for we had not yet drawn any camp equipage. We received one blanket apiece, and had that charged up, the amount to be taken out of our pay.

I am not writing a history of the Mormon Battalion, but am relating my individual experiences in that detachment of the United States army, as I recollect them; so it will not be expected of me to tell much of what others saw, or to narrate events as they remember them, but as they impressed themselves upon my mind at the time of occurrence.

Just before our last farewell to friends at the Missouri River, and preparatory to taking up our line of march, we were formed into a hollow square, and President Brigham Young, with Heber C. Kimball and others of the Apostles, came to our camp, rode into the square, and gave us parting blessings and instructions. The words of President Young, as they fastened themselves upon my memory, were in substance as follows: "Now, brethren, you are going as soldiers at your country's call. You will travel in a foreign land, in an enemy's country; and if you will live your religion, obey your officers, attend to your prayers, and as you travel in an enemy's land, hold sacred the property of the people, never taking anything that does not belong to you only in case of starvation; though you may be traveling in an enemy's country, do not disturb fruit orchards or chicken coops or beehives, do not take anything but what you pay for—although it is customary for soldiers to plunder their enemies in time of war, it is wrong—always spare life when possible; if you obey this counsel, attending to your prayers to the Lord, I promise you in the name of the Lord God of Israel that not one soul of you shall fall by the hands of the enemy. You will pass over battlefields; battles will be fought in your front and in your rear, on your right hand and on your left, and your enemies shall flee before you. Your names shall be held in honorable remembrance to the latest generation."

Heber C. Kimball and other prominent men of the Church confirmed what President Young had said, and all bade us an affectionate farewell, with "God bless you and spare your lives."

Thus we set out in good cheer on our journey of more than two thousand miles in a section of the continent wholly unknown to us.

In the month of July, from about the 20th, we passed down through the towns and villages along the river, for two hundred miles, to Fort Leavenworth. The heat was excessive, and the roads dusty, when we started out. A great part of the way we had only a small ration of food, for it did not seem to be in the country, and we suffered much from want. We took regular turns in standing guard around the camp and in herding the stock. Heavy rains came on, and for several days we pressed forward amid such terrible storms as I never had experienced before. With less than half rations, and that badly or insufficiently cooked, from lack of proper utensils and experience, and having to lie on the ground without any bedding save one blanket each, it is a wonder the entire camp were not down sick instead of a few. But with all this hardship there were no desertions and few complaints. Everything seemed to move harmoniously among the men.

The command crossed the river at Fort Leavenworth, Kansas, and soon afterwards we drew a tent to each mess of six men. This afforded us great relief at nights, protecting us from the dews and rain; but in the daytime the whiteness of the tents seemed to intensify the heat so that there was no comfort in them. While at Fort Leavenworth we washed our old clothing and made ourselves as comfortable as possible. Soon we drew camp equipage and rations from the government. We got flintlock muskets, and accoutrements consisting of bayonets, cartridge-boxes, straps and belts, canteens, haversacks, etc., also a knapsack each. We drew our first pay, forty-two dollars each, sent part of it to our families, and fitted ourselves out with new clothes and shoes.

With all the paraphernalia of soldiers, we seemed so burdened as to be able neither to run nor to fight. Then to be obliged to travel all day under a broiling sun, or in driving rain or fierce winds, across sandy deserts and over trackless mountains, going sometimes sixty to ninety miles without water, in an enemy's country—kind reader, you may picture such scenes in your imagination, but it is impossible for you to realize the conditions except by actual experience therein. It is equally impossible for me to find language to describe fitly the situation at that time at the United States military post of Fort Leavenworth.

The place being an outfitting station for United States forces in the war with Mexico, all was bustle and activity; steamboats were unloading material, and teams filled the streets; many of the new recruits were very rough indeed, and drinking and fighting seemed to be their pastime; myself and companions were amazed and shocked at the profane and vulgar language and vile actions that we were compelled to listen to and witness; with all else, squads of soldiers were being drilled, the bugle sound was frequent, as were also the beating of the drum and the playing of the fife; everywhere the men were preparing for victory or death, and many were so reckless they did not seem to care which came.

As our battalion was preparing quietly for the great march before us, a band of very small Mexican mules was brought in to be used as teams in our transportation department. The animals were unaccustomed to harness, and very wild, so there was a detail of men from each company assigned to do the harnessing. It fell to my lot to engage in the work, and great was my surprise to see one of those little mules dragging three to five men about the yards. I thought I was able to handle one of the little long-eared animals myself, but had the conceit taken out of me in quick order by having my hands burned with the rope, as I was jerked and dragged about in fertilizer in the yards— there being an abundance there. But we accomplished our work, with some sport and considerable cost to our patience and muscular energy.

From the 10th to the 15th of August, companies A, B, and C moved out on the Santa Fe road, and in two or three days were followed by companies D and E. Our esteemed colonel, James Allen, having been taken ill, ordered Captain Jefferson Hunt of company A to take command until the colonel should recover and settle up the business of outfitting the battalion.

Our route lay over rolling hills, through some timbered country and some prairie. The weather was warm, and there was much suffering, especially from lack of drinking water, this being scarce. The sick felt the hardship particularly, and there was quite a number down with chills and fever; such water as was obtainable was of poor quality, warm and unhealthy, and added to the number of the sick.

Each company had a large wagon and three or four yoke of oxen to haul the tents and camp equipage, and one issue of rations, I think it was for one week. The government had assigned a doctor to our command, George B. Sanderson of Platte County, Missouri. He proved to be so cruel and tyrannical as to incur the ill-will of every man in the command. He had immediate charge of the hospital wagons, and no matter how ill a man was, he was not allowed to ride in the company's wagon until he had reported to this cruel quack, who had to be honored with the title of physician and surgeon. With his permission a man was allowed to crawl into his company's wagon, which was filled nearly to the bows with tents and other camp equipage. Sometimes there would be five or six crowded in together, some shaking with ague and others burning with fever. Our company wagon was called the Gray Eagle; John Gilbert was the teamster, and did all in his power to favor those of his comrades who deserved it.

Besides the company and hospital wagons, there were sutlers' or merchants' wagons—speculators that are permitted to follow the army for what they can make off the troops. They carry in stock such things as they know from experience the soldier most needs, and many luxuries; they had almost everything to entice the famishing soldier, who had to stand guard over them and their stores. Many times, through hardships, we seemed compelled to patronize them. Our suffering was their opportunity, and they were not slow to take advantage of it. Their prices were enormous, and their bills never failed to reach the paymaster by each payday; after these were paid, the soldier came in for the balance, if there was any. Some were very unfortunate through sickness, and had to patronize the sutler, or merchant; others were unwise in their purchases; and thus the eight dollars a month wages often was spent before it was earned.

Our commissary and ammunition department included over a hundred wagons; the three or four pieces of artillery followed close in our rear, in charge of a wagonmaster and assistants.

The usual order of marching, as I remember it, was: an advance guard; then the colonel and his staff; next came the body of the command; then a rearguard, the baggage and hospital wagons, etc. Only on special occasions was the main body of the battalion permitted to march at will, as long as it remained between the front and rear guards. When the country was specially rough, and roads had to be made, the road hands, or, in military language, the sappers and miners, were allowed extra rations, and had to start out very early with the advance guard.

CHAPTER V.

CROSSING OF THE KAW RIVER—INDIAN FARMERS—FIERCE STORM ON STONE COAL CREEK—CROSSING A CREEK WITH PRECIPITOUS BANKS—RUINS OF AN ANCIENT CITY—WAGONLOAD OF SICK UPSET IN A STREAM—SAD NEWS OF COL. ALLEN'S DEATH—DISPUTE OVER HIS SUCCESSOR—MILITARY RULES DISREGARDED IN SETTLING THE QUESTION—TROOPS DISSATISFIED—SICKNESS IN CAMP —HARSHNESS OF THE NEW COMMANDER, LIEUTENANT COLONEL SMITH—BRUTALITY OF THE DOCTOR—DOSES OF OBJECTIONABLE MEDICINE IN AN OLD IRON SPOON—IN THE COMANCHE INDIAN COUNTRY—ABUSE FROM LIEUTENANT COLONEL SMITH—SCARCITY OF FUEL—BUFFALO CHIPS—COOKING FOOD UNDER GREAT DIFFICULTIES—INCREASE OF SICKNESS—UP THE GRAND VALLEY OF THE ARKANSAS—DETACHMENT OF SICK SENT TO PUEBLO— MIRAGES—HERDS OF BUFFALO—ON THE SICK LIST—REACH THE ROCKY MOUNTAINS—PREHISTORIC RUINS—IN MEXICAN VILLAGES—ARRIVAL AT SANTA FE.

WE crossed the Kaw River about the 17th of August, being ferried over in flat boats by some half civilized Delaware and Shawnee Indians. Where we crossed the river it was from three to four hundred yards wide. The country in the neighborhood seemed to be well adapted to farming. The Indians had good crops of corn and water-melons, and knew as well as white men how to charge for them. These Indians were an intelligent-looking people, having log cabins for dwellings.

From the Kaw we traveled to Spring Creek, over a beautiful country, and there joined the companies that had preceded us. We met with rainstorms that made it very disagreeable for us at night, when two of us would spread one blanket and lie down on it. It would wet through at once; and though we had tents over us, we often slept on the wet ground, in wet clothes.

Moving onward to Stone Coal Creek, we there endured one of the severest storms of wind and rain that any of us ever had experienced. Nearly every tent was blown down; several government wagons were overturned, and others were sent rolling before the wind as though they were express or stage coaches; many men fell on their faces and held to the shrubbery to avoid being carried away by the violence of the hurricane, while others not so fortunate as to be able to catch hold of a shrub were driven some rods before the blast. Some were bruised and others badly frightened, but none received serious injury; and although everybody was thoroughly soaked, not even the sick seemed to be unfavorably affected in health by their experience.

The storm over and our clothing dried, we resumed our march. Coming to a deep creek with precipitous banks, we had to hold the wagons back with ropes and let them down gradually to the bed of the stream; then a number of men with ropes, on the opposite side, assisted the teams in drawing the wagons up the steep bank. We passed over some very fine land to a place we named Allen's Grove, and camped. Next day we came to the ruins of a city of the dim, distant past; the stone walls were yet visible to the traveler. That night we rested on

Beaver Creek. On the 25th or 26th, while traveling through a beautiful country of rich soil, one wagon with five or six people was upset into a creek, and the occupants received a dangerous ducking, though I do not recall any serious results following.

It was on this day that a messenger from Fort Leavenworth overtook us, bringing the sorrowful news of the death of our esteemed commander, Colonel James Allen. It was a sad blow to us, for all had learned to respect, and, indeed, even to love him. Yet I have felt sometimes that it was a kind providence to him that he was taken from us, for his nature was too kind and sympathetic to have forced his men through what the Mormon Battalion had to endure before reaching its destination.

Colonel Allen's death left a vacancy in the command that was not difficult to fill according to military rules, as the next officer in rank should have occupied his place. But plain as is the military law on the subject, there arose a dispute, and much feeling was worked up. The council of officers decided that, as Captain Jefferson Hunt of company A had been placed in charge by Colonel Allen till the latter should rejoin the command, he should continue in that position. Accordingly, he led the battalion to Council Grove, where it was learned that Lieutenant Colonel Smith was on the way, intending to assume command. Thus the quiet of the camp was again disturbed, and much feeling manifested. There were many warm discussions between the officers and among the soldiers as well.

It was at Council Grove that Lieutenant Colonel Smith, Major Walker, and G. B. Sanderson overtook us. The question of command was further discussed, Captain Hunt standing up for his rights. But in the council, Captain Nelson Higgins of Company D (my company) moved that Smith should be recognized as the commanding officer; this was seconded by Captain Davis of Company E; all the officers but three, viz.: Laron Clark, Samuel Gully, and Wesley W. Willis, voted for the motion, and the question was settled. Lieutenant Colonel A. J. Smith took command, to the disgust of the soldiers, a large majority of whom, if not all, were quite dissatisfied. Next day we reached Diamond Springs, where the battalion was inspected by Lieutenant Colonel Smith.

At this time there was much sickness in camp, chills and fever and mumps. This condition was produced by frequent changes of drinking water, and by poorly-cooked food, as many times we had to depend on dry weeds for fuel. When a man became sick, it had been the custom for him to crawl into the company wagon. Our new commander soon dropped on the kindness of the teamster, and put an end to it without mercy. The commander was so rough and ungentle, and had so much pomposity and assurance, that the whole command was disgusted, and almost all were angry. He ordered the sick out of the wagons, and directed that before they could ride they must be reported by the doctor as unable to walk, and had to take a dose of the doctor's drugs from his old rusty spoon. We soon began to realize that we had fallen into bad hands.

The doctor often talked to the men as though they were brutes. He was very unfeeling, and the men would not respond to his sick call ("Jim along, Josey") when it was possible for them to walk alone. When we stopped he would sit in front of his tent with his book on his knee, a long chest of medicine before him, a colored man for his body servant, and a hospital steward standing in front of the wagon. At sick call, everyone who could not walk had to be taken before the doctor's tent, and there be seated or laid down, sometimes on the wet ground, then, like going to a mill, wait for his grist, or dose of calomel. There was not much chance to miss it, for, when a man's name was called and responded to, the hospital steward was ordered to give him such and such a dose, and the old iron spoon, with its contents of we knew not what, was presented in the presence of the doctor. Under these circumstances we began to feel at least the rigors of military rule.

About this time we entered the Comanche Indian country, and on September 2 camped on Cottonwood Creek. The Indians were said to be very hostile, yet we had no trouble with them. I think it was here that we began to see signs of buffalo, and the prairie dog villages. Timber was very scarce, and the country was more uninviting than that we had passed over.

Shortly after Lieutenant Colonel Smith took command we were drawn up in line, and some military laws were read to us. At the end of almost every sentence there was the word death, as punishment for infraction of the law. We were then talked to in a most offensive and domineering manner, until some of us began to wonder what we had done to merit such severity and downright abuse.

We were tired and footsore, and suffered much from lack of water. The country showed such a sameness of forbidding features that the journey became very monotonous and tiresome. Fuel was so scarce that we had to dig trenches two or three feet long, and eight or ten inches wide and a foot deep, fill these with dry grass, and start a fire and pile on buffalo chips, with which to do our cooking. The result was our food often was half raw and badly smoked, and many of the men were brought down with severe diarrheal complaints. As many had traveled the road in advance of us, even buffalo chips for fuel were so scarce that often we had to go for miles to gather them.

When we reached Pawnee Fork we found it a very difficult stream to cross. The wagons had to be let down the steep bank with ropes, by the men, and had to be taken up the opposite bank in the same manner.

The events narrated here will indicate that it is not all of a soldier's duty when on a long march to tramp all day with musket and accoutrements and knapsack, but the soldier on such a journey as we had must push and pull wagons up hill, hold them back when going down hill, haul them through deep sands, and help them and the teams out of quicksands; he must stand guard and night-herd stock; must press on, over rough or smooth ground, rain or shine; must wade rivers, and when crossing streams is not allowed to take off his clothing, but has to plunge into the water, and then travel on in wet clothes; besides, there are many other experiences that are far from pleasant.

We pushed along the best we could to the Arkansas River, through a very uninviting country, in which we began to find brackish water and saleratus. We traveled up the broad river bottoms of the Arkansas eighty to one hundred miles, the water being poor and unhealthy. Many were added to the corps of "Jim along, Joseys," and had to be led or carried by their comrades to the unfeeling doctor, many times to be cursed at by him, and then to take a dose from his nauseating spoon. Quite a number of the sick were badly salivated by the drugs given them.

About September 15 or 16, we crossed the river where the roads fork, one going toward Fort Benton, and the other leading to Santa Fe. There we parted with Captain Nelson Higgins, he having been detailed to take a small squad of men and the families to a Spanish town called Pueblo, some hundred miles away, there to winter. Meanwhile, we pushed our way over barren plains and sandy deserts to the Cimmaron River. We saw deceptive rivers, ponds and lakes; we chased after them for miles sometimes, till we found that, like jack o' lantern or will o' the wisp, we could not get nearer to them. Finally we learned that they were mirages—a peculiar reflection of the sun upon the great plains or sandy deserts. It seemed impossible for the inexperienced to discern the difference between the mirage and a body of real water.

In this barren country we saw immense herds of buffalo; in our long march we came to ponds of water made perfectly filthy by the buffalo, and rendered offensive by the broiling hot sun, the liquid being almost as thick as gruel; but we were so terribly famished with thirst that we were glad to get even such foul water.

When the Cimmaron River was reached, there was good water, and good feed for our stock, but our rations were reduced one-third, and we were pretty well worn down.

On the 18th or 19th of September it was my place to be on guard. I had stood the journey very well, but by this time had become affected by the alkali, and that day was so badly afflicted with diarrhea as to be almost unable to drag myself into camp. But rather than march to "Jim along, Josey," I took my place on guard. That night there came on one of the most terrible storms I ever have experienced. I had to brace myself with my musket to stand. From that date I have never been free from pain in the right limb, near the instep, caused by the severe exposure. Next day it became necessary to go on the sick list, to remain several days.

About the 23rd we began to come to timber in the hills, and having been for nine or ten days with nothing but grass and buffalo chips for fuel, we were in a situation to appreciate the change. Soon we were among the sand-hills, where traveling was hard, and passed the Rabbit Ears (Black Peak and Agua Fria Peak), two high mountain peaks. In this mountainous region we found traces of the inhabitants of a past age, in old stone walls and in numerous irrigation canals long since dry.

On the 2nd or 3rd of October we came to the Red River. The mountain air was bracing, but there were many men who yet remained sick. About this time the command was culled over by Lieutenant Colonel Smith and the doctor, and all who were considered able to stand a forced march to Santa Fe were ordered forward on the double quick.

The sick men were left to take care of themselves as best they could, with the broken down teams of the command to look after. My lot was still with the invalids, and of course I had to remain. Yet we were only about two days behind the strong men who left us in the mountains; we reached Santa Fe on October 12th, having passed through several Mexican villages, the houses of which were low and flat-roofed, and covered principally with cement and tile. We saw the very small Mexican sheep and goats, the people milking the latter, by sitting at the back end, in an earthen pot, and there milking regardless of anything that might drop into the vessel intended for milk only.

From the appearance of Santa Fe we had no reason to doubt that it was between three and four hundred years old; for it looked at least that far behind the times. Mexicans and Indians, badly mixed, made up the population. Their costume, manners, habits, and in fact everything, were both strange and novel to us, and of course were quite an attraction. Many of the people looked on us with suspicion, and if it had been in their power no doubt they would have given us a warm reception; others appeared to be pleased, doubtless because it made trade better for them, and on that account they seemed very friendly. They brought into camp, for sale, many articles of food; the strongest of these were red pepper pies, the pepper-pods as large as a teacup, and onions (savoyas) as large as saucers, to be eaten raw like turnips.

A few days' rest and change of food at Santa Fe, and the command was ready to resume its arduous march.

CHAPTER VI.

EXEMPLARY CONDUCT OF THE MORMON TROOPS—LIEUTENANT COL-
ONEL P. ST. GEORGE COOKE ARRIVES AND ASSUMES COMMAND—
A WELCOME CHANGE—ANOTHER DETACHMENT OF SICK, ALSO
THE LAUNDRESSES, SENT TO PUEBLO—SELECTING MEN TO CON-
TINUE THE JOURNEY TO CALIFORNIA—REDUCING THE BAGGAGE
—DIFFICULTIES OF THE 1,100 MILES JOURNEY AHEAD—POOR
EQUIPMENT THEREFOR—LEAVE SANTA FE—ROADS OF HEAVY
SAND—ON ONE-THIRD RATIONS—HARDSHIPS INCREASE—GALLED
FEET AND GNAWING STOMACHS—MORE SICK MEN FOR PUEBLO—
LEAVING THE LAST WAGONS—MULES AND OXEN IN A PACK
TRAIN—IN AN UNKNOWN COUNTRY—HUNTING A PASS OVER THE
MOUNTAINS—ALARM OF AN ENEMY—A BEAVER DAM—CROSSING
THE RIO GRANDE DEL NORTE—GREAT SUFFERING AMONG THE
TROOPS.

WHILE we were in Santa Fe, Colonel Sterling Price came in with his cavalry command, and soon the town prison was filled with them, so that it became necessary for a guard from the Mormon Battalion to be posted at the prison. I do not recall that any of our command was put into the prison, though it is possible one or two might have been, for a few of them got rather too much wine; but it was a very few who acted that way. There were many invalids of other commands left to garrison Santa Fe, and they caused considerable disturbance, many of them getting into prison.

It seems that word had gone ahead to the Mexican town that the Mormons were a very hard class of outlaws, consequently at first we were looked upon as "toughs" of the very worst kind. But when the people had an opportunity to see our superior conduct in contrast with that of the other troops, they realized the true situation, and male and female thronged our camp in friendly visit.

It was on October 13, 1846, that Lieutenant Colonel P. St. George Cooke assumed command of the Mormon Battalion, having been designated for that purpose, and by this proceeding we were liberated from the little tyrant Lieutenant Colonel A. J. Smith.

By order of Colonel Cooke, Captain James Brown of Company C took command of all the sick that were unable to continue the journey to California; also of most of the laundresses, and a few able-bodied men, with directions to go north to Pueblo, and join Captain Higgins. In order to determine who were not able to continue the march to California, we were drawn up in line, and the officers and Dr. Sanderson inspected the whole command. The doctor scrutinized every one of us, and when he said a man was not able to go, his name was added to Captain Brown's detachment, whether the man liked it or not; and when the doctor said a man could make the trip, that settled the matter. The operation was much like a cooper culling stave timber, or a butcher separating the lean from the fat sheep.

My desire was very strong to continue the overland journey, and when the doctor neared me, I braced up and tried to look brave and hardy. To the doctor's inquiry, "How do you feel?" my answer was, "First rate." He looked at me suspiciously and said, "You look d——d pale and weak," then passed on, and I was greatly relieved at having gone safely through the inspection.

In order No. 8, Colonel Cooke called the particular attention of the company commanders to the necessity of reducing baggage as much as possible; that means for transportation were very deficient; that the road was almost impracticable, much of it being in deep sand, and how soon we would have to abandon our wagons it was impossible to

3

ascertain; that skillets and ovens could not be taken, and but one camp-kettle to each mess of ten men.

Colonel Cooke very properly and correctly pointed out that everything seemed to conspire to discourage the extraordinary undertaking of marching the battalion 1,100 miles, for the much greater part of the way through an unknown wilderness, without road or trail, and with a wagon train. He said the battalion was much worn by traveling on foot, marching from Nauvoo, Illinois; their clothing was very scant, there was no money to pay them, or clothing to issue; the mules were utterly broken down; the quartermaster's department was out of funds and its credit bad; animals were scarce, and those procured were inferior and deteriorating every hour from the lack of forage. All this made it necessary that such careful preparation as could be should be made in advance.

It can be easily seen from this statement that the condition and prospects of the battalion were not very encouraging; yet there were very few of the men who had the least desire to retrace their steps—they knew what they had passed through, but looking ahead they tried to hope for the best, realizing, just as they had been told, that the country through which they had to travel was an unknown region.

With the colonel's orders carried out, we got ready to move, and about the 21st of October we left Santa Fe and traveled six or eight miles to a stream called Agua Fria (cold water). Grass for animals was very short, the nights were very cold, and our road was in heavy sand almost from the start. Our advance was slow, for the best teams had been taken for extra service or express duties in other departments. Besides, there was added to our already overburdened animals the load of sacks, packsaddles, lashing-ropes, etc., necessary in the event of being compelled to abandon the wagons, so we would not be entirely without means of transportation. There was also the burden of sheep pelts and blankets to use under pack saddles, and as most of these were bought second-hand, they were well stocked with the insects commonly called "greybacks."

In a short time we drew near to the mountains, and the weather became colder. Having but one blanket each we began to use the pelts and saddle-blankets to splice out our scanty store of bedding. Thus we proceeded over sandy roads, through the towns and villages of Spaniards, Indians and Greasers—the surroundings presented being of such a sameness that the journey became very monotonous.

Soon after leaving Santa Fe our rations were reduced to one-third the regular amount allowed by law to the soldier. A detail of men was called as a substitute for mules, to move and to lighten the loads of the ammunition wagons. Each soldier was required to carry sixty-four rounds of cartridges that contained each a one-ounce ball, three buck-shot, and powder enough to send them where they should be, besides the heavy paper they were wrapped in, and extra flints for the firelock—about two hundred ounces added to the already overburdened soldier.

Now the soldier must wade the tributaries of the Rio Grande del Norte, sometimes waist deep and more, and is not allowed even to take off his shoes, or any of his wearing apparel. An officer, perched on his white mule on some point or eminence overlooking the whole command, with a hawk's eye for keen military experience, calls to this or that squad of men, with a horrid oath, as if they were brutes; often he curses the men until they long for a battle where perchance someone would remember the tyrant with an ounce ball and three buckshot. And yet, if that feeling were not quenched in the soldier's bosom it would not require an engagement with the enemy to accomplish the deed. But, praise God, that feeling quickly passed off as the men marched along, their clothes wet, and their thick soled cowhide army shoes partly filled with sand—the chafing and galling of the flesh without and the gnawing and grinding of the stomach within defied the mind to dwell upon any one subject for long at a time.

Is it any wonder that under these conditions fifty-five of our comrades wore down and collapsed so they had to go on the sick list and it became necessary for Lieutenant W. W. Willis to take command of that number of invalid soldiers, and join Captains Higgins and Brown at Pueblo? This company of sick and exhausted men left us, on their return, about the 10th or 12th of November.

About this time, the quartermaster was ordered to leave the remaining two heavy ox-wagons, while the company commanders were directed to reduce their tent-poles two-thirds; that is, to cast away all the upright poles and use muskets instead, and to put gores in the back part of the tents so they could shelter nine men in place of six; we were also to leave one-third of the campkettles.

Then came some sport in putting packs on a number of our mules and worn-out oxen. Some of these, which did not look as though they could travel a hundred miles further, when the crupper was put in place would rear up, wheel around, and kick in a most amusing style; nor did they cease until their strength failed them.

When this sport, if sport it may be called, was over we began to realize in a small degree the gravity of our situation. Our guides were "at sea," so to speak. We were in an enemy's land, with not a soul in camp who knew anything of the country. Men had been sent ahead to hunt a route for us to travel, and every time, on their return, they reported impassable barriers ahead—rough, high, steep mountains, without springs of water or creeks, or sandy plains, and barren deserts that it would be impossible to cross. In this dilemma we had to bear to the south, along the river, in hopes of finding a pass to the west.

One night, while camped near the Rio Grande del Norte, we heard a great noise as though a band of horses were crossing the river. This created quite an alarm, as there had been rumors of Mexicans revolting. For a short time it was thought it was Mexican cavalry crossing to attack us by night, but on the colonel making inquiries of the guides it was learned that the noise proceeded from beaver playing in the river. After watching and listening for a time, all settled down, contented that there was no enemy at hand.

On resuming our march next day, we passed through a grove of cottonwood trees, and saw where many of them had been cut down by the beaver. Some of the trees were two feet or more in diameter, had been cut off in long sections, and a surprisingly large dam had been constructed by the beaver across the river. This dam had caused to be formed a large pond, in which the beaver congregated at certain seasons, for sport. Thus the mystery of our midnight disturbance was solved to our satisfaction.

We passed along the sandy road to a large bend in the river, which Colonel Cooke decided was the place where we would cross the stream. He stationed himself on an abrupt point of rock, from which he could view the whole proceeding. Men were detailed from each company to follow the wagons through the river. In order to avoid a rocky ridge the stream had to be crossed twice within quarter of a mile. There were very heavy quicksands, and if the teams were allowed to stop one minute it was doubtful whether they could start again; consequently the precaution of having men close at hand was very important, though the average soldier did not understand the real reason for forcing him into the water without stripping off at least part of his raiment.

The crossing was made early in the day, and the water was very cold, as I had ample evidence, being one of those detailed to attend the wagons. Our comrades took our muskets over the point while we lifted at the wagons. As the water was waist deep, when the men would stoop to lift it would wet our clothing very nearly to the armpits; our shoes also were filled with sand.

Wet and cold, almost chilled, we continued our march through deep sands, pushing and pulling at the wagons till our clothing dried on our bodies, our shoes became so dry and hard that walking was very painful and difficult, and our feet became raw. If this had been all, we might have had less reason to complain; but when an irritated officer (not all the officers pursued such a reprehensible course, but a few of them did) swore at us as if we were brutes, when we were already burdened almost beyond endurance, it is no wonder there was an impulsive desire to retaliate. For my own part, my feelings never were so outraged, and the desire for revenge never ran so high and wild as then. But we cooled down, though our physical sufferings were not lessened; as we tramped on through the sands we became so weak it was almost impossible to keep our ankles from striking together as we walked, and our hard and dry shoetops would cut our ankles till the blood came.

CHAPTER VII.

IT was but a little while after this that we left the Rio Grande del Norte, and pressed on toward the west. One day, while passing up a brushy canyon, my place being with the advance guard, in the rear of the road hands, I had occasion to step into the brush by the roadside. While there, out of sight, Col. Cooke and staff and guides came along and stopped right opposite me, so close that I dared not move lest they should see me. As they came up, the colonel inquired of the guides if there were no fruit or berries that men could live on; the reply was, no, not a thing. They were talking about some place ahead that the guides were acquainted with. The colonel then asked if there were no trees that had bark something like elm bark, which men could live on for a few days; but the answer was that there was neither fruit, roots nor bark, that the country was a barren waste.

Upon receiving this information, the colonel exclaimed,

"What can we do?" In response, the suggestion was that the guides did not know unless some of the stronger men and mules were sent on a forced march to the first place in California, where they could get a bunch of beef cattle and meet us on the desert with them. There was some further conversation, when it was ended by the colonel exclaiming, with a despairing oath, "I expect the men will starve to death!"

The deep gloom of sadness hung over those who knew of the situation. All of the men, however, were not informed of the gravity of the position we were in. At that time we were drawing less than half rations. The fresh meat we had was more like glue or jelly than beef. The plan had been adopted of slaughtering the weak cattle first, so that the stronger animals could travel faster. When an animal became too weak to hold up one end of a yoke, or to carry a packsaddle, it was slaughtered, and the flesh issued to the men. Not a scrap of the animal would be left on the ground; the hide, intestines—all was eaten; even the tender or soft edges of the hoofs and horns would be roasted, and gnawed at so long as a human being possibly could draw subsistence therefrom. Many times we were without water to wash the offal. The bones would be carried along, broken up, and boiled and re-boiled, in some instances as long as there could be seen a single "bird's eye" (the name given to solitary spots of grease that would come to the surface) of grease rise on the water; then each man was eager for his share..

Sometimes cattle became so weak that men were left with them to come up to the command after night. On one occasion, when an old ox could not be got into camp and had to be left four or five miles back, men were sent bright and early next morning, to bring him in. It snowed that night, and in camp things generally were disagreeable. The ox was brought in, slaughtered, and issued to us for rations. If any man had failed to get his share of that white ox at that time there might have been a row, but a fair distribution maintained peace. The place of our camp was called White Ox Creek, and we laid by for one day to rest and refresh ourselves.

From there we traveled over a rough country, but one that evidently had been inhabited ages ago, for we found stone walls, pottery by the acre, and old and dry canals—their former source of water having disappeared. We found in a rock a deep and large hole with water sufficient to supply the command; we secured it by drawing all night, until everything was watered. Then we moved on, and next night camped without water. We passed many old mines, supposed to be of silver and copper, and there were said to be gold mines in the vicinity. Late at night we traveled, and were on the march early the following morning. All day we pressed forward as rapidly as possible, there being no water, and late at night the command came to a place called Dry Lake.

That was the hardest day for me that came in the experience of the whole journey. I had been run down so low with a severe attack of dysentery that I could travel no longer, and laid down. My thirst was intense, and it did not seem possible that I could live till morning. It seemed that everyone was traveling as best he could, for the rearguard passed me without taking any notice. Men went by, looking like death, their mouths black, their eyes sunken till it was difficult to recognize them. Some eyes had a staring glare, which looked as if the monster death were close at hand. Yet the men staggered on, their feet hitting each other, tit for tat, as one was dragged past the other. The hopes of these men were greater than mine, for I had ceased to march. This was the first time I had felt there was little reason to hope that I would ever reach camp again, for I supposed that all the men had passed me. The sun's rays

faded away on the eastern mountain tops, and the brigh
orb dropped beneath the western horizon.   For a moment
I felt that with me the vital spark would soon sink below
the mortal horizon, as if to accompany the king of day.

Just when my hopes were flickering as does a candle when the wick has all but burned out, there came to
my ears the sound as of the tinkling of a tin can that seemed
to keep time with a soldier's step as he marched. Gradually
the sound became more distinct until its approach was a
certainty.   Then my uncle, Alexander Stephens, came in
sight.   He had been left to bring up an old spotted ox which
had failed, and had driven the animal into the shade of a
rocky cliff, where the ox laid down, while the driver hunted
around and found a dripping of water as it seeped from a
crevice in the rock.   He had quenched his thirst and filled
his canteen, resting in the meantime, then followed on the
trail, pricking the ox with his bayonet.

When Uncle Alexander Stephens came up he handed
me his canteen, and the draught of water quickly revived
me.   I did not think myself able to rise to my feet, but with
a little assistance I got up, and took hold of the packsaddle.
My knapsack, musket and accoutrements were lashed to the
ox, and by a final effort we reached Dry Lake camp, by
halting at short intervals along the four miles we had to
travel.

Wretched, wretched indeed, was the condition of the
command that night.   It is doubtful whether at any time
in the long march the men suffered more than they did then
and the forty-eight hours preceding.   Next morning, at the
doctor's call, many had to be helped by their comrades to
the place designated for the sick.

For myself, two men sat me upon the ground, and held
me up till my time came to be questioned.   Dr. Sanderson
called out, "What is the matter with you?"   When he received the information asked for he remarked gruffly: "I've

a d——d great mind not to report you sick. I never saw such a d——d set of men in my life. They will not report till d——d nigh dead." I answered that it did not matter to me whether he entered me on the sick list or not, for I could not walk. At this he said sharply. "Not a d——d word out of you or I'll make you walk."

Then he ordered the steward to give me a dose of castor oil and laudanum, stating the quantity. The steward, William Spencer, said, "Isn't it a rather heavy dose?" to which the doctor responded with a curse, telling him to do as he was ordered. At that the dose was poured into a tea-cup, filling it half full. It was given to me, the steward saying in a low tone of voice, "If you do not throw it up it will kill you." I was assisted back to the company's wagon, and soon vomited the medicine, but not until it had changed my countenance so much that the lieutenant of my company, Cyrus Canfield, did not know me. He came and ordered me out of the wagon, telling me to go to my own company. It was sometime before he could be convinced who I really was, then remarked that I looked so near dead that he could not believe it was I. But when he recognized me he was very kind, and was willing to do anything he could for my relief.

For four days I lay in a dull stupor, when that phase of the disease was checked, and a very high fever set in. My sufferings were so terrible that some of my messmates came into the tent, anointed me with oil, then administered to or prayed for me; and although burning with a high fever till it seemed that I could not live, I was instantly healed, so that when they took their hands off the fever was entirely gone, and I was wet with perspiration. From that time I began to gather strength. That was my first experience with the ordinance of healing by the laying on of hands by the Elders of the Church of Jesus Christ of Latter-day Saints.

CHAPTER VIII.

ON THE SUMMIT OF THE ROCKY MOUNTAINS--CROSSING THE BACKBONE
OF THE NORTH AMERICAN CONTINENT—REVIEW OF THE JOUR-
NEY—GRAVES OPENED BY WOLVES—MUTILATED BODIES--AN UN-
PARALLELED JOURNEY OF HARDSHIP—THE PROSPECT AHEAD—A
MATTER OF LIFE AND DEATH—START DOWN THE PACIFIC SLOPE--
DESCENDING THE CLIFFS WITH WAGONS—ONE VEHICLE SLIPS
AND IS REDUCED TO KINDLING WOOD AND SCRAP IRON—INTO A
NEW CLIMATE--CHANGE IN THE CHARACTER OF VEGETATION--
WILD HORSES AND CATTLE—ATTACKED BY WILD CATTLE—SEV-
ERAL MEN HURT AND ONE MULE GORED TO DEATH--A NUMBER
OF CATTLE KILLED—SUPPLY OF BEEF—REACH THE SAN PEDRO
RIVER—TRAVELING THROUGH A HEAVY GROWTH OF MESQUIT
AND CHAPPARAL--APPROACH THE MEXICAN GARRISONED TOWN
OF TUCSON—NEWS OF APPROACH OF A LARGE AMERICAN ARMY
SENT TO THE MEXICANS—ORDER ISSUED BY COLONEL COOKE.

AT the camp at Dry Lake, which we reached between
November 20 and 25, we laid over a day, and a party
was sent ahead to cut a road over the divide.   I was too
weak for four or five days to take much interest in what
passed; and in the meantime the command reached and
crossed the divide, or summit of the Rocky Mountains—
the backbone of the North American continent—where the
waters are divided, flowing on either side to the Atlantic
and Pacific respectively.

For eighteen hundred miles the Mormon Battalion
members had made a hard and weary march.   Starting
from Nauvoo, on the Mississippi River—the "father of
waters"—as exiles, they had passed over a lovely country,
yet at a season of the year when travel was difficult, to the
Missouri River.   At the latter point the battalion was
mustered into service, and moved over an excellent country
two hundred miles to Fort Leavenworth; thence through
what is now the state of Kansas, passing over a goodly land

to the Great Plains, a timberless country, where water is scarce. There they began to be footsore and leg-weary, and to suffer severely from heat and thirst. Soon they came to the desert, and for nine days tried cooking their shortened rations over "buffalo·chip" fires, with fuel even scarcer than it was poor; often having very little water, and that brackish, so that men and hearts began to grow weak and ill.

At this point in the long journey they commenced passing the open graves of soldiers, many of whom laid down their lives in the advance companies. Their graves were open for the reason that wolves had dug up the dead bodies and devoured the flesh from the bones; the blankets in which the bodies were wrapped were torn to shreds, while in some instances the carcass still hung together, except that the fingers and toes had been eaten off by wild beasts. The road was also strewn with dead horses and cattle, so that as the battalion advanced the gruesome sights became more frequent and therefore excited less comment. And in turn the battalion contributed a share of dead to the lonely graves of the plains.

Then, on the sandy roads, there was the rough order to put the shoulder to the wheel and help the jaded teams; and the battalion waded creeks and rivers with quicksand bottoms, or lifted or pulled at ropes in lowering or raising their wagons over rough and precipitous places—in what appeared at that time a rough and worthless country, which may not have changed greatly since.

At times they were called forward to tramp sand roads for teams, and then to return and pull at ropes or push at wagons which, without assistance, the teams could not control. Then when Santa Fe was passed the journey was proceeded upon with reduced rations, down the difficult country along the Rio Grande del Norte. Onward the struggle continued, over sandy deserts and through a

rough, mountainous region, where the hardships were
intense, and where there seemed no eye to pity and no
hand to pass even a drop of water to moisten the parching tongue. It was not human capability, it was the divine
power that sustained them in such extremities as they had
to endure.

It was thus the renowned Mormon Battalion toiled and
struggled on their journey to the summit of the lofty
Rocky Mountain range—the crest of the continent— a
journey whose details of privation, and peril, and patient
courage, cannot be told in human words, and never can be
realized except by those who experienced it. So many lofty
mountain spurs had been crossed, that the final ascent
seemed quite gradual.

Leaving now this general survey of the past, I recall
that from the lofty eminence we had reached on our march,
the descent was very abrupt and difficult, through the rugged defiles to the west. But with the battalion it was a
case of life and death. That was no place to remain, there
was no earthly help at hand, no way to life open but to
trust in God and persevere in the onward movement. So
with the pick-axe and crow-bar we commenced to clear the
most feasible road down by chopping away the shrubbery
and brush and removing that and the rocks.

After much of the baggage had been taken down the
mountain one way by pack animals, long ropes and guy-
ropes were attached to the wagons and the descent with
them began by another way. The wagons were lowered
for a distance of half a mile or so, men standing as best
they could on the mountain side, letting the vehicle down
gradually, then holding it till other men could get a fresh
footing and lower it still further. Thus one by one the
wagons were let down in safety, all but one. By some
mishap that got adrift from the men, and to save their lives
they had to let it go until there was nothing of it but scrap-

iron and kindling-wood. As there was already an abundance of the latter around us, no one was desirous of descending to the rugged depths of the ravine to secure even a relic of that terrible descent.

It was thought by our commander and guides that it would require from six to eight days to make the descent, but thanks to the tact and skill of some of our men who had been accustomed to frontier life, the work was done in two days, and we were again where the wagons could stand on partially level ground.

In a very brief space of time we found ourselves plunged into a warm climate, where we could not see any plant or shrub that we had been acquainted with before. There was some small, scrubby ash, sycamore and black walnut, but everything, even to the rocks, had a strange appearance. We also had entered the land of wild horses and cattle, which roamed the hills by thousands. The wild cattle became excited at the rumbling wagons, and gathered thickly along our way.

At last the muskets commenced to rattle, partly through fear, and partly because we wanted beef. Finally a herd of wild cattle charged our line, tossed some men into the air, pierced others with their horns, knocking some down, and ran over others, attacking one light wagon, the hind end of which was lifted clear from the road. One large bull plunged into a six-mule team, ran his head under the off-swing mule, throwing him entirely over the near one and thrusting his horn into the mule's vitals, injuring our animal so it had to be left on the ground, where it expired in a few minutes. There were several men and mules roughly used and bruised, just the number I do not now recall. The attacking party lost twenty or twenty-five of their number killed, with many others badly or slightly wounded.

We had plenty of beef for a few days, and might have

secured much more. I never understood the reason why
we were not allowed to lay by and "jerk" an abundance
of meat for the subsequent use of the command, but the
stop was not permitted. Many of the men felt greatly disappointed and indignant because we were denied the privilege of availing ourselves of this splendid opportunity of
replenishing our scanty rations. We were half starving
at the time, and perhaps if we had been allowed to lay by
a few days we would have gorged ourselves to our injury.
It may be that would have been more serious than to have
stormed, as some did, at being ordered to march on.   It is
possible this was the view taken by our commander, though
we never knew.

Continuing our advance to lower levels, the climate
was mild and pleasant.   Our course was northwesterly until we passed a deserted ranch called San Bernardino, in
what is now Arizona, and followed down the San Pedro
River.   I think this was the south fork of the Gila River.
There was some good country along this lovely stream. It
was there we first saw the mescal and mesquit, the former
being the plant from which the Mexicans distil their whisky (pulque), the latter a tree somewhat resembling the
black locust, but growing with a very spreading habit, making it difficult to travel among.   In many places it had to
be cut down and cleared away before we could proceed.
There was another scrubby tree-growth which the Spaniards call chapparal.   This brush grew very thick in places,
so that in cutting it away travel became very tedious.

Here the guides told Colonel Cooke that if we followed
along the stream it would be a hundred miles farther than
if we cut across the bend, but if we took the latter route
we would have to pass through a Mexican fortified town,
where a body of soldiers had been left to guard it as an
outpost.   At that time it was impossible for us to learn the
strength of the place; but it was thought that we might get

some supplies of provisions and some animals. At the same time there was considerable risk that we would have to fight, and perhaps get defeated, in which case it would be not only a loss of property but of life as well.

On December 12 and 13 we followed down the San Pedro, our course being nearly due north, near the base of a mountain extending towards the Gila River. The guide, Leroux, with others, returned from an exploration of the table-land to the west, leading to Tucson. They found a party of Apache Indians and some Mexicans distilling mescal, and learned from them that the Mexican garrison at Tucson numbered about two hundred men. The interpreter with the guides, Dr. Foster, had thought it proper to go to Tucson, and Leroux told the Mexicans to inform the commander at Tucson that an American army was approaching en route to California; that the advance guard numbered about three hundred and sixty men, and if it stopped to drill it would give time for the main army to come up; that the strength of the main army could be judged by the size of its vanguard; and that if Foster did not rejoin the advance guard by a given time it would be understood that he was a prisoner at Tucson. Upon learning what had been done and said, Colonel Cooke issued the following order:

"Headquarters Mormon Battalion, Camp on the San Pedro, Dec. 13, 1846.

"Thus far on our course to California we have followed the guides furnished us by the general. These guides now point to Tucson, a garrison town, as on our road, and assert that any other course is one hundred miles out of the way, and over a trackless wilderness of mountains, rivers and hills. We will march then to Tucson. We came not to make war on Sonora, and less still to destroy an important outpost of defense against Indians. But we will take the straight road before us and overcome all resistance, but

4

shall I remind you that the American soldier ever shows
justice and kindness to the unarmed and unresisting?   The
property of individuals you will hold sacred; the people of
Sonora are not our enemies.

"By order of Lieutenant Colonel Cooke.

"P. C. MERRILL, Adjutant."

CHAPTER IX.

ON the 14th the battalion ascended to the plateau,
traveling up hill for eight or nine miles, when it
struck the trail leading to Tucson.   Colonel Cooke selected
fifty men, with whom he pushed forward.   Passing the
vanguard, he soon reached water, where he found four or
five Mexican soldiers cutting grass.   Their arms and saddles were on their horses near by, easily accessible to our

men. But these had no wish to molest them, and the Mexicans appeared to pay little attention to us.

The colonel learned from a Mexican sergeant that rumors of a large force of American troops coming had reached Tucson, and great excitement prevailed in the town. Of course the colonel, who was possessed of generalship as well as a stern sense of discipline, took no pains to disabuse the Mexicans' minds, and thus possibly expose our little army to unnecessary peril. Indians who had seen us from a distance had overestimated largely our numbers, and thus served to impress the people of Sonora with the accuracy of the statement made by the guides.

The colonel also learned from the Mexican sergeant that the commander of the garrison had orders from the governor not to allow any armed force to pass through the town without resistance. A message was therefore sent to the commander by this same sergeant, saying that the people need not be alarmed, as we were their friends and would do them no harm, as we wished merely to purchase supplies and pass on.

The next day we traveled about twelve miles, passing a distillery, and camped without water. The battalion marched in front of the wagons, to protect the provisions. Here a new (to us) species of cactus proved very troublesome. It was jointed, and when an animal rubbed against the thorns it broke loose at the joints, and sections about three inches long would stick fast to the animal. The same variety of cactus is found in southern Utah.

This day a corporal, the son of Cassaduran, commander of the Mexican post at Tucson, and three Mexican soldiers were met with. They showed no signs of fear until Colonel Cooke ordered them arrested, when they seemed terribly frightened. On arriving at our camp, the corporal was questioned by the commander as to Dr. Foster. He said (and it proved to be true) that Foster was under

guard, but had been requested earnestly to come with
them, and had refused. He had feigned indignation at being
arrested, lest the Mexicans should be suspicious as to our
numbers and should get reinforcements and fight us. As
he anticipated, his conduct inspired them with terror.

One of the Mexican prisoners was released and sent
to the garrison with two of the guides, one of whom took
a note to the commander of the post, demanding Foster's
release and stating that the other three Mexicans were
held as hostages. About midnight, Dr. Foster was brought
into camp by two officers, one of whom was authorized to
arrange a special armistice.

Colonel Cooke sent a proposition to the Mexican commander that he deliver up a few arms as a guaranty of
surrender, and that the inhabitants of Tucson would not
fight against the United States, unless released as prisoners
of war. The Mexican prisoners also were released. Our
camp at this time was about sixteen miles from Tucson;
and on our advance the following day, when a few miles
out, a cavalryman met us with a note from Captain Cassaduran, declining the proposition to surrender. We were
thereupon ordered to load our muskets and prepare for an
engagement. We had not traveled far, however, before
two other Mexicans met us, with the news that the garrison
at Tucson had fled, and had forced most of the inhabitants
to leave the town. They also had taken two brass pieces
of artillery with them. A little later in the day, about a
dozen well armed men, probably soldiers in citizens' dress,
met and accompanied the battalion to Tucson. But before
passing through the gates a halt was ordered.

That morning, when we were striking camp for the
march into Tucson, Dr. Sanderson opened up again by
remarking that "every d——d man who could stand alone
ought to fall into line." Our first move was to form ranks
with everything in proper order to make an assault or re-

ceive a charge. Then we moved out in line of battle. When within three or four miles of the fort a stop was made, we were faced to the right, and the command came to forward march, double-quick time. At that the whole column moved on a smart trot. Some of us, at least, thought we were advancing upon an enemy that had been discovered by the commander; but when we had gone pell-mell over cobblerock and gullies, through brush and cactus, for a distance of nearly three quarters of a mile, we received the command to halt. Then came orders to left face, file left, march. This move brought us back into the road, where we filed to the right and marched on to the fort.

At the gates of the fort, Colonel Cooke made a brief speech, stating that the soldiers and citizens had fled, leaving their property behind and in our power; that we had not come to make war on Sonora; and that there must not be any interference with the private property of the citizens.

We then marched through the town, where a few aged men and women and some children brought us water and other small tokens of respect. We made no halt in the village, which had contained some four or five hundred inhabitants, of which number all but about a hundred had fled. Our stop was made about half a mile down stream from the place.

In the town we made purchases of wheat, corn, beans and peas, which we parched or boiled. We were so near starved that we could not wait for this food to be more than half cooked before we ate it. There was no general supply purchased at Tucson, but each man or mess obtained as much as could be with the scanty means on hand.

On the night of December 17, Albern Allen and his son Rufus C. Allen had been placed on picket guard above Tucson, with orders that if any body of men, say ten or more, appeared, an alarm was to be fired, and the guards were to run into camp. Sometime between midnight and two o'clock a body of Mexicans put in an appearance, and the alarm was given as ordered. The bugle sounded at the colonel's quarters, and soon Lieutenant George Oman, who was officer of the day, rushed through the camp, shouting, "Beat that drum; if you cannot beat the drum, beat the fife!" The drum-major, R. D. Sprague, obeyed the order, and hit the drum. Immediately the stern voice of the colonel shouted to cease that music. In less time than it takes to tell it, lights sprang up through the camp. Then came the sharp command from the colonel, "Dust those fires!" and the flames went out; the adjutant rushed through the camp with orders to the officers to form their companies into line, the men were commanded to fall in, and all was rustle and bustle.

The writer had been up relieving his stomach of half-boiled wheat, corn and peas, and had just got settled back in bed when the alarm was fired, so he heard all that was going on. As we all slept in our pantaloons, the first thing I thought of in that country of prickly pears was my boots; and while reaching for these and bumping heads with comrades, some of the men whose muskets were used for uprights for the tent thought these the first articles in the emergency and seized them, the tent coming down and the ridge-pole making another bump on heads. At the same time we were all trapped in the fallen tent, which was pinned down tight. I was trying to get the left boot on the right foot, and my footwear being rather small I had no easy job. All being caught in the tent-trap, the thought came how easy it would be for a body of Mexican cavalry in a charge to cut us to pieces, and we soon burst through the tent and fell into line.

For the first time in the whole march the writer brought up the rear in getting to his place, and received a rebuke from the officer in command, George P. Dykes. Right here, however, in that brief experience, I learned a lesson I have never forgotten, namely, order in dressing and undressing. We had been in the habit of putting our clothing anywhere and each throwing his on top of another's, if convenience appeared to suggest it, so that in the dark it was difficult for each to get into his own raiment. I realized then how important it was to have "a place for everything and everything in its place;" hence to put every article of wearing apparel down so that in the darkest hour of night I knew where to place my hand on it, and when armed always to have my weapons in the best possible order and where the hand might be laid on them without any mistakes.

Notwithstanding all the confusion, it seemed to me we were in line of battle in very short order, awaiting an attack of Mexican cavalry. There was a few minutes' breathless silence after we were ready for the assault, and no enemy appearing, reconnoitering parties were sent out to ascertain the true situation. We were held in readiness an hour or more, then learning that everything was quiet, were permitted to retire to our tents, but not without some apprehension of danger until the dawn of day, which came bright and peaceful, and we began our march out on what was known as the Ninety-five Mile Desert, which lay between us and the Gila River.

After the first day's march on that awful stretch of barren waste, we began to straggle along, and before the Gila was reached the command was scattered along on the clay beds and sand strips for twenty miles. We traveled night and day, not stopping at any one place more than six hours.

The command was in a most deplorable condition on this journey. Many were the men that lay down by the wayside without a hope that they would live to reach water, and often thinking that they were behind the command. But after they had rested for a few hours and perhaps dozed long enough to dream that they died on the desert, and that the wolves that were howling around were dragging their emaciated carcasses over the sands or perchance in the alkali pools, so strongly impregnated with poisonous stuff that it would consume, in a short time, the flesh if not the bones also, then the thought of home and loved ones would come; and what was sometimes last, though not the least, would be the memory of the promises which the servants of God had made when we left the dear ones of home. Then the worn and weary soldier would stagger to his feet, survey the surroundings, and perhaps would catch sight, in the distance, of some comrade who was staggering and reeling onward toward the setting sun, and would follow in his path.

So the almost dead soldier would go on, his feet playing pit-a-pat as they dragged past each other, until his limbs would refuse to carry him farther, and down he would go and repeat the agonizing experience of a few hours previous. He would also chew a buckshot or two to induce moisture in his parching tongue, and would offer an earnest prayer from his humble soul—a further exertion which he would not have brought his wearied mind to do if it had not been for the confidence he placed in the promises of God, made through His faithful servants.

Thus, dear reader, the renowned Mormon Battalion passed forward across the great Gila Desert, almost without a human reason to hope that they would reach the goal, and only able to accomplish their aim through divine grace. When they succeeded in reaching the banks of the river, their clothes were so tattered and torn that it was with difficulty they could cover their nakedness.

CHAPTER X.

ON THE GILA RIVER—PIMA INDIAN VILLAGE—WELCOME GIFTS FROM
THE PIMAS—AMONG THE MARICOPA INDIANS—ASLEEP ON THE
TRAIL—VISIT FROM A BEAR—LOSS OF PROVISIONS THROUGH AN
ATTEMPT TO FLOAT A QUANTITY DOWN THE GILA—HARD TRAVEL-
ING—CROSSING THE COLORADO RIVER—GLOOM IN THE CAMP—
LOWER AND UPPER CALIFORNIA—TERRIBLE MARCH OVER THE
TIERRA CALIENTE, OR HOT LANDS—DIGGING WELLS FOR BRACKISH
WATER—ADVANCE GUARD REACH A MOUNTAIN SPRING—WATER
CARRIED BACK TO REVIVE THE FAINTING TROOPS—LAST SPOON-
FUL OF FLOUR USED—DIVIDING THE RATIONS—IN THE CANYONS
OF THE SIERRA NEVADA—HEWING ROADS THROUGH ROCKS AND
BRUSH—FEEDING ON LIVE ACORNS AND GREEN MUSTARD—NEWS
OF VICTORIES BY UNITED STATES TROOPS IN CALIFORNIA –PRE-
PARING TO ENGAGE THE RETIRING MEXICAN ARMY—FIRST HOUSE
SEEN IN CALIFORNIA—BEEF WITHOUT SALT—TRADE FOR ACORN
MUSH—HEAVY STORM AND FLOOD IN CAMP—A FEW POUNDS OF
FLOUR SECURED—DANCING IN MUD AND WATER—RECEIVE OR-
DERS TO GO TO LOS ANGELES—DISCOVER A BODY OF TROOPS IN
LINE OF BATTLE—ADVANCE TO THE ATTACK—SUPPOSED FOE
PROVES TO BE FRIENDLY INDIANS—PRESENCE OF THE MORMON
BATTALION PREVENTS AN INTENDED ATTEMPT BY MEXICANS
TO RETAKE CALIFORNIA, ALSO AN UPRISING OF CALIFORNIANS
AGAINST THE UNITED STATES—ON A BATTLEFIELD WHERE GEN-
ERAL KEARNEY HAD FOUGHT—RELICS OF THE ENCOUNTER—
PROPHECY OF PRESIDENT BRIGHAM YOUNG AND ITS FULFILL-
MENT—SOURCE OF HIS INSPIRATION.

WHERE we reached the Gila River it was a lovely
stream, four or five rods wide; but the country
was covered with alkali grass and mesquit brush. We
rested part of a day, then proceeded down the river eight
or ten miles, coming to a Pima Indian village. The Pima
Indians were superior to any that we had fallen in with
heretofore. They were an agricultural people, peacefully
inclined, and kind and loving toward each other. Those in
the village appeared the picture of good health. They

came and went by twos, the males and females keeping,
each sex, to themselves. They seemed the most affectionate people I had ever met; happy and innocent in appearance—a large and handsome class of persons. Each
Indian was wrapped in a large home-made blanket.

The Pimas had corn, wheat, pumpkins, beans, and,
I think, peas. Some of the Indians noted our wretched
and starved condition, and cut up a lot of pumpkins—as we
cut them for cows. These they boiled, and handed to the
soldiers as the latter passed by and took the proffered food
in anything they could get to hold the steaming hot vegetables. The men were indeed thankful for these favors,
although they came from Indians.

It was between the 20th and 25th of December when
we left the Pima Indian village, and passed down the Gila
River to a broad, open, fertile valley in the Maricopa
Indian country. At the Maricopa Indian villages we met
many fine specimens of the native inhabitants. We traded
brass buttons for food. One brass button had more purchasing power than a five dollar gold piece.

It was some five or six days before we passed out of
the Maricopas' farming country. There was a large bend
in the river, and we traveled three days over a rough,
sandy country before we came to the stream again. On
this march we camped without water. The writer was one
of those who stood guard around the stock. The feed was
so scarce that we were kept running all night. I was so
completely worn out next day that at about eleven a. m. I
sought rest by dropping out of the command and hiding
from the rearguard behind a clump of brush that grew on
a sand knoll. No sooner had I laid down than I fell into a
sound slumber, oblivious to all danger.

When the writer awakened from that sleep the rearguard had passed on long before; the sun had changed
position so that the drowsy soldier felt perfectly lost, but

gradually he came to realize that it was three or four
o'clock p. m. Some six or eight feet from where he had
been lying he found fresh bear tracks, telling him of the
wild beast that had been viewing him while wrapt in slumber. He hurried forward on the trail, and reached camp
just as the night guards were being posted and his comrades were becoming greatly concerned for his safety.

Our route lay down the river, through deep sand and
mesquit brush, where we had not only to chop and clear
away the brush, but had to push and pull the wagons until
our souls as well as our bodies were worn out. We
gathered mesquit and a kind of pod to feed our mules. We
were six days traveling sixty miles, to the crossing of the
Colorado River, or Red River, as it was called by some.

The reader will not wonder that on reaching this
point a mountain of gloom rested upon the whole command,
causing the men almost to despair as they, on the 10th day
of January, 1847, stood on the banks of the swift-flowing
Colorado—the stream being half a mile wide at that place—
with no alternative but to wade across, pulling and pushing
at the wagons, then to cut and burn their way out, through
the thick brush on the bottom land, to the bench or bluff
that opened out on a barren desert, known to the Mexicans
as Tierra Caliente, or the Hot Lands.

Now the command entered upon another soul-trying
march. The route from the crossing of the Colorado was
over the northeast corner of Lower California, some sixty
miles above the Gulf of California, then into the southeastern part of Upper California. The stronger men, with
a little extra ration, preceded the main army, to dig wells
in the desert.

No sooner was the almost hopeless march commenced
than men began to lag behind, so that when the advance
guard came to a halt at any part of the journey, others
were miles behind. The first day we came to a well that

General Phil. Kearney and his men had dug, but it had caved in so badly that it was almost as much work to clean it as to dig a new one; and when it was cleaned, our men dug another. The water was scant and brackish. We remained at that point only until the rear of the command caught up, then proceeded on our way, stopping but a short time in any one place, until we reached Cariza, a splendid spring near the base of the Sierra Nevada range of mountains. The first men to reach water filled kegs and canteens, lashed them to the stouter animals, and hastened back to succor and revive the famishing men who were bringing up the rear.

On that terrible march many of the weaker men despaired of ever reaching water. We passed several, who, with sunken and glazed eyes and blackened mouths and looking as ghastly as death, stammered to us as we passed them: "Goodby, I shall never live to reach water. I cannot go a step farther, but shall die on this spot." Poor fellows! I verily believe that if they had not been resuscitated by the water that was carried back, their words would have been painfully true before the rising of another sun.

If it had not been for some fresh mules and beef cattle that we met on this tedious march, we never could have got through with the wagons, and possibly would have lost some men, as our flour had given out and we were reduced so near to starvation as to eat every particle of the worn-out beef ox; even the tender part of the horns and hoofs, and the intestines, were broiled on the coals and eaten, without water to wash them.

In our mess, the last spoonful of flour was made into a thin gravy by stirring it into some water where some of our glue-like beef had been boiled. This so-called gravy was divided among the men by spoonfuls, then the pan was scraped with a table knife and wiped into a spoon, and with the point of the same knife it was divided into seven parts. Each man watched the division; and I do not believe there was one man out of the seven but would have fought for his share of that spoonful of pan-scrapings. Nor do I believe there was one of them who would have robbed his comrades. For the last three or four hundred miles we had been in the habit of cooking the food, and dividing it into seven equal parts. Then one man would turn his back, and the cook or the one who made the division would touch each morsel and say, "Who shall have that?" whereupon the one whose back was turned would say, so and so, calling each messmate by name, until all had been "touched off," as we used to call it.

From our camp at the spring we passed into the canyons of the Sierra Nevada. The days had been excessively hot on the desert, and it was very cold and frosty in the mountains at night. We soon came to where the canyons were too narrow for our wagons; then with crowbar and pickaxe and sledge we went at the jagged rocks until the pass was sufficiently widened, and with our shoulders to the wheels or by tugging at ropes we got our train to the summit.

It was while passing through this range of mountains that we first saw live-oak acorns. They were bitter as wormwood; yet we ate considerable quantities of them, and as we descended the western slope they became very abundant, and served for a change. As we passed down to the valleys we found green mustard, which was boiled and eaten without pepper or salt.

About this time one of our guides or interpreters brought word from the governor of San Diego that several battles had been fought by the California troops and United States forces, and that we might meet a large Mexican army retreating to Sonora. In consequence of receiving this news, Colonel Cooke ordered a drill. We had secured a few beef cattle and some fresh mules, and with this increase of strength and the prospect of engaging the Mexicans we were spurred on from one mountain summit to another, pushing and pulling the wagons—a business we were well versed in, from oft repeated lessons.

At Warner's Ranch, we came to the first house we had seen in California. Mr. Warner hailed from the state of Massachusetts. From him the colonel purchased two or three fat beeves. The beef was good, yet we had nothing to eat with it, not even pepper or salt for seasoning, and it did not satisfy the cravings of hunger. We rested a day at the ranch, and some of us wandered off up the creek in hopes of finding wild fruit or game. We came to a small camp of Indians who were engaged in hulling and leaching live-oak acorns, then pounding them to a pulp in stone mortars; this was boiled to a thick mush in home-made earthen pots. The writer bantered one of the old ladies for about three or four quarts of that cold-ochre mush, by offering her the belt that held his pantaloons in place. She accepted the offer, and he, being without proper utensil to receive his purchase, substituted his hat for a pan, and the mush was scooped into it. Then when he found himself in the dilemma of his pantaloons threatening to desert him, he seized the alternative of holding up that portion of his attire with one hand, and carrying his hat and its contents in the other, and proceeded to camp, where his purchase was divided and devoured as a sweet morsel.

From Warner's Ranch we traveled over low hills and camped on a little narrow flat between two hills. In the night it came on to rain terribly, and the flat was so flooded that we awoke to find ourselves half-side deep in water. At dawn one of the boys crawled out of the water and wet blankets, and crowed; for he had learned that the men who had been sent back to recover some flour which had been left in the boat had come in with about four hundred pounds.

Soon every man in camp had heard the glad tidings of the arrival of this expedition, about which there had been much anxiety.

In a short time the writer was called on by the orderly sergeant of his company, D, to go with him and receive the portion of flour to be issued to the company. At the door of the tent where the flour was being divided we met Col. Cooke, who was sitting with his head down, as if in deep study. Some of the boys had found a fiddle that had fared better than its owner, and near by one of them struck up the tune of "Leather Breeches Full of Stitches," or some similar lively air. Immediately a number of men formed a couple of French fours and began dancing in water half to their shoe tops. The colonel caught the sound, started up, and inquired what it was. Some one replied, "Oh, nothing, only the boys are dancing and making merry over the prospect of getting a little flour." The colonel shrugged his shoulders and remarked, "I never saw such a d——d set of men before in my life. If they can get out somewhere so they can dry their clothes and have a little flour they will be as happy as gods!"

Doubtless the colonel could call to mind often having seen us stagger into camp, and perhaps could remember a dozen or so of us rush to where his mule was being fed corn mixed with beans, which the well-fed mule would object to by throwing his head first one way, then the other, scattering the half-chewed corn and beans in the sand, where the hungry soldiers would pick it from, rub it in their hands, and eat it raw; for to the famishing soldier beans are not so objectionable.

I am reminded at this point in my narrative that three croaking ravens had followed the command nearly all the way from Santa Fe, for the bits that escaped the soldier's eye. Surely if it had not been for the ravens' keener vision they would have left in disgust, and would have given us a very hard name. Even the wolf might have told his fellows not to follow such a greedy lot, which did not leave a bone till it was pounded and boiled and re-boiled till it could not be scented, and if perchance a bit was found it was too hard for even wolves' teeth.

From this camp we moved to the west under orders from General Kearney to go to Los Angeles. While on the march toward that point, just as we emerged from a canyon, we heard the drum and fife in an open valley. Soon we saw a military force forming in line of battle, and as we drew nearer we discovered their spears or lances gleaming in the sunlight, and officers dashing up and down the lines giving commands. Our advance guard slowed up, and we were ordered to form in line of battle. Every officer took his place, the command dressed in proper order, and, as we advanced, comrades looked into each other's faces as if to say, "How do you feel about it?" One asked Alexander Stephens the question, and received a prompt reply, "First-rate. I had as lief go into battle as not. If we must die, the sooner the better, for it seems that we must be worn till we starve and die anyhow. I do not fear death a particle." Others were heard to say as much, and although the ashy look of death shone in many faces, from the privations undergone, I do not think there was a tremor in any heart, or a single man who showed the white feather.

As we drew near the force in our path, there was a dead silence, as if awaiting the order to wheel into line and open fire, for we were within rifle range. Just then two of the opposite party came out on horseback to meet us. The colonel sent two of our interpreters forward, and the command was halted. Soon our guides returned and stated that the supposed foe was a band of Indians which had had a battle with Mexicans in the vicinity a few days before, and the Indians had returned to bury their dead. They had taken us for enemies, but their fears were turned into joy on discovering that we were American soldiers.

With all our bravery, there was a sigh of relief when we heard the news that our supposed enemies were friends. It was now late in the day, and both parties went into camp within a short distance of each other. Friendly visits back and forth were made that evening. The Indians were dressed in Spanish costume and were armed the same as the Mexicans; as I remember them they displayed bravery, and some skill in Mexican military tactics.

Next day we proceeded on our way, and passed down a dry wash, the bottom of which was mostly lined with a whitish cobblestone, upon which the feet of some comrade showed blood at every step for a hundred yards or more. I cannot now recall the man's name. We continued our march from that place, and afterwards learned that the Mexicans had intended to make an effort to regain California, but the timely arrival of the battalion prevented any attempt to execute the movement.

So far as I can remember, it was between January 23 and 27, 1847, that we passed over a battlefield where General Kearney and his little command had fought and beaten the Mexicans. There lay broken swords and firearms, and dead horses and mules; and there also were the graves of the slain, while all around the blood-stained soil was plainly within our view, fixing the scene upon our memory.

Here came to our minds the words of President Brigham Young, in his farewell address to the battalion, in which he said: "You are now going into an enemy's land at your country's call. If you will live your religion, obey and respect your officers, and hold sacred the property of the people among whom you travel, and never take anything but what you pay for, I promise you in the name of Israel's God that not one of you shall fall by the hand of an enemy. Though there will be battles fought in your front

5

and in your rear, on your right hand and on your left, you will not have any fighting to do except with wild beasts."

Here I pause and ask: Who on earth dare to make, of himself, such a promise, under the circumstances and in the name that this promise had been made? And yet over three hundred men who heard it could stand up after they had filled the time of their enlistment, and before high heaven and all the world could bear testimony to the literal fulfillment of those words spoken eight months before, in the camp in Missouri Valley, two thousand miles distant. I ask the honest reader: From whence came such foresight, if not from the Eternal God, the Creator of the heavens and the earth, and all things therein? To Him we ascribe all honor and glory, power and praise, for our success in that great, wonderful and unparalleled march of twenty-five hundred miles made by infantry. Who shall say that God had not made bare His arm in support of that ever memorable Mormon Battalion? But as yet the whole task of the battalion had not been completed.

CHAPTER XI.

ORDERS had been received changing our destination from Los Angeles to San Diego, passing by way of the Mission San Luis del Rey. When we reached the San Diego Mission we passed it by and camped between it and the town. It was en route to this place that we came in sight of the waters of the great Pacific Ocean, a view that was most pleasurable to us, and which we hailed with shouts of joy, as we felt that our long march of starvation was about over. We were now drawing five pounds of fair beef, with- out salt or pepper.

Another day's march, and we had completed the journey over the nation's highway across the continent. We were allowed one day at San Diego, when we were ordered back to the San Luis del Rey Mission. There was some dis- appointment, but the order to return was obeyed without murmuring. It was thought we would meet the enemy, as it was said there was a force of about eighteen hundred Californians, under General Flores, lurking in the mountains northwest of San Luis del Rey Mission, but we did not see them. At the Mission we were required to do fatigue duty, as it was called, which included cleaning up the place, it having been neglected a long time. At this place the following was issued by Col. Cooke:

"HEADQUARTERS, MISSION OF SAN DIEGO,
"January 30, 1847.

"Lieutenant Colonel commanding congratulates the battalion on its safe arrival on the shores of the Pacific Ocean, and the conclusion of its march of over two thousand miles. History may be searched in vain for an equal march of infantry; nine-tenths of it through a wilderness, where nothing but savages and wild beasts are found, or deserts where, for want of water, there is no living creature. There, with almost hopeless labor, we have dug deep wells, which the future traveler will enjoy. Without a guide who had traversed them, we have ventured into trackless prairies, where water was not found for several marches. With crowbar and pickaxe in hand, we have worked our way over mountains, which seemed to defy aught save the wild goat, and hewed a passage through a chasm of living rock more narrow than our wagons. To bring these first wagons to the Pacific, we have preserved the strength of the mules by herding them over large tracts, which you have laboriously guarded without loss.

"The garrison of four presidios of Sonora, concentrated within the walls of Tucson, gave us no pause; we drove them out with their artillery; but our intercourse with the citizens was unmarked by a single act of injustice. Thus marching, half naked and half fed, and living upon wild animals, we have discovered and made a road of great value to our country.

"Arrived at the first settlement of California, after a single day's rest, you cheerfully turned off from the route to this point of promised repose, to enter upon a campaign, and meet, as we believed, the approach of the enemy; and this, too, without even salt to season your sole subsistence of fresh meat.

"Lieutenants A. J. Smith and George Stoneman of the First Dragoons, have shared and given valuable aid in all these labors.

"Thus, volunteers, you have exhibited some high and essential qualities of veterans.   But much remains undone. Soon you will turn your strict attention to the drill, to system and order, to forms also, which are all necessary to the soldier.

"By order of Lieutenant-Colonel P. St. George Cooke.
    [Signed.]   "P. C. MERRILL, Adjutant."

It is stated by Sergeant Daniel Tyler, in his "History of the Mormon Battalion," that February 4th was the date of the reading of the order.   Its spirit and tone were an agreeable surprise to us, as the general tenor of the colonel's course had been so different, apparently, that we did not look for him to do the battalion justice.   Yet if he had been less stern and decisive, it would have been worse for us. We had stern realities to deal with, consequently like means were necessary to overcome the obstacles we had to contend with.   It required push and vim to enable the battalion to perform the heroic deeds demanded of it, and a sympathy that would have caused the men to shrink back instead of seeing that every one stood to his post of duty would have been a fatal error.   After all, Col. P. St. George Cooke was a good military commander, maintaining excellent military discipline; and for one the writer feels to say, Peaceful be his sleep.

It was about the 4th or 5th of February when we got

back to the mission, and the order given, with others, was
made known.   The other orders included such directions as
to trim the hair so that none came below the tip of the ear,
and shave the beard all but the mustache.

We were informed that we had no right to think in
acting for ourselves—that the government paid men to think
for us, and it was our duty to obey orders.   We were
allowed very little time in which to wash our rags and hunt
down the insects that had waged a continuous warfare on
us all the way from Albuquerque or the Rio Grande del
Norte to the coast; yet we turned on the creeping foe, and
never relented till we routed him, nor showed any quarter
till the last one was gone.   We also had to repel an attack
from the nimble flea in great numbers, in which we realized
that this impudent insect did not care where he hit.

While we were still living on beef alone, without pepper or salt, we were ordered out on squad drill, which
seemed to continue about eight hours per day.   The reason
given for this was the supposed threatened attack from
eight hundred Californians in the mountains; and further,
the rumors that Col. John C. Fremont, with eight hundred
or a thousand men, claimed it was his right, and not Gen.
Kearney's, to dictate to the United States forces in California.   In fact, it was reported that Col. Fremont was in
open hostility to Gen. Kearney, who was military governor
of California by orders from Washington.   Under these
circumstances, we were kept in constant readiness, not knowing the moment we would be called into active service.

Our training daily was one hour for each pound of
beef issued, the beef costing less than a cent a pound to the
government.   Sergeant Tyler says our rations were five
pounds a day, and I say it was not half enough, for we were
ravenously hungry all the time.   If the reader doubts this, let
him try the ration for a little while, and doubt will disappear.

About February 25 we obtained bolted flour and

some other supplies of provisions that had been brought from the Sandwich Islands, by Major Sward, to San Diego, and thence to San Luis del Rey by mule team. In the meantime we had received a small amount of unbolted flour, brought by Lieutenant Oman and a small detachment of the battalion sent out for the purpose. Then the beef rations were reduced; so that during the whole twelve months' service we did not once have issued to us the full rations allowed by the government to the American soldier—if we had full rations in one thing, another was lacking. Either the government made a great saving from regulations in feeding us, or a steal put money into some contractors' pockets.

Day after day the duties of soldier were performed, drilling, out on detached duty, or marching here, there and everywhere, early and late, by day and by night, just to suit the fancy of some of our officers, and not always upon real occasion for the movements. It would seem that in many respects the soldier's life is much like a faithful wife's; and in others much unlike a woman's work. Like hers, in that the task seems never done, busy all day and up at every hour of night in response to calls of first one child, then another, or even to the exploits of some mischievous cat, her rest broken and her life worn away; unlike hers, in that she usually has a dry shelter, regular meals, and a place to lie down when she can rest, while the soldier in time of war never knows where he will make his bed at night, often is without food and drink, having to move at the word of command over deserts, rocks, mountains, plains and rivers—a stranger to the locality he may call his home. But the toils of both are necessary, she to rear the nation's pride and strength—a soldier in the right; he to protect her and himself, to defend their country's rights and avenge her wrongs.

Returning to the narrative of garrison duty, it appeared

to me the hours of drill were more than Sergeant Tyler's account will admit of; but I shall not dispute with him, as I write from memory. I do recall that roll call came at daylight, sick call at 7:30 a. m., breakfast call at 8:40, drill at 10 a. m. and 3 p. m., roll call at sundown, tattoo at 8:30, and taps at 9 p. m., after which lights must be out except in case of sickness. All must be silent then, as the men are supposed to have retired for the night.

On or near the 20th of March, companies A, C, D and E took up their journey to the Puebla de Los Angeles. We traveled over a hilly country, where there were numerous herds of cattle and bands of horses. In some places we passed down to and along the sandy beach around big bluffs over which, so we were told, the Californians, some years previously, had driven thousands of horses and cattle to rid the country of them, as they had overrun the place so that all were suffering for food. This story seemed confirmed by the great amount of bones that we saw among the rocks and sands at the foot of deep declivities along the seashore.

On the way to Los Angeles we passed a stone church that had been badly shaken; the walls had been good mason work, but now were mostly broken down. We were told that an earthquake did the damage, and that some three hundred people had been killed. On by the San Gabriel River we went, arriving at Los Angeles in about four days' march from where we had started out. We marched into the main street and stacked our arms as if to say, "We have possession here."

Most of the citizens stood aloof, looking as if the cause they had supported was lost, but soon the merchants brought out buckets of whisky and wine, which they set before the command, inviting us to help ourselves. Some accepted the invitation rather freely, while others refrained from touching the beverages. We returned to the river at night, and camped.   In a day or two we were marched about two miles up the stream, and above the town, where we again ran out of provisions and had to go hungry; nor did we break our fast till 11 a. m. next day.

At this time the air was full of alarming rumors.   A revolt of Californians was talked of; then it was Fremont who was said to be in rebellion against General Kearney's authority; and again, a powerful band of Indians was ready to pounce down upon us.   It was not very unexpectedly, therefore, that we received orders to occupy the most commanding point overlooking the town.   Soon after this we learned that a supply of provisions for the command had been landed at San Pedro, about twenty-one miles distant, and teams and wagons were sent at once, under an escort of soldiers, the writer being one.   We returned next day, heavily loaded.

About this date, the command began the erection of a fort, or rather began to throw up earthworks.   Lieutenant Rosecranz was ordered with a small detachment to Cajon Pass, a narrow opening in the Sierra Nevada range, about eighty miles east of us.   The object was to guard the pass against the advance of any foe, for, as has been said, there were many rumors of impending danger.   In a short time, Lieutenant Pace, with twenty-nine officers and men of the battalion—the writer being one of the number—received orders to relieve the detachment of Lieutenant Rosecranz. Pace's command had just reached the Rosecranz party, finding the latter in the act of striking camp, when a dispatch came by pony express ordering us to return as well.

On our march out, the wild cattle, which were there by thousands, became excited and began to bellow and crowd toward us.   We could see them for miles coming on the run.   They closed in quickly until we were surrounded by them on three sides, with a deep gulch or very brushy ravine on the fourth.   We retreated in double-quick time

to this gulch, and were compelled to remain in what shelter
it afforded until the next day, before we could pass on in
safety.

The unsettled state of the country kept us constantly
busy.   Our fort was pushed to completion, and we having
obtained what artillery Colonel Fremont had, the twelve or
fifteen pieces now in our possession were placed in proper
position for defense.   Everything was made as complete
as could be, and the warclouds began to give way.   Fremont had been placed under arrest for insubordination or
rebellion, I do not recall which, and this contributed to the
peace of the country.

A Spaniard was hired to haul a liberty pole from San
Bernardino Canyon, a distance of eighty miles, and as he
dared not undertake the journey without a military escort,
Corporal Lafayette Shepherd and fourteen men, among
whom the writer was included, were sent to protect the
Spaniard and help get the pole down to the fort.   On that
trip we camped on the present site of San Bernardino City,
then a wild and lonely wilderness, with not a house or farm
in sight.   At that time the country abounded in wild cattle,
bear, and other wild animals.

Just where we came out on the plain we camped for
the night, and in the morning our Spanish friend went out
into the hills to see if he could kill a deer.   Soon he came
upon a party of Indians jerking beef, and he shot into their
camp.   They came out, returned his fire, and gave him
chase.   We were getting breakfast when he dashed into
our camp, shouting that the Indians were upon us, and for
us to get our guns.   Of course, we complied, and were
ready in short order, but as no Indians came, the Spaniard
insisted that we go in and rout them, as they were killing
the citizens' cattle, and our commander had given a
promise of protection from this.   Hastily we saddled our
mules and started, expecting every moment to meet the

Indians, who were on foot. We found no one before we came to the campfires, around which was strewn considerable beef. Soon we discovered the Indians fleeing up the mountain, and on our jaded mules we gave chase, but when we reached the summit the Indians were going up the opposite ridge. We dismounted and poured a few volleys into the brush above them. They did not fire back. I do not think any harm was done. They were fleeing for their lives and did not show any opposition to us, and we had no desire to harm them, but simply to demonstrate to the Californians that as United States soldiers we were ready to protect them and their property, as was promised by our officers.

We hastened back to the fort with our charge, the logs in the rough being about fifty feet each, the two making a pole between ninety and ninety-five feet long when completed, which was done by the members of the battalion at the fort.

Another event about this period was an order by Colonel Cooke for a detail of good marksmen and trusty men to go through the town and shoot or bayonet all the dogs to be found in the streets. The colonel had notified the town authorities of his intention. Accordingly the detail was made and ammunition issued. The writer was one of the trusted marksmen. We sallied forth in the town of Los Angeles, where the dogs were more numerous than human beings, and commenced our disagreeable and deadly work. Muskets rattled in every street and byway, dogs barked and howled in every direction, and women and children wept to have the animals spared. But military orders had to be obeyed, for the dog nuisance had become intolerable. After that, there were sanitary orders sent forth, and the streets were cleared of the dogs and a great amount of bones and other rubbish.

With all this cleaning up, there still was tolerated the

greater nuisances of liquor drinking, gambling, the most lewd and obscene conduct that could be imagined, Sabbath breaking by horse racing, cock and bull fighting, men fighting and knifing one another—indeed, the Sabbath was the greater day for all these vices.

Bull fighting was carried on inside of a square of one to four acres surrounded by one-story adobe flat-roofed houses, on which spectators would climb, and thus have an excellent view of the whole exhibition of cruelty and bravado and jeopardy to life. Numbers of the wildest and most ferocious bulls were taken, and were brought into the arena one at a time. The animal was turned loose, and a man would tease him into fury with a sharp lance. A horseman would charge and make thrust after thrust at the maddened bull, striving to pierce him just behind the horns, the aim being to cut the pith of the spinal column at that point. If this were done, the animal would fall dead on the spot. As a general thing, the bull was more apt to gore the rider's horse, and give the rider himself a very close call; but a number of very expert horsemen were kept in readiness to lasso the bull or cast a blanket over his eyes and thus blindfold him until his tormentor got out of danger. In this cruel sport many horses were sacrificed, and sometimes the riders as well. It was not an unusual thing for a hundred or more of these wild bulls to be collected at a time, and the bloody sport to be kept up three or four days and perhaps more. Sometimes a grizzly bear would be captured and turned loose with a wild bull, the death of one and perhaps both being the result. The whole populace seemed to enjoy this cruel sport, shouting and screaming thereat all the day long. Males and females, of all ages and conditions, met on a common level to witness this wild and reckless amusement.

Horse racing took place on the principal streets. One popular part of this pastime was to secure an old male chicken; this was buried all but the head in a hole in the street, the soil being packed in as tight as could be and have the bird live. An Indian stood by to rebury the fowl as fast as the horsemen resurrected him by seizing him by the head when riding past at full speed. The aim was to swoop down, seize the cock's head, pull the bird out of the hole, and hold to the head to the end of the contest, which was indulged in by a dozen or more. When one rider tore the bird from the hole all the others would charge on him and try to capture it. The possessor would strike right and left, to hold his prize, until the poor fowl was torn to pieces. Often the bird fell to the ground alive, was buried again, and some one else would lead in the dash for it. Just before the rider reached the fowl, a horseman on either side would lash the horse unmercifully, so that the rider could not slow up to get a better chance at the exposed head. This game would be continued till some one carried the fowl's head to the end in triumph.

It was said that a scheme existed to draw the attention of the Americans during the most exciting of these sports, and then raid our camp; but if this ever was thought of it failed, for with us everything was kept in readiness for an emergency, and sometimes we lay at night with loaded muskets and fixed bayonets. Besides, we had become very proficient in military tactics, and every man had learned well his duty as a soldier.

The fort having been completed, and every reasonable anticipation for surprise in the return of the Mexican forces or for an uprising having been cut off, on the morning of the Fourth of July, 1847, the Stars and Stripes was hoisted on the pole in triumph, and floated in the breezes from the Pacific Ocean—I think the first time that glorious banner waved from a liberty pole in California, although Commodore Sloat had raised the American flag at Monterey on July 7, 1846.

CHAPTER XII.

THE members of the Mormon Battalion had been purchasing horses and mules and a general outfit for a
return to our friends at the close of our term of enlistment,
which was drawing nigh. At the same time, Col. Stephen-
son, of the New York volunteers, and other commissioned
officers, were making strenuous efforts to have us re-enlist
for another twelve months, or six months at least, telling us
they had authority to impress us if they chose, but they
preferred to have us come as volunteers. It had been
reported that although the Californians had been whipped,
there was not concord, and that as soon as the Mormon
Battalion left the country the Californians would revolt and
make an effort to overthrow United States supremacy; but
while we remained there was no fear.

Now, as there were many of the battalion who had
spent all their wages—ninety-six dollars for their year's
service—it may have appeared to them that the only thing
to do was to re-enlist. Horses could be purchased cheaply,
and provisions were not high, but some money was needed.
Consequently, one company re-enlisted under Capt. Davis
of company E, while the rest of the command were busy

preparing for their journey east to meet the Saints somewhere, they knew not just where.

Comparatively few of our command had acquired sufficient knowledge of the Spanish language to do their own
trading, and these acted as interpreters for their comrades.
The writer happened to be one of the few who had made
some success in picking up the language. On one occasion, when hunting the town and adjacent country for such
articles as we needed in our outfit, he became fatigued and
went into a cafe for a cup of coffee. On entering the
restaurant he found, besides the landlord, three or four
good-appearing Spaniards, who soon began to question him
about the United States and its people. Their questions
were being answered in a courteous manner, when the
attendant, who was a tall, fine-looking Spaniard, interposed
with the remark that America was a fine country, but her
soldiers were cowards and babies. The writer was alone,
and scarcely knew how to treat the insult; besides, there
was a possibility that it was intended as a joke. Therefore, he felt that it would be improper to be too abrupt in
replying, and said, quietly, that America was a good
country and her soldiers were the bravest of the brave.

At that moment the Spanish-Californian stepped back
and brought out an American hat that had been cut through
on the side by some sharp instrument. Said he: "Here is
one's hat—I killed him in battle. He was a great baby."
Reaching back, he brought out a dragoon's sword and a
holster, with two iron-mounted U. S. pistols. His eyes
flashed, and he mimicked the dying soldier, saying all the
Americans were cowards. My blood was up, and I taunted
him by asking him how it was, if the Americans were such
cowards and babies, and fled from the Spaniards on the
battlefield, that the Americans had taken the country.
Pointing to the Stars and Stripes floating over the fort on
the hill, I said, "That shows where the brave men are; it is

the Californians who are cowards and babies." In an instant a pistol was snapped in my face, and I saw the fire roll from the flintlock. Quick as a flash, I caught a heavy knife that was handy, leaped on to the counter, and was bringing the weapon down on the head of my assailant, when both of us were seized by bystanders, and were disarmed. I started for camp, but was dragged back to compromise the affair. When I re-entered the room the proprietor was priming his weapon with mustard seed. He said it was all fun, and we should make up. The spectators were anxious to settle, and offered to treat. Some of the Spaniards expressed regret at the occurrence. The matter was dropped, though I never was convinced that that Spanish attendant did not have murder in his heart.

On another occasion I had an unpleasant experience with another Spaniard. It was when I was on guard duty at the prison in Los Angeles. A very large, well dressed Spaniard came across the street from a drinking saloon and gambling den. He wore a large sombrero worth about eight dollars. He had been gambling and drinking, but was not drunk. Said he, "I have lost all my money, and I want to leave this hat with you for four dollars. If I do not bring the money back, you may keep the hat; it is worth eight dollars, and will sell for that any day." His offer was rejected, when he showed some displeasure, again urging the loan, and promising to bring the money back in a short time. Finally he prevailed, left the hat and took the money.

In two or three hours the Spaniard returned, saying he wanted his sombrero, at the same time promising to bring the money next day. Of course this proposition was rejected, whereupon he showed considerable temper, but at last said it was all right, he would find the money; and added, "Come over to the saloon and have a drink of wine, and we will be good friends." Thinking that would settle the matter, I còmplied with his request. He had on a long Spanish sarapa, or blanket, and as we neared the door he stepped ahead, leaned over the counter, and said something to the bartender. As I entered the door I was again asked for the hat, and he in turn was requested to hand over the money. He grew angry, threatened, and finally challenged me to fight. As I squared off to meet his impending assault, the Spaniard drew a large bowie knife for a thrust at me, but was stopped by some bystanders. I was at the time nineteen years of age, and my young blood was thoroughly aroused. I rushed for my musket, which was loaded and had bayonet fixed, and with the hurting end foremost I was quickly back at the saloon, forcibly declaring my readiness for the conflict. The bystanders closed in and called for peace, the four dollars was soon raised, and the sombrero found its way back into the hands of its angry owner, who displayed considerable effect of the liquor he had been drinking. But I learned an impressive lesson, namely, to avoid the companionship of men who drink intoxicants or who follow games of chance for a livelihood. Even if a man does not indulge himself, those who do are liable to ask favors, and if these are not granted the next thing is insult, which often ends in bloodshed, or did in those days in California. In illustration of the light estimate of human life, I can recall a man's foot being kicked about the street, and no more notice being taken of it than if it were an animal's.

As to Spanish character, the writer can say from a close acquaintance that when the Spaniards are sober and friendly, they are very friendly, hospitable and polite, being very good company; in fact, we seldom met with a more wholesouled and agreeable people. Yet it is doubtful if there are any people who will resent an insult quicker and more seriously than they will. They are brave and manly; yet those who are of mixed blood, such as the Greasers, are low, degraded, treacherous and cruel. In California there were a few of the higher class, many more of a medium kind, and still more of the lower class; so that in summing up the total of California's inhabitants in 1846-7, the country was only half civilized and thinly inhabited.

At that time the country was wild, being overrun with wilder horses, cattle, sheep and goats. In places wild oats and mustard abounded, in many sections the mustard being as high as a man's head when on horseback, and so dense that a horse could be forced only a few feet through it. In the foothills and mountains wild game was very abundant, consisting of elk, deer, bear, and smaller game. Along the water courses and on the lakes waterfowl was plentiful. There were millions of acres of uncultivated land, as good as any on the globe. The climate is scarcely equalled anywhere. The chief products of the soil then were wheat, barley, beans, peas, apples, peaches, plums, apricots, pears, dates, figs, olives, grapes, black pepper, spices, and many fruits not named here. These all seemed to grow very near to perfection, especially when properly cared for. The greater part of the labor was performed by native Indians, and that too with the most primitive tools. The buildings were low, being one-story adobe, with flat roofs covered with cement, or a natural tar that exuded from the earth; sometimes tile was used, but I do not remember seeing one brick building or shingle roof in all the land.

Under the conditions which existed, it was no easy matter for a hundred and fifty men to get an outfit together to travel over the mountains east, as that number of the battalion intended to do; but having commenced before we were discharged from service—say some time in June—to purchase our horses, saddles, and everything necessary for a pack train, we were partly prepared for the journey when the day came for us to be mustered out.

CHAPTER XIII.

MORMON BATTALION MUSTERED OUT OF SERVICE—ONE HUNDRED AND
    FIFTY MEMBERS ORGANIZE TO RETURN EAST TO THE ROCKY
    MOUNTAINS—START ON THE JOURNEY—DIFFICULTIES OF THE
    ROUTE—DEALING WITH WILD HORSES AND CATTLE—STAMPEDE
    OF A PACK ANIMAL—CHASE INTO AN INDIAN CAMP—LOST ALL
    NIGHT IN A SWAMP—SUFFERING ON THE DESERT FOR LACK OF
    WATER—ARRIVE NEAR SUTTER'S FORT—ON THE SITE OF SACRA-
    MENTO—PARTY DECIDE TO REMAIN OVER FOR THE YEAR, AND
    OBTAIN EMPLOYMENT—MEET CAPT. J. A. SUTTER AND JAMES W.
    MARSHALL—PROPOSITION TO CAPT. SUTTER—ENGAGED TO WORK
    ON A SAWMILL—PROCEEDINGS AT THE MILLSITE—MILL STARTED
    UP—THE WRITER ENGAGED TO DIRECT INDIANS LABORING AT
    THE TAIL RACE—CONVERSATION WITH MR. MARSHALL—MAR-
    SHALL TALKS ABOUT FINDING GOLD—HE AND THE WRITER MAKE
    A SEARCH FOR GOLD, BUT FINDING NONE, DEFER THE INVESTI-
    GATION TILL NEXT MORNING—MARSHALL'S FAITH IN HIS BEING
    SUCCESSFUL IN DISCOVERING THE PRECIOUS METAL.

ON the 16th of July, 1847, the close of the Mormon
    Battalion's term of enlistment, we were called into
line, and an officer passed along as in ordinary inspection.
Then, without further ceremony, he said, "You are discharged." I do not think one-half of the command heard
him, he spoke so low. Some of us thought he may have
felt ashamed because of his conduct toward us on our march
to Santa Fe. He was the little bigot, Lieutenant A. J.
Smith.

Thus we bade adieu to United States military authority
and returned to the ranks of civil life. One hundred and
fifty of us organized ourselves into hundreds, fifties and
tens, and were soon on our way to meet our friends somewhere, as we supposed, in the Rocky Mountains east; and
still we did not know just where. We sought information
as best we could, and the most that we could learn was that

by following under the base of the Sierra Nevada range
six hundred miles we would come to Sutter's Fort, where
we could obtain further information as to the best route to
where we supposed we would find our friends.

It was about the 20th of July when the first company
moved out on the intended journey; and in three or four
days the remaining hundred followed. We passed Gen.
Pico's ranch about twenty miles northward, and from there
crossed over a mountain so high and steep that it made our
heads swim, and it was with difficulty that we could sit on
our horses. In places, it was impossible for us to dismount,
for lack of room. Two mules lost their footing and fell
twenty-five or thirty feet before they could regain a foot-
hold, and it was very hard work to get them back on the
trail. We traveled some eighteen or twenty miles from
Pico's ranch to Francisco ranch, where we joined the fifty
who had preceded the main body, and were waiting for us
to come up.

A meeting was held, at which it was decided to purchase forty or fifty beef cattle, which was done at not to
exceed four dollars per head. The course of our journey
from this time was northward. The country where we were
traveling was a wilderness of hill and dale, deep gorges,
and brush, so that the first two days we lost ten or fifteen
head of beef cattle. It was decided to make sure of the
remainder by slaughtering and jerking or curing the beef,
and next morning there came a battle with the cattle, which
had become wild and ferocious, plunging at the men on
horseback everywhere, so we had to shoot them down as
best we could. After stopping two or three days to jerk
the beef, we proceeded on our journey.

Many of our horses were bronchos, or wild, when we
purchased them, and gave us much trouble. The packs
would get loose and turn under the animals, which would
run and kick, scattering things as they went. One day

Alexander Stephens, William Garner and I had a horse stampede with its burden. I gave pursuit, and as I had no thought of anything but capturing the animal, I chased it about three miles, right into an Indian camp. The Indians must have seen me coming and fled. Their fires were burning, pots boiling, and camp equipage laid around. From appearances there must have been fifteen to twenty families; their tracks were thick and fresh. The runaway horse seems to have been so excited that, like its pursuer, it ran in among the camp before observing the danger; then it turned and I secured it with a lasso. At that moment I recognized the peril of my own position, in the possibility of being ambushed by Indians. It may be needless to state that I got out of that place in a hurry; although I had lost sight of the camp and was confused for a little time till I found my trail.

Upon returning, I met my two comrades, who had had all they could do to take care of the other pack animals, and were very anxious about me. It was getting late in the day, and the company had passed out of sight. We followed as fast as we could, but darkness overtook us and we soon found ourselves wandering in the bullrushes and marshes of the east end of Tulare Lake. Turn which way we would we could not find any trail out. At last we found a spot more solid than the surroundings; we halted and felt around in the darkness; every way we went it was mud and water. The night was so dark that we could not see each other or the horses, and finally we tied the animals together so we could hold them, took off the pack, and waited around till daylight. I do not think either of us slept fifteen minutes that night. We had nothing to make a fire with, and if we had, it would not have been wise to have attracted savage Indians with one. Early in the morning we prepared to seek a way out, and to our surprise, discovered close by a bullrush boat which an aged Indian was pushing through the rushes. The boat had been made by twisting and braiding the rushes together, and reminded us of what the prophet says about embassadors going forth in vessels of bullrushes. We could not learn from whence the Indian came or whither he was going, nor yet his errand. We bade him good day, and soon found the trail of our company. After going three or four miles, we met some of our men who had been sent in search of us; they had passed the night in great anxiety concerning our safety. Thankfully we reached the camp to have a bite of food and proceed on our journey, grateful that we yet had our hair on the top of our heads, where the darkey says "the wool ought to grow."

Our journey took us over cold mountain streams, some of which we forded, carrying our baggage on our heads and making from three to five trips each way; others we built rafts for, by tying dry logs together with our lash-ropes, piling them with baggage, and drawing them over or pushing them with poles, the men swimming their horses and often themselves. These streams were quite numerous. Among those I remember were the Tulare, the San Joaquin River, and others. The crossing of these streams was hard on man and beast, the water being cold close to the mountains, and the work hazardous owing to the rapid currents and boulders in the channels of the rivers. On this journey we were two days on dry plains, and suffered almost to death; some of our horses became so thirsty that their eyes turned white as milk and blind as bats; they staggered against anything they came to. Some of the men gave out entirely, and if it had not been for some of the stronger men and horses that pushed forward and then returned to aid the others, many of the latter never would have been able to have reached camp. Men had their tongues swollen and eyes sunken and glazed; some could not drink water when t was brought to them, until their lips and mouths had been bathed and some of the liquid poured into their throats. Fortunately for the writer, he was one of the stronger ones who went ahead and returned to his comrades the last day on the desert; the scene was terrible beyond the powers of description.

Fully five hundred and fifty miles of that journey was made without seeing a house, or a white woman or child. There were many Indians and their ranches, but the savages gave us no particular trouble. We pressed forward till August 26, when we came to the American River, two miles above Sutter's Fort and about a mile and a half from the Sacramento River, at the point where the city of Sacramento now stands. The locality was then a forest of cottonwood timber and undergrowth.

When we reached the vicinity of Sutter's Fort a consultation was held, at which it was decided that most of the party would remain until next year, and obtain employment where they could. Captain John A. Sutter and James Marshall contemplated building a gristmill and also a sawmill, but had no skilled workmen to perform the task. Accordingly, a committee was appointed from our number, who informed Captain Sutter that we had among us carpenters, blacksmiths, wheelwrights, millwrights, farmers and common laborers; that we were in need of horses, cattle, and a general outfit for crossing the mountains early the next summer, and that if we could not get all money for our pay we would take part in supplies for our journey; the committee also inquired what the prospect for employment was. Captain Sutter gave the committee encouragement, and asked them to call on him again in two or three days.

The result was, that between August 29 and September 5, from forty to sixty of us called on Captain Sutter. Some were employed to work on the gristmill; others took contracts on the mill race. The race was seven or eight miles long, and was also intended for irrigation.

Between the 8th and the 11th of September, Alexander Stephens, James Berger and the writer started for the site that had been selected by Mr. Marshall for the sawmill; we were the first Mormons to arrive at the place. Peter L. Wimmer and family and William Scott had preceded us a few days, having two wagons loaded with tools and provisions; the teams were oxen, and were driven by two of Captain Sutter's civilized Indians. Some weeks after we went up, Henry W. Bigler, Azariah Smith, William Johnston, and Israel Evans, members of the Mormon Battalion, came to the camp.

Upon our arrival at the millsite, work was begun in earnest. The cabin was finished, a second room being put on in true frontier style. While some worked on the cabin, others were getting out timbers and preparing for the erection of the sawmill. The site was at a point where the river made considerable of a bend, just in the bank of what appeared to be an old river bed, which was lowered to carry the water from the mill.

Between January 15th and 20th, 1848, the mill was started up. It was found that it had been set too low, and the tail race would not carry off the water, which would drown or kill the flutter wheel. To remedy this defect, several new pieces of timber were needed, and all hands were put to work within ten or fifteen rods of the tail race, getting out the timbers.

Part of the time I was engaged in directing the labors of a gang of Digger Indians, as I had picked up sufficient of their dialect to make them understand me clearly. It had been customary to hoist the gates of the forebay when we quit work in the evening, letting the water through the race to wash away the loosened sand and gravel, then close them down in the morning. The Indians were employed to dig and cast out the cable rock that was not moved by the water.

On January 23, I had turned away from the Indians and was with the white men. Mr. Marshall came along to look over the work in general, and went to where the tail race entered the river. There he discovered a bed of rock that had been exposed by the water the night before. the portion in view in the bottom of the race being three to six feet wide and fifteen to twenty feet long. Mr. Marshall called me to him as he examined the bed of the race, and said: "This is a curious rock; I am afraid it will give us trouble." Then he probed a little further, and added: "I believe it contains minerals of some kind, and I believe there is gold in these hills."

At this statement I inquired, "What makes you think so?" He answered that he had seen blossom of gold, and upon my asking where, he said it was the white quartz scattered over the hills; on my inquiring further as to what quartz was, he told me it was the white, flint-like rock so plentiful on the hills. I said it was flint rock, but he said no, it was called quartz in some book he had read, and was an indication of gold. He sent me to the cabin for a pan to wash the sand and gravel, and see what we could find. I went to a cabin which had been built near the millsite by Alexander Stephens, Henry W. Bigler, James Berger, Azariah Smith, William Johnston and myself, and in which we were doing our own cooking. I brought the pan and we washed some of the bedrock that we had scaled up with a pick. As we had no idea of the appearance of gold in its natural state, our search was unsuccessful.

Mr. Marshall was determined to investigate further, but it was no use that night. He rose and said: "We will hoist the gates and turn in all the water that we can tonight, and tomorrow morning we will shut it off and come down here, and I believe we will find gold or some other mineral here."

CHAPTER XIV.

ARRIVAL OF MEMBERS OF THE MORMON BATTALION AT SUTTER'S
FORT OPENS THE WAY FOR THE DISCOVERY OF GOLD IN CALI-
FORNIA—JAMES W. MARSHALL OUT EARLY ON JANUARY 24,
1848—"HE IS GOING TO FIND A GOLD MINE"—REGARDED AS A
"NOTIONAL" MAN—"BOYS, I HAVE GOT HER NOW!"—TESTING
THE SCALES OF METAL—"GOLD, BOYS, GOLD!"—FIRST PROCLAMA-
TION OF THE GREAT GOLD DISCOVERY—SECOND AND THIRD TESTS
—ALL EXCITEMENT—THREE OR FOUR OUNCES OF GOLD GATH-
ERED—AGREE TO KEEP THE DISCOVERY SECRET—FIND THE
PRECIOUS METAL FARTHER DOWN THE STREAM—HOW THE
SECRET LEAKED OUT—MORE DISCOVERIES—FIRST PUBLICATION
OF THE NEWS MADE IN A MORMON PAPER—WASHING OUT THE
METAL—FIRST GOLD ROCKER—GATHERING GOLD—PART TAKEN
BY MR. MARSHALL, THE MORMONS AND CAPTAIN SUTTER IN
THE DISCOVERY—MISFORTUNES OF SUTTER AND MARSHALL—
ACCOUNT OF THE GOLD DISCOVERY CERTIFIED TO BY SEVERAL
EYE WITNESSES.

IT is my understanding that when Captain Sutter and Mr. Marshall were contemplating the erection of the two mills, an apparently insurmountable obstacle confronted them in the inability to get and pay for the skilled labor necessary for portions of the work. This obstacle was removed by the proposition our committee had made to Captain Sutter at the first interview; and in the two or three days' time asked in August, 1847, by the captain, a decision was reached to go ahead. Therefore, if it had not been for the opportune appearance of the mustered-out members of the Mormon Battalion, the sawmill would not have been built that winter, nor would the discovery of gold have been made at that time. But for the action of those Mormons in connection with the enterprise proposed by Captain Sutter and

Mr. Marshall, in offering the desired class of labor upon the terms they did, the state of California might have waited indefinitely to have been developed and to be christened the Golden State, and the entrance to the bay of San Francisco might never have received the title of the Golden Gate.

Resuming the narrative of my association with Mr. Marshall on the afternoon of January 23rd, I will state further that each of us went our way for the night, and did not meet again till next morning. I thought little of what Marshall had said of finding gold, as he was looked on as rather a "notional" kind of man; I do not think I even mentioned his conversation to my associates. At an unusually early hour in the morning, however, those of us who occupied the cabin heard a hammering at the mill. "Who is that pounding so early?" was asked, and one of our party looked out and said it was Marshall shutting the gates of the forebay down. This recalled to my mind what Mr. Marshall had said to me the evening before, and I remarked, "Oh, he is going to find a gold mine this morning."

A smile of derision stole over the faces of the parties present. We ate our breakfast and went to work. James Berger and myself went to the whipsaw, and the rest of the men some eight or ten rods away from the mill. I was close to the mill and sawpit, and was also close to the tail race, where I could direct the Indians who were there.

This was the 24th day of January, 1848. When we had got partly to work, Mr. Marshall came, with his old wool hat in his hand. He stopped within six or eight yards of the sawpit, and exclaimed, "Boys, I have got her now!" Being the nearest to him, and having more curiosity than the rest of the men, I jumped from the pit and stepped to him. On looking into his hat I discovered ten or twelve pieces or small scales of what proved to be gold. I picked up the largest piece, worth about fifty cents, and tested it with my teeth; as it did not give, I held it aloft and exclaimed, "Gold, boys, gold!" At that, all dropped their tools and gathered around Mr. Marshall. Having made the first proclamation of the very important fact that the metal was gold, I stepped to the work bench and put it to the second test with the hammer. As I was doing this it occurred to me that while en route to California with the Mormon Battalion, we came to some timber called manzanita. Our guides and interpreters said the wood was what the Mexicans smelted their gold and silver ores with. It is a hard wood and makes a very hot fire, and also burns a long time. Remembering that we had left a very hot bed of these coals in the fireplace of the cabin, I hurried there and made the third test by placing the metal upon the point of an old shovel blade, and then inserted it in among the coals. I blew the coals until I was blind for the moment, in trying to burn or melt the particles; and although these were plated almost as thin as a sheet of note paper, the heat did not change their appearance in the least. I remembered hearing that gold could not be burned up, so I arose from this third test, confident that what had been found was gold. Running out to the party still grouped together, I made the second proclamation, saying, "Gold, gold!"

At this juncture all was excitement. We repaired to the lower end of the tail race, where we found from three to six inches of water flowing over the bed of rock, in which there were crevices and little pockets, over which the water rippled in the glare of the sunlight as that shone over the mountain peaks. James Berger was the first man to espy a scale of the metal. He stooped to pick it up, and found some difficulty in getting hold of it, as his fingers would blur the water, but he finally succeeded. The next man to find a piece was H. W. Bigler; he used his jack-knife, getting the scale on the point of the blade, then, with his forefinger over it placed it in his left hand.

As soon as we learned how to look for it, since it glittered under the water in the rays of the sun, we were all rewarded with a few scales. Each put his mite into a small phial that was provided by Marshall, and we made him the custodian. We repeated our visits to the tail race for three or four mornings, each time collecting some of the precious metal until we had gathered somewhere between three and four ounces.

The next move was to step and stake off two quarter sections, beginning at the mill, one running down the river and the other up. Then we cut and hauled logs and laid the foundation of a cabin on each of them; one was for Sutter, the other for Marshall. This matter being finished, Mr. Marshall was prepared to dictate terms to us, for every tool and all the provisions in that part of the country belonged to Sutter and Marshall. They had full control, and we were depending on the completion of the mill for our pay. Marshall said that if we would stay by him until the mill was completed and well stocked with logs, he would supply us with provisions and tools, and would grant us the first right to work on their gold claims. We all assented to his proposition, and also agreed that we would not disclose the secret of the gold discovery until we learned more about it and had made good our claims. Not having the remotest idea of the extent of the gold deposits, we pushed the mill as rapidly as possible; for as yet we had not received one dollar's pay for our four months' labor.

Soon there came a rainy day, when it was too wet to work. H. W. Bigler thought it a good day to hunt ducks, so he put on an old coat, and was gone all day.

When he returned, we said, "Where are your ducks?"

He said, "Wait a while, I will show you; I have got them all right."

Finally he drew an old cotton handkerchief from his pocket; in the corner of it he had at least half an ounce of gold tied up. For a while all were excited, and he was asked a great many questions like the following: "Did you find it on Sutter's claim along the river?" "How far is it from here?" "All in one place?" "Is there any more?" "How did you get it, you had no pick or shovel?" "Can you find the place again?"

He replied that he had found it down below Sutter's claim, along the river where the bedrock cropped out along the bank, and in little rills that came down the hills to the river, indeed, everywhere that he found the bedrock cropping out.

"Then you found it in more than one place?"

"Yes, more than a dozen."

It was now proposed that we keep this discovery a secret, as the discovery in the race had been kept. So the mill work was pushed with vigor to completion. But in the meantime Marshall had felt it his duty to inform his partner of the discovery. Accordingly, he wrote a letter stating the facts, and sent me out to find a strange Indian who would take it to Captain Sutter, fearing that if he sent it by someone who was acquainted with the circumstances the secret might leak out. About this time Wm. Johnston found that he had some urgent business below and must go there, and did so; he went to the gristmill and along the camps on that mill race. Then somehow or other the bag came untied and our old cat and all the kittens ran out, and to the camps they went, until everybody heard of the gold discovery. But, like all great truths, people were slow to believe the story.

In a short time, however, Sidney S. S. Willis and Wilford Hudson, whose curiosity had been aroused, began to feel that they would like a little venison; and with that for an excuse they took their guns and set out on foot, having been assured that by following up the river they would come to the sawmill, which they succeeded in doing the first day. I think it was only a thirty-five miles journey. I believe they stayed one day and two nights with us; then, after a thorough examination of the bedrock, sand and gravel, and the surroundings, they gathered a few specimens, among which was one nugget worth about five dollars—the largest by long odds that had been discovered up to that time.

As Willis and Hudson passed back on their way home, they discovered a small ravine or creek in which there was some of the same kind of bedrock which they had seen at the mill race, and by picking around in the sand and gravel they discovered quite a rich prospect. That was just above what was afterwards called Mormon Island, about twelve or fifteen miles above the gristmill, and about the same distance below the sawmill. Then they returned to the mill, told their story, and showed the specimens to the boys. Some of these went to Sutter's Fort, to a little grocery store kept by a Mormon named Smith, who came around Cape Horn to California by the ship Brooklyn. The story of the find was told, and specimens exhibited to Smith, who wrote to Samuel Brannan. The latter was publishing a paper in San Francisco at the time; and from that press the news went forth to the world. Brannan was a Mormon Elder, and the press was owned by a company of Mormons who had sailed from New York around Cape Horn, and were presided over by Samuel Brannan.

From one hundred to one hundred and fifty Mormons flocked to Mormon Island; then people from every part of the United States followed, and the search for gold commenced in earnest. With jack, butcher, and table knives, the search was made in the crevices, after stripping the soil from the bedrock with pick and shovel. Next, we conceived the idea of washing the sand and fine gravel in tin pans, but these were scarce and hard to get hold of. Alexander Stephens dug out a trough, leaving the bottom round

like a log. He would fill that with sand and gravel that
we scraped off the bedrock, and would shake it, having
arranged it so as to to pour or run water on the gravel;
finally he commenced to rock the trough, which led to the
idea of a rocker.   His process caused the gold to settle at
the bottom; then he arranged the apparatus on an incline
so that the gold would work down and also to the lower
end of the trough.   At short intervals he would turn what
was collected into a tub of water, and at night it would be
cleaned and weighed on a pair of wooden scales that
Stephens made also, using silver coins for weights, counting the silver dollar equal to one ounce of gold.   This
rocker led to the renowned gold rocker; I am under the
impression that Stephens made the first rocker ever used
in California.

The next and last process that we used in gathering
gold was to spread a sheet on the sandy beach of the
river, placing some big rocks on the corners and sides to
keep it well stretched.   We then would fill in the rich dirt
on the upper edge, and throw on water to wash the dirt
down into the river, leaving the gold on the sheet.   Occasionally we took up the sheet and dipped it into a tub of
water, washing the gold off the sheet into the tub.   At
night we would clean up our day's work, averaging from
twelve to fifteen dollars each.   Our best paying dirt was
carried on our shoulders from Dry Gulch, fifteen to sixty
rods to where we could find water to wash it.   We made
buckskin pouches or wallets to carry the gold in; it was
not dust, nor yet nuggets, but small scales.

Sutter's capital and enterprise and Marshall's shrewd
sagacity have been given the credit of the great gold discovery in California.   The facts are, that James W. Marshall discovered the first color; in less than an hour six
Mormons found color as well, and within six weeks Mormons had discovered · it in hundreds of places that Mr.

Marshall had never seen, the most notable of which was Mormon Island, to where the first rush was made, and from where the news was spread to the world. As to Sutter's enterprise and capital, he furnished the graham flour and mutton, wheat and peas, black coffee and brown sugar, teams and tools, while we, the members of the Mormon Battalion, did the hard labor that discovered the metal. It is also true that we were in Sutter's employ at that date, and that we did not get paid for our labor. I worked one hundred days for the firm, and never received a farthing for it. I heard a number of other men say they never got their pay. It was our labor that developed the find, and not Marshall's and Sutter's, and we were never paid for it; when we went for a settlement we were told by Captain Sutter that he could not settle with us, for his bookkeeper had gone to the mines, and his books were not posted. He cursed Marshall and the mines, and declared that he was a ruined man; that the discovery was his ruin, for it had drawn off his laborers and left everything to go to rack, and that he was being robbed.

I do not wish it to be understood that I charge Sutter and Marshall with being dishonorable, for I do not. I think they were honorable men in a business way. The fact is, they were completely overrun with all classes of people, and were confused, so that the people took advantage of them, their business was undermined, and there was a general collapse of their affairs and of every industry and business. The cry was, "Gold! Gold! More Gold! Away to the gold fields!" Every other enterprise was sacrificed in the rush for gold.

With due respect to Captain John A. Sutter and James W. Marshall, to whom the world has given the credit for the great gold find, I believe that if they had been taken out and shot to death the day of the discovery, they would have suffered less, and would have met their Maker just as

7

pure, if not more honored in this world, than to have lived
and endured what they did.   As far as I am concerned, I
say peace to their remains, for on this earth they have been
greatly wronged, if I have read their history correctly.
Like a lynching scrape where there is an outburst of the
people, it is very difficult to find those who are responsible
for the crime.   Regarding the wrongs did these men, it
seemed as if the whole population of that locality picked on
them.

I will add here, that my account of the gold discovery
in California was submitted in 1893 to the following members of the party who were at the place in January, 1848,
and who were the only survivors within my reach at the
time: Orrin Hatch and William S. Muir, Woods Cross,
Davis County; George W. Boyd, and H. D. Merrill, Salt
Lake City; and Israel Evans, Lehi, Utah County, Utah.
They united in giving me a certificate that they knew this
account to be a true and correct statement of the discovery
of gold in California, at Sutter's mill race.

CHAPTER XV.

PREPARE TO LEAVE CALIFORNIA—SNOW IN THE MOUNTAINS CAUSES A WAIT TILL THE LAST OF JUNE—DISCOVER A RICH GOLD PROSPECT —LEAVE IT TO MAKE THE JOURNEY OVER THE MOUNTAINS—NO REGRETS AT ABANDONING THE MINES IN ANSWER TO THE CALL OF DUTY—CAMP ORGANIZED IN PLEASANT VALLEY—START ON THE TRIP—THREE MEMBERS OF THE PARTY AHEAD, LOOKING OUT THE ROUTE, FOUND MURDERED BY INDIANS AT TRAGEDY SPRINGS—COVERING THE BODIES—STAMPEDE OF ANIMALS— GUARDING AGAINST HOSTILE INDIANS—CROSSING THE DIVIDE IN SNOW—THE WRITER FOOLED—TAKE TWO INDIANS PRISONERS— CUTTING A ROAD—HORSES STOLEN BY INDIANS—PURSUIT TO CAPTURE THEM—IN CARSON VALLEY—ALONG HUMBOLDT RIVER— AT STEAMBOAT SPRINGS—OVER THE DESERT—MEMBER OF THE PARTY WANTS TO KILL INDIANS—THE WRITER'S EMPHATIC OB-JECTION—INDIANS WOUND STOCK—ADDISON PRATT AS A LUCKY FISHERMAN—WRITER TRADES WITH AN INDIAN—THE RED MAN'S TRICK—WRITER PURSUES HIM INTO THE INDIAN CAMP—ESCAPE FROM DANGER—JOURNEY TO BEAR RIVER—HOT AND COLD WATER SPRINGS—REACH BOX ELDER—VIEW THE GREAT SALT LAKE—ARRIVE AT OGDEN, WHERE CAPTAIN BROWN AND SOME SAINTS HAD SETTLED—JOURNEY TO THE MORMON CAMP ON WHAT IS NOW PIONEER SQUARE, SALT LAKE CITY—HEARTILY WELCOMED BY RELATIVES AND FRIENDS—REJOICING AND THANKSGIVING.

IN June, 1848, some thirty-seven members of the Mormon Battalion rendezvoused at a flat some six or eight miles from Coloma, California, near where the first gold discovery was made. This assemblage was preparatory to crossing the Sierra Nevada mountains at or near the head of the American River; for we had learned that it was next to impossible to take wagons at this time of the year by what was called the Truckee route, and as we had become accustomed to pioneer life it was thought we could find a better route, so it was proposed to open up one by the way stated. We had been successful in get ing a few hundred dollars each from the mines, and had fitted ourselves out with wagons and ox teams, seeds and tools; for our protection on the journey we bought of Captain Sutter two brass Russian cannon, one a four pounder and the other a six-pounder.

Some of the company, eight or ten, had pitched camp at the site selected, and were waiting for others who were tardy in getting their outfit. Early in May, a party consisting of David Browett, Ira J. Willis, J. C. Sly, Israel Evans, Jacob M. Truman, Daniel Allen, Henderson Cox, Robert Pixton, and, I think, J. R. Allred, went out about two or three days ahead, and found the country covered with deep snow, so that at that time it was impracticable to go forward with the wagons; the party therefore returned to the main camp, and waited till the last of June. During this wait, David Browett, Daniel Allen and Henderson Cox, being anxious to be moving, started a second time to search out the route, and were surprised at night and all were killed by Digger Indians. They had been gone some eight or ten days before the main body got together, and about twenty days before we started. Alexander Stephens and I, it seems to me, and some two or three others, did not join the party, as I remember, until June 29.

The day before starting from the gold diggings on our journey was kind of an off-day, in which the writer had some spare time and wandered off from camp, with pick and shovel. up into a dry gulch, where he soon struck a very rich prospect of gold, about a quarter of a mile from water. This was about 11 o'clock a. m. By sundown he had carried the rich dirt down in his pantaloons, and washed out forty-nine dollars and fifty cents in gold; yet kind reader, strange as it may appear, he, with his partners, hitched up and rolled out the next morning, and joined the main camp at what we called Pleasant Valley, but now, I think, known as Dutch Flat. I have never seen that rich spot of earth since; nor do I regret it, for there always has been a higher object before me than gold. We had covenanted to move together under certain conditions, and those conditions existing we were in honor bound to move the next day. We did move, leaving that rich prospect without ever sticking a stake in the gulch, but abandoning it to those who might follow. Some may think we were blind to our own interests; but after more than forty years we look back without regrets, although we did see fortunes in the land, and had many inducements to stay. People said, "Here is gold on the bedrock, gold on the hills, gold in the rills, gold everywhere, gold to spend, gold to lend, gold for all that will delve, and soon you can make an independent fortune." We could realize all that. Still duty called, our honor was at stake, we had covenanted with each other, there was a principle involved; for with us it was God and His kingdom first. We had friends and relatives in the wilderness, yea, in an untried, desert land, and who knew their condition? We did not. So it was duty before pleasure, before wealth, and with this prompting we rolled out and joined our comrades in Pleasant Valley.

At our camp in Pleasant Valley we organized with Jonathan Holmes as president, and with captains of tens. Then there were chosen eight or nine vaqueros or herdsmen, to take charge of all the loose stock from 4 a. m. till 8 p. m.; but in the main the herdsmen were the chief pioneers for the camp. I remember only a few of them: W. Sidney, S. S. Willis, Israel Evans, Jacob M. Truman, Wesley Adair and James S. Brown.

The date of our start from Pleasant Valley I cannot now recall, further than that it was between the 25th of June and the 1st of July. We made slow progress, for the road was very rough. About six of us rode ahead, and looked out and marked the route. We would go ahead half the day, and then return to meet the train, often finding them camped, the men working the road, cutting the timber, rolling rock, and digging dugways, or mending wagons. Sometimes we had to lay over a day or two to make the road passable.

Thus we pushed forward on our journey till we came to a place we called Tragedy Springs, for near a beautiful spring at this place we found the remains of the three brethren who had preceded us, they having been murdered by Indians, and buried in a shallow grave. We first found bloody arrows, then stones with blood on them, then the nude bodies, partly uncovered; these were recognized by Daniel Allen's purse of gold near by. Our feelings cannot be described through the medium of the pen, therefore I must leave these to the reader's imagination. We built a wall of rough rock around the grave, then covered it with flat stones to protect the bodies from wild beasts, This was the best we could do, for the bodies were so decomposed that we could not do more. The names of the deceased and manner of death, with proper dates, were cut in a large tree that stood near by.

The night we came to Tragedy Springs was very dark, and our camp being in a dense forest of large trees, the darkness was intensified. Guards were at their posts around stock and camp, when suddenly, from some cause we never knew, the stock stampeded. This raised a great excitement, and before it subsided one of our cannon was discharged; as it belched forth its stream of fire, and the sound of the explosion echoed in forest and hills, the animals were stampeded still worse, only a few horses that had been securely tied remaining. We were compelled to lay by for two days to get things together, but we finally did so, recovering all our stock.

We made another start, going to a place we called Leek Springs, because of there being so many leeks growing wild. We had to stop over and mark our way among rocky ridges. Thence we moved on, musket in one hand, or in a handy place to the teamster, with his goad or whip in the other hand, the train moving in close order and constantly on the alert for an attack by man or beast.

We ascended a very high spur of the Sierra Nevada range, on the south side. When we reached the summit the wind blew as if it were the middle of November. As we crossed over we came to a large snowdrift; on the north side of the mountain our wagons rolled over the snow as if on marble pavement, but when we came to where the sun had shone in the latter part of the day, our wagons went down to the hub, and four were capsized and some of them badly broken. The others succeeded in reaching the bottom in safety. It took us till after dark to pick up the pieces and get them together to be ready to start the next morning.

We all gathered around the campfire and discussed the subject of standing guard, when the writer remarked that there was no need of guards—that he would agree to take care of all the Indians that would come around that night, for it was so cold and disagreeable that he supposed no human being would come there from choice. Just then someone inquired what an object on a rock was. Some said it was an owl, others that it was an Indian. Two or three of us took our guns and sallied forth to settle the dispute finding to our surprise two Indians with feathered headdresses on, and with long bows, and quivers full of arrows. They were within easy bowshot of us. The party had the laugh on the writer for once.

We took the Indians prisoners, disarmed them, and prepared a place for them to sleep, after giving them their supper. The writer was one called on to guard them, and he promptly complied. The Indians made good company, though they were very nervous, and we had to threaten them frequently to keep them from making a break for liberty. At midnight the guards were changed, and at dawn we made ready to descend to the camp below, arriving there just as the Indians moved off; we had released our prisoners. The Indians soon began to come in from every quarter, all armed. We moved in close order, every man well armed. The savages numbered three to our one; they flanked us and we could see them on every hand, in threatening attitude. In this situation we had to chop and roll logs out of the way, move rock, and make dugways, lifting at and holding wagons to keep them from turning over. Consequently, our progress was slow, and the journey very hazardous. Finally, when we had worked our way carefully along the difficult route, passing over the summit of the great Sierras, which divide the waters of the great deserts from those which flow to the Pacific Ocean, the threatening red men slunk out of sight, and we found a rough camping place, where we lay all night upon our arms, but nothing came to alarm us.

We continued down the canyon and came to a more open country, camping by a river bend where there was good feed, water, and fuel. We had begun to feel more safe from the red men, yet that night they stole in past our guards and took some of our saddle horses which were tied within four or five rods of our wagons. The Indians escaped, and were detected only by our guards hearing them cross the river; this was about 4 a. m. Early in the morning we learned more definitely our loss, and eight or ten of us gave pursuit, following the trail across a sandy country and over the foothills, ultimately succeeding in the recovery of all our horses but one, and for that we captured an Indian pony that had the distemper, as we discovered after it had been turned into our herd. That was one of the hardest day's rides that the writer remembers in all his experiences, for we put our horses through all they could live for.   Every moment we were liable to ambush, for the Indians divided into three parties and we did the same. One of our party supposed he had killed an Indian, or certainly wounded him, just as he entered into the thick brush.

It was late the next day when we resumed our journey, and that night we camped in Carson Valley, where we looked on an extensive plain or desert.   Being unable to discern any evidences of water, we turned to the north, just under the base of the mountains, traveling over a very hard route, until we came to the Truckee River, where we entered the old emigrant road.   We followed that road till we came to the sink of the Humboldt, then called St. Mary's River.   The distance was said to be forty-five miles; be that as it may, we were twenty-four hours covering it, and I do not think we had any rest or sleep during the whole trip.

We passed the wonderful Hot or Steamboat Springs. I remember seeing a dog run up to one of them as if to lap the water, and as he did so his feet slipped into the edge of the pool.   He was so surprised at the heat that he gave one yelp of pain and jumped into the middle of the spring, stretched out his legs, and never gave another kick. In a very short time the hair was all scalded off him.   The incident reminded me of the story of a Dutchman who, when he came to a hot spring, ordered his teamster to drive on, as hell could not be more than a mile away.   We did not feel to blame the Dutchman, if the springs were like this; for, from the surroundings, hades did not appear to be far off, and we passed on without any desire to linger about the dreadful place.   It was about 4 a. m. when, as we approached the Humboldt River, our horses and cattle hoisted their heads, began to sniff, and broke into a trot; from that they started into a run, and we had enough to do to keep up with them till they reached the water.

We had a short rest, and resumed our journey, for there was no food for our stock, and the water was brackish, so we traveled eight or ten miles and camped for the night. As the grazing was still short, we made a very early start, and were soon joined by two Indians, who remained with us all day and were very friendly. When we camped they stopped with us, and as we had been told the place was a dangerous one for Indians, the presence of these two caused a suspicion that they were spies, and probably would signal their fellows when to attack the train.

We had been in camp only a short time when a white horse was led in. The animal had a slight wound on his wethers and a mark of blood some six inches down on his shoulder. This wound had been caused by the horse rolling on some burned willow stumps, one of the men having seen him roll; and there were on the animal the black marks from the charred wood. Yet some of the camp insisted that the wounds were from Indian arrows. At this time some one came up from the river and caused a flame of excitement by saying he had seen an Indian skulking in the brush, although he admitted that it might have been a bird or a wild animal, for, while he saw something move, he was not in a position to say just what it was. The discussion now waxed hot, and one man leveled his gun at one of the Indians, declaring he would shoot him. The writer was standing near by and caught the gun to prevent such an act, and was in turn threatened with being shot, when the trouble was stopped by others interfering.

That night, when the camp was called together as usual, for prayers and consultation, and prayers had been said, the same man who had threatened to shoot the Indian moved that we lay by the next day, hunt down all the Indians we could find, and by killing rid the country of the "d—d black rascals." This startling proposition seemed to stun the senses of the men for a moment, for no such spirit had invaded the camp before; our motto being peace on earth, good will to man.   The proposition was so repugnant to the writer's feelings that he made his maiden speech in strongly opposing the motion, declaring that if such a cruel step were taken he would be a swift witness against all who engaged in the wicked and savage action; he also asserted that he would inform on them at the earliest opportunity, for as yet the Indians in that vicinity had done us no harm, and it was as much murder to kill one of them as to kill a white man.   Others sided with the writer and the matter was dropped.

We passed on up the river until we came to near the narrows or canyon.   There some of our stock was wounded by Indian arrows.   I do not recall just how many were injured or died from their wounds.   The Indians who did the damage kept out of our sight.

I must mention Elder Addison Pratt, who joined us at Sutter's Fort, as he was returning from a five years' mission to the Society Islands, in the South Pacific Ocean.   He was a great fisherman, and it was along this part of the route that he used to catch the little speckled trout in such numbers as to attract both our admiration and our gratitude. He would go where no one else would ever think of finding fish, and would meet with wonderful success.   In fact, some of the party were so astonished at his good luck that they declared he could catch fish in a cow track.   He was a good, jolly soul, and made the best of everything.

Our train journeyed on in peace till we came to Goose Creek, where the writer traded a mare to an Indian, for a mule.   The red man was given several articles for the difference.   He sauntered around for a little while, then mounted the mule, and away he went, taking the articles with him.   The writer pursued alone for four or five miles, and first thing he knew was too near the Indian camp to turn back, so he rushed in among them, dismounted, changed the mare for the mule, and rode off. The Indians looked surprised and frightened, and made no resistance. I never realized the hazard I had taken till the danger was over; then I was glad to rejoin my fellow-travelers.

We crossed Goose Creek Mountains and again struck out into the trackless desert, pioneering our own way, rolling the rocks and cutting the road. We reached the Malad, a very difficult stream to cross, but we succeeded in getting over without serious damage. From there our route lay to the Bear River, which we crossed in safety by blocking up our wagon boxes. I think the crossing was made just above where Bear River City is now located. From there we traveled southward under the base of the mountains to where we found two springs, one of hot water and the other of very cold water, within a very few feet of each other; they flowed in the same gulch or ravine. Along this route we had naught but an Indian trail to guide us. When we reached Box Elder we thought it the finest place we had seen since leaving Carson Valley.

While in California we had learned that the Latter-day Saints had settled near the south end of the Great Salt Lake; and as we had been in sight, from the mountains, of the north end of the lake for some days, we began to feel that we were nearing a place of rest. We journeyed on till we came to the Ogden and Weber rivers, where we found that Captain James Brown, of company C of the Mormon Battalion, and a few of the Saints had settled; the country looked very wild. We still pursued our way southward, till we reached the present site of Salt Lake City, entering the Sixth Ward Square—now Pioneer Square—where the Saints had built houses and a stockade. I think the date of our arrival at this place was the 28th of September, 1848.

We were heartily welcomed, by relatives and friends, after our long and tedious march of near four thousand miles, and our more than two years' absence from those we loved and who loved us. Our meeting and greeting were far more joyous and precious than the glittering gold we had left behind. Neither our friends nor ourselves had any regrets for our having left the gold fields when we remembered our marching away, over two years before, to the tune of "The Girl I Left Behind Me," for we were so very glad to find her again, no matter if it were in a desert. We all rejoiced, and gave thanks to God for His protecting care and our safe return to the bosom of friends.

CHAPTER XVI.

CONTENTMENT AMONG THE SAINTS IN GREAT SALT LAKE VALLEY—
RUDE DWELLINGS AND SHORT RATIONS—TRYING EXPERIENCES—
RESCUE OF MORMON BATTALION MEMBERS FROM STARVATION—
CARRY NEWS OF THE CALIFORNIA GOLD DISCOVERY TO THE
EAST—RE-UNION OF MORMON BATTALION MEMBERS—ADDRESSES
BY THE FIRST PRESIDENCY AND OTHERS—SETTLING A NEW
COUNTRY—ORGANIZATION OF MINUTE MEN—COLD WINTER—THE
GOLD FEVER—TENOR OF THE PREACHINGS AND PROPHESYINGS
OF THOSE TIMES—INSTRUCTING THE PEOPLE IN INDUSTRIAL
PURSUITS—POLICY TOWARD THE INDIANS.

NOTWITHSTANDING the fact of the aspect in the Great Salt Lake Valley being gloomy, most of the people were contented with their lot, although the experiences of 1847 and 1848 had been anything but encouraging. Some of the inhabitants were living in log cabins, others in dugouts, and still others in wagons, while some who did not have the latter had built brush sheds; almost everybody was living on short rations, crickets and grasshoppers having destroyed most of the crops. The whole face of the country was brown and dry, except small streaks along the water courses. There was no provender for our stock, and we could only turn them out upon the range, and trust them and ourselves to a kind Providence. Timber for fuel was in the mountains, and higher up in these there was timber for fencing and building purposes. In order to get either, we had to make roads at great expense, building bridges and cutting dugways, sometimes going in armed companies to protect ourselves from the threatening Indian tribes. A long brush bowery was built in the town; we met there for religious services, and for all other purposes that made it necessary for the people to be called together.

October 6, 1848, a general conference of the Church was held, and the people as a rule felt blessed, although there were a few who were very much discouraged as the rations grew short and the cold weather pinched more closely.

Some time in October, news reached us that a small detachment of the Mormon Battalion coming from California was starving to death on the western deserts. Their old comrades in arms soon gathered supplies and fitted up a team, and six or seven of us went out to give assistance. We met the suffering company at the point of the West Mountains, about two days earlier than we had expected. The men were suffering, but not quite so badly as we had been led to believe from the word we had got. It was snowing when we met them, and continued to do so the greater part of the night and of the next day, so that we suffered much from cold before we reached shelter, for everything was soaked through. The company brought considerable gold, which was exhibited to many of the people.

Some of our comrades were not so fortunate as to find their families in the Great Salt Lake Valley, so they pushed on to where these had been left, in Iowa or Nebraska. Those men bore the news of the great gold discovery in

California, and, as evidence of the truth of their story, showed the precious metal they had secured. Thus the Mormon Battalion not only was at the discovery of gold in California and took part therein, but bore the news thereof eastward, until it spread to the world, causing great excitement.

The last detachment of the battalion for the season having arrived in the valley, a feast was prepared, and a re-union of the soldiers and their friends was called. It was made as grand an affair as could be under the circumstances, Presidents Brigham Young and Heber C. Kimball leading out with liberal hands. We were welcomed in royal style; interesting speeches were made by the First Presidency of the Church, and also by the officers and soldiers of the battalion.

From that time things moved quietly, people making roads and getting out timber for various purposes, herding stock, fencing, and so on. At length the Indians began to run off and kill the stock. A meeting was called and one hundred men selected to enroll themselves as minute men, the writer being one of the company. We were required each to keep a horse on hand, and to be ready at a minute's warning to march to any point of attack. We had to fit out ourselves, as there was no quartermaster's department on which officers could issue requisitions and have them honored. We had to provide our own provisions, and everything necessary for a campaign, at our own expense. Most of the young men having horses of their own, and many of them having become expert horsemen, a full quota was furnished for the company. We had turned over to the Church authorities, for the public defense, our two brass Russian cannon. The minute men met for drill at regularly appointed times.

The winter of 1848-9 was quite cold. Many people had their feet badly frozen. For one, the writer suffered so severely from this cause that he lost every nail from the toes of both feet. In February and March there began to be some uneasiness over the prospects, and as the days grew warmer the gold fever attacked many so that they prepared to go to California. Some said they would go only to have a place for the rest of us; for they thought Brigham Young too smart a man to try to establish a civilized colony in such a "God-forsaken country," as they called the valley. They further said that California was the natural country for the Saints; some had brought choice fruit pips and seed, but said they would not waste them by planting in a country like the Great Salt Lake Valley; others stated that they would not build a house in the valley, but would remain in their wagons, for certainly our leaders knew better than to attempt to make a stand in such a dry, worthless locality, and would be going on to California, Oregon or Vancouver's Island; still others said they would wait awhile before planting choice fruits, as it would not be long before they would return to Jackson County, Missouri.

This discouraging talk was not alone bv persons who had no experience in farming and manufacturing, but by men who had made a success at their various avocations where they had been permitted to work in peace, before coming west. Good farmers said: "Why the wheat we grew here last year was so short that we had to pull it; the heads were not more than two inches long. Frost falls here every month in the year—enough to cut down all tender vegetation. More, James Bridger and Gudger, who have been in this country ten years or more, say that corn cannot be raised anywhere in these mountains. In fact, Bridger has told President Young that he will give a thousand dollars for the first bushel of corn raised in the open air here, for he says it cannot be done."

It was at this time of gloom that President Young stood before the whole people, and said, in substance, that some people had misgivings, and some were murmuring, and had not faith to go to work and make their families comfortable; they had got the gold fever and were going to California. Said he: "Some have asked me about going. I have told them that God has appointed this place for the gathering of His Saints, and you will do better right here than you will by going to the gold mines. Some have thought they would go there and get fitted out and come back, but I told them to stop here and get fitted out. Those who stop here and are faithful to God and His people will make more money and get richer than you that run after the god of this world; and I promise you in the name of the Lord that many of you that go, thinking you will get rich and come back, will wish you had never gone away from here, and will long to come back but will not be able to do so. Some of you will come back, but your friends who remain here will have to help you; and the rest of you who are spared to return will not make as much money as your brethren do who stay here and help build up the Church and kingdom of God; they will prosper and be able to buy you twice over. Here is the place God has appointed for His people. We have been kicked out of the frying-pan into the fire, out of the fire into the middle of the floor, and here we are and here we will stay. God has shown me that this is the spot to locate His people, and here is where they will prosper; He will temper the elements for the good of His Saints; He will rebuke the frost and the sterility of the soil, and the land shall become fruitful. Brethren, go to, now, and plant out your fruit seeds." Stretching his arms to the east and to the west, with his hands spread out, he said: "For in these elements are not only all the cereals common to this latitude, but the apple, peach and plum; yea, and the more delicate fruits, the strawberry and raspberry; and we will raise the grape here and manufacture wine; and as the Saints gather here and get strong enough to possess the land, God will temper the climate, and we shall build a city and a temple to the Most High God in this place. We will extend our settlements to the east and west, to the north and to the south, and we will build towns and cities by the hundreds, and thousands of the Saints will gather in from the nations of the earth. This will become the great highway of the nations. Kings and emperors and the noble and wise of the earth will visit us here, while the wicked and ungodly will envy us our comfortable homes and possessions. Take courage, brethren. I can stand in my door and can see where there is untold millions of the rich treasures of the earth—gold and silver. But the time has not come for the Saints to dig gold. It is our duty first to develop the agricultural resources of this country, for there is no country on the earth that is more productive than this. We have the finest climate, the best water, and the purest air that can be found on the earth; there is no healthier climate anywhere. As for gold and silver, and the rich minerals of the earth, there is no other country that equals this; but let them alone; let others seek them, and we will cultivate the soil; for if the mines are opened first, we are a thousand miles from any base of supplies, and the people would rush in here in such great numbers that they would breed a famine; and gold would not do us or them any good if there were no provisions in the land. People would starve to death with barrels of gold; they would be willing to give a barrel of gold for a barrel of flour rather than starve to death. Then, brethren, plow your land and sow wheat, plant your potatoes; let the mines alone until the time comes for you to hunt gold, though I do not think this people ever will become a mining people. It is our duty to preach the Gospel, gather Israel, pay our tithing, and build temples. The worst fear that I have about this people is that they will get rich in this country, forget God and His people, wax fat, and kick themselves out of the Church and go to hell. This people will stand mobbing, robbing, poverty, and all manner of persecution, and be true. But my greater fear for them is that they cannot stand wealth; and yet they have to be tried with riches, for they will become the richest people on this earth."

My dear reader, the writer stood on the Sixth Ward Square, Salt Lake City, in the year 1849, fifty-one years ago, and heard the foregoing spoken by President Brigham Young. Now it is 1900, and I bear my testimony to the literal fulfillment of most of those sayings, and that portion which has not yet come to pass I most assuredly believe will do so. I entreat the reader of this to pause and reflect. Was there divine inspiration in this matter, or not?

About the same time, Parley P. Pratt, one of the Twelve Apostles, told the people to save the hides of their cattle, tan them, and make boots and shoes for their families. He said that in the mountains there was spruce, pine bark, and shumac, with tanning properties; advised that they be gathered, and the beef hides tanned; and predicted that the time would come when leather would be tanned here, and boots and shoes would be manufactured and exported. It was also stated that we would raise sheep here, and would manufacture woollen fabrics and export them.

As the writer walked away from meeting that day, in company with some old and tried men, who had been mobbed and robbed, and driven from their homes, and whom he looked upon almost as pillars of the Church, one of them said he had passed through such and such trials in the past, but that that day, 1849, was the darkest he ever had seen in the Church. The thought of trying to settle this barren land, he said, was one of the greatest trials he had met. There were some three of the party particularly whom the

writer thought were staunch men; one of these asked another what he thought of the preaching that day, and got
the reply that it would do "to preach to d——d fools, but not
to men of sense"—that it was insulting to a man's better
senses, it was absurd to think that it was possible to manufacture anything for export from a country like this, where
we were more likely to starve to death than to do anything
else. Now, after half a century has passed away, the writer
refers to the manufacturing and mercantile establishments in
these mountain valleys to establish which were the divinely
inspired utterances of that day.

On one occasion in 1849, President Heber C. Kimball,
when preaching to the people, exhorted them to be faithful as Saints, to cultivate the earth, and let others dig the
gold. He said it was not for the Saints to dig it, but the
time would come when they would learn to use it, and not
abuse it, or the power that it gives; they would possess it
by millions, and the time would come when people would
be willing to give a bushel of gold for a bushel of wheat,
when judgments and calamities would be poured out on
the nations of the earth. He declared that people would
come here by thousands, yea, tens of thousands would yet
flee to Zion for safety; they would come with their burdens
on their backs, having nothing to eat, and the people here
would have to feed them; others would bring their gold
and silver, and envy the people here their peace and comfort, for God would temper the climate so that the Saints
would be able to raise everything they needed. Elder
Kimball further said: "Brethren, build good, large gran-
aries, fill them with wheat, and keep it against the time when
it will be needed. Some people think we have passed the
day of trial, but let me tell you that you need not fear that,
for if you are faithful you shall have all the trials you can
bear, and if you are not faithful you will have more, and
will apostatize and go to hell. Some people have come

from the eastern states and the old country and said: "Brother Kimball, O that we could have been with you in Kirtland, in Jackson county, and in Nauvoo, and shared the trials of the Saints with you!" Brethren, hold on a little while, and you shall have all the trials you will be able to stand; for God has said that He will have a tried people, so you may prepare yourselves; for before the roof is on the temple that we will build here, the devils will begin to howl, and before the capstone is laid you will begin to have your trials. Your leaders will be hunted as wild beasts; we shall not be with you, and men will be left to themselves for awhile. Then is the time that you should be filled with light, that you may be able to stand through the days of trial. Now, you can leave your bench-tools on the work-bench, and your plows and farming tools in the field; and can lie down and go to sleep without locking or bolting your doors; but the time will come when, if you do this, your tools will be stolen from you. These mountains will be filled with robbers, highwaymen, and all kinds of thieves and murderers, for the spirit of the old Gadianton robbers lurks here in the mountains, and will take possession of men, and you will have to watch as well as pray, to keep thieves away. Therefore, brethren, begin now to take better care of your tools; attach locks and bolts to your doors, and do not wait until the horse is stolen before you lock the door." Elder Kimball referred to the fact that the young men were becoming restless and did not know what to do; they ran hither and thither to the mines, and became rude and uncultivated. Said he: "Let me tell you, boys, what to do. Marry the girls and build homes for yourselves. Do not leave the young ladies to take up with strangers who will marry them and then desert them. If you do not marry them, I counsel the middle-aged and old men to marry the girls and treat them well, and let them have the opportunity to obey the first command of

God to man, to multiply and replenish the earth. Brethren, take to yourselves more wives; for if you do not, the time will come when you will not be permitted to do so. Seek wisdom by faith and prayer; study and read all good books; study the arts and sciences; build good schoolhouses, and educate your children, that they may be able to perform the great work that will come upon them."

Some of the most practical and best informed men in the community were called to deliver free lectures on farming, stockraising, etc., for many of the people had come from manufacturing centers and had no experience in agricultural life, consequently these people needed instruction, and it was given in every industrial pursuit that was practicable at the time, and that by experienced men. Thus the people were incited in their labors to subdue this wild and then desert land—for it was barren and waste in the extreme.

President Brigham Young also instructed the people to treat the Indians kindly, and divide food with them, "for," said he, "it is cheaper to feed than to fight them. Teach them that we are their friends. Indeed, treat every man civilly and kindly; treat every man as a gentleman until you prove him to be a rascal—then let him alone."

The foregoing is the tenor of the teaching and preaching to the people in 1848 and 1849, in what is now the State of Utah.

CHAPTER XVII.

SCARCITY OF FOOD IN THE GREAT SALT LAKE VALLEY—WILD VEGETA-
    BLES FOR GREENS—FAIR PROSPECTS FOR CROPS—CLOUDS OF
    CRICKETS LAY BARE THE FIELDS—PEOPLE STRUGGLE AGAINST
    THE PEST ALMOST TO DESPAIR—VAST FLOCKS OF SEA GULLS, AS
    THE CLOUDS OF HEAVEN, COME TO THE RESCUE—DESTRUCTION
    OF THE CRICKETS—PEOPLE PRAISE THE LORD—THE WRITER IN-
    VITED TO A MEETING, ORDAINED A SEVENTY, AND CALLED WITH
    OTHERS TO GO ON A MISSION TO THE SOCIETY ISLANDS—WORDS
    OF PRESIDENTS BRIGHAM YOUNG AND HEBER C. KIMBALL—PREP-
    ARATIONS TO TRAVEL TO CALIFORNIA WITH AN EMIGRANT
    COMPANY—DESCRIPTION OF THE ROUTE BY CAPTAIN JEFFERSON
    HUNT—START ON MY MISSION—PROPHECY BY PRESIDENT WILLARD
    RICHARDS—BATTLE WITH INDIANS AT PROVO AVERTED BY APOS-
    TLE C. C. RICH—PROSPECTS OF UTAH VALLEY TO SUPPORT POPU-
    LATION—OVERTAKE THE EMIGRANT COMPANY—DISCUSSIONS AT
    BEAVER RIVER—COMPANY STARTS FOR WALKER'S PASS—TURNED
    BACK BY SCARCITY OF WATER—EXPERIENCE ON THE DESERT—
    DISSENSIONS IN THE COMPANY—FUTILE ATTEMPT TO SEND SOME
    OF THE MEMBERS BACK—APOSTLE C. C. RICH FORESEES FURTHER
    TROUBLE, AND ENDEAVORS TO SAVE THE MORMON PART OF THE
    TRAIN BY ADVISING THEM TO RETURN TO THE OLD SPANISH
    TRAIL—METHODIST AND CAMPBELLITE MINISTERS INCITE THE
    COMPANY AGAINST THIER MORMON GUIDE, CAPTAIN HUNT—MAIN
    COMPANY DISREGARDS CAPTAIN HUNT'S WARNING OF DANGER,
    AND LEAVES THE OLD SPANISH TRAIL TO SEARCH FOR THE
    ROUTE THROUGH WALKER'S PASS—MORMONS GO WITH CAPTAIN
    HUNT ON THE SOUTHERN ROUTE.

WHEN seed time came that year, provisions were
    very scarce. People dug segos and thistle roots,
and gathered cow cabbage, as we called a plant that was
found in the canyons. We ate these as greens, cooked the
hides of beef cattle—in fact, gathered everything eatable,
and worked hard and put in our crops. These started out
with fair prospects for harvest until the grain was from one
to six inches high. Then there came down from the moun-

tains myriads of black crickets, their bodies nearly as large
as a man's thumb. They entered upon wheat and corn
fields, and swept or ate every green thing before them.
Field after field was cleared of vegetation. Whole families
with their chickens moved out to their farms and made
war upon the crickets. Men, women and children fought
from morning till night, and still the enemy advanced from
field to field. Men almost despaired, women wept, and to
all human appearance our cause was lost. The crickets
ate the crops so close into the ground that they could not
start again. The people held fast meetings and prayed for
protection. I am not positive that there were any special
meetings for that purpose, but it was customary to fast and
pray the first Thursday in each month.

Almost everybody was in despair, and the enemy did
not seem to be diminished in numbers. With their war
cry, or ce-ce, the crickets advanced, and, seeming to call
up their reserve forces, with a bold front kept up their
march. Then there came from the west and northwest
what seemed to me might be justly called the clouds of
heaven, or perhaps more properly the clouds of salvation.
These were white sea gulls, which flew so close together and
were so numerous as to form a cloud wherever they went.
They covered almost the whole farming district north and
southeast of the city—the main farming district in Salt Lake
Valley at that time; they visited Davis County and other
places as well; and when they lit down the fields looked as
though covered with snow. The gulls came at sunrise
and returned to the west at sundown, after having gorged
and disgorged themselves the entire day, being tame as
chickens. They kept up the work of deliverance day
after day, as the crickets continued to come down from the
mountains. I believe that was the first time this kind of
birds had been seen by any of the settlers. When they
had completed their work of mercy they went away,

leaving a grateful people who returned thanks to the Giver of every good gift. The Saints in the valley then were united and their meetings were well attended.

One Sunday, Brother Jedediah M. Grant came down from the stand, took the writer by the arm, and asked him to take a walk. The request was granted readily, and I was led to Brother Lorenzo Young's house on City Creek, where we found the First Presidency, some members of the Twelve Apostles, and some of the first council of the Seventies. There the writer was ordained to the Priesthood of a Seventy, and his name was enrolled in the third quorum. Shortly after that he was invited with others to attend a council meeting of the First Presidency and Twelve Apostles, in President Kimball's schoolhouse. When we got in and were seated, President Young said, "Brethren, if any of you have anything to say, say on." There being no response, the president rose to his feet and said, "I move that Elders Addison Pratt, Hyrum Blackwell and James S. Brown take a mission to the Society Islands, in the South Pacific Ocean." President H. C. Kimball said, "I second the motion." The question was put and unànimously sustained, and the president turned to me and asked, "Brother James, will you go?" The answer was, "I am an illiterate youth, cannot read or write, and I do not know what good I can do; but if it is the will of the Lord that I should go, and you say so, I will do the best that I can." The president then took a seat near me, placing his right hand on my left knee, and said, "It is the will of the Lord that you go, and I say go; I am not afraid to risk you. And I promise you in the name of the Lord God of Israel that if you go you will be blessed, and do good, and be an honor to yourself and to the Church and kingdom of God. Although men will seek your life, you shall be spared and return to the bosom of the Church in safety."

This council was on Sunday evening, some time in

September, 1849, and we were to start no later than the 10th of October; indeed, we were instructed to get ready as soon as possible, so that we could join a company of emigrants which was organizing to go through to California by the southern route, as it was too late to go by the northern route.

As Elder Addison Pratt and I had agreed to go sowing wheat together on Monday morning, I thought I could speak to him without any notice being taken of it. I said to him, in a low tone of voice, that I guessed we would not sow much wheat next day. President H. C. Kimball jumped from his seat as quick as a flash, and pointing his finger directly at me, said, "What is that, Brother Jimmie?" When I told him what I had said, he continued, "Jimmie, it is not for you to sow wheat or to reap it, but your calling is to sow the good seed of the Gospel, and gather Israel from this time henceforth. Mind that, now; let others sow the wheat." From that time I felt a weight of responsibility that I had never thought of before.

We then went to preparing for our journey. Apostle C. C. Rich had been called to go through to California, so he and Brother Pratt and I fitted up a team, I having a good wagon and one yoke of oxen; they each furnished a yoke of oxen. In a few days we were ready for the start. We had a rodometer attached to our wagon, to measure the distance.

In the meantime, the emigrants called a meeting before taking their departure. They had employed Captain Jefferson Hunt of company A, Mormon Battalion fame, to be their guide, as he had come through that route with pack animals. He was invited to tell them what they might expect. He described the route to them with the roughest side out, lest they might say that he had misled them by making things more favorable than they really were. In concluding his remarks he said: "From Salt

Springs, we cross to a sandy desert, distance seventy-five miles to Bitter Springs, the water so bitter the devil would not drink it; and from thence away hellwards, to California or some other place. Now, gentlemen, if you will stick together and follow me, I will lead you through to California all right; but you will have to make your own road, for there is none save the old Spanish trail from Santa Fe to California, by the Cajon Pass through the Sierra Nevada Mountains."

The emigrant company consisted of about five hundred souls, and one hundred wagons and teams, the latter in poor condition. Feeling in high spirits, the company moved out between the 1st and 8th of October. C. C. Rich, Francis Pomeroy and I remained to follow up on horseback, in three or four days. Pratt and Blackwell, taking our team, started with the main body. They got to the Cottonwoods, when one of my oxen became so lame that they could not proceed any farther. Blackwell returned to inform me of the situation, and I went down and traded with John Brown, late Bishop of Pleasant Grove, for another ox, mine having been pricked in shoeing. Then they overtook the main company, and all proceeded together.

On the 8th we followed. I started out alone, to meet with the others at Cottonwood. As I passed the home of Dr. Willard Richards, counselor to President Brigham Young, Dr. Richards came out and met me; he took me by the right knee with his right hand, as I sat on my horse, and said, "Starting out on your mission, I suppose?" I replied, "Yes, sir." "Well, Brother James, I am glad, and sorry; glad to have you go and preach the Gospel, and sorry to part with good young men that we need in opening up a new country." At that he gave my knee an extra grip. Stretching his left hand out to the southwest, his chin quivering and his eyes filling with tears, he said, "Brother James, when you are upon yonder distant islands, called to preside over a branch of the Church of Jesus

Christ of Latter-day Saints, men will seek your life, and to all human appearance, there will be no possible escape: then look unto God, and His angels shall draw near unto you, and you shall be delivered, to return home to this people. Do not stop to write to Brother Pratt, your president, to Brother Brigham, or to me, for you will require the immediate protection of God. Then put your trust in Him, and He will deliver you; for I promise you in the name of Israel's God that you shall be delivered from your enemy and return to this people. Goodbye, and God bless you." Need I tell the reader that my mind was greatly impressed by those prophetic words, their inspired character being established so vividly in my later experience? Prophetic I knew them to be, and impressive they were indeed; and the impression has been deep and lasting.

I then went on to Brother Jacob M. Truman's, on Big Cottonwood Creek, and stayed with him that night. Next morning I passed on to Brother William Bills', where I met with Brothers C. C. Rich and F. Pomeroy, and we proceeded on to Provo by the Indian trail, having been joined by Alexander Williams, with whom we stayed.

At Provo we learned that the citizens and Indians had had some trouble, and there was considerable excitement, as there were but few settlers at that place and the Indians were quite numerous. The latter were singing war songs and working up a spirit of war preliminary to making an attack that night or next morning, as was supposed. The people were preparing to receive them as best they could. Guards were posted around the camp, and men put on picket duty, so that any enemy might be discovered readily.

The Indians made no move until after daylight; but just before sunrise they started from their camps in force, to attack us. We advanced to meet them, so as to prevent heir assailing us in the small fort, where the women and children were.   The savages marched up as if to give us open battle.   We formed across the road, and each man took his post ready for action.   I always have believed that if it had not been for the presence of Apostle C. C. Rich, and his cool, conciliatory action, there would have been bloodshed, for there were some very hot-headed white men, who would have preferred war to peace.   Through Brother Rich's influence, the cause of the trouble was looked into, a conciliation effected, and war averted, so that after breakfast we of the missionary party proceeded on to what was called Hobble Creek—now the city of Springville, with a population of over two thousand souls.   I remember that we thought the place would be capable of sustaining eight or ten families, or a dairy, believing there was not enough water for more.

From Hobble Creek we passed on from one small stream to another, expressing our opinion as to the capacity of the water supply; and in no instance did we suppose that there was water sufficient for more than fifteen families, judging from what we could see then.   Again, the barrenness of the country was such that it did not seem that more than seventy-five or a hundred head of cattle could find feed within reach of water.   Now thousands of head of horned stock and horses are sustained at the same places.

We kept on our way until we overtook the wagon train on Sevier River.   We came up with the emigrants just as they were ready to move on, but did not find them so full of glee as they were on the start from the city.   Still, we rolled on very peaceably until we came to Beaver River, where the country began to look more forbidding.   Then the ardor of the emigrants began to weaken.

At this place the company was joined by a man named Smith with a pack train of about seventeen men; also James Flake, with thirty Latter-day Saints; besides, there were

William Farrer, John Dixon, H. W. Bigler, George Q
Cannon, and others, whose names I do not now recall.
Smith felt confident that he could find Walker's Pass, in
the Sierra Nevada Mountains. This supposed pass had
been spoken of often, but men had been disappointed as
often in finding it, or rather in not finding it. Smith's story
excited our whole camp so that there was a general desire
to try the new route, and go down through the canyon and
out on to the sandy desert. The whole company except
a very few favored the idea of leaving the route they had
hired a guide for, and they urged Captain Hunt to strike
out and look for water. He said, "Gentlemen, I agreed to
pilot you through to California on the Old Spanish Route
by the Cajon Pass. I am ready to do so, and am not
under any obligations to lead you in any other way; and if
you insist on my doing so you must be responsible, for I
will not be responsible for anything. On this condition, if
you insist on changing your route, I will do the best I can
to find water, but I do not have any reason to hope for success when I leave the trail."

The company hurrahed for the Walker Pass, and
Captain Hunt struck out a day ahead while the company
shod and doctored their lame and sick stock for one day.
Then we moved out ten miles on to the plain southwest of
where Minersville, Utah, now stands, and camped.

Sometime in the night Captain Hunt came into camp,
so near choked from the lack of water that his tongue was
swollen till it protruded from his mouth; his eyes were so
sunken in his head that he could scarcely be recognized.
His horse, too, for the need of water, was blind, and staggered as he was urged on. Their stay had been thirty-six
hours, on the sands, without water. About 2 o'clock
next morning our stock stampeded from the guards and
ran back to water. Two-thirds of the men went in pursuit,

and animals and men did not return to camp till 2 o'clock in the afternoon.

By this time confusion and discontent abounded in camp. A committee was appointed to inquire into the condition of every team, and to ascertain the food supply, with the avowed intention of sending all back who failed to have what were considered the requisites for the journey. I think that one-third of the company, our wagon included, were found wanting when weighed in that committee's balances. But when we were ordered to return, those who gave the command found that they were without authority and no one would heed them. So the discontent was patched up for a time, and we proceeded on to Little Salt Lake Valley, where we struck the old Spanish trail again. Then the company began to split up, some going on after night, and others stopping.

Brother C. C. Rich told me that it had been shown to him that there was going to be trouble, and he felt led to believe that if we would go with the pack train he could at least lead the brethren there back on to the trail and save them. This was in the night, as we slept together in the wagon. He awoke and asked me if I were awake. Finding that I was, he told me what would befall the company. To save the brethren and all who would heed him, he purchased some ponies and went with the packers.

As we passed along the Spanish trail—said to be three hundred and fifty years old—on the great desert, we could follow the route by the bones of dead animals in many places. It is said that many fierce battles have been fought between Mexicans and Indians along this trail. So far as we were concerned, although it was known that the Indians were very hostile, they gave us no trouble.

When we reached what is called the Rim of the Basin, where the waters divide, part running into the Colorado River and on to the Pacific Ocean, and part into the Salt

Lake Valley, the company called meetings, and several made speeches, saying there must be a nearer and better route than that on which the Mormon guide was leading them. One Methodist and one Campbellite preacher in the company said that they had started to California, and not hellwards, as the Mormon guide had stated at the outset, quoting what Captain Hunt had said just before starting. Others claimed that they had been on the mountains, and upon looking west had seen something green, which they asserted was an indication of water. Some of them celebrated the proposed separation from us by boring holes in trees then filling these with powder and firing them, exploded the trees in symbol of the break-up of the company.

Next morning all but seven wagons turned off to the right, toward the supposed Walker's Pass. We preferred to follow the guide. The company was thoroughly warned by Captain Hunt of the danger of dying from lack of water. In our party there were eleven men, two women and three children. The main company expressed pity for us and tried to persuade us to go with them, but we felt confident that our course was the safest, notwithstanding their superior numbers. They seemed to rejoice at their conclusion, while we regretted it for their sakes. Thus we separated, the emigrant company heading for Walker's Pass, and our small party continuing on the old Spanish trail, or southern route to California.

CHAPTER XVIII.

CAUGHT IN A SNOWSTORM—VIA THE SANTA CLARA AND RIO VIRGEN TO
THE MUDDY—NEWS OF SAD DISASTER TO THE EMIGRANT COM-
PANY—MAKING CHARCOAL AND NAILS—AN APOSTLE AS A BLACK-
SMITH—SEARCHING FOR WATER ON THE DESERT—CROSSING AN
ALKALI STREAM—DISCOVER GOLD NEAR SALT SPRINGS—HURRY-
ING ON OVER THE DESERT—CATTLE POISONED AT BITTER
SPRINGS—KILLING ANIMALS TO RELIEVE THEIR SUFFERINGS—
FIRST WAGON OVER CAJON PASS, GOING WEST—SEVERE JOURNEY
TO THE SUMMIT OF THE PASS—ALL GET OVER SAFELY—SENSE OF
GREAT RELIEF—GRASS AND WATER IN ABUNDANCE—OVERTAKEN
BY SURVIVORS OF THE EMIGRANT COMPANY—THEIR STORY OF
TERRIBLE SUFFERING—DIVIDE PROVISIONS WITH THEM—CELE-
BRATING CHRISTMAS, 1849—CONTINUING THE JOURNEY NORTH—
SPANISH WARNING IN A CEMETERY TO INDIANS—CRUELTY OF
THE SPANIARDS TO THE INDIANS—THE WRITER PLACED IN
CHARGE OF THE COMPANY—DIRECTED TO GO TO THE GOLD
MINES.

WHEN the company had separated the weather was
very threatening, and it soon began to snow very
fast.   We pulled on until late in the afternoon, and camped
on the mountain. Next day we came to some Indian farms
where the savages had raised corn, wheat and squash. We
passed on to the Santa Clara, followed it down for three or
four days, and found a written notice to those who came
that way: "Look out, for we have killed two Indians
here."   With this warning, we felt that we must keep a
vigilant guard all the time.   From the Santa Clara we had
a very long drive across the mountain and down a long, dry,
rocky slope until we came to the Rio Virgen.   We went
along that stream three or four days; where we left it we
found a cow with an Indian arrow sticking in her.   We
next passed over a high plateau to a stream well named the
Muddy.   There we laid by and doctored and shod our
lame cattle.

9

While we were on the Muddy, Brother C. C. Rich and party came down the stream to us, bringing sad and heartrending news from the great emigrant company, which had broken into factions and become perfectly demoralized and confused. Some had taken packs on their backs and started on foot, their cattle dying, their wagons abandoned. All were despondent, and unwilling to listen to anybody. I think, from the best information we ever got of them, I would be safe in saying that four-fifths of them met a most horrible fate, being starved or choked to death in or near what was afterwards called Death Valley. In after years the miners of Pahranagat found the irons of the wagons very handy for use in their pursuits.

On the Muddy we burned charcoal and made nails to shoe our cattle, having to throw the animals down and hold them while Apostle C. C. Rich shod them. Brother Rich did his work well, for the shoes never came loose till they wore off.

From the Muddy I accompanied Captain Hunt and Henry Rollins twelve miles and found some small pools of water about two miles to the right of the trail; I went back to turn the packers to it, while Captain Hunt and Henry Rollins went ahead in search of more pools of water and found some. George Q. Cannon and I stayed there as guides for the wagon train, and turned them off to the water. When the train arrived, about 11 o'clock p. m., we had to dip water with cups and water the stock from buckets. Then we pressed on till daylight, made a halt long enough to take breakfast, and pushed on, for there was no feed for our stock.

About 2 p. m. we came to the Los Vegas, where we rested a day, then continued our journey over mountains and across dry deserts from day to day until we reached a stream of water about three rods wide. It was so strong with alkali that we dared not allow our cattle to drink of it, but put the lash to them so that they could not get a sup as we crossed it twice. Thence we traveled across a very sandy desert for twelve miles to the Salt Springs, where the train went around a point of the mountain. A. Pratt and I, with three or four others, followed on a small trail that passed over a notch of the mountain. While going through a narrow pass, Brother A. Pratt said it looked as if there might be gold there. At that we went to looking in the crevices of the rock, and in a few minutes one of the party found a small scale, and then another. Among the rest, I saw the precious metal projecting from a streak of quartz in the granite rock. From there we went over about one and a half miles to the Salt Springs, and met with the teams. Several of the party journeyed back to look further for the gold. I took along a cold chisel and hammer, and chipped out some at the place I had found, but as our teams were weakening very fast and there was neither food nor water at that place to sustain our stock, we had to push on across the sandy desert of seventy-five miles, day and night, until we came to the Bitter Springs.

These were the springs that Captain Hunt had told the emigrant company about before they left Salt Lake City, that from thence it was "away hellward to California or some other place." It certainly began to look that way now, when our cattle began to weaken and die all along the trail. The springs would have been as properly named if they had been called Poison Springs, instead of Bitter, for it seemed that from that place our cattle began to weaken every moment, and many had to be turned loose from the yoke and then shot to get them out of their misery.

We had to shoot one of Brother Pratt's oxen to end its suffering. This act fell to my lot. Oh, how inhuman and cruel it seemed to me, to drive the patient and faithful dumb animal into a barren desert, where there is neither food nor drink, to goad him on until he falls from sheer exhaustion, so that he bears any punishment, to make him rise, that his master sees fit to inflict, without giving a single moan, then to walk around and calmly look him in the face and fire the deadly missile into his brain, then leave his carcass to the loathsome wolves and birds of prey!

In looking back over a period of fifty years since then, the writer cannot call to memory a single act in his life that seemed so cruel and ungrateful as that; and still there was no earthly means to save the poor creature from a more horrible death, which would have come if he had been left in that driving snowstorm, when his whole frame shook with cold, there to lie and starve—one of the most miserable deaths that the human mind can conceive of. Of the two evils we chose the least by ending the suffering in a moment, when it would have taken hours if it had not been for this act of mercy, as we call it after taking in the whole situation.

From Bitter Springs our team took the lead to the end of the journey, or to Williams' Ranch, being the first team that ever crossed over the Cajon Pass going west, as I remember. Ascending to the first pass from the Bitter Springs our situation was most gloomy. In mud and snow, with darkness come on, every rod of the road became more steep and difficult. The summit was two miles ahead and the nearest team half a mile back. We moved by hitches and starts, and could only make three or four rods at a time. Two of us pushed at the wagon while the other drove. Our guide was a few feet ahead, marking out the road, and saying, "Crowd up, boys, if possible. Let us wallow on over the summit, for it is our only salvation to cross and try to open the road if possible for the weaker teams."

Finally, with a shout of triumph, we reached the summit in two feet of snow, at 11 o'clock at night. Our guide

told us to go on down and build fires at the first place where
we could find anything for our stock, and he would go
back and cheer the rest on as best he could.

The descent being quite steep, we soon made the distance of three or four miles to where there was but about
six inches of snow, and where we found some feed.   Our
matches were all damp, and we were wet as could be. We
split up our spare yoke and struck fire with flint and steel,
crawled into the wagon, and started a fire in the frying-pan.
Then, as there was plenty of fuel, we made a roaring fire
outside, took a bite to eat, and turned in for a few moments'
rest, being satisfied that the others of the party had halted
before they reached the summit, and as the guide was with
them we thought they would take a rest and come on at
daybreak.

This conjecture proved right, for about 4 o'clock a. m.
Captain Hunt hallooed to us and called for a cup of coffee.
He seemed to be chilled to the bone, so we soon stirred
the fire and got him something to eat.   He told us all the
teams would make the riffle, but for us to have a good fire,
for some of the men would be chilled nearly to death.
Then he directed us to go ahead until we found feed for
the stock, and he would remain until the company came
up.   We advanced about ten miles, and halted for our cattle to feed and rest.   In the meantime we discovered the
company coming down the slope of the mountain.   Our
feelings, as well as theirs, were much relieved at the sight,
as we beheld each other, and when they had rested their
teams they came on to our camping place for another stop,
while we moved ahead to the Mohave River.   When we
reached that stream, I presume that we felt as pleased as a
man liberated from a life sentence in a dungeon, for we
had reason to feel assured that we would succeed in our
journey, as we had only one more hard scramble of thirty
miles, and had pleasant weather and plenty of feed and

water for our stock, with time to rest in.   Some shouted :
"Daylight once more; thank God for our deliverance!"

It was while we lay here that some of the company
which had parted with us at the Rim of the Basin came
up to us with packs on their backs, half-starved.   The
story of the condition of their comrades was horrifying
beyond description.   Men, women and children suffered
death alike by thirst and starvation.   This painful episode
affords one more instance of where the majority had been
wrong and the minority right.   The new arrivals said that
when we parted from them they were sorry for us.   But
now we were more sorry for them than they had been
for us.

We divided our food the second or third time to relieve these starving people, then pursued our course up
stream for nine or ten days.   There we rested our cattle,
did some hunting, and replenished our food supply with
wild meat, principally venison, quail and the gray squirrel.
We found plenty of wild grapes, and also discovered that
the raccoon lived in that part of the world.

It was about the 17th of December when we crossed
the Cajon Pass, in the Sierra Nevada Mountains; from
thence we moved via the Cocomonga Ranch to Williams'
Ranch, arriving there on December 24th.   At Williams'
we found C. C. Rich and party; we joined in with them
and had a good Christmas dinner.   There we traded for
new supplies to last us up to the gold mines on the Mari-
posa and the Stanislaus rivers, in northern California, or
the upper country.   The writer acted as pilot, interpreter
and quartermaster for the company of something like fifty
men.

It was about the 27th of January when we left the
ranch, from which we traveled to Los Angeles, thence
twenty miles to the north, where C. C. Rich and ten or fifteen men left us, and H. Egan took charge of the company

as captain. We followed up the Santa Barbara road at the rate of fifteen miles per day. The roads were very rough and hilly. The whole country was still in a very wild state. We were frequently warned to be on our guard for bandits, which were said to be roaming in the locality. We passed in peace, however, nothing out of the general routine happening until we arrived at the San Antonio Mission. The alcalde invited me into the chapel. To me, at that time, it seemed to be very grand, so attractive was the decoration. The alcalde, then opened the gates of the cemetery, in which I saw a pillar of burnt adobes with four Indian skulls on it, for the rest of the Indians to see what they might expect if they committed any outrages on the citizens.

From all that I have learned about Spain's treatment of the red men, it has been very cruel, yet the Spaniards claimed their methods were necessary in order to Christianize the aborigines. At that time the Indians in California were more cruelly treated than the slaves in the south; many of them had scars on their backs ten or twelve inches long, caused by the lash of the Spaniards.

We continued our journey up towards San Francisco until the 11th of February, when we arrived at a town called the Mission San Juan. There we received a letter from Apostle C. C. Rich; it was dated February 8, 1850. The mission was old and dilapidated, and at that date was occupied by a very rough class of men. The surrounding country was very beautiful and fertile.

About 7 o'clock that same evening Captain Howard Egan assembled the company together, and called on the writer to take charge. Then he went forward to overhaul the company that had preceded us. Next morning we continued on our journey, crossing a deep stream of water, and going to near Fisher's Ranch, where we received a few lines from Captain Egan, ordering us to stop the ox teams and forward the mule teams to San Jose to get provisions. We obeyed, and purchased a beef animal and dried the meat.

When Captain Egan returned to camp he told me that Apostle C. C. Rich thought I had better continue with the company on to the mines, until I saw or heard from him again. Accordingly I did so.

Retracing our steps about four miles, we turned to the left on a trail that led us to Gilroy's Ranch, thence to Rancho Pacheco. There we met a Frenchman who directed us across the mountains. Meantime our company appointed six of us to precede the wagons and mark out the road, as we were again entering into a wilderness with no roads except Indian and wild animals' trails.

CHAPTER XIX.

JOURNEYING TOWARD THE GOLD DIGGINGS—THREATENED BY WILD HORSES—DIFFICULTIES OF TRAVELING—CONVOCATION OF THE FEATHERED CREATION—REJOIN OUR FRIENDS—FERRYING ACROSS A RIVER—STRIKE A GOLD PROSPECT—ON A PROSPECTING TOUR—AN AGREEMENT THAT FAILED—INSTRUCTED TO GO TO SAN FRANCISCO TO PROCEED ON A MISSION—TRIP TO STOCKTON—GAMBLERS, SHARPERS AND MINERS AT THAT PLACE—A TEMPTATION OVERCOME—ARRIVE IN SAN FRANCISCO—WELCOMED BY SAINTS—RECEIVE KIND TREATMENT—ON BOARD A VESSEL BOUND FOR TAHITI.

ON the second day of our journey toward the mines we were confronted by a band of wild mustang horses. Two of our men who happened to be half a mile ahead of the other four of us were cut off from us by the wild animals, so that the confusion of the situation was such that we did not rejoin them for three days. The band was about three hours in passing us, and the trail was one mile in width. We thought it a low estimate to say that there were seven or eight thousand horses. There seemed to be hundreds of the finest animals dashing up and down, flanking the main herd, and driving, and shaping the course followed. To save ourselves and our horses from being taken in by them, we tied our horses' heads close together, and then stood between them and the wild band with our rifles in hand ready to shoot the leaders or any stallion that might attempt to gather in our horses, as we had heard that they did not hesitate to attempt to do when out on the open plains as we were. We supposed from all that we could learn that they had been to the San Joaquin River for water, and were returning over the plains to the foothills for pasture. The noise made by them as they galloped past us was like distant, heavy thunder, only it was a long, continuous roar or rumbling sound; we stood in almost breathless silence, and mingled fear and delight, and viewed the magnificent picture. At last the animals passed, and we heaved a sigh of relief.

We proceeded on for about four hours, when we had to call another halt and take similar precautions, and for the same reason, except that there were only about five hundred horses. When they passed we steered our course for the lower end of the Tulare Lake, where, so we had heard, a ferry had been located a few days before. As there was no road to travel, we thought we would go high enough and then follow the San Joaquin River down until we came to the crossing.

Night overtaking us, we camped by a slough where bear tracks, large and small, were in great abundance. For fear of Indians we dared not make much fire, so we passed a very lonely night, being filled with anxiety about our lost comrades, not knowing what had become of them; for, as near as my memory serves me, this was our second night camp since they were separated from us. To add to our troubles and gloom, the night was intensely dark, and a drizzling rain was falling.

Suddenly our horses all broke from us. We followed them by the sound of their feet as they ran, and after a long chase through swamps and sloughs we succeeded in capturing them. Then the next trouble came. We had lost one man and all our pack, and were without supper. Being out of hailing distance, it was by mere chance that we found our man and camp late in the night. Our horses had become so frightened that it was necessary to sit up till morning, to keep them quiet; so that only two of us could get a dreamy snooze at a time.

Next morning dawned and our friends were still missing. We journeyed on, passing down the sloughs to the river. At times it seemed that the whole feathered tribe had met over our heads and all around in one grand carnival, to consult over the advent of the white man into that swampy country. We had never before beheld such a grand aggregation of waterfowl, and the writer has never seen its equal since. For a time, we could not understand each other's talk, because of the clatter. Our next surprise was about five hundred elk which passed in front of us, but the deep sloughs between prevented our replenishing our scanty store of rations.

Soon we were pleased at falling in with our lost friends. They had found a lone wagon trail towards the river. We dispatched two of our party to meet the main company, and the rest of us followed the wagon trail to the river, where we found a man named Woods who had got there three days ahead of us, with a rowboat and a small supply of provisions and groceries. Salt pork and hard sea biscuit were selling at seventy-five cents per pound, and everything else proportionately high. The boat had just been launched.

The next day, when the wagons came in, we took

them apart and crossed in a boat, all except my wagon; it being heavy and having the rodometer attached to it, we got a cable rope and thought to tow the wagon over with the load, but when it had reached the middle of the river, which was about fifteen rods wide, the rope parted and the wagon turned over and over. Then Irwin Stoddard jumped in and made the rope fast to the hind axle, and as he could not manage the pole of the wagon, I jumped in to help him. Between us, we liberated the pole, so that after great exertion and hazard of life we finally succeeded in saving the vehicle, but we were thoroughly chilled through. We did not cross our animals till next morning, when we drove them in and they swam over, and we were soon on our way to and up the Merced River. Six of us proceeded ahead of the teams, traveling on horseback, to see what we could learn that would be of benefit to the company.

On the third day, I think it was, we came to a small mining camp called Burns' Diggings, on the south side of the Merced River. There we struck a very good prospect, and stopped until the main company came up. As it was evident that we could take from twelve to fifteen dollars per day to the man, we advised the company to begin work there, as the country was so muddy and soft that we could not make much headway in traveling higher into the foot hills. They agreed to accept our advice; then came a quite laughable performance. Those who had been the very worst drones in camp were now the first with the pick and washpan. They pitched into the creek as if they expected to scoop up the gold by shovelfuls, leaving their teams hitched to their wagons; while those who had been on hand early and late, taking a more methodical view of things, first formed the camp, got their dinner, and then went quietly to prospecting up and down the creek. By this time our drones decided there was no gold there, and that they would go where there was some. What a lesson

we learned there of human nature! The next day, however, things settled down a little more like business, after
it was ascertained that some had been making from fifteen
to twenty-five and fifty, and some even as high as one
hundred dollars per day, to the man. Next day, Captain
Egan and five others of our number were elected to go
further up into the mountains and prospect for the company,
while the others dug gold. The latter were to keep an
account of all they earned, and when we returned they
were to give us an equal share with those who stayed and
worked.

On these conditions six of us set out on horseback and
with pack mules. When we got well into the mountains
it began to rain and snow so that we were not able to do
much but cut browse for our horses. The snow became
so deep that we had to go ahead of our horses and break
the road so as to get out. We were soaked to the skin,
and our bedclothes were all wet. Our provisions were
almost gone; so we set out for our camp, after spending
ten days in a most miserable condition. We traveled in
snow two and a half feet deep from 2 p. m. until 6 a.
m. before we succeeded in reaching camp, when we found
that Apostle Rich had been there, and the men had sent
every dollar's worth of gold they had dug in our absence
to Stockton for supplies of provisions, clothing, tools, etc.,
so there was none left to pay us our proportion.

As Apostle C. C. Rich had brought word that Brother
A. Pratt desired me to meet him in San Francisco by a
certain date, I packed up my effects, sold my oxen to
Captain Jefferson Hunt for two hundred dollars, and bade
adieu to the rest of the camp, who owed me one hundred
dollars, and they yet owe it.

I traveled in company with C. C. Rich and Howard
Egan. On the 20th of March, when we got out of the
hills, we took the main road to Stockton, crossing the

Merced, Tuolumne, and Stanislaus rivers, all tributaries to the San Joaquin River.   We arrived in Stockton on March 28th.   The place was at that time a point of debarkation where freight was landed for the many mining camps. There were a few trading establishments and warehouses, and three or four large gambling houses in and around which were gathered freighters, packers, and one of the most motley gangs it has ever been my lot to see.   Bands of music were in the gambling halls.   At one of these I noted twelve tables, four men at each, armed with bowie knives and revolvers; and to me it looked as if there were more gold and silver exposed on those twelve tables than six mules could draw.   On the street and around the door, calling on the passers-by to come in and have a free drink and listen to the music, were men whom I soon learned were called cappers, or ropers-in, to the gambling hall; they would steam men up with drink, get them to gambling, and rob them.   Sometimes men would come in from the mines with their buckskin wallets containing three to four hundred dollars' worth of gold. They would stand around with perfect strangers and drink free whisky until they became dazed, then would set down their wallets of gold on a card, and the next moment their money would be taken up by the gambler, who would continue dealing his cards as unconcernedly as he would knock the ashes from his cigar. The poor, silly miner would turn away with a sickly look, having not even enough left to get him a change of clothing.   He would go into the street with his old miner's clothes on, without a dime to pay for his supper or to get a night's lodging.   Sometimes thousands of dollars would change hands in a few moments.   This was in the spring of 1850, when the strong, with revolver and bowie knife, were law, when gamblers and blacklegs ran many of the towns in California.

By this time I imagine that the reader asks what, as a

missionary, I was doing there. I might answer by quoting the saying of Christ, that it was not the righteous but the sinners that He had come to call to repentance. But I will not offer this excuse, for it was not applicable; and as open confession is good for the soul, I will make one, hoping that it may be not only good for my soul, but be a warning to all who read it. I was twenty-one years old at the time, and was alone on the street. I did not know where to go or what to do. My companions had left on business, and as I started along the street I met with an old time friend who appeared very much pleased to see me. His pleasure was reciprocated. He asked me to go in and have something to drink; I thanked him and said that I was not in the habit of indulging. He said, "Oh, come in, and have a little wine for old friendship's sake. There is no harm in a little wine; come, go in and hear the music, anyway." With that I turned in with him to the largest gambling den in the town. The place was packed with men of almost every nationality. This was the house I have described.

In the time of great excitement, it must be confessed, the writer was tempted to lay down a purse of one hundred dollars, as he had that amount with him. But the next instant the thought came to him, Would you try to beat a watchmaker or a gunsmith at his trade? The idea was so absurd that he then thought how foolish it was to try to beat these professional gamblers at their own game. Then the disgrace that attached to the act became so repulsive to his nature, that he felt ashamed that he ever had been tempted; and to this day, in a life of seventy-two years, he has never gambled. He has always felt thankful that that simple thought came to him at that time and place.

As soon as I could arrange a little business that detained me at Stockton, I boarded a steamboat called the *Captain Sutter*, bound for San Francisco, paying twenty-five dollars for a seventy-five mile ride on the crowded deck. I paid two dollars for a dinner that consisted of tough beef, poor bread. and a cup of tea. Such were "times" in California in 1850.

We landed at the great wharf in San Francisco about 8 o'clock that evening, April 5th. I went up town, where the streets were crowded, then returned and slept on the deck of the boat. Next morning, I took my trunk to the Boston House, and leaving it there, sought friends. I was not long in finding Brother Morris, who directed me to Brother Cade's, who, together with his good lady, received me very kindly. He inquired if I had any place to stop at, and when I told him no, he said, "Stop and have dinner with us, then bring your trunk here and stay until you can do better, if you can do with such fare as we have. We are old and cannot do very well, but you are welcome to stay with us as long as my old lady can cook for us."

With thanks, the writer accepted the kind offer, and from there visited the Saints in San Francisco. I met Amasa M. Lyman and Charles C. Rich, two of the Twelve Apostles, also found Addison Pratt, my fellow missionary. Brother and Sister Cade were not willing that I should stop over night at any other place, or pay for my washing. The good old lady said she had money enough to last her while she lived and pay for the washing of my clothes. Sister Ivins, who lived near by, sent for my clothes and had them well laundered. While I stayed there, Sister Cade presented me with five dollars and a nice silk handkerchief, and the old gentleman gave me a good inkstand. Sister Patch, who lived near by, gave me five dollars and a silk vest, and many of the Saints showed us favors.

On April 19th we carried our trunks on board the brig *Frederick*, Captain Dunham commanding. The fare was one hundred dollars each, in the cabin. We returned on shore and stayed over night, and having received our instructions and blessings from Apostles A. M. Lyman and C. C. Rich, we boarded the vessel at 6 o'clock a. m., April 20, and sailed away to the southwest, for the island of Tahiti, South Pacific Ocean.

CHAPTER XX.

SAILING FOR THE SOUTH PACIFIC—SEVERE ATTACK OF SEASICKNESS—BECALMED IN THE TROPICS—INTENSE HEAT—MARQUESAS ISLANDS—CANNIBALS—REACH TAHITI—LAND AT PAPEETE—MEET WITH FRIENDS—HEARTY WELCOME—PREACHING TO THE NATIVES—ANIMOSITY OF PROTESTANTS AND CATHOLICS TOWARD THE MORMONS—JEALOUSY OF FRENCH GOVERNMENT OFFICIALS ON THE ISLAND—WATCHED BY DETECTIVES—SIX NATIVES BAPTIZED—LEARNING THE LANGUAGE—RUMORS OF AN INTENTION TO EXPEL THE MORMONS—ELDERS B. F. GROUARD AND T. WHITAKER ARRESTED—APPEAL FOR AID—THEIR RELEASE AND RETURN TO THEIR MISSIONARY LABORS—MEET WITH BROTHER PRATT AGAIN—INTERVIEW WITH THE GOVERNOR—THAT OFFICIAL REFUSES ELDERS PRATT AND BROWN PERMISSION TO VISIT ANOTHER ISLAND—SCARCITY OF FOOD AT HUAUA—EATING SEASNAILS AND BUGS—STRANGE DISHES OF FOOD—ALMOST PERISH FROM THIRST—VISIT TO TIARARA—ACQUIRING THE LANGUAGE.

LEAVING San Francisco on April 20, 1850, the wind being fair, we made about eight knots per hour, and soon lost sight of the land over which the Stars and Stripes waves. The writer became very seasick, and remained so for the voyage. He was seven days without an action of his bowels, and he could not retain any kind of food on his stomach until we got down in the tropics, when two flying fish flew aboard ship at night, and the steward cooked them for the sick man. That was the first thing he had a relish for. The captain said that if he had ever heard of anybody dying of seasickness he would have had no hopes of getting the writer ashore.

The monotony of the voyage was broken only by vast

fields of seaweed, so dense that it greatly impeded our progress. Seabirds and fish were very plentiful, and many times attracted the attention of the voyagers, who caught several kinds of fish, including dolphin, shark and porpoise. The fishing afforded some amusing sport, the writer gaining courage enough at one time to crawl out on the jibboom and catch one fish.

The most trying event of the whole voyage was a calm in the torrid zone, where we lay for eight days; it was said that in that time we gained only eight miles. During that calm all the pitch broiled out of the seams of the deck, making it leak so that it had to be recalked and repitched. It became so hot that a man could not endure his bare feet on it, and if it had not been for the seamen throwing water on deck it seemed that we could not have lived through the terrible ordeal. Finally a gentle breeze came to our relief, and we were wafted in sight of the Marquesas Islands. We passed so close to these that the captain expressed a fear that we were in danger of being attacked by the natives of Nukahuia, the principal island. He said they were cannibals, and that small vessels had been captured by the natives coming off in such numbers, in canoes, as to overpower the crews. Hence he thought it dangerous to be so close with such light winds as we had. The wind soon freshened to a gale, and thus our fears were allayed as we bore down close along to the northward of the Tuamotu group, sighting some of them, to Tahiti, on which we landed on May 24, 1850.

Tahiti is the principal island of the Society group; it is said to be eighty miles in length, varying from two miles at the isthmus to forty miles in the widest place. The highest mountain summit is said to be five thousand feet or more. The capital, Papeete, is in latitude 17 degrees

10

32 minutes south, longitude 144 degrees 34 minutes west. The islands were invaded by the French in 1843. In 1847 the war was concluded, but not until much blood had been spilled and the country laid waste. Then a French protectorate was established there, and consequently, at the time we arrived, we found ourselves under the French flag, and had to apply to Governor Bonard for permission to go on shore. This was granted, but very reluctantly, and we paid the secretary three francs for each of us.

Once on shore, we found Brother Pratt's old friends, Hamatua and Pohe, who treated us very kindly and on May 25th got our baggage from the vessel, then took us in their boat around the northeast of the island to their home in a little village called Huaua, where we were met by their families and six or seven Church members. It seemed to be impossible for them to rejoice any more than they did, and under the circumstances we could not be treated with greater kindness. They provided us with the best the land produced, making us cordially welcome.

Brother Pratt preached to them, while I was deaf and dumb, so far as the spoken language was concerned; but the actions of the natives spoke louder than words. When it came to meal time, they spread before us roast pig, and fish, taro, fais, bananas, cocoanuts, sweet-potatoes, popoie, oranges, pine and vee apples, doavas, bread fruit, etc. We had appetites equal to the occasion, and felt no remorse for not having done justice to the table, or to the chest which was a substitute for a table.

We soon learned that the Protestant ministers and Catholic priest were very much prejudiced against us, and were doing all they could to prevent the people receiving us into their houses, advising them not to hold any conversation with us, or attend our meetings. We also learned that the government officials were jealous of Mormon influence, and that a watch was kept over us, in other words, the natives said that detectives were on our track, and that a ship of war had been sent to Tubuoi for Elders B. F. Grouard and T. Whitaker, who were on that island as Mormon missionaries, and who had been accused of speaking against the government. It may be imagined, therefore, that in all respects our stay was not so pleasant as otherwise it might have been.

As it was, however, we made the best of the situation. Brother Pratt preached and talked much of the time to a few who gathered around, and he soon baptized six persons. I studied the language by committing a few words to memory, then forming them into sentences, and having them corrected by the natives. Then, when I heard one tell another what to do, I watched what was done. I collected many sentences, and walked the beach till I committed them to memory. At first it seemed a very difficult task to catch the sounds, but in a short time I could begin to understand, and then to talk. For a change I would rest myself from studying the language by practicing reading and writing, having provided myself with copybooks and other necessary material before leaving San Francisco.

The home we had been made so welcome to was situated a few rods from the beach, and between two little streams of water that came tumbling down from the steep precipices in the background into a small valley, which was heavily timbered. There were some six or seven small huts or dwellings and twenty-five or thirty people all told. No business was carried on further than gathering the fruit that grew, uncultivated, in abundance for the needs of the population; and with little effort they caught fish as they cared to consume it. As most of the people of the village were quiet and peaceable, it will be understood why we called the place our lonely retreat, or lonely Huaua. We visited other villages occasionally, and tried to interest the inhabitants and preach to them, but in vain. They would give us food, and sometimes offered to keep us over night, but as a rule they were very cold and indifferent towards us.

Under the circumstances the best we could do was to study the language and prepare ourselves for future usefulness as the way might open. Meanwhile, many rumors were in circulation about the French driving the Mormons out of the country; and the Protestant ministers and Catholic priest seemed to spare no pains to spread all the slanderous stories they ever had heard about the Mormons. So many rumors were in circulation that we did not know what to believe, so we remained in suspense till July 17, when, to our surprise, Brother Grouard came in through a heavy rain and told us that he and Brother Whitaker had been brought from Tubuoi, where they had been building a small schooner for the use of the mission. He said they had been arrested on the charge of speaking against the French government. They had landed that morning from a ship of war, and he had got permission to come and see us, but had to return that evening so as to be at the trial next morning. He had left a horse five miles back, because the road was so rough that he could cover the distance on foot quicker than on horseback, and had no time to lose. He greatly desired that Brother Pratt and I should be at his trial. Said he, "I am innocent, but I do not know what they will prove, and we want you to stand by us." So it was agreed that Brother Hamatua and I should go on foot early next morning, and Brothers Pratt and Pohe would come as soon as the wind quieted down, as it was then too high to venture out in the boat.

Brother Hamatua and I set out early in the morning, in a heavy rain, which continued to pour down till we reached Papeete, at 11 o'clock, when we met Brother Grouard coming from his trial, he having been discharged. He said Brother Whitaker would also be acquitted, although the prejudice against them was very strong.

Brothers Grouard and Whitaker thought the government would board and lodge them at least till it got ready to return them home again, but in this they were mistaken, so they and I did the best we could for ourselves. We soon learned that the steamship *Sarien* would leave for Tubuoi in three or four days, and the brethren would be taken back on that. Brother Grouard sought the permission of the governor for Brother Pratt and me to go on the *Sarien* with him. This was refused on the ground that two Mormon missionaries were enough on that island. The governor did not wish any more to go until he knew more about them.

The wind kept so high that Brother Pratt did not reach Papeete until Brothers Grouard and Whitaker had been acquitted and had gone. I had started home, and was overhauled by Brother Grouard, who said something had broken on the ship and they had to stop to repair it; that he could not remain to see Brother Pratt, but would stay with me as long as he could. He had only a few moments to stop, so I proceeded about six miles, when I learned that Brother Pratt was on the way by boat. Upon obtaining this information I went back to the house where we had stayed two or three nights, finding the place barren and uninviting. Everything was very lonely with no friends there. I feared that I would be alone that night, but at last Brother Pratt came. The boat had stopped, with our bedding and provisions, three or four miles up the coast. Although the night was very dark, and the road lay through the woods and across creeks, Brother Pratt thought we had better try to make the boat for the night, as we had to give up going to Tubuoi.

This course was followed, and we found our friends and bedding all right. Not being satisfied, however, with the situation, we went back to Papeete next morning, to see the governor ourselves. When we met him, Brother

Pratt asked the reason why we could not be free to go where we chose. He replied that there had been some trouble with Mr. Grouard, and as it was his business to look after government affairs, he wished to inquire into the matter further before permitting more American missionaries to go there. Said he: "While I do not wish to interfere with religion, it is my duty to keep peace, and if you will call again in a month or six weeks, I will let you know more about it."

At this we went to the boat, and with our friends returned to lonely Huaua. Indeed, if it had not been for our friends Hamatua and Pohe and their families, our stay at the place for some time after this would have been very uncomfortable. Food had become very scarce, so that we had to eat seasnails, and bugs that played on the surface of salt water pools. These bugs were about the size of the end of a man's thumb; in form and action they very much resembled the little black bugs found along the edges of our fresh water streams, and called by some people mellow bugs. I submit that a dish of these, without pepper or salt, was a strange sight to present to a white man—their legs sticking out in all directions; yet, when a man has gone long enough without food, they become quite tempting, and he is not very particular about the legs, either.

We also had other strange dishes set before us. When other food failed, the natives would go to the mouths of small fresh water streams, and dig in the sands, just where the high tide flowed, and at a depth of twelve to eighteen inches they would find a something that resembled young snakes more than anything else I can compare them to. They were from six to ten inches in length, had a snake's mouth, and a spinal column, or we should have called them worms; they were without fins, or we might have called them eels. The natives had a name for them, but I have forgotten it. When they were boiled in salt water—put a quart or two into a pot of cold seawater, then hang them over the fire and see them squirm a few moments—they were ready for the missionary's meal, taken without pepper or salt. When cooked, a person seizes one by the head and extracts it from the dish, or the banana leaf, as the case may be. He retains the head between his thumb and forefinger, then takes hold of the body with his teeth, draws it through these, and thus strips off the flesh in his mouth. He then lays down the head and backbone, and repeats the operation until he has completed his repast.

Just a moment, my friendly reader; we have another dish for you on the Society Islands, that you may enjoy better. It is a peculiar kind of fish, very rare indeed, for they seldom appear more than once or twice in a year: then they are present by myriads. They come up out of the sea into the fresh water streams so thickly that they can be dipped up with a frying-pan or bucket. Sometimes the natives dip them up with an open bucket, or with a sack having a hoop in the mouth, thus taking them by bushels. These fish are of a dark color, and from half an inch to an inch and a quarter long. When boiled they look like boiled rice, and a man can eat about as many of them as he can grains of that vegetable. When they are eaten with the cream of the cocoanut they are quite palatable. This dish is not very common, as I remember seeing it in only three or four places.

Besides the dish named, we had a small shellfish called maava. It lives in a shell so much like a snail's that we called it a seasnail. It was cooked in the shell, and was quite acceptable for a change in hard times. We also had a large shellfish called pahua; again, we had a jelly-fish which, when taken and laid in a dish, very much resembled the white of an egg; it had neither scales nor bones, and was eaten raw, without pepper or salt.

Still another course of food which we had was wild

boar from the mountains. I can only say that the flesh is
hard and tough. Brother Pratt shot a boar with his shotgun. This pleased the natives very much. I also gave
chase to one which led me so far away from water that I
felt I should die of thirst and heat. On my descent returning, I came to a lone cocoanut tree that had plenty of nuts
on. I tried in vain to climb the tree; then I clubbed the
nuts that were only forty feet or so up, but finding that it
was impossible to obtain drink in that way, I sat down in
the shade in despair, and felt for a moment that I could not
live to reach water. At last my nerves became somewhat
steadied, and I took aim at the stem of a nut, it being not
so thick as my little finger. The bullet cut one stem entirely away and passed through another close to the nut.
Thus two cocoanuts dropped, and hopes of life sprung up
anew, only to perish, for I found it impossible to open the
nuts. After a brief rest, I started down the mountain
again, and succeeded in reaching a cocoanut grove where
an old man was throwing down nuts. I told him of my
suffering and he hastened down, opened a nut, and gave
me a drink that was most refreshing. May he receive a
prophet's reward, for he gave me drink when it seemed
that life was fast ebbing away. The welcome draught refreshed me so that I gained the village early, being wiser
for the experience of following wild boars in the mountains
away from water. Although the temptation came to me
several times afterward, I never chased a wild boar again;
but at one time I killed one which appeared to be about
two years old, without a chase. This, and hunting ducks
and fishing a little, greatly relieved the monotony of our
involuntary stay.

For a change from our living at Huaua, I went to visit
Pohe, nephew of my old friend Hamatua, who lived at
Tiara, three miles up the coast, making my home with him.
I visited among the people there, and by hearing none but

the Tahitian language spoken, I progressed very fast therein; indeed my progress astonished the natives at Tiara, who said, "The Lord helps the Mormon missionaries learn our language, for in three months they speak it better than other foreigners do in five years."

CHAPTER XXI.

OFFER OF TRANSPORTATION TO THE ISLAND OF TUBUOI—APPLY TO THE
GOVERNOR FOR PERMISSION TO GO—TROOPS ON PARADE—SUITE
OF QUEEN POMERE—CALL ON THE GOVERNOR—CONVERSATION IN
THREE LANGUAGES—DIRECTED TO COME AGAIN NEXT DAY—PUT
OFF BY THE GOVERNOR—LATTER REFUSES THE PERMISSION
ASKED—HIS PREJUDICE AGAINST THE MORMONS—DEMANDS A
STATEMENT OF THEIR DOCTRINES—NOT REQUIRED OF OTHER
DENOMINATIONS—WRITER'S INTERVIEW WITH THE GOVERNOR—
RETURN TO HUAUA—OTHER ELDERS REQUESTED TO ASSEMBLE
THERE -BITTERNESS OF PROTESTANT MINISTERS—NATIVES COM-
MENT ON MORMONS LEARNING THEIR LANGUAGE QUICKLY.

DURING my stay at Tiara, news came to Brother Pratt that a schooner from Lurutu was at Papeete, and that the captain had proffered to take us to Tubuoi free of charge. On receiving this message I returned at once to Huaua. Brother Pratt requested me to visit Governor Bonard, and see if we could get permission to make the trip, it being near the time when we were to call on him again. It was necessary for us to give him eight days' notice of our coming, and as the vessel was to sail in ten days, there was no time to lose.

On August 9th I set out, two native boys accompanying me. When we reached Hapape, we saw there about four hundred soldiers. Then we met Governor Bonard and staff, and after them saw Queen Pomere and suite, all in their military dress. It was difficult to tell which made the

finest appearance.   On our arrival in Papeete we were told
that the troops had gone out on dress parade and review,
preparatory to sailing to the island of Huhine, to settle
some trouble between the natives of that island and some
shipwrecked foreigners.   It was late when we reached
Papeete, and we went to the house of a native named Didi,
staying over night; he was very kind to us.   I also met
with the owner of the Lurutu vessel, who told me he would
take us to Tubuoi free of charge, if we wished to go.   He
seemed very friendly toward us.

The next day, August 10th, I went to see the governor.   I met a sentinel at the gate, who ordered me to
halt.   Then he called for the officer of the day, who told
me to wait till he gave notice to the governor.   The officer
went in, and soon returned and beckoned me forward.   I
advanced past a second sentinel, when the officer ushered
me into the presence of his excellency, who rose from his
seat and met me.   When we had shaken hands, he very
politely bade me to be seated, and then said pleasantly:
"Do you speak English?"   This question being answered
in the affirmative, he said, "Me speak lete." Then we
entered upon a conversation.   As I understood a little
French, and both of us could speak a limited amount of
Tahitian, we made a jargon of one-third English, one-third
French, and one-third Tahitian.   Then we laughed heartily
at each other because of our novel attempts in the three
languages.   The governor invited me to call next morning,
when his French captain, who could speak English, would
be there.   Then, with French politeness. he bowed me out
and off.

Next morning I went, and met the governor going to
church.   He said he had forgotten it was Sunday, so I
would have to wait an hour or two, and come again.
This I did, being stopped by the sentinel as before, going
through all the ceremonies of the previous visit, and being

ushered into the same room.   I met the English-speaking captain, to whom I made my business known.   Said he, "The governor declines to grant your request."   I was not disappointed, for I was well satisfied from what I had learned the day before that that would be the result, but as the talk had not been very conclusive, I had called for a clearer understanding, hoping the governor might yield when he understood us better.   In this I was mistaken, however, as it seemed the governor was thoroughly filled with prejudice against even the name of Mormon Elder.

I asked Governor Bonard his reasons for detaining us where we were.   He said that in the first place he had no proof that we were good men, and he wished to know what we would preach, and what our doctrines and faith were. I told him that we preached the Gospel which Jesus Christ and His Apostles preached, and could produce our credentials, if he desired to see them.   He said no, he did not wish that of us; neither did he wish to interfere with religious matters, but it was for peace in the country that he wished us to stop there; for if we and everybody who desired it were allowed to set forth new doctrines among the people, and get them divided among themselves, they would be fighting, and it was his place to keep the peace. Said he, "Before you go from this island, I wish to know more about your doctrine."   I told him that was what we wished him and every good man to know, and to embrace it if he would.   Then he said that he desired the Mormon Elders to get together, and make a declaration of what they would preach and how far they would obey the laws. I replied that that was just what we wished to do, but if he refused us the privilege of going to Tubuoi we did not know when we could get together.   Said he, "You had better write to your friends at Tubuoi, and have them come here.   Your faces are strange to me, and you are from a foreign country.   We have no proof that you are good men.

The doctrine you preach is new to me and if you will gather all your white brethren, and make a declaration of the doctrine you preach, and how far you will obey the laws of the land, signing your names to it, then, if I accept of it as being good doctrine, you will have liberty to go anywhere you wish, and have our protection." My answer was that we had no objection to acquainting him with our doctrine.   I asked him if he made the same requirement of other denominations that he did of us, and received the information that he did not.   Upon this, I inquired why he made it of us, and he stated that there had been some difficulty already with B. F. Grouard. "Well," said I, "did you not acquit Grouard?"   "Yes," he said, "but we would like to look further into the matter, and if possible prevent further trouble."   They had lost two good seamen going after Grouard, and one fell overboard on the return trip, but they succeeded in rescuing him.

When I found that I could not prevail on the governor to allow us our liberty, I left and visited the captain of the *Lurutu*.   With him I boarded his novel vessel.   It was of very frail construction; all the stays and braces were made by hand from the bark of a tree called by the natives burson, and resembling somewhat the basswood of the Eastern and Middle States.   The captain said he sailed by the sun by day, and at night by the moon and stars, but in cloudy weather by instinct, or guess.   I asked if they did not get lost sometimes; he said no, they were well acquainted with the sea.   They had been three years in building the schooner. It would carry about forty tons.   The crew conveyed the products of their island three hundred and sixty miles to Tahiti principally, but occasionally to other islands.   To me the vessel appeared a frail craft, and wholly without comforts, for white men at least.

Having satisfied my curiosity about the strange craft, I returned to Huaua on August 11, and reported results to

President Pratt, who wrote immediately to the different Elders to come and sign with us the document the governor had suggested. The mails were so irregular and uncertain that we had not the remotest idea when our release would come, for if ever our letters were received by the Elders, it might be three or even six months before they could get a passage to Tahiti. Thus the reader can see that we were doomed to tarry almost as prisoners in the little valley of Huaua, which was only about eighty rods wide by one hundred and fifty in length, being bounded on the south by high, steep mountains, that were almost impossible to cross, at least by a white man not accustomed to climbing them; and on the northeast the open sea rolled and surged upon the rocks and the sandy beach, to within fifteen rods of where we slept, our heads being not more than ten feet above high water mark. This was not all; for the Protestant ministers were very bitter against us, and so prejudiced that it was useless for us to try to enlighten them in regard to ourselves or our faith. They seemed to spare no pains in spreading their venom among the people, and in every way possible intimidated the natives so that our friends were but few, though our enemies had no power over them. With the aid of a book, however, we could improve in the language, and did so to the extent that when we had been there five months the natives who were not of us said, "Surely the Lord is with the Mormons, for in five months they speak our language better than other foreigners do in five years. No one can learn our language like the Mormon Elders unless the Lord helps them." Thus encouraged, we bore our imprisonment the best we could.

CHAPTER XXII.

ON September 5th, 1850, I met with the opportunity of
going to Papeete in a boat that was passing. My
friends took me out in a canoe to the larger vessel. I was
very seasick. The wind was so high that in two hours we
were in Taunoa, where we stayed over night. On the 6th
we got to Papeete, where I received a letter from B. F.
Grouard. I answered it the same day. We found friends
who treated us very kindly; then returned to our lonely
retreat, traveling through a heavy rainstorm all the way.

We continued our studies without anything to vary
the monotony until October 2nd, when President Pratt
and Hamatua, and three children from the latter's family, took their blankets and went into the mountains for
a change, while I made a visit to my friend Pohe to get my
books, which had been left with him. When I returned I
continued my studies alone until Brother Pratt and party came
back; then, on September 15th, I went to Papeno, duck-
hunting. As Sister Hamatua had some relatives there, she
and her stepdaughter accompanied me, thinking that my
stay would be made more pleasant. Sister Hamatua was
between fifty and sixty years of age, was well versed in

the scriptures, and as true to her religion as anyone I have ever met. She had never had any children of her own, and yet she had taken three young babes, from their birth, and nursed them at her own breast, and gave them suck and reared them. I think one mother had died at her child's birth, and with another child the young mother had cast it away to die, as it was illegitimate, and she denied its being her child. The third had been promised to Sister Hamatua before its birth, and at that time she claimed it and took it home the same hour. I saw the children, and the natives bore witness to the truth of the narrative here given. The youngest child was princess of Tubuoi, her name was Aura, and at the time I write of she was a bright girl of eight years.

We went on our journey to Papeno, passing down along the cliffs of rock and precipitous and deep, dark caverns that were almost impassable. The shrieking and howling of the wind as it was forced up through the crevices in the rocks by the surging waves from the open sea, combined with the dangers of the route, had such an effect on my nerves that I have never desired a repetition of the hazardous trip, though I traveled many times on the Brom (state road), parallel with the perilous path. I had no desire to pass over or even to think of the jeopardy we were in on that terrible trail. Suffice it to say, that we reached our journey's end in safety, and stayed with the governor of the village, who treated us very kindly. We returned next day, the 16th of September. On our way we saw a ship heading for Papeete. This gave us hope that we would get some news from the outer world.

September 22nd, Pipitila and I started for Papeete, thinking we would meet with the Elders, or at least get some word from them. All that we could learn was that they were expected in Tubuoi instead of in Tahiti. We stayed in Taunaa, where we met with friends who treated

us well.   One old man said that he had become tired of
the English ministers, for they preached one thing and did
the opposite.   Said he, "I have been a fool that has no
eyes all my life.   I have belonged to the Protestant church
ever since it has been here, and still I am like a fool, for I
am black or dark in my heart.   I have tried ever since the
missionaries came to get light.   They came and went back
and died, and still I am a fool, and darkness fills my soul, for
I never learned before that Christ was baptized.   You have
given me the first light that I have ever had on the Gospel."
We returned to our home on September 25th and found
all well.   On October 3rd friends from Tiara came to visit
us, and for a time broke the monotony of our island-prison
life.

Nothing out of the usual happened till November 6th,
when I was ready to start on a trip of inquiry.   A little
girl came in and said there was an old white man out at the
creek, and that he was asking for Brother Pratt.   In a few
minutes Brother S. A. Dunn came in, and to our great surprise and joy he brought word that Brother Pratt's family
and a company of Elders had arrived at Tubuoi, all well.
He had letters for us, too.   I received one from my father
—the first word that I had had since 1847.   I also had a
letter from my old friend and comrade, Jonathan C. Holmes,
stating that my Uncle Alexander Stephens had been
wounded in a battle with the Ute Indians in Utah County,
but that he was getting around again very well.

Brother Pratt received letters from the First Presidency
of the Church, also from Apostles Amasa M. Lyman and
Charles C. Rich, all bringing good news and words of
encouragement to us.   Elder Dunn told us that he had
called on Governor Bonard, who seemed very pleasant and
who told him that as soon as we would get together and
make a statement of what we would preach, and signed
the same, we would have liberty to go where we chose,

and should have the protection of the French government.

November 8th we wrote as follows to the governor:

"Whereas, we, the undersigned, have been requested by his excellency, Governor Bonard, of Tahiti, to make a statement of the intentions of our mission to the Society Islands, in compliance therewith we proceed to give the following:

"1st.   To preach the everlasting Gospel, which brings life and salvation to the children of men. 'For I am not ashamed of the Gospel of Christ, for it is the power of God unto salvation to every one that believeth, to the Jew first, and also to the Greek.'—(Romans 1: 16.)

"2nd.   To teach the people by precept and by example the habits of virtue and industry, which are so desirable to the happiness and prosperity of civilized life.

"3rd.   To observe and keep the laws of every land wherein we dwell, so far as it is required of preachers of the Gospel in Christian countries; and to teach and admonish the people to observe and keep the laws of the land.

"Huaua, Tahiti, November 8, 1850.

"[Signed] ADDISON PRATT,
"SIMEON A. DUNN,
"JAMES S. BROWN."

We started on November 10th to see the governor and present to him the foregoing.   Traveling on foot, we went to Papeno, where we were very kindly received by the governor, at whose house we stopped over night. Many of his friends called to see and greet us.   On the 11th we proceeded to Papeete, arriving there in time to pass the guard and be ushered into the governor's office, where we were received very coldly.   The governor was engaged talking with two officers.   We stood until observed, from a side room, by a French officer, who invited us (speaking in English) to come in and be seated; he then called an interpreter. When the latter came he looked over the article that we had presented, and rejected it. Then he produced one which the governor had had drawn up, and which he read as follows:

"On my arrival at Tahiti, two or three persons styled Mormon missionaries were residing either at Tubuoi or at the Pamutus. As they were already there, I thought it proper to allow them to remain, considering the small number of persons forming the mission, upon conditions, however, that they attended strictly to the laws which govern the lands of the protectorate, not interfering in any way with politics or civil matters, but solely religious, with which I have no intention whatever to interfere.

"Now that a large number of persons attached to the Mormon mission request permission to reside at the Society Islands, tending to create a sort of church government embracing all the lands of the protectorate of France, to create, it might be said, a new existence in the population of the islands, it is now my duty to interfere.

"I requested to be informed as to what are the means of the Mormons for their living.

"1st. From whence the society of Mormon missionaries derive the power of forming themselves into a body?

"2nd. What are the forms of government and the discipline which govern this society?

"3rd. What guarantee of morality and good conduct do they require from members appointed as missionaries for the foreigners?

"4th. What guarantee do they require before conferring grades and offices on natives?

"5th. What duty do they require either from foreigners or from native members, not including religious dogmas, with which I shall not interfere?

"6th. What number of religious services do they hold weekly or monthly?

"7th. Finally, what morals do the Mormons preach?

"These questions put, and satisfactorily answered. This is what it is my duty to make known to the Mormon missionaries: As men, they, as all foreigners, are permitted to reside in the islands of the protectorate, and have a right to French protection by conforming themselves to the laws of the country; as missionaries, with an open pulpit which might consequently give them great influence over the population, and create, as it were, a new power, it is my duty to impose conditions that they guarantee, consequently:

"1st. The Mormon missionaries shall bind themselves to preach their religion without interfering in any way or under any pretext with politics or civil matters.

"2nd. They shall withhold from speaking from the pulpit against the religion established in the islands of the protectorate, or the laws and the acts emanating from the authorities.

"3rd. They shall not exact from the inhabitants of the islands of the protectorate any tax, either in money, labor, provisions or material.

"4th. They shall not inflict penalties upon any one, either in money, labor, provisions, or material, for failing to comply with the rules of the religion they preach.

"5th. They cannot acquire land in the name of the society, without the approbation of the protectorate government.

"6th. No person can be allowed to unite himself with them, as a Mormon missionary, in the Society Islands, before having signed that he adheres to the present declaration, and whenever proof might be made of guilt of an infringement of these articles, it would occasion his exclusion from the islands of the protectorate.

"The persons calling themselves Mormon missionaries, and who sent a delegate to me whom I could not recognize officially, are hereby informed that before I can authorize them as a society they must reply categorically to the questions which I have put to them; that until then their residence is illegal, and I refuse, as it is my duty to do, all authorization to the Mormon missionaries to take up their residence. Moreover, it is my duty to inform them that when they are constituted a society no meetings, except on days regularly known as days of prayer and preaching, can be held without the permission of the authorities, on pain of being prosecuted according to law."

When this long and proscriptive roll had been read and strongly emphasized, we were handed a copy, and the interpreter said we could make such answers as we saw fit. At this we went to a quiet place, and on November 12th President Pratt wrote out the following reply:

"As it has been requested by his excellency, the governor of Tahiti, to give answer to certain questions that he has propounded to us, we herein comply:

"1st. First, as it is declared in the New Testament of our Lord and Savior Jesus Christ, that they that preach the Gospel shall live off the Gospel, we are sent forth by the authority of the Church to which we belong with expectation that those to whom we preach will contribute to our necessities, so far as life and health are concerned, of their own free will. Second, we have no authority from those who sent us to the islands to form ourselves into a body compact, either civil or religious, nor have we any intention of so doing. Third, the reason of our going to Tubuoi is this: I, Addison Pratt, arrived at Tubuoi in the year 1844, in the capacity of a missionary of the Gospel of Jesus Christ. I remained there in that capacity about nineteen months, and when I was about to leave there I was invited, by the authorities of the island then in power, to return to them with my family, and reside with them as their preacher. They wished also to be instructed in the arts

and sciences of civilized life.   After I left Tubuoi, I went
to Anaa, to assist Mr. Grouard in his missionary labors,
having been sent for by request of the people living there. I
remained at Anaa about nine months, and while there a
general conference was held, by the people we had baptized, on the 6th of October, 1846.   At that meeting a
request was made by the people of whom Aniipa was
head, to send by me to our Church, in North America, for
more missionaries to assist Mr. Grouard and myself, as the
Gospel had spread in several islands of that group.   The
company that has arrived at Tubuoi are the missionaries
who have been sent for, as I returned to North America
in the year 1847 and laid the minutes of the conference
held at Anaa, and the request of the people of Tubuoi,
before the Church.   A part of that company now at
Tubuoi are preachers of the Gospel, and a part of them are
mechanics and husbandmen; they have brought with them
tools and seeds for carrying out the object for which they
were sent.

"2nd.   The forms of government by which the society
is governed are those set forth by Jesus Christ and His
Apostles, as laid down in the New Testament, to which we
have referred.

"3rd.   We request them to be strictly virtuous in every
sense of the word, observing and keeping the laws of the
land wherein they dwell, and teaching the people so to do.

"4th.   We request of them all that is contained in the
articles.

"5th.   We request of them what is contained in the
third article and nothing more.

"6th.   We have no stated times for religious services
except upon the Sabbath; we hold semi-annual conferences.
Besides these, we are subject to the will of the people.

"7th.   We preach to and admonish the people to keep

all the commandments of God, and strictly obey the laws of the land wherein they dwell."

Our answer was signed by Addison Pratt, Simeon A. Dunn and James S. Brown, and was presented to his excellency, who objected to the first statement, about our means of support. He said he wished men to get a living in a more honorable way than that. The second paragraph he did not like. He seemed to dislike scripture references. We told him we had been reared to work, that we still expected to labor for our living, and that a part of our people had come to work and a part to preach the Gospel.

After he had interrogated us to his satisfaction, and placed about us all the restrictions that seemed possible, the governor told us that if we would go with Mr. Dugard, one of his officers, he would give us permits to reside among the islands of the protectorate, after we had signed the articles he presented to us.

As we left the governor's presence, Mr. Dugard told us that, as it was getting rather late, we had better call at his office the next morning at 8 o'clock, and he would attend to our case. We complied with his suggestion but did not find him at home. The lady of the house told us to call at 2 o'clock and he would be there. In a short time we met the interpreter who advised us to call at 11 o'clock, which we did, finding the official ready to wait on us, as we supposed; but instead, he directed us to go to a certain notary public, who would give us our permits. We did as intructed and obtained the documents, paying three francs each. Thus we were permitted to go as ministers of the Gospel among the islands of the French protectorate.

CHAPTER XXIII.

RETURN TO HUAUA—HEAVY RAINSTORMS—REFUSAL OF AN OFFER TO
BE CARRIED OVER A STREAM—PERILOUS SWIMMING FEAT—EPI-
SODE WITH A WILD BOAR—START ON A TRIP AROUND THE ISLAND
—OBTAIN A LOAF OF BREAD—PEOPLE NOT DESIROUS OF LISTEN-
ING TO THE MORMON ELDERS—CUSTOMS OF THE NATIVES—REPU-
TATION OF PROTESTANT CLERGY ON TAHITI—WITH THE CHIEF
MAGISTRATE OF UAIRAI—ACROSS A SMALL BAY IN A CANOE—
FRENCH GARRISON AT THE ISTHMUS—WITH MY FRIEND POHE—
REVIEW OF A HARD JOURNEY—AGAIN AT HUAUA.

AS there were no vessels bound for where we wished
to go at this time, on November 13th we started on
our return from Papeete to Huaua, but it rained so hard
that we had to seek shelter after traveling six miles. We
came to a creek about two rods across, and began to take
off our shoes preparatory to wading it. Just then a
sprightly little woman came along and told us she would
carry us across on her back. She said, "There are little
sharp shells and rocks that will cut your feet, and they will
not hurt mine, for I am used to them. My feet are tough,
but you are not used to going barefoot like us, and your
feet are tender. I will gladly carry you over free rather
than see you cut your feet." She plead with such earnest-
ness and so innocently that it became almost a temptation,
especially as she would have considered it a great honor
to carry the servants of God, as she was pleased to call us.
Said she, "You need not be afraid that I will fall down with
you; I can carry you with ease." When her very kind
offer was declined, she seemed very much disappointed.
We tried to console her by telling her how greatly we
appreciated her kindness, then proceeded on our way, but

owing to the heavy rain soon called at a native's house, where we were pleasantly entertained. He spread the best food he had. This was put on the bed. He also asked us to take seats on the bed, offering as an excuse, "The fleas are so bad we have to get up there to be out of the way, or they will get in the food."

We accepted the situation with thanks, and felt that we were right royally treated. The people from around flocked in until the house was so thoroughly packed with humanity that the fleas had a fine opportunity to gorge themselves. The people did not seem to be much annoyed by them, but talked and sang till 11 o'clock, when we turned in for the remainder of the night, concluding that the fleas had been so feasted that they were willing to let us slumber in peace, which we did.

November 14th we resumed our journey, only to be driven in by the rain, but not until we were thoroughly drenched. Having met with our old and well tried friend, Hamatua, when the storm subsided we continued our journey to Papeno. A call was made on the governor of that district, who told us that the river was so swollen that it was not safe for white men to attempt to cross. He said the natives could go over safely, but we could not do so, and told the party they were welcome to stay with him all night. The writer thought that if a native could cross the river he could, so he prepared for the attempt. The stream was about fifteen rods wide. The governor, himself a very large and powerful man, said, "If you go I will go with and assist you, for you cannot cross there alone. Two natives have been swept down to the sea and drowned. If I go with you we can cross safely, but I am afraid to have you go alone." At that both of us got ready to cross. He took hold of my right arm close to the shoulder. We waded in till the swift current took our feet from under us, then we swam with all our power, and finally gained the opposite shore by swimming three times the width of the river. The governor could have turned and swam back again without any trouble, but I had quite enough to satisfy my conceit, and ever since have been willing to acknowledge that a native can beat me in the water.

Brothers Pratt and Dunn were well satisfied to wait for the water to fall before they tried to cross, and by late in the evening the stream was down so that they came over with comparative ease. We stayed with some very good friends, and on the 15th of November reached home. All were well. Things went on as usual until the 28th, when the natives came running and said a wild hog had come down from the mountains and was at the next door neighbor's, with his tame hogs. The people wished us to come with bubus (guns) and shoot him. On a previous occasion, before I could understand the natives, a wild hog had come down and was with the hogs of our host. There was great excitement among the natives, so Brother Pratt hastened and got his shotgun, and went out and killed the hog. He told me to hold on with my gun, and would not let me know what the excitement was until it was over. Now, the natives shouted that Prita's (Pratt's) gun was the strong one, that he was the brave hunter and knew how to shoot, but that my weapon was too small a bore—it could not kill if I hit the hog. But on this occasion I outdistanced the old gentleman with my small-bore rifle. I shot the hog just behind the shoulder; it ran a few jumps and fell in the thick brake. As the animal was out of sight, and the natives could not see any evidence of its having been hit, they blamed me for not letting Brother Pratt get there first, saying he would have killed the hog and we would have had something to eat. Brother Pratt good naturedly joined in with them; they looked disappointed, and tried to laugh me to shame, but in the height of their ridiculing me a lad who had followed the track a rod or two into the brake shrieked out in terror: "Here is the hog, dead! I was near stepping on him before I saw him!" The laugh was turned.

The hog was soon dressed, and the natives had to examine my gun. They concluded that both Brother Pratt and I were good gunners, and had good weapons. The hog was a boar, a year and a half old or more, and if it had been fat would have dressed two hundred pounds. All were well pleased for it was a time of scarcity of food.

On December 2nd Brother Dunn and I started to go around Tahiti on foot, passing by Papeete. Hametua Vaheni, John Layton's wife, and the two small girls of the house, went with us to Papeete. We stayed at Faripo the first night, with Noiini, who was very kind to us. Next morning we proceeded on our way to Hapape, where we stopped at the house of Teahi, a relative of Hametua Vaheni. There we took breakfast, and continued our journey to Taunoa, where we remained over night with Tamari. There we left our baggage while we went on to Papeete to see what news we could get. We spent most of the day to no purpose, returning to where we had stayed the night before.

Next morning, the 4th, we started without breakfast. On the way we purchased a loaf of bread—a rare treat to us, as we had not even seen bread for several days. We ate it as we walked along, stopping at a small brook to get a drink. At Wamau, a man invited us into his house. As it had begun to rain we accepted his kind offer with thankfulness. Upon entering the house we were requested to take a seat upon the bed. Some very fine oranges were set before us, and soon the house was filled with young people mostly, who seemed very desirous of learning who we were, where we were from, and what our business was. We told them, and they appeared to be very much disappointed. We soon found that they had no use for us, so we went on

our way and soon came to a cemetery in which was a large
monument of masonry with an iron cross on it.   At one
grave there was a candle burning.   We were told by some
of the people that in the time of the war a great battle
had been fought there between the natives and the French,
and that the monument had been built in honor of a great
French general who had fallen.

From there we passed on through a large cocoanut
grove, and in a short time came to a small village called
Tapuna.   We turned into a house and not finding anyone
at home, sat down for a rest.   In a little while we were
discovered by some of the villagers, who invited us in, and
as is usual among that people, inquired of us, saying, "Who
are you, where do you come from, where are you going,
and what is your business here in our land?"   When we
informed them that we were ministers of the Gospel, they
were very much pleased, but when we told them that our
Church was called the Church of Jesus Christ of Latter-
day Saints, commonly known as the Mormon Church, they
almost invariably showed signs of disappointment, and
seemed to have less interest in us.   Still there were some
in almost every village who were kind enough to keep us
over night, give us the very best they had, and often go
with us a little way on our journey the next day.   They
never failed to have a hymn sung, and often a chapter from
the Bible read, and would call on us to offer prayer.   Then
the eldest of the young men who had called in—sometimes
there were ten or fifteen—would shake hands with us, followed by all the rest, apparently according to age.   The
young women then would do likewise, observing the same
rule, after which the older people would follow, the women
coming first in this case, such being their custom.

Before we left Tapuna, one man desired us to visit his
mother, who was sick with consumption.   We complied
with this wish, but found that she had no faith in the Gos-

pel. From there we passed on to an English missionary's home, the headquarters of one Mr. Chisholm. He was not in, so we passed on to the next house, where, according to what the people said, a very dissipated missionary had lived, and the other had come to take his place. We were told that the newcomer was no better than the old one, for both were drunken and lustful and behaved very badly with the women. Such was the general reputation, among the natives, of the Protestant clergy at that date.

We went on till we were called into a house where the people said they wished to know what we had to say of religion. As soon as they learned that we differed from their views they displayed no further concern in us, and we departed. After wading many streams, and getting very tired and hungry, we reached a village called Uairai, where we were invited in to have a meal. We had been indoors but a few minutes when the people of the village came running in as if to a dog fight or a monkey show; for it was rarely they saw two white men traveling as we were, they being accustomed to seeing the missionary in a hammock carried by four stout men.

When we had been there a short time two men came in with a message from the governor or chief magistrate of the village, desiring us to call at his residence. As soon as we had partaken of refreshments we complied with the request, the whole assemblage of people following us. We found his honor holding some kind of meeting with the more aged people, the exact nature of which we did not learn. He invited us in, gave us seats, and shook hands with us very warmly. He then stood before us and said, "Who are you, where do you come from, what is your business here, and where are you going?" We answered that we were ministers of the true Gospel of Jesus Christ, and were traveling to preach to all people that were willing or wished to hear the Gospel of salvation. "Well," he said, "that is what we want here, but I must see the French governor and our ministers before I can give permission for any one to preach."

When the meeting was over he came to us again and said he would be pleased to have us stop over night with him. We accepted his kind invitation to visit his house, and all the congregation followed, for a time seeming very desirous of learning from us the true Gospel. We conversed with them quite awhile and there was not one to oppose us, but all seemed very well pleased with what we had to say.

Supper over, we returned to the house of Miapui, where we had left our valises, and where we spent the night, being well treated by our host and by all who called on us.

Next morning our host accompanied us on our way until we met his brother, whom he instructed to see us across a small bay that extended up to the base of the mountain, which was so steep that we could not go around its head. We were taken across in a canoe, paying a dollar and a half. The man said the use of the canoe cost him that amount, but he would take nothing for his services. He then conducted us through a thick forest of timber and underbrush to the Brom (state) road.

We next proceed to the isthmus, to a French fort garrisoned by one company of soldiers. The isthmus is about one and a half miles across. From there we turned to the northwest, towards Huaua, as it was too rough, steep and dangerous to proceed closely along the coast. We traveled homeward till 1 o'clock p. m., when we came to a little hamlet called Otufai. There we met a man named Aili, who invited us to dinner. We accepted his courtesy and while there the school-teacher called and asked us to go home with him. We also availed ourselves of this kind invitation, finding the teacher, whose name was Tuamau, very friendly. We spent the night with him, being treated well, but he did not evince much interest in what we had to say on religious matters.

The following morning it was raining very hard, and for a time it seemed that we were weatherbound; but breakfast over, it cleared off, and we proceeded on our way to Hitia, where we stopped at the house of Fenuas and got dinner. Then we went on to Tiara and visited with our friend Pohe (in English, dead), or, as he was sometimes called, Mahena Toru (third day). He made us feel very much at home. This we were in a condition to fully appreciate, for we had traveled on foot in the hot sands and sun about one hundred and fifty miles, until we felt that we were almost parboiled. We had waded many streams of water, which, though very disagreeable, helped to make our journey more tolerable, through being cooling. The sharp rocks and shells in the water courses made us pay penance instead of pennies for crossing them. Sometimes the streams were so swollen and ran so swiftly as to be very dangerous, because the crossings were so near the sea that if a man were to lose his footing he was liable to be carried into the billows, from whence it would be almost if not quite impossible to escape.

On the 9th of December we passed down three miles to Huaua, where we found all our friends well, and some prospects of getting an opening to preach.

CHAPTER XXIV.

ON the 16th of December I set out from Huaua on a short journey to a small hamlet called Tapuna. Everywhere I went the people were complaining of the great scarcity of food; still they managed to furnish me with plenty, treating me very hospitably. About the 20th I returned to Huaua and preached to the people. On the 29th and 30th I attended to my correspondence.

January 1, 1851, I started for Tarepu, finding the roads quite muddy. It rained heavily, so that all the streams were so swollen as to make my journey very hard and tiresome. The majority of the people were rather surly and indiffer-ent, so much so as not to invite me in out of the storm, so I had to pass along to where I found more hospitality. The trip altogether was a hard and ungrateful one. I had to swim some of the watercourses, and barely escaped being carried into the sea. I got everything I had with me, even to my watch, thoroughly soaked. Then I sought a place sheltered from the view of the passers-by, and there dried my clothes. As I was alone almost all the time on this trip, I felt it to be long and tedious, without any profitable results, as far as I could see. Yet I remembered that my experience was that of a fisherman; and as my calling was to fish for men I did not complain, but continued my journey to Hitia. There I called on one Mr. Baff, a Protestant minister. I left a copy of the Voice of Warning for him to read. When he returned it he sent a note thanking me for the privilege of perusing it, but he did not express an opinion of the work. I never had the pleasure of meeting the gentleman again.

Having been informed that Elders Pratt and Dunn had an opportunity of going to Tubuoi, I hastened back to Huaua, to find that they had not yet engaged their passage. After resting two or three days, Brother Pratt sent me down to Papeete to secure passage for them on Captain Johnson's schooner, which was expected to sail in a few days. I met Mr. Johnson, with whom I made a contract, and returned next day. Then, on January 13th, all hands went down to Papeete. We found that Brother John Layton had come from California, and brought letters for us from the Elders who had been sent to the Sandwich Islands.

Mail matters considered and answers written, the program was changed so that Elder Dunn did not go to Tubuoi, and as Brother Pratt had to wait a few days before he could start, part of the native family that had accompanied us remained to see him off, while the others returned with Brother Dunn and I to lonely Huaua. In the meantime we learned that Priest John Hawkins was expected down from Anaa in a few days, when Brother Dunn was to return with him to Anaa.

When we were at Huaua without Brother Pratt, the place seemed doubly lonesome. On January 30th, I went to Papeete and learned that Brother Hawkins had arrived with some native brethren from Metia, and that all had started in their canoes for Huaua, to which place I repaired the next day. All were well. The native brethren went back to Papeete, and Brother Hawkins and wife stayed at Huaua a day or two; then he also went down, returning to us in eight or ten days, accompanied by Elder Joseph Busby, from Tubuoi. The latter said that he had started for home, if it was agreeable to the brethren. He told us that it would be two months before the brethren would come with their new schooner, which they were building.

March 2nd, all hands went to Taunua, to a sacrament meeting. We met in a house close down by the beach, where we saw the vessel that Brother Busby sailed on for home. There were sixty-seven brethren and sisters at the meeting, and we had a very good-spirited time. We returned to Huaua; and it was on March 12th, when, in company with our old, faithful friend and brother, Hamatua, and family, I set sail in a whaleboat for Papara. We had a fine breeze till we came to a hamlet called Otura, where we stayed one night and were well cared for by our host, a brother in the Church. On the 13th we continued our voyage by sea, having to row most of the time, for there was no wind. We reached our destination, Papara, on the 14th, and stopped at the house of Purua, a brother of Hamatua, who had died, and his widow had sent for Hamatua to come and move her and her family to his home. We found our friends here very kind, and well pleased to meet us.

While at Papara, many people came in to see us. These manifested a desire to know who I was, and my business there, but showed great reluctance in shaking hands with me. I learned that the cause of this diffidence was that they were afraid of the Protestant ministers. For a while they kept very shy of me. I called on their minister, Mr. Chisholm, and presented him with a Voice of Warning, which I asked him to read; but when I held it out to him he said no, he would not read it or anything the Mormons had; "but," said he, "I want to exhort you, and show you that you are deluded." I asked what he knew about our Church to cause him to be so excited. He said he had had a letter from Simeon A. Dunn, one of our Elders, and that public opinion was enough to satisfy him that we were false teachers and deceivers of the people. At that he called one Mr. Davis from a side room. The latter was totally blind, and had spent most of his life on the islands. Both of them reviled at me, and rehearsed many of the old slanders about Joseph Smith and the Mormons. I left them in disgust, returning to my friends, where I found many people congregated. These were quite sociable.

Soon a messenger came from the minister and asked what kind of baptism we believed in. When I said that we believed in immersion, that seemed to please the people very much, as I turned to the third chapter of Matthew and showed them that Christ was baptized in that manner. From that time the house was thronged with people anxiously inquiring for the doctrines we taught.

On March 16th I was sent for by a sick man, who wanted to be anointed. When I told him about the order of the Church, and that he should repent and be baptized for the remission of his sins, and thus become entitled to the blessings of the Gospel, he said that it was of no use to him for he was a great sinner and could not repent in one day. Then he said, "I shall have to remain sick." He had his own way to look at things, and as we were unable to convince him otherwise, we returned to our stopping place.

Shortly after this I was called to see a young woman who had been under medical treatment by the Protestant ministers for four months. Her name was Maui. She had been reduced to a mere skeleton, and was unable to stand alone. When I came, she said she had heard of the doctrine that I had preached to the people, and knew it was true, "for," said she, "it is all in the Bible." She was the foremost scholar of the district, and was highly respected by the ministers as well as by the whole people. When it became known that I had been called to see her, it aroused an excitement, and many people came together, insomuch that the house could not hold them all. As I talked with her on the first principles of the Gospel, she would say, "Yes, that is so, for it is in the Bible;" and she said, "I am willing to be baptized now, for I know that what you tell me is the truth." I asked the consent of her parents and of her young husband, who readily acceded to her desire. Then I told them that if they would take her to a suitable place by the creek, I would meet them there and attend to the baptizing. Accordingly, they carried her to the creek, some ten or twelve rods away, where I met them, prepared for the work. There were probably one hundred people assembled. After singing and prayer, I went into the water and the friends of the young woman helped her to me, I having to aid in holding her on her feet while I said the baptismal ceremony. When she came up out of the water she thanked God, saying, "I am healed of the Lord," and walked out of the water and home without assistance, although her friends offered aid. This excited the people so much that some of the young woman's particular friends prepared to come into the water of baptism, but the older ones prevailed on them to wait a while, saying maybe they would all go together.

When I had changed my clothing and had gone to where the new convert was, I found her sitting on the bed and praising God, bearing her testimony that she was healed of the Lord, and that we had the true Gospel. The baptism of this young woman was the first that I had administered, she being my first convert. The house where we had assembled was crowded to overflowing, and when I had confirmed her I returned to my stopping place, the people following me. There must have been at least three hundred of them. Several brought bedding and camped under the trees around the house, while others were preparing a feast for the occasion, in which they roasted eleven big hogs, and gathered fish, fruit and vegetables for the roast.

This was too much for the Protestant ministers, for, as I was sitting at a table expounding the scriptures to the people, in came a lusty Frenchman in citizen's clothes. He took a seat among the people for a short time, then slipped away and donned his police uniform, with belt, sword and pistol; then, with a comrade similarly attired, he reappeared at the door and asked me if I had a permit from the governor. I told him I had one at home, but not with me. At that he, in a rather rough tone of voice, bade me follow them. Without hesitation I did so, and about a hundred of the people came after us to the mission station, where I was ushered into the presence of Messrs. Chisholm, Howe and Davis. All of them were what were called English or Protestant missionaries. Mr. Howe acted as chief spokesman or prosecutor, while Mr. Chisholm filled the role of justice, Mr. Davis appearing to be his assistant. Thus arrayed, they told me that I had been arrested and brought before them because I had raised a very unusual excitement among the people, and I could not produce a permit from the government as a resident on the island. They said I was capable of making much disturbance among the people, and the decision they had come to was that if I would not agree to leave the place by 8 a. m. next day I would be locked up in a dungeon until I did agree to leave.

Of course I consented to depart at the appointed time, thinking I could get my permit and return in a few days Then they told me I was at liberty, but they did not release me until they had scored me unmercifully with their tongues for belonging to such a set of impostors as "Old Joe Smith and the Mormons" were. Said Mr. Chisholm, "You are a fine young man, capable of doing much good if you had not been deceived by that impostor, Old Joe Smith." They told me to cease my preaching and deceiving the people, and that I had better go home. At that I pocketed their insults and left them. Many of the people followed me to my stopping place, some of them shouting triumphantly for the young Mormon missionary, and calling shame on the English ministers.

A house full of people had assembled, and we sat up till a late hour that night talking on the principles of the Gospel. Early next morning our boat was filled with the family and provisions, and we sailed at 8 o'clock. I put on a fisherman's suit and took the helm, facing outward from the shore. I did not have any particular object in view at the time in doing this, yet it seemed to serve a purpose, for we had sailed but a few miles when we saw two mounted gen d' armes come out of the woods to the sandy beach, where they stopped and watched our boat till they seemed satisfied there was no missionary on board, and passed on. Then it occurred to us that if I had not been in the unintentional disguise they would have stopped our boat and arrested me, for they were well armed, and could have reached us easily with their firearms. As we afterwards learned, they passed on to where we had come from and made a thorough search for me, going through houses, turning up the beds, and scouring the coffee groves and every place the supposed Mormon missionary could have hidden. Then they and the Protestant missionaries called a meeting of the people and thoroughly warned them against the Mormons, and especially against young Iatobo (James), as they called me. At this mass meeting Mr. Baff, one of the oldest of the English missionaries, appeared with the others I have mentioned.

There was another incident that seemed to be very providential, though disagreeable at the time. The wind died away to a perfect calm, and when we came to an opening in the outlying coral reef, we thought that by going out through the opening we might catch a breeze, and could hoist the sail and make better headway; so we steered for the open sea. There we found that we had to row all day before we could get back within the reef. Thus we were carried so far from the land that passers-by could not discern who we were, and we were kept from the gen d' armes till sundown. Then we landed away from the thoroughfare, in heavy timber. In that way we escaped our enemies, for next morning we were off and out in the open sea soon after sunrise. We rowed all day and till 11 o'clock p. m., then landed in an obcsure place, and were up and off again by sunrise, putting out to sea and keeping there till we reached the western passage to the harbor of Papeete. There we went ashore near a large American tile establishment's wholesale and retail department. Just in front of this lay a large American warship. The water was very deep, so that the vessel was moored to the shore, the gangway resting upon the street, where a great many people had gathered.

As soon as we landed I stepped into the retail department referred to, on some little errand. In a couple of minutes or so I was confronted by the Rev. Mr. Howe, who has been mentioned before. He was a fine-looking English gentleman of thirty-five or forty years of age. He came up and shook hands with me, saying, "Mr. Brown, are you aware that the gen d' armes are in search of you? You must have been in hiding somewhere. They have searched Papara for you, and now are searching this town, and there is great excitement over your actions. You had better be cautious what you are about." I could not understand at first what he meant, so I asked him what I had done to create such a great excitement as to have the police hunting for me. I said I had not been in hiding at all, had not thought of such a thing. He replied, "Why, sir, you have gone and plunged a young lady head and ears into the cold water, and we have had her under medical treatment for four months, and expected her to die. Now you have endangered her life by plunging her into cold water. She is one of the most talented and smartest women of this island. We have taken great pains to educate her, and she is widely known and respected by everyone who knows her."

"Well," said I, "what harm have I done? She was healed of her sickness, as she and her mother testified to me before I left, and every person who was present can bear witness of the same."

"Ah, well," said he, "you have such a fierce countenance and expressive voice as to excite a person under the most excruciating pain until they would not realize they had any suffering at all. She may relapse and die, then you will have grave responsibilities to meet for your unwarranted act." He continued talking, turning to intimidation and abusive language until he said it was a great pity that one of my natural endowments lacked in educational attainments, for if I had been taught in Greek or Latin I would have understood that baptism was *baptiso* in Latin, and meant merely the application of water, and not to plunge people head and ears in the shameful and ridiculous manner that he said I had done.

By this time we were talking so very loud as to attract the attention of all around. Finally Mr. Howe said, "Do you teach the people that baptism is essential to the salvation of man or the soul?" I told him I did. "Then," said he, "you teach a lie, and I will follow you up and tell the people that you are a liar and teach false doctrine." As my calling as a missionary would not admit of a violent retaliation, I merely said to him that in my country that would be very ungentlemanly language for one minister to use towards another, but I supposed it was some of the

Greek and Latin that he had been learned in. Then I turned away from him.

My action brought a tremendous cheer from the Americans on board the warship, and from all who understood the conversation. The people assembled hurrahed for the Mormon boy. At that my antagonist turned very red in the face. Some of the natives ran up to him, pointing their fingers at him, and shouting, "Look how red his nose is! The Mormon boy has whipped him!" They rushed around me to shake hands, and seemed as if they would carry me on their shoulders. It should be understood that we talked partly in English and partly in Tahitian, so that all could understand in a general way what we said, for we had grown very earnest if not heated in our discussion.

Soon after this I went up through the town and there learned from several people that there had been much excitement over my having baptized the sick young lady, and that the police had searched the place over for me. I realized then that if it had not been for the calm weather we had had at sea we would have got into town just at the height of the excitement, and I would have been locked in prison. So, thanks for the calm, although when we were in it we wished for wind that we might make better headway; but that delay gave time for reflection, and for the news of the young lady's convalescence to reach Papeete, so that I could pass on my way without further insult.

CHAPTER XXV.

SEVERAL BAPTISMS—VISIT PAPARA AGAIN—COLDNESS OF THE PEOPLE—
BITTER EFFORTS OF THE PROTESTANT MINISTERS—NATIVES VISIT
ME IN SECRET—ANTI-MORMON MASS MEETING—FOOLISH AND
VICIOUS SCHEME TO ENSNARE THE WRITER—IT IS EASILY DE-
FEATED—RETURN TO PAPEETE—MORE BAPTISMS—DEPARTURE OF
ELDER DUNN—I AM LEFT ALONE—BRETHREN COME FROM TUBUOI
—ELDERS APPOINTED TO LABOR IN DIFFERENT ISLANDS—THE
WRITER ASSIGNED TO THE TUAMOTU GROUP—LEAVE ON THE
ELDERS' SCHOONER, THE RAVAI OR FISHER—MEET WITH CON-
TRARY WINDS—DRIVEN TO VARIOUS ISLANDS—ENCOUNTER A VIO-
LENT STORM—IN GREAT PERIL—VESSEL BEYOND CONTROL—
STORM CALMS DOWN—REACH TUBUOI—FIRST PREACHING OF THE
GOSPEL THERE, IN 1844.

WE reached our home at Huaua on the 20th of March, and found all well. On the 23rd I baptized Tereino and Maioa, and on the 24th Brother Dunn baptized two other persons besides Brother Hamatua and two of his children. Then I sailed for Papara, after providing myself with the permit that I lacked on our previous visit. We stopped at Taunua the first night, the 25th, having had to row all the way.

On the 26th we reached Papara, where the people acted very coolly towards us. There was one friend, how-ever, who dared invite us in and provide us with food and lodging. On inquiry, we learned that the young lady who had been ill and was healed at her baptism was sound and well, and had been so from the time she was baptized. We also learned that Messrs. Howe, Chisholm, Baff and Davis had called the people together after the baptism, inquired of them where I was, had the town searched for me, and had sought diligently to learn if I had spoken against them or against the French government; but they failed to learn anything of this kind on which to base an accusation against me, and had to content themselves by telling the people all the foul slanders they had heard against the Mormons and Joseph Smith, and by warning the people against us, saying that if they took us in or bade us Godspeed they would not be permitted to partake of the sacrament in their church, and if they went to hear us preach they would be excommunicated. They sent a delegation to the young lady whom I had baptized, to see if she had been healed, and through being intimidated she said no. Her relatives had quarreled over the matter, some being in favor of her saying that she was not, while others said that she was healed. The report that the delegation made to their masters, however, was that she said she had not been healed; when I went to see her, she ran out to meet me, and told me that she had not been sick one day since she had been baptized.

By such means as those I have named, the ministers sought to turn the people against us, and strongly forbade them to show us any favors whatever; and when the natives could come secretly and talk with us they would explain, "Now, if we come openly and investigate your doctrine and are not satisfied with it, then we will be turned out of society. For that reason we dare not receive you or come and talk openly with you. Our hearts are good towards you, but we are watched by the police, so that we dare not be friendly with you where we can be seen."

As soon as the ministers learned that we had returned, they called another meeting, at which they seemed to take delight in abusing and vilifying the Mormons in general and me in particular. When the meeting was over, they called two pretty young women, and privately told them to dress themselves as nicely as they could and perfume themselves and make themselves as attractive as possible, then to take their Bibles and hymn books and get into conversation with the Mormon missionary, Iatobo (James). They were to be very sociable and friendly to me. They had been told also that they would learn that the Mormons were licentious deceivers, and that my actions would show that I was a licentious rascal and would lead them astray. Orders were also given them that when they had proved this they were to return and report to the ministers. I came into possession of this information regarding the scheme through the spirit of discernment, and by the confession of the parties themselves.

The young ladies came as instructed, and the moment they entered the door and I inhaled the perfumes I had the discernment of their mission and the instructions they were under from their ministers. Nevertheless they were welcomed in and took seats just in front of and close to the writer, on a mat. In the blandest and most pleasant manner they began to make scripture inquiries, accepting every answer as final, and assenting to all I had to say. They became more and more sociable and bold, until at length one of them raised on her knees, and placing her open Bible upon the writer's knee, at the same time looked him squarely in the face with her most pleasant smile. He at once moved his chair back, and said to them, "You have not come here with the object that you profess to come with, but your mission is a deceptive one, and you have been sent here by your ministers to try to deceive me, thinking to lead me into lewd and wicked practices that I am a stranger to. Now, if you wish anything of that kind you must return to your masters who sent you, and tell them that if they wish you to be accommodated in that way, they will have to do it themselves, for Mormon Elders are not guilty of such practices, though they have proofs that the ministers are. And I exhort you to be ashamed and to repent of your sins, and be baptized for their remission, and you will know that what I have told you is true."

At this rebuke, they both confessed openly that every

word I had said was true, and that they had been sent for
no other purpose than the one I have stated.   As they had
come straight from the minister's house, they wondered how
the writer could tell them so directly what their ministers
had ordered them to do, and how he came to read their
mission so accurately.   They said, "*No te varua tera*" (that
is of the Spirit); for no one else could have told him so correctly.   At that they took their leave, and I heard no more
of them or their mission.

The ministers called another meeting on March 29th.
I attended that, and after service asked permission to speak
a few moments.   This being granted by Mr. Davis, I merely
gave notice that I was a minister of the Church of Jesus
Christ of Latter-day Saints, there on a mission to teach the
true Gospel, and if any wished to hear me I was at their
service, if they would permit.   There was no response, so
a hymn was sung, and the people dispersed.   At night a
few came to hear me, but seemed to be under such restraint
that there was no pleasure in talking to them.

We spent several days at the place without any success, owing to the great prejudice of the people, and the
unwarranted hatred of their ministers.   Then we left for
Papeete, starting on April 2nd, and arriving at our destination at daylight on the 3rd.   Having had to row all the
way, we were very tired, so stopped to get some needed
rest.   In the evening we baptized one person, Maua.   On
the 6th we attended meeting with about twenty of the Tuamotu Saints, then the boat and the others of the party went
home while I tarried till the next day, going home by land
to Hapape, where I found a boat bound direct for Huaua,
so I took passage on it, and was wafted there speedily.

It was on April 19th that I started for Otumaro.   On
the 21st we got to that place, where I stayed while the
others of the party made a visit to Papara.   On their return I joined them and proceeded to Papeete, where I left

the boat again and walked the remainder of the journey. The next day the rest of the party came up by sea; and on the 29th we baptized three more persons.

While at Otumaro, some Matia brethren came from Hitia after a missionary or two. Matia is a small island about ninety miles north of Tahiti. Brother Dunn, being very tired of Huaua, concluded that he would go with them, they taking his trunk and bedding on their shoulders and marching off, apparently in triumph. They insisted that I should go with them as well, but having been left in charge of the mission on Tahiti, I did not feel at liberty to leave, as Brother Pratt had told me to remain there until the new schooner should arrive. Therefore I turned alone to my missionary labors. On the 29th I baptized Tuane; and at Huaua on May 4th I baptized Tafatua and Tafai, who had been baptized by Brother Pratt; they confessed that they had been led astray, but desired to return to the true fold. The same day I administered the sacrament to twenty-one souls.

Just at dark on May 12th, 1851, we heard a gun fired at sea. We hastened to the beach, and, sure enough, it was our long-looked-for brethren on their new schooner, which was named the Ravai (Fisher.) Brother John Hawkins having joined us, he and Hamatua went off in a canoe to get the news. They found all well. Next day we joined them in the harbor of Papeete, and remained with them on board the schooner and wrote letters.

On the 15th Brothers Pratt John Layton, Hawkins and the wives of the last two, as well as some of the native brethren, sailed in a whaleboat for Huaua, while we stopped at Hapape and took a nap, and at 2 o'clock a. m. started back, reaching our destination at daylight on the 16th. We rested on the 17th, and on the 18th, in council, Elders Thomas Whitaker, Julian Moses and two native brethren were appointed to labor as missionaries on Tahiti; Elders

John Hawkins, Alviras Hanks, Simeon A. Dunn and James S. Brown were appointed to labor among the inhabitants of the Tuamotu group of islands.

On May 19th, Brothers Pratt, Layton and Hawkins set out for Papeete, and at 3, p. m. Brothers T. Whitaker and Pohe, with their families, started for Pueu in a boat belonging to some of their relatives. On the 21st, the schooner—the new one built at Tubuoi, and commanded by Benjamin F. Grouard—called with the brethren who went down the day before on board. She was bound for Anaa, two hundred and ten miles east, or nearly so. When they got opposite Huaua, Captain Grouard came ashore and said they desired me to accompany them, as they intended to call by Tubuoi before returning to Tahiti.

In fifteen or twenty minutes I was ready, and we soon boarded the little vessel. She was thirty-five or forty tons burden, had poor accommodations on board, and was insufficiently supplied with provisions. We started, but the wind being contrary, we soon had to change our course, so that on the 24th we sighted Riroa, and on the 25th we touched at Uratua and got some cocoanuts. In consequence of the strong current there, we could not make much headway, but in trying to beat around it we sighted Anutua. On the next tack we came to Aunua, where we went ashore and found a small branch of the Church. The Saints were very kind to us, showing every favor they could, and pressing us to allow one of our number to remain with them. But it was not considered proper to grant the request, so we held two meetings and preached to them, giving them all the cheer and comfort that we could, and then left. They seemed to appreciate our visit and counsel as only Latter-day Saints can.

Again we sailed for Anaa, but the strong wind and waves prevailed against us, so that we were driven so far from our course that we sighted Faraua on May 31st, and on June 1st we encountered a very heavy storm, commencing at 5:30 and continuing till 11 p. m., when it seemed to abate a little. At 7 p. m. all sails had been taken in save the foresail, which was close-reefed, and as the vessel was beyond our control, our best seamen being willing to admit that they could do nothing for us, the helm was lashed down, and all hands went below. The hatch was securely fastened down, leaving only two of our best and bravest men lashed on deck with slack rope. Everyone seemed to realize our peril, and that we must rely alone on the Almighty to save us from destruction. There was land all around, and the wind and currents were so strong that it was impossible, with the means at our command, to direct the course of our little Fisher. I must leave the friendly reader to draw his own conclusions as to the condition we were in, for I have not the ability to describe it. Suffice it to say that through the mercies of the Lord we were spared to find ourselves perfectly landlocked by three islands, namely, Anutua, Apatai and Aunua. Again getting control of the vessel, we put into the harbor at Apatai, that being considered the safest place. There we found some Church members, and were treated very kindly. We remained there until the 6th, holding meetings and preaching to the people.

Apatai is one of the islands of poison fish, and we felt the effects of these slightly before we left. We had a fair wind for Anaa on the 6th, when we started, but it soon died away and we were left to drift with a very strong current. On the 7th we found ourselves drifted down by the side of Anutua. Having some natives of that island on board they were sent ashore. Jonathan Crosby went with them, and returned with the boat. From thence we had a pleasant voyage to Anutua. There we went ashore and preached to the people. Brothers Grouard's and Hawkins' wives also landed.

We left them on the 9th, and sailed for Tubuoi. Having a fair and strong wind, we were wafted to Matia, where we left some passengers belonging to that island. We also took in a small supply of provisions, as our store was very scanty. Then we continued towards Tubuoi, having a favorable wind till we got within eighty miles of our destination. Then a strong headwind forced us to change our course, so that we put into a small island called Loivivi. This was on the 17th. The island does not exceed four miles in length and two in width; there were three hundred and eighty-three people living on it. They had the wildest and fiercest look of any that we had met on our cruise, yet they behaved very well to us. On the 18th we sailed again for Tubuoi, and on the 20th we cast anchor at that island, which lies between the twenty-third and twenty-fourth parallels, south latitude. It is only twelve or fifteen miles in length, and from a distance resembles the tops of mountains in a plain. Its inhabitants numbered four hundred, all told.

It was on this island that the Gospel was first preached in this dispensation, in the islands of the Pacific Ocean. This preaching was by Elder Addison Pratt, July 12, 1844. He was accompanied by Elders Noah Rogers and B. F. Grouard, they having been sent by the Prophet Joseph Smith, from Nauvoo, Hancock County, Illinois, U. S. A., in the year 1843. Knowlton Hanks was one of the missionaries who left Nauvoo, but he died on the voyage from Boston to Tubuoi, after the vessel had rounded Cape Horn.

CHAPTER XXVI.

HEARTY WELCOME IN TUBUOI—START FOR TUAMOTU—REACH PAPEETE,
TAHITI—VISIT TO HUAUA—LEAVE TAHITI—WRITER GETS RELIEF
FROM SEASICKNESS—BROILED FISH AND COCOANUTS—IN A SCHOOL
OF WHALES—THROWN INTO A CORAL REEF—TOTAL WRECK IMMI-
NENT—THREE PERSONS GET ASHORE—BOAT GOES OUT TO SEA—
WRECK OF ELDER DUNN'S PARTY—THREE DAYS IN THE SEA,
CLINGING TO A CAPSIZED BOAT—CLOTHING TORN OFF BY SHARKS
—SKIN TAKEN OFF BY THE SEA AND SUN—REACH THE ISLAND OF
ANAA—RECOGNIZED BY A MAN WHO HAD SEEN ME IN A DREAM—
PREACHING AND BAPTIZING—MANY OF THE NATIVES CHURCH
MEMBERS—MAKE A RUDE MAP OF THE CALIFORNIA GOLD FIELDS
—TELL OF HAVING BEEN IN THE MORMON BATTALION—CATHOLIC
PRIESTS ELICIT THIS INFORMATION AS PART OF A SCHEME TO
HAVE ME EXPELLED FROM THE ISLAND.

WHEN we landed on Tubuoi on May 20th, we found the people feeling well. They were greatly pleased to see us, and we rejoice to meet with and preach to them. We traveled from village to village preaching, and visited the people from house to house, being received everywhere in the most friendly manner.

On July 1st and 2nd we attended to correspondence, and on the 3rd everything was in readiness and we sailed with a cargo of cattle for Tahiti. Elder A. Hanks and the writer were bound for the Tuamotu group of islands. On the 6th, after a pleasant voyage, with the exception of sea-sickness, we landed at Papeete, Tahiti, all well.

Our captain said that he would only remain in harbor a day or two, then would sail for Anaa. As I desired to visit the brethren at Huaua, fifteen miles up the coast, I started at 4 p. m., afoot and alone, and reached my destination the same evening. I was surprised when the whole family, men, women and children, leaped from their beds and embraced me, and wept for joy. Some refreshments were provided, and we then turned in for the remainder of the night.

I stayed there until the 8th, and met with Elders Julian Moses and T. Whitaker, who accompanied me to Papeete, where we arrived at 1 o'clock p. m., and found the vessel being prepared to sail. Brother Hanks was detained in getting his permit until it was too late to get out of the passage till the 9th, then the wind came straight into the passage, so that we had to drop anchor till late in the afternoon. We managed to get clear that night, but the wind being contrary we did not lose sight of land till the 10th; then we had a perfect calm for two days. Late in the evening of the 12th we got a light breeze. This day was the first time in my life that I could say that I was well at sea. Never before that evening had I gone below and enjoyed a meal of victuals; but from that time on I could take my rations with the rest except in a storm.

On July 13th we sighted and passed Metia, and sighted Tikahau; the 14th Matea was in view, and we passed along close to the weather end of Riroa; the 18th we were near Uratua. There two boats were let down, one to pull up through the lagoon of the island, twenty miles long, to where Brother Hawkins lived, and the other to fish. About 11 p. m. we neared the village when the natives came and conducted us to the place. They spread some broiled fish and cocoanuts before us; and of course we were thankful to get that, for there was no other food on the island. This was all that some of the inhabitants ever had to eat on their own island, save an occasional pig or a chicken. After the refreshments we turned in for the night.

Next morning we were feasted as best the people could do. We preached to them, then sailed away; for our schooner was waiting for us. We next headed for Riroa, as we could not get a wind for Anaa, which we had been trying to reach from the time we left Tahiti.   On the 21st we passed through a school of whales to the harbor. Again we encountered a strong current coming out of the passage, and a headwind.   Then, in trying to beat up into the harbor, our vessel failed to stay, and we were driven into the coral rock, which stood up in the water like tree-tops.   Crash we went, and the vessel began to quiver and jar.   All hands and the cook had an awful scare, and for a few moments it looked as though our vessel would be a total wreck, and we be all spilled into the raging billows, among crags and rocks.   But thanks to the Lord, this was averted.   Three of us succeeded in gaining the shore in safety, and the vessel put to sea for the night, coming in on the 22nd to anchor.

On shore we were feasted on broiled fish, cocoanuts and roast pig.   The people seemed overjoyed at our visit. We called a meeting and preached to them, encouraging them in their religious duties.

It was while we were on this island that we heard from Brothers Dunn and Crosby, who were well.   We also heard from Manahuni and party, who left Tahiti at the same time that we departed on our first cruise.   They sailed for Anaa, in a small, open boat called the *Anaura*, the same that Brother Grouard made many trips in from island to island, and in which he had many narrow escapes.   But Manahuni and his party of six brethren and sisters had a much severer experience than any former party.   Their boat capsized in a heavy storm, the same that we had been caught in on our former cruise.   They lost everything save their lives, and these were preserved only by clinging to the keel of the boat for three days and three nights.   Finally the boat righted itself, and they drifted to the island of Tikahau, but not till the last rag of clothing had been torn from their bodies by sharks, and much of the skin—all of the cuticle— had sloughed off through their being in the salt water and hot sun so long. But their lives were spared to them, and they were nourished by the kind people of Tikahau, until they were able to reach the island of their destination, Anaa.

A fair wind for Anaa came on July 26th, so we left for that place. At dawn on the 28th we sighted the island, and at 10 o'clock a. m. we landed at Tuuhora. As we neared the shore I was seated in the stern of the boat, when a man came bounding through the water and passed all our party till he came to me. Then he reached out his hand, which had in it five pearls wrapped in a little rag, and said, "Here! I have seen you before. You have come to be our president, for you have been shown to me in a dream. Welcome, welcome to our land!" Just then he turned his back for the writer to get on, and in this way took me to the shore, where the people soon prepared a feast of welcome, as is their custom when their friends come to see them. No feast, no welcome.

The feasting over, with Brothers Hanks and Hawkins I visited the branches, the three of us traveling together, preaching and baptizing the people, who came forward in large numbers to receive the ordinance. August 5, 1851, Brother Hanks left for Taroa, and Brother Hawkins for Arutua. I had been appointed to preside on Anaa, and commenced my labors in that duty. On the 6th I was instructed, by Elder B. F. Grouard, to travel and preach, to reorganize the branches wherever it was necessary, and to organize and teach schools as I might find it prudent; in fact, to do all things pertaining to my calling as a missionary. Thus I started out alone.

One of the first things I found after I began my labors was that there were four Catholic priests on the island, building four stone churches; that they had about thirty natives employed on them, and that no others would attend their religious services; it was claimed that there were about nine hundred persons belonging to the Mormon

Church, most of them being members in good standing. There were no natives there belonging to the Catholic church.

On one occasion soon after my arrival, I was being questioned, in a conversation, about California and the gold fields, and also about my birthplace and the city of my residence. I took a sheet of paper and sketched a rough outline of the gold fields. One of the natives who apparently had been greatly interested in the narrative, asked for the sketch. It being given to him, he went off and soon returned with a large sheet of drawing paper, on which he requested me to draw a map, on a larger scale, showing my birthplace, where Salt Lake City was from there, and the location of the gold fields. Then the question was asked, how I came to be in California at so early a date. I told them I went there in the Mormon Battalion, in the service of the United States, during the war with Mexico. Little did I think I was mapping out the outlines of a foundation for a wicked and false charge to be preferred against me by the Catholic priest. Neither did I have the remotest idea that my rude sketch would be used in crediting me with being a civil engineer of no mean ability, nor that my having been in the army of the United States would entitle me to the dignity of a highly educated military graduate from some United States army school; nor was I aware that my walk and carriage were that of an officer in the military establishment of my government. Yet the sequel will show that all this was the case.

CHAPTER XXVII.

ON August 7th I was solicited by the chief men of Putuhara to assist them in organizing a school. Indeed, the whole people were anxious to have me aid them in this, therefore I took hold as requested. They had no school at that time, and were looking for a white Elder to start one, as they themselves had but a vague idea of the proper order or rules to govern such an organization. The writer did not have the remotest idea that he would meet with the antagonism of the Catholic priests in this matter, as there was a unanimous desire for him among the people, who had rejected the offer of the priest stationed at that place. However, I soon heard that the priest was displeased because the people had rejected him and supported us by sending their children to our school, and by feasting me and showing me marked preference in many ways. Our house was crowded to its full capacity every evening, while the priest sat alone in his studio.

On August 12th we had thirty-six students; by the 14th the school had increased to sixty-five. The priest came to the door, looked in, then turned short on his heel, and went away without speaking, yet showing his displeasure in his manner. Soon he got a house to run opposition in school work, but he failed to get pupils. Then he became very cross and snarly at every one he came in contact with; at least, so said the people.

In company with some of my friends, I went to Otapipi on August 15th. We met a man with a letter from the head Catholic priest, for me. It was in the Tahitian language, and began as follows: "Iarran Iatobo, i te Atua" (James, how do you do in the Lord?) and continued, translated into English: "This is what I have to say to you: Do not trouble our schools, and we will not trouble yours. If you do so again, I will send for the governor's aide de camp, and we will have you tried before him. You must not trouble us any more." It closed with "Tidar Paran Iaraan ae, Tavara" (That is all the talk. Good bye to you.) As we had not knowingly interfered with their schools we did not make any reply, but continued our journey to Otapipi, and held a prayer meeting at that place at 3 o'clock p. m. While there I saw a priest and his two attendants coming across the lake. They landed, and came straight to the house where we had put up. The priest walked in without hesitation, and politely offered to shake hands. We met him as politely, and took his hand. Then he asked if we had received a letter from the priest below. We informed him that we had. "Well," said he, "we don't want you to interfere with our schools, and we will not with yours." At the same time he threatened me with the governor's authority, if we did not "walk straight." After some discourse, I asked him what kind of a God he worshiped. He said a spirit without body or parts; but he failed to find any Scripture to support his belief, and the people who had gathered around laughed at him, making him feel very much out of temper. On August 16th he called a few children together and spoke briefly to them in

Latin or some language that I did not understand. Then he departed for another village.

Soon after this, the people prepared a feast in honor of our visit. The food consisted of roasted fish and fowl. Many little presents were also brought, such as could be made from the fiber of the cocoanut husk, mats, shells, etc. When all was laid before us, the spokesman said, in substance, in the Tahitian language: "James, as a token of our great love and respect for you, the servant of God, we, the people of Otapipi, Anaa, have collected of all the varieties of food that our land affords, and a few articles of use. Here is a pig, there is a fish, and fowl, and here are cocoanuts. This is meat and drink for us, and all that is produced in our land. We wish you to accept it from all of us as your true friends, and we wish you to eat and be full. Be our president and teacher in the Gospel, and a teacher of our children; for we are glad to have you come to our land as a father and guide. Our hearts are full of gladness that God has sent you to our land, that we may be taught to love the true and living God, for we have always been in the dark, and did not know there was a true and living God to love and worship. Now we have no more to say. Amen."

The foregoing is a fair representation of the addresses made to us on occasions such as that was. That night the house could not hold all who came to search the Scriptures and sing sacred hymns. Three persons offered themselves for baptism, and were put off till Sunday, the 17th, when I preached on faith, repentance, and baptism for the remission of sins. At the afternoon services, I exhorted the people to be faithful, told them the conditions on which they could be admitted into the Church, and said that all who felt to accept those conditions might be accommodated that evening, as I had three candidates to wait on at the close of the services.

When the meeting was over, the whole congregation gathered down by the seaside. We sang a hymn and prayed, and I went down into the water and remained there until I had baptized thirty-five souls. When these were confirmed, the people remained together to a late hour before they would disperse. On August 18th, agreeable to the request of the people and with the approval of the rulers of the village, I opened a school, classified the students, and chose teachers for each class, then laid down rules to govern them. The feasting was continued from day to day to August 24th. On Sunday, the 25th, I preached from the second chapter of the Acts of the Apostles. At the close of the meeting three persons presented themselves for baptism, and we attended to the ordinance. One of those baptized was Mahia, who, forty years later, presided over the entire mission, being, at the latter time, totally blind. Besides the three mentioned, sixteen others were baptized, and all of them confirmed.

On the 26th, the school was continued in good order. That day the news came that the Catholic priest had taken charge of our meeting house at Temarari, although the house was built and owned by the Latter-day Saints. The priest claimed the right to control it in the interest of his church; and the Saints requested me to come and help them regain possession of the house. With two of the natives, I started on the 27th, quite a company, male and female, following us. When we arrived a feast was prepared; the people gave us a perfect ovation. We held meeting that evening, the 28th, and I preached from the twelfth chapter of Luke.

At the close of the meeting the bell was rung for school. In came the priest to take charge, but as he had no right to the hour, and the people did not want him to teach, but desired me to take charge, I told them that when they settled the dispute about the house, if it was desired by the whole people and their officers that I should proceed, I would do so. They arranged to settle the matter in a day or two.

On the 30th I received a letter from Elder T. W. Whitaker, of Tahiti, and I wrote to the white Elders. The same evening I had a call from two of the Catholic priests, whose names were Tavara and Harara. Evidently they were very much disturbed in their feelings, as the people were still feasting with and showing every respect possible to me, while they passed the priests by with a cold nod.

Sunday morning, August 31st, I preached on the attributes of God. At the close of our meeting the priests rang the bell and came marching in with their lamps and images, demanding possession of the house. We told them we had business matters to attend to, and were not ready to give up the place. Nevertheless, they piled their things on the table in front of me as I sat writing. They had as much as two or three men could carry. They crowded their things right into my way, so I asked what they meant by such conduct, and who had invited them there before we got through with our business. They replied that it was their time for meeting, and demanded the house, claiming it was a public building, and that they had a right to hold their meetings in it. I said that it had been built and was owned by the Mormon people, and that we did not propose to be disturbed by the intruders until we had finished our business. At that they flew into a rage and threatened us with the law, as they had done before, but finally they cooled down, carried their things out, and waited until we were through and had left. Then they held their services. I do not think they had over six persons in their congregation. They dispersed quietly, and at 10 o'clock a. m. we held meeting again. I preached on faith and baptism. One hundred and thirty people attended our meeting. In the evening I baptized and confirmed twenty-five persons.

On Monday, September 1st, I took up school by request of the people and their peace officers. On the 4th we had thirty students. On the 5th, two native Elders went with me to Tuuhora. We received a call from a priest; also held a prayer meeting, but few people attended it. On Sunday we held three meetings, administered the sacrament, baptized nineteen souls, and confirmed them. On Monday, the 8th, we organized a school with fifty students, and with the peace officers selected a teacher for each class. The Catholic priest called on me and forbade me changing his hours of school. As I had not attempted to interfere with him or his schools, I came to the conclusion that he was seeking an occasion against me under the law, as they had threatened me with before. I knew they were jealous, for where I stopped the people would throng around me and the priests were left alone.

When the older people had gone through some morning exercises that day, desiring on my part to prevent further trouble with the priest, I sent him word that as soon as we got through with the younger classes he could occupy the building, but not before, as he had threatened to do. Just as the messenger returned, the priest rang the bell most spitefully, and then came rushing into the school room, his eyes flashing angrily. Our school was greatly disturbed. I advanced, and asked him civilly if he wished to attend our school. He said yes, evidently misunderstanding me. I pointed him to a seat, saying we were much pleased to have our school increase, and would he please give me his name. I must confess that I felt a little mischievous, and to retaliate slightly for their constant meddling in our affairs. He saw the point, flew into a rage, and sent for the landholders of the place to have me put out of the house. The landholders came, and told him they did not wish to have me disturbed, as they had sent for me to come and take up a school; that the people preferred me to him; that he was the one who had made the disturbance, not me, and that he must give way and cease his interference.

Not satisfied with that decision, the priest sent for the governor and chief men of the town, who came, and with them a large crowd of citizens. When the governor had heard both sides, he confirmed the decision of the land-holders, and called for a vote of the people to say which of us should teach school. The vote was unanimous against the priest. Then the governor told him that as the people did not want him he must leave the house at once, and not disturb me or my school any more, for none of the people had any use for him, as he had witnessed; they had all voted against him, and all wanted Iatobo.

At this, the priest took up his books and slates, and after accusing me of everything that was mean and low, and calling the Mormon people the vilest names, he withdrew. Later, he wrote a letter to Governor Bonard, of Tahiti, and circulated it for signatures. We learned afterwards that he got thirty signers. I believe that eleven were French traders, and the other nineteen were natives whom the traders had in their employment. We also learned, at the cost of inquiry, that the priest's letter contained the charges upon which I was subsequently arrested. But at that time we continued our school in peace.

On September 12th I was feasted in royal style by non-members of the Church. They called on one of the native Elders to deliver the address, which he did in a most eloquent manner. I responded in the usual way, and accepted their kind offering. The cook disposed of the spread to the great satisfaction of the whole assembly, on such occasions all present being directly interested in the distribution of the eatables.

About this time the writer had a remarkable dream. He dreamed that God appeared, and told him to go to a field of his earthly father's, and replant where the birds and squirrels had destroyed the grain. Then his father appeared and showed him where to begin the labor. When he had been furnished with seed and a hoe, he went to work, and the replanting was soon done. Then he was shown a field of wheat that, in the spring of the year, was about eight inches high. The ground was quite wet, and the grain was growing nicely. While he was gazing on the bright prospects, a herd of cattle came in, breaking down the fence. They seemed to trample everything they came to. Then he heard a voice say, "Drive them out;" and as he attempted to do so, a fiery red bull made a charge toward him so that it seemed impossible for him to escape being gored to death; but as the animal lowered its head to make the deadly thrust, the writer seized it by both horns and bore its head to the earth. The animal was coming with such force that it turned a somersault, both horns being sunk to the head in the earth, and the bull's neck being broken. Then a black and white bull, very peculiarly marked, came up in the same fierce manner, only to meet with a similar fate. At that the herd cleared the field, but not until much damage had been done.

When he awoke, the writer felt that there was more trouble ahead for him, but he did not know from what source it would come. Of the priests who had given so much annoyance, one had fiery red hair, and another was white and dark spotted, or freckle-faced.

CHAPTER XXVIII.

ON September 19th, Nihiru, a native brother, came with his canoe and gave the writer a free passage to a village on the east end of the island, called Tematahoa. We arrived in the evening and found a great deal of sickness among the people. Just at dark on the 20th, a brother named Pasai came from Temaraia with a sick man to have him anointed and administered to. I attended to that and he was healed.

On the 21st, Sunday, I preached on the signs, gifts of healing, etc. There were about two hundred and fifty persons in the congregation. In the evening I baptized and confirmed eighteen persons. Monday morning I opened school with twenty-eight pupils; next day there were forty-one.

On the following day, September 24th, a man and his wife came to me with a child three and a half months old. They said that a short time before their child had been taken sick in the night, and they had talked to each other of having it anointed. At this, the child spoke, and stated in plain words, like an adult, that it would not be anointed. It said many words as plainly as any person could do. From that time it grew worse to the day it was brought to me to be administered to. The parents said they did not belong to the Church, but desired to be baptized, for they believed the Gospel as the Mormon Elders taught it. Their names were Tauahi and Taui. We baptized them and one other person, then administered to the child, which lay limp as if dead. We could not tell whether it was dead or alive. However, when we took our hands off its head, it opened its eyes and looked as if nothing was the matter. Then it nursed as any healthy child might. There were many people gathered there, and all were astonished at what had taken place. Finally the babe went to sleep as if nothing had been wrong with it, and the whole company rejoiced at the great change that had come. They said that truly it was the Almighty who had healed the child through His servant.

I turned and gave my attention to some writing that was necessary, and the crowd became unusually quiet. In a few minutes a strong rushing or movement among the people attracted my attention, and as I turned to face the people there appeared to be an ashy paleness over the faces of the whole assembly. All seemed terrified and speechless. At that moment an aged couple, a man and his wife, entered the door and went straightway to where the sleeping infant lay. They bowed down over it and kissed it, and then went through some ancient heathen ceremony that I could not understand. Then they walked direct to their canoes and sailed across the lake to where they had come from. From that moment the relatives of the child began to mourn and say that it would die; and sure enough, inside of an hour it was a corpse. The parents were asked why they had lost faith and given up the child. They said the old people who had kissed the babe had power with evil spirits, and had afflicted it in the first place; that their power had been broken by the Priesthood, and they could not reunite it with the babe until they could come and touch it; and when they had done that, the parents and all concerned lost faith, and could not resist the influence that came with the old pair of witches, as we think they would be called by some civilized people. I must confess it was a strange thing to me. I had never before witnessed anything so strange.

It was on the 27th of September that the child died. On the same day a Scotchman came and brought me a few sea biscuits. I was very thankful to him for the favor, for bread was such a rarity in that part of the country as to give a man some satisfaction in seeing it, even though he might not have the pleasure of eating it. Thanks to the benevolent Scotchman. I regret that I have forgotten his name. The next day I preached on the resurrection of the dead, and baptized and confirmed eighteen persons into the Church.

Before leaving my reminiscences of this place, I will narrate two incidents of some note to me. In one, we were called to see a man who had been confined to his room the greater part of a year with a swelling in his hip and thigh. On examination it was found that his whole hip and thigh were filled with a thick and very noxious pus. No one in the village dared to lance it, but when I told him his condition he insisted that I should cut it whether it killed or cured. I hesitated to comply with his wish until all his immediate relatives had been consulted, and had given their assent. Otherwise, the superstition of the people was so great that if in the operation the patient succumbed the operator would have the gravest responsibility to meet. But when all concerned had given sanction, and each had assumed his or her responsibility, I performed the operation most successfully, the wound discharging at least six pints of the most offensive matter, and the patient being greatly relieved from his terrible suffering. The operation was performed with a penknife, for in that country at that time the only surgical instrument ever used for cutting was a shark's tooth or a scale from a broken bottle.

In this case the operation seemed to the people very little less than a miracle. The news thereof spread all over the island, insomuch that the operator acquired much practice in similar cases, such as swollen jaws, boils, carbuncles, etc., and though he performed many operations, he never received one cent as pay. If the people had toothache, he was called on and performed the operation of extraction, in some instances using a rusty nail, or any kind of an old iron, in place of a hammer or mallet, to punch the tooth out. His best dentist tool was his rifle bullet mold, using both ends for forceps. He never failed to give satisfaction, for there were neither dentists nor surgeons in that part of the world.

The other incident, and a very singular one, which occurred at that place was this: On one occasion seven very rough characters came into our sacrament meeting. Some of them were said to be from an adjacent island. They came, took seats at the back of the hall, and behaved very rudely, making loud remarks and threats about the young ladies of the choir. When they partook of the sacrament they said that when the meeting was out they would administer the sacrament in a very different manner to that in which the Mormons did it. Sure enough, at the close of the meeting they pushed along through the congregation till they came to the young ladies, and made wicked propositions to them, which were very quickly spurned. Then they passed on, still making their boasts of what they would do at nightfall. But they failed in carrying out their threats, for in a very short time three of them were stricken

14

down with violent cramps, so terrible that all three were corpses before the next morning. The other four had strong symptoms of the same complaint, and inside of a week they were dead also. The people said it was the power of evil spirits that had been sent to destroy them, that they might not be permitted to carry out their wicked purposes. The whole people were so excited that they shot off guns, blew horns, built large fires, prayed and shouted in wild confusion, to drive away the evil spirits; and many people were smitten with sickness and some died.

On the 29th of September we sailed for Putuhara. The wind blew a gale, and we had a fearful passage, but succeeded in reaching our destination in safety, and in time for evening meeting, when we preached to a large congregation. October 1st, I baptized and confirmed three persons. On the same day the roughest people of the island assembled to feast and dance. It seemed that to quarrel and fight was the principal number on their program, and they appeared to indulge in everything that was wicked. They killed pigs, chickens and dogs, roasted all alike, and ate them with great relish. They also ran through the streets with torchlights and firebrands, and the confusion was so great and turbulent that it looked more like an actual battle of savages than a dance. All ages participated, from the child of tender years up to the old grayheaded man and woman, all of them two-thirds naked, and some of the children entirely nude.

I had seen Indians in their warpaint and dances, but this excelled in confused savage deeds anything I ever beheld before. It seemed that they never knew what order meant. Yet, strange to say, at the first tap of the church bell they reminded me of a turkey gobbler which, when in full strut, seeing a dog run at him, drops his feathers so suddenly that he does not look like the same bird. So it was

with that savage-looking lot. At the first tap of the bell
they became as silent as if dead, then retreated to their
hiding places, and not another yell was heard from any of
them, so great was their reverence for religious services.
At one time, though, it did seem that they could not be
silenced short of bloodshed, for there were two opposing
parties mixed up together.

When the confusion was straightened out and peace
apparently restored, the parties separated, only to come
together again later, with more roast pigs, chickens and
dogs.   Then they ate of their feast until full, when some
unwise person of one party made an insulting remark about
the other party.   Quickly the participants in the feast
formed for battle, armed with clubs and stones.   At that
moment one man from each party ran for the ormatua
(missionary).   I went out and stepped up on to a large
chest, at the same time calling aloud for peace.   Strange as
it may seem, although their clubs and stones were raised to
strike fatal blows, and the women and children were shrieking and crying, the moment the natives recognized me
among them they dropped their ugly weapons and listened,
and the spokesman of each party came forward to plead
his particular case.   I caught the spirit of the situation and
addressed them briefly on the subject of peace, order and
good will to all, and exhorted them to leave their grievances to two or more of their cooler and wiser men to settle.   This they agreed to do; then they joined forces and
made an attack on the writer, not for blood, but of love and
respect.   Men and women seized on to him, embracing him
and shaking his hands until he was nearly smothered and
almost borne to the ground.

I would not have it understood that this great reverence and respect was shown to me for any superiority that
I would claim; but it was a man's calling as a minister of
the Gospel which they held sacred before the Lord.   So

long as he did not betray their confidence, the minister's influence was almost unbounded, and with all their faults the natives had many most estimable qualities.

From this great excitement, and the accounts that he had heard from time to time, the writer was led to inquire into the manner of warfare, the traditions and the superstitions, as also into the causes for and cannibalism of the islanders. Their wars usually had an origin in very trivial causes, such as family quarrels, thefts, politics and disputes over land or over fishing waters. At one time the islands had a dense population, and the strong would go on the warpath for conquest, one village or island being pitted against another. Their ariis (kings), as they call them—I think it would be more proper to designate them as chiefs, as the Indians do —attain power through brave and heroic acts, and the great havoc they make among their adversaries. Their weapons consisted chiefly of spears made from fish bone and hard wood, stones and slings, clubs, and a rudely fashioned glove made by winding bark and shark's teeth together in such a way as to have the teeth stand out thickly on the inside of the hand. With this latter weapon they would grapple with and tear out each other's entrails. They had rude drums and some kind of whistles for musical instruments.

In war, the two parties approach each other, dancing, boasting and threatening, until within a few feet of each other, when they leap at and onto one another in a hand-to-hand conflict, fighting as wild beasts, to a finish. Their mothers, sisters, daughters and aunts prepare themselves with strong baskets made from the cocoanut leaf, and swing these on their backs; then (each with a sharp rock or a seashell in her hand) they enter the battlefield in rear of their nearest male relative. When the latter has dispatched his man or disabled him so that the women can finish him, he engages another adversary, while the woman beheads his victim, puts the head into her basket, swings it on her back, and continues to follow her male relative to victory or death.

When a war is over, and the victorious party returns home, each family has a place for the captured heads, where they are put in rows, being set some six or eight inches below the surface of the ground, and easy of access. This was done so that when any question arose as to the bravest family, or the member of a family to take the first place as dictator or chief, the mori, or place of skulls may be visited and a tally made, when the one with the highest number of skulls or heads is given the coveted position. In these contests they also count the heads taken by their ancestors, as far back as they can find them, no matter how many generations they cover. Thus the family with the most skulls gets the place sought, which is generally that of chief or king.

When a battle is ended, the victors pass over the ground, often bleeding from their wounds, and starved and well nigh exhausted from being without food. The islanders have a tradition that whatever gives them pain they should eat. So if they are wounded by a sharp stone which by any means has fastened itself into a man's flesh, or by a sliver, they extract and eat it, saying, "You are my enemy, you never shall hurt me more." Thus they seem to satisfy the vicious spirit of revenge. This strange proceeding may have had something to do with the origin of cannibalism. Still, I am rather inclined to think it had its beginning in starvation, and to that was added the spirit of revenge. Thus the appetite was cultivated until, with very slight pretext, human life became sacrificed to a depraved and vicious appetite. These practices and others seemed to be justified in their savage minds, insomuch that they did not scruple in gathering up the slain and feeding upon them.

His curiosity having been awakened in searching into heathen life, the writer made inquiries at the most authentic sources of information for further light on this custom.   In one case he found an old lady who was the last of the fifth generation back.   Her intellect seemed bright, although she could not open her eyes except with her fingers. When questioned in regard to cannibalism, she lifted her eyelids and said, "I have followed my fathers, brothers, husband and sons in battle, and we ate our victims as we would eat pork or fish."   When asked if she had eaten white man's flesh, she replied, "Yes; we captured some white men on a small schooner and ate them."   The next inquiry was whether there was any difference in the taste of the white man's and of the native's flesh.   "Yes," said she; "the white man's flesh is hard, tough and salty, while the flesh of the native is sweet and tender."   Then came the question as to what part of the human body was preferable to eat.   She said the heel and the hand of a fourteen year-old girl were the sweetest morsels of flesh she ever ate. Being asked if she did not have feelings of remorse when they had committed actions like these, her answer was: "Not a bit, it was in our days of heathendom; but now, since the Gospel has come to us, we have no desire for anything of that kind, though formerly we took pleasure in our practices, for our minds were very dark."

CHAPTER XXIX.

HOLD CONFERENCE IN PUTUHARA—INSTRUCTIONS TO THE SAINTS— GO TO OTAPIPI—OPPOSITION AT TEMARAIA—OFFICIALS BRIBED BY CATHOLIC PRIESTS — ARRIVAL OF A FRENCH WARSHIP— THE WRITER IS ARRESTED WHILE EXPOUNDING THE SCRIP- TURES TO THE NATIVES — CAUSE OF ARREST IS FALSE AC- CUSATION BY CATHOLIC PRIESTS — I PLEAD NOT GUILTY — ORDERED TAKEN TO TAHITI — PAINFUL PRISON EXPERIENCE —CANNIBALS IN CUSTODY — START FOR THE SHIP—SYMPATHY OF THE NATIVES — HURRIED INTO THE SHIP'S BOAT — IN A SCHOOL OF WHALES—A FRIGHTENED BOAT LOAD—ON BOARD THE WARSHIP — UNCOMFORTABLE QUARTERS — QUESTIONABLE FRENCH COURTESY—AMONG COCKROACHES, FILTH, AND INCON- VENIENCES—SOFT SIDE OF A PLANK FOR A BED.

LEAVING the revolting subject of cannibalism, I will return to our missionary labors.   Peace and quiet hav- ing been restored, the people assembled in Putuhara on October 5th for conference, Elder James S. Brown presid- ing.   After reports of the various branches had been made, as presiding Elder I reported the condition of the Church generally on the island, made a few opening remarks, and called on the different Elders to speak.   One after another these referred to themselves and the people generally hav- ing a desire for me to write home to the Church authorities, to get a missionary to each village.   All spoke of their love for the Gospel, and their wish to have it preached on all the adjacent islands.   There was such enthusiasm among the people that it seemed unwise to hold a lengthy conference. The zeal of the people there was such that it well nigh drove them into a frenzy; so after the business of the con- ference had been done, I addressed them on the object of a house of worship, that it was a place in which to worship the true and living God, and not a dancehouse or a place to have lawsuits, quarreling, fighting, and worshiping of idols in, as they had been doing. A motion was made and carried that our building be kept exclusively for a house of worship. Thus everything else was forbidden by the landholders. At the close of the conference eight persons were baptized and confirmed.

The schools of the different villages met on October 6th, to read and spell in friendly contest. October 7th, the school in Putuhara had increased to one hundred pupils. That day the rougher element of the place assembled again in their wild dancing; they sold their jewelry for fat dogs and pigs. On the 11th, the non-Mormon women of the place prepared a great feast for us, and turned it over with pride, saying, "Here is a token of our love for you, and we desire you to accept it and remain in our town and teach us of the Lord."

We preached on Sunday, the 12th, and on that day also baptized and confirmed five persons. Next day, school was opened with one hundred pupils. A great deal of sickness was reported in the town. On the 14th, school was continued in good order, and we departed in a small canoe for Otapipi, where we found the people pleased to see us. The school there was intact. Next day I wrote to Elder Alviras Hanks that I had heard of his having been cast away on another island.

Sunday, October 19th, I preached, and baptized two persons. On the 24th I went to Temaraia, where I met with more opposition from the Catholic priest, with regard to school matters, and learned that he had bribed Governor Telidha, also Parai, the mouthpiece of the town, as he was called. Having them for his backing, the priest was very bold and defiant, and no doubt thought that by keeping up an excitement the Catholics would gain some support for the foul and false charges which he had made against me. By the means I have named, the priest got a decision against us, and for the first time we were compelled to yield, but much against the people's desires. Still, all settled down from high excitement to peace and quiet, till October 28th, when the French frigate *Durance* made its appearance northwest of the island.

The warship had on board the governor's aide de camp, who landed at Tuuhora with his guards. On the 29th he crossed the lagoon to Temaraia, where we were. At 8 p. m., while I was engaged in expounding the scriptures to a few of the natives, in came a French gen d' arme and a native officer. They presented me with a warrant, which, being in the French language, I could not read. The officers stood for a minute or so, when I gave them to understand that I was unable to decipher the document. Thereupon the native officer said that it meant that I was to appear before the governor's aide de camp, down at the stockade, at 9 o'clock, and if I did not come willingly, they had orders to drag me there like a dog. They being armed with swords and pistols, I thought it wisest to go willingly, especially as there was no chance to do otherwise. The officers were quite haughty, yet somewhat nervous, for they had been told that I was prepared to make a strong resistance. Of course, I accompanied them readily and without a word, and was soon ushered into the august presence of the governor's aide. I found him seated in a small room, in which were four or five other officers and a few soldiers armed with muskets and cutlasses. When I entered, the interpreter arose, read a long list of charges, and asked for my plea. I answered not guilty to each accusation.

It will be remembered by the reader that when I first landed on the island I sketched, at the request of some of the natives, a rough outline of the United States, pointing out my birthplace, also Salt Lake City, and where gold had been discovered in California. From that time the

Catholic priests had conspired to entrap me, to break my influence, and to close my schools.

The charges against me began, as near as I now remember them, and with memory refreshed from brief notes taken at the time, by an assertion that I had subverted the laws of the French protectorate; had interfered with government schools; had hoisted the American flag; had enrolled some three thousand men for the American government, to be controlled by the Mormon Church; had armed the men; was a civil engineer of no mean ability; had ordered the people to demolish some of the towns, and rebuild with better fortifications; that my walk and general movements indicated military ability, and undoubtedly I had been brought up at a military school in the United States; that I had mapped out plans of defense; had great power with the native people, and was capable of doing much mischief in the country. These, and many other charges of a frivolous nature, were in the list, all of them without the slightest foundation in fact, except that I had much influence with the people.

I stated that I proposed to prove myself innocent of every one of the accusations made. To this the officer made answer that they had the most positive proof to establish the charges, which were very serious. He gave me two hours to settle my business, and see friends, when I would have to return to the stockade and stay where the governor's aide thought proper. The next day I was to be taken on board the man-of-war, and go as a prisoner to Tahiti, for trial.

Upon receiving this information, I claimed the right to be tried where I was accused of having committed the offense, and where I had the witnesses in my behalf. "No;" said the officer, "your crime is too great to be tried before any less authority than the governor." I asked to have witnesses summoned, and the officer inquired if I had any way of taking them to Tahiti. He knew, of course, that I was helpless in that regard, and being so answered, told his men to take me in charge. Accordingly, they marched me to where the arrest had been made.

I gathered up some of my effects, bade goodbye to my friends, and returned to the stockade. There I was ordered to a seat under an open shed till daylight, being guarded by two lustful police, who took unwarranted liberty with some lewd females, behaving most shamefully in the prisoner's presence. My friends brought bedding for me and attempted to spread it, but were rudely driven away by the guards, who took turns at pacing in front of me, while the other interested himself with the females spoken of, who were void of shame.

That night I was mortified and disgusted as I never had been before with peace officers. At last the long night wore past, and dawn appeared. Then close to my right, in a stockade, I saw about fifteen native cannibals, who could barely hide their nakedness. They had been captured by French soldiers on some island in the north, and were accused of killing, upon different occasions, the white crews of three small schooners. They were also charged with eating their victims, as well as robbing and scuttling the schooners.

I took my last glance at those fierce-looking monsters just at sunrise on October 30th, when I was called before the aide de camp to sign my name four times in English, and four times in the Tahitian language. Then I was ordered into a filthy old boat that was used to collect oil. The boat's crew were rough and dirty, and scoffed and jeered at me and otherwise made the sail across the lagoon to Tuuhora as disagreeable as they could.

When we landed at Tuuhora it was among about one hundred and fifty French marines. They, too, must jeer, and satisfy their curiosity by gathering around and imperti-

nently staring me in the face, jabbering together and laughing, while the natives met me with sympathy expressed in
their countenances.   Two soldiers kept close to me, however, and did not allow much opportunity for conversation
with anyone. I was served with a bowl of fish broth and
a small piece of bread, and when this was eaten I was
ordered to the landing, to one of the boats from the warship.   By this time there were probably five hundred native
people gathered.   These followed to the boat, declaring
that where their missionary went they would go, too, and
saying, "It is the Catholic priests who have done this, with
their lies."

The news of the arrest had been heralded during the
night to every village, and boats and canoes were coming
in, laden with sympathizing friends, not only Church members, but full as many that did not belong to the Church.
They said, "E mea hama teie" (a shameful thing, this).
The excitement became so general that the guard was increased to about twenty armed men, and the prisoner was
urged to hurry into the boat. As the water was from shoetop to knee-deep between the shore and the boat, I attempted to take off my shoes and turn my pants up, but I
was forbidden to stop, and was crowded into the vessel.
When I reached it, it was full of sympathizing men, women
and children, weeping and accusing the Catholic priests.
Fully five hundred people lined the shore, some with rolls
of bedding, while others were laden down with baskets of
cocoanuts.

When the guards arrived with their prisoner, the boat
was ordered cleared, and as the native people were rather
slow to obey the command, the soldiers pricked them with
their cutlasses and bayonets. I was urged into the boat,
which was soon manned, and the boatmen soon pulled from
the shore, while many scores of people wept aloud, shrieking out my native name, "Iatobo, Iatobo; no te Catholic

te i a ne peapea" (James, James, of the Catholics this trouble). They waved handkerchiefs as long as we could see them.

As the boat was going out to the ship, it ran into what seemed to us to be hundreds or even thousands of whales. For a while the sea seemed to be black with them. At the same time the boatmen took in their oars and became pale and still as death, lest the monsters should take fright and knock us into eternity and the boat into splinters. The oarsmen were better aware of the danger than I was, and were ashy pale. Indeed, it may have been the same with me for aught I know, for I did not see my own face as I saw theirs. But I had been where cattle stampeded, where the wild buffalo was rampant, or wild mustangs were charging by thousands on the plains by night and by day; had been surrounded by packs of fierce and hungry wolves; had been in the brush when grizzly bear were thick around, or when rattlesnake and deadly viper hissed in my ears; and I had been chased by savage Indians; still I do not remember a time when I felt that every hair on my head was trying to get on end more than I did for a few moments as these great sea monsters glided past so near that we could almost put our hands on their long, black backs, while they shot by swiftly, spouting the briny spray almost in our faces. The thought of the loss of the boat did not concern me so much as it did to think how easy it was for a whale, at one stroke of its monster tail, to make of us convenient shark's food. While in this truly great peril, minutes seemed hours to us, and when it passed we breathed freely again, and soon gained the great warship that was lying off shore, for there was no harbor or anchorage at that island.

I was next required to try a new experiment, to me, that of climbing a rope ladder up the side of a ship as the latter rolled and pitched in the waves. After a struggle I succeeded in reaching the deck in safety, there to be sur-

rounded by the marines as though I had been a wild beast.
When their curiosity had been satisfied, I was ordered
down on to what was called Swaltses' battery, the gun
deck.   There I found that as I walked my head came in
uncomfortable contact with the beams of the upper deck,
and at each one I had to duck my head. This greatly
amused the marines, and they got a mopstick, a broomstick,
or any kind of a stick.   Some would press the sticks on
the sides of their noses, while others held theirs back
of them, poking their sticks up so as to hit the beams
above.   Then they would form into a squad and
march by and duck heads with me, while some were
giving commands which I supposed meant, "Left, duck,
left duck"—at any rate, that was the action.   Then they
would shout and laugh.

Soon meal time came, and I was conducted into the
hold of the ship, and there assigned to a small, filthy room.
There was an old chair in it, and a bunk without bedding.
The room swarmed with cockroaches, which seemed to be
thicker than flies.   I was served with a bowl of fish broth,
and one small loaf of bread and a bottle of wine, for the day's
rations.   Then an officer called me to follow him to the
upper deck and to the bow of the ship, where he made me
understand, by unmistakable motions, that I was to use the
chains for a water closet.   In disgust I remembered that I
was among Frenchmen, the most stylish, the proudest, and
the most fashionable people in the world.   I was an American, "honored" with two uniformed and armed French attendants, who never left me alone only when I was in my
room, following me everywhere, allowing none to obstruct
my path, and even being careful to keep me from falling out
through the portholes, as, when I leaned over a big gun to
look out upon the deep, they would take me by the arm,
lead me away, and show me the big hole in the deck, and
my room.

By this time the writer began to understand French courtesy, under some conditions, and to realize his own situation. He asked himself what the outcome would be, he reviewed every action performed on the island of Anaa, and could not see wherein he had trenched upon anybody's rights or done anything against the law. He failed to discover one intentional or other wrong; so he felt to trust in the Lord, and made himself as contented as possible, though he found the boards in the berth as hard as American boards, notwithstanding that they were French lumber.

CHAPTER XXX.

VOYAGE TO PAPEETE—IN A TAHITIAN DUNGEON—CRUEL TREATMENT—WRITE TO FRIENDS—KINDNESS OF THE AMERICAN HOTEL KEEPER—BROUGHT BEFORE THE GOVERNOR—FALSE CHARGES READ, AND PLEA OF NOT GUILTY ENTERED—PERJURED TESTIMONY AGAINST ME—FORBIDDEN TO LOOK AT, OR EVEN CROSS-EXAMINE WITNESSES—SECRECY OF THE ALLEGED TRIAL—DEMAND MY RIGHTS AS AN AMERICAN CITIZEN—CONFUSION OF THE GOVERNOR—RETURNED TO MY CELL—AMERICAN CONSUL TAKES UP MY CASE—GIVES BONDS THAT I WILL LEAVE THE PROTECTORATE—ELDERS AND FRIENDS CALL ON ME—MY VISITORS ALLOWED TO SAY BUT LITTLE, AND SOMETIMES EXCLUDED—DECISION OF THE GOVERNOR THAT I MUST LEAVE THE SOCIETY ISLANDS—FAIR TRIAL REFUSED ME—LETTER FROM THE AMERICAN CONSUL—TAKEN TO THE CONSUL'S OFFICE—ADVISED TO LEAVE—ELDERS DECIDE THAT I SHOULD GO OUTSIDE OF THE FRENCH PROTECTORATE—SET SAIL FROM PAPEETE.

ON November 3rd, 1851, we set sail for Tahiti, and on the 6th made the port of Papeete, having had a rough voyage. When the ship anchored, a police boat came alongside, and the prisoner was ordered to try his skill at climbing down the rope ladder. He promptly obeyed orders, and soon found himself locked up in a cobblestone dungeon, six by eight feet, quite damp, and so dark that not a ray of light penetrated it anywhere. For his bed he had a board dressed out like a washboard. He had a good mattress and pillows and blankets of his own, but they were locked up in an adjoining room and he was denied the use of them. What the object was he never learned, unless it was done to punish him. He remained in that condition fourteen hours out of the twenty-four, and was fed on bread and water that was very filthy. The water was kept in a small keg in a corner of his cell, and was thick with a green, moss-like substance. In an opposite corner was a different kind of French water closet to that he had on shipboard—a keg which was never emptied during the prisoner's stay there. Unlike the water keg, it was replenished often. As to the result of such conditions in that hot climate, I leave it to the reader to conjecture; for I had enough of it without dwelling further on the subject.

On November 7th I wrote letters to Elders Thomas Whitaker and Julian Moses, the brethren who had been assigned to labor on Tahiti. On the 8th, one Mr. Lampher, proprietor of the American hotel in Papeete, sent me a prime dinner. It was received with thanks, and was duly appreciated.

On the 10th I was called out by the turnkey; immediately an armed soldier took position on either side of me, while a sergeant stepped directly in front, then moved three steps in advance, and gave the command to forward march. In this order we passed two lines of sentinels and went to the governor's mansion, where we met another officer, who commanded a halt, and I was directed to be seated for thirty minutes. Then I was called into the governor's office, where I was confronted by his excellency and seven officers. They were in full uniform and had sidearms.

Each had in his hands what appeared to be notes. I was at once ordered to be seated, and the very profligate son of a Protestant professor acted as interpreter, read the long list of charges spoken of, and asked for my plea thereto. I answered not guilty.

Then the trial began. They placed on the witness stand a native named Tania, who had been admitted recently to the Catholic church. He had been posted in what he should say, but seemingly had some pangs of conscience, for when he stood up he turned his eyes toward me, then to the court, and back to me, and answered the questions in a hesitating way, his confusion being so great that the governer, through the interpreter, ordered me not to look at the witness, as he said my countenance was so fierce and vivid as to baffle the most substantial witness. I was not permitted to ask a question, not even to cross-examine the witness.

The next testimony came from a man who had been brought to Papeete a prisoner, but who had been discharged without the formality of a hearing, evidently that they might have him for a witness against me. Both he and the preceding witness were put on the stand without being sworn. Not a single spectator was permitted to be present, so I concluded that if it was a court at all that was trying me it was a military court martial.

When I saw how onesidedly things were going, I arose and asked the court what right it had to try me with closed doors, not even allowing me the opportunity to defend myself. I told them I was an American citizen, and claimed my rights as such under existing treaties and international laws. I quoted law that I had never read or heard mentioned, for it was given to me of the Lord in the hour that I had need. I can never forget the expression on the faces of those officers. Not one of them would look me in the eye. As I spoke, every face was turned downward. At the conclusion of my remarks I was marched back to the filthy cell, without another word being said.

About this time Mr. W. H. Kelly, the American consul, called on the governor, and on making inquiries about me and my alleged crime and arrest, was told that I was a very dangerous man, a man learned in treaties and international laws. "Why," said the governor to Mr. Kelly, "he can quote more of them than my officers, and he has great power and influence with the native people. He is undoubtedly a military man of no mean ability. For these reasons he cannot be permitted to take up his residence as a minister under the French protectorate." I learned the foregoing from Mr. W. H. Kelly, who told me that he had to sign bonds to the amount of fifty thousand francs, and that sum would be forfeited if I did not leave the protectorate by the first vessel sailing from port, or if I was known to preach another discourse under the French government.

That evening Elder T. Whitaker called at my cell with two pies for me. We were allowed to speak but few words to each other. When the prison door had been locked again, I wrote to Elder B. F. Grouard, who, as I learned from Brother Whitaker, had arrived in port. November 11th, my old friend Pahe called with a basket of fruit, which was admitted, but the giver was permitted to say scarcely a word.

I had a call on the 12th from Elders S. A. Dunn and Julian Moses. Their short visit gave me much satisfaction, as they brought news from home. On the 13th Elder Grouard and some other friends called with some food, but they were not admitted, the food being passed in to me by a murderer.

On November 14th I was called before the governor's aide de camp, who said, "I suppose you have heard the decision of the governor and his council?" I told him no. He then said, "They have decided that you must leave the protectorate by the first vessel sailing from port, or you will be detained until you are willing to comply with that decision." I asked if they intended to send me away without a fair trial. He said yes; that the governor had it in his power to send out anyone that raised a disturbance in the country. I asked him to show that I had raised a disturbance. He said, "It does not need proof, for the Mormon missionaries have caused the government a great deal of trouble, and the decision is that you must go by the first vessel leaving port, or remain in prison till you agree to do so." With this, I was satisfied that there was no redress for the wrong that was being done me.

I was then marched back to the cell, where I received a letter from W. H. Kelly, the American consul. It read as follows:

"CONSULATE OF THE UNITED STATES, TAHITI,
November 14, 1851.

"*Mr. James Brown:*

"DEAR SIR:—Having been informed, through the governor of the protectorate, that you are a state prisoner in Papeete, charged with the crime of rebellion and attempting to subvert the laws of the protectorate established on the island of Anaa, I am bound to furnish the honorable secretary of state of the United States with all charges and punishments to which the citizens of the United States may render themselves amenable, under the laws of the countries in which they may reside.

"You will therefore oblige me by furnishing me with an unbiased and clear statement of the facts connected with your arrest and imprisonment. I do not wish to know what has been told to you, or of what you have heard from others, but simply the truth of the whole transaction.

"This letter will be forwarded to his excellency, Governor Bonard, who will, through the proper channel, have it forwarded to you.

"I remain, sir, your obedient servant,

"W. H. KELLY,

"United States Consul."

Elder B. F. Grouard kindly came down and wrote my reply to Mr. Kelly. This was on November 15th. The same day I was called out into the yard, when a sergeant and two soldiers took me in charge and marched me along a back alley to the rear of the consul's office. Then the sergeant stepped forward and notified Mr. Kelly that they had brought their prisoner to him, and without further ceremony the officers disappeared by the same alley by which they came.

Mr. Kelly welcomed me to his office, and congratulated me on regaining my liberty. Then he told me of his visit to Governor Bonard, the conversation they had had, and about his signing the bonds for my release. He said, "Mr. Brown, the French authorities are afraid of you. They say that you are a highly educated man, and that you are capable of doing much mischief in the country. Now you have your liberty in and about my office, but you must not go off alone in any by-place, for the French are a very excitable people, and they will watch every move that you make, and would shoot you if they could find you alone in the brush or where they could do it without being detected. Now, I have got horses, and will accompany you to any place you may wish to go, to visit your friends or to settle up what business you may have to do. But you must not be caught alone, for the French fear that you could raise an army and cause much trouble. As your friends are in town, you and they had better have a consultation here in my office, and see what you can do."

Accordingly, the Elders came into the consul's office,

and together with him said the best thing they thought could be done was that I should go on board the little schooner *Ravai*, and that they get it ready for sea as quickly as possible, so as to leave port before any other vessel did, for if I did not go the fifty thousand francs would be forfeited.   The schooner was the vessel owned by the Saints of Tubuoi, and commanded by Captain B. F. Grouard; it was bound for a cruise among the Tuamotu group of islands before going to the island of Raivavai, four hundred miles southeast of Tahiti, and outside of the protectorate.   It was thought that we could make the cruise intended, and then go on to Raivavai without any danger of forfeiting the pledge.   Conformably with this conclusion, the vessel was got ready, and on the 17th we sailed from Papeete.

CHAPTER XXXI.

LEAVING TAHITI UNDER THE ORDER OF BANISHMENT—SUPPLY OF PRO-
VISIONS EXHAUSTED—CAUGHT IN A CALM—SUFFERING FROM
LACK OF FOOD—REACH TUBUOI—GO ASHORE UPON INVITATION
OF THE QUEEN—SAIL FOR RAIVAVAI—MEET ELDER PRATT THERE
—LEFT ALONE ON THE ISLAND—SAVAGE CHARACTER OF THE
NATIVES—THE GOVERNOR A FRIEND—VISIT FROM HOUSE TO
HOUSE—PEOPLE GENERALLY UNWILLING TO RECEIVE THE GOS-
PEL—COUNCIL DECIDES THAT I MUST LEAVE THE ISLAND OR BE
KILLED—A TIME OF EXCITEMENT—STORM PASSES FOR AWHILE—
BAPTIZE TWENTY PERSONS—NOTED CHIEF AND THE HEIRESS TO
THE THRONE JOIN THE CHURCH—MORE BITTERNESS AND EX-
CITEMENT—TWO PARTIES OF NATIVES MEET TO ENGAGE IN BAT-
TLE—MANAGE TO RECONCILE THEM AND PREVENT BLOODSHED—
FURTHER THREATS AGAINST THE MORMONS—SOME CHURCH
MEMBERS FEEL TO RETALIATE, BUT ARE RESTRAINED—PASSEN-
GERS ARRIVE WITH FALSE AND SCANDALOUS STORIES ABOUT
THE MORMONS—PERSECUTION INCREASES—THE FEW SAINTS ON
THE ISLAND BECOME SORROWFUL AND DISCOURAGED—PROTEST-
ANT MINISTERS ADVISE EXPULSION OF THE SAINTS—RENEWAL
OF THE FAITH AND ZEAL OF THE CHURCH MEMBERS.

AS we were leaving the Tahitian harbor we encountered
a strong headwind, and beat our way against wind
and waves until our little schooner became somewhat disabled. Provisions began to be scarce, and everything
seemed to be against us. Finally we changed our course,
heading for Tubuoi. When we got within about eighty
miles of that island, our food supply became exhausted;
we had not one mouthful on board, and were in a dead
calm for some time. Then a gentle breeze sprang up and
wafted us to port, where we arrived on November 29th.
Before this relief, however, we suffered considerably from
lack of food.

I supposed that I had to remain on board the schooner

until it was ready to sail for Raivavai; but when Pitamai Vehene, the queen, heard that I had been banished she came off in her own canoe and invited me to go ashore with her, saying, "This is my island, and the French have no right here. I will be responsible for all the trouble that may arise." As the brethren and general authorities of the island thought it was safe to do so, I accepted the invitation, going ashore in the queen's canoe, and remained on the island till December 8th. Then I boarded the little schooner again, and we started for Raivavai, where we landed on the 9th, and found President Pratt in good health.

On December 10th, Elder Pratt sailed away in the schooner, leaving me to take his place in presiding over the interests of the Church on the island. Brother Pratt's friends became my friends, and gave me food and shelter. There were eight Church members on the island; all the rest of the inhabitants, three hundred and eighty-three in number, opposed us, many of them being the most savage and rudest I had met—in fact, they were scarce removed from cannibalism. Some of them did not hesitate to tell of their experiences in eating human flesh, and that they had sacrificed infant children to their idols. They showed the coals before their heathen gods, where they had roasted their babes. Some of them felt proud to relate these things, saying it was in their heathenish days, before the Gospel had come to their land, but now they thought it very bad, and they had no disposition to repeat their evil deeds.

I was shown to the house of Governor Fate, who received me very kindly. He and his wife had received the Gospel on Anaa, and although he was the legal heir to the throne, as they called it, through his joining the Church he had lost much of his influence. But he was a very good man, rendering me all the assistance in his power, while I visited from house to house, trying to make the acquaintance of the people. I went to every home on the island, endeavoring to inform the people on the Gospel, but they were unwilling to give heed, and treated me with marked indifference, often passing by and looking as surly as mad bulls.

The island was not to exceed fourteen miles in circumference, its high and very rugged peaks penetrating the clouds, which nearly always were hanging over and about. The mountains were so steep as to defy all but the wild goats, of which there were some hundreds among the cragged rocks. It was said that the beginning of the existence of these animals on the island was that a sea captain had turned three or four pairs of them loose some years before, and they had increased to hundreds.

Having satisfied my curiosity by traveling over and around the island, visiting the ancient places of worship and seeing the heathen gods and places of skulls and sacrifice, I again called at every house, trying to become more friendly and sociable with the people; but the same stolid feelings still prevailed. I attended their meetings, told them my business in the land, and asked the privilege of preaching to them. Part were favorable, and part were not. I baptized a few, and that caused much excitement.

A council was called to adopt some way by which the islanders could get rid of Mormonism and the American plant, as they called me. Some proposed to fasten the "plant" on a log, and tow it out to sea, where the sharks would eat it, while others suggested burning or making a roast of me.

At last the matter was carried so far that it was decided that I must leave the island or be killed. I learned that they had just about decided on the latter course, so I hastened to go before the council to try and allay their feelings, if possible, and appease their wrath, but I found it utterly impossible to reason with them. My presence, instead of having a conciliatory effect, created the wildest confusion. I was confronted by a native called Tabate, who was a very stout, heavy set man, and who exclaimed, "I will slay you!" At that moment my friend, Governor Fate, stepped between us, and some of the more peaceably disposed took hold of Tabate, while my friends insisted that I leave the house to save bloodshed, saying that Tabate was a very desperate man, but if I left the room they thought the council could restrain him. Accordingly I withdrew with my friends. The council had a hot time of it for awhile, but finally the more consistent party prevailed, so that the matter passed over for the time being. Still, a bad feeling rankled in their bosoms, and I could hear threats that the more rabid party was going to have a fat missionary for a roast.

Although this bitterness continued with many of the people, I baptized some twenty souls, and blessed several infants. I also administered to the sick, and, as I can now remember, all were healed but one child, which died of hip disease, it being a mere skeleton when I was called.

Other councils were held to see what could be done to get rid of the "plant Mormonism, from America," before it spread over the island and became master. But the friends and relatives of those who belonged to the Church would oppose any harsh measures, saying, "Wait until our missionaries of the English church come and we hear what they say."

Now, Elder Pratt had baptized one man who was seventy-five or eighty years of age. He was one of the first born, and his feet had never been wet in salt water. His name was Tauteni (thousand), because he had slain so many people in war, and he could count skulls in his mori or place of skulls, with the best of them. He was well acquainted with the taste of human flesh; had been a great high priest of the natives in their heathenish days, and was supposed to have great influence with the spirits of men. He had a grand-daughter who was said to be the heir to the throne. This girl was brought forward by the old man for baptism. He had reared her, and her parents being willing, I baptized her. This created great excitement and another council was held, where feelings ran so high that it was very hard to conciliate our opponents. But the old man told them that it was his and her father's fault, and not the missionary's, that she was baptized. The girl, whose name was Teraa, also declared that it was by her wish and not mine that she became a member of the Church. This cooled them down a little, but occasionally local difficulties would arise, and the natives would take sides and arm themselves for war. One time I heard the shrieks of the women, and the warwhoops of and commands given among the men.

Although, one day when I was stopping at a village called Tatake, I had heard that there was going to be a battle fought, such rumors were so frequent that I did not pay much attention thereto till I heard the warwhoops and shouts. Then I jumped up, ran out, and beheld thirty to forty men coming from the upper village, Anatomu. They were armed with muskets, and were in their war costumes, dancing and going through the manœuvers peculiar to the natives just before going into an action. At the same time another party was approaching from the inland village of Atibona. These, too, were ready, and with their drums, whistles and shrieks made quite a showing. Still there were some among them inclined to conciliation rather than war.

With my friends, I went out and plead with the two parties to be reconciled, and finally we prevailed so that both bodies of men retired without fighting, and a few of each party met and shook hands, some of both parties seeming friendly to us for a time.

For a short time after this we had comparative quiet, yet threats came about the Mormons, and there was talk of taxing us for the support of the Protestant church. Our brethren claimed rights in the school and meeting houses, but were refused these; then they threatened to burst open the houses, and came to me to get my sanction to do so; but I could not consent to being a party to such a movement, knowing that would give the enemy the pretext they wanted, in order to carry out their threats. My party was not pleased with my position, and threatened to break in the houses anyway, and assert their rights to occupancy. I told them that if they did I would disown them; that they could not be my brethren if they indulged in anything of the kind, as it was for us to be on the side of peace and defense, and not to be aggressors. Finally they said they would obey my counsel. Then things passed along more smoothly for a time.

Soon a schooner came from the island of Ruruta, with about one hundred passengers on board. They brought the alleged news that all the American Elders had left Tubuoi, and were going home. These passengers also seemed to have been well posted in all the old slanders about the Church, and with many new ones about the Elders. These slanders were industriously circulated by the new comers, who said that the people of Tubuoi were glad that the Mormons had left their land. From these stories, and the persecutions the Saints had endured on the island, the few Church members grew sorrowful and discouraged. When I went from Anatomu to Tatake, I found two of the native brethren and two sisters very sad, and as soon as we met they gave vent to their pent-up feelings, wept bitterly, and said that I had to leave the island, and they intended to follow me, no matter where I went. I told them not to fear, and tried to pacify them as best I could.

At our next appointment for a meeting there were but

five out of thirty attended. This seemed strange, for there always had been a full attendance; but now everyone was sad and gloomy. The spirit of mobocracy seemed to thrive on the filthy slanders that had come by the Ruruta schooner. Meetings were called and threats made. Clouds of darkness lowered and filled the atmosphere; the spirit of death seemed to hover around, for the boisterousness of the people had given way to a sullen, murderous disposition, more to be dreaded than when there was abundance of noise and threats.

At this time two young Protestant ministers came and made three or four inflammatory speeches, telling the people that they had admitted a wolf into the fold, and if they did not get rid of him the ministers would not call again. "Drive him off, and pluck up that American plant, or it will overshadow your land, and control you," said they. Thus the wild and heathenish passion was fanned into a lively flame of renewed persecution. Yet, strange to say, when the spirit of death seemed to rest most heavily upon us, the brethren and sisters returned to me with renewed zeal, and all but two men stood firm thereafter.

CHAPTER XXXII.

ABOUT the 5th of May, 1852, the whole people were called to assemble at the village of Tatake and prepare a feast, and at the same time to decide definitely what to do with the Mormon minister and his pipis (disciples). Everything was excitement. The young braves came armed with muskets, shouting and yelling, saying they were going to have a fat roast for tomorrow, while the old councillors, twenty-five or thirty in number, came with slow, quiet steps and grave countenances, and filed into the schoolhouse just at dark. Then the people gathered, loaded down with roast pig, and fruit, fish and poultry. They kindled fires and began shouting, singing and dancing.

Soon the young braves were dancing around the house that they were in; for by this time every member of the Church had come to one place. The mob seemed to be fully enthused with the spirit of murder, as they shouted, "Tomorrow we will have a fat young missionary for a roast!" Just then they fired a salute, seemingly under the foundation or sill of the house—a frame building. Then they commenced to tear down the post and pole fence that enclosed the premises. This fence, together with other wood, was piled up in a heap, as people in timbered countries stack timber to burn it off their land. Then the natives covered the wood with coral rock, as if they were going to burn a lime kiln. They kept up a continual howl all the night long, firing their guns, singing their war songs, and burning their camp-fires.

While this was going on, we held prayer and testimony meeting, never sleeping a moment the whole night. Many times we could hear the crowd outside boasting what a fine, fat missionary roast they were going to have enanahe (tomorrow.)

Daylight came, and the village was all alive with people, as in America on the Fourth of July, at a barbecue. Soon the feasting began. The council had been all night in deciding what they would do with the Mormons and their minister. The provisions at the feast were apportioned to each village according to its numbers, and subdivided among the families, so that a full allowance was made for the Mormon pupu (party). They sent to me the portion of ten men, saying: "Here, this is for you, Iatobo (James), eat it and get fat for the roast," laughing contemptuously as they did so. By this time the whole people were in high glee, eating, drinking, talking, laughing and jeering, as if all hands were bent on pleasure only. When the feasting was over, all became silent, and it seemed as though everybody had gone to sleep.

By 1 o'clock p. m. all were astir again. Two great ruffians came into my apartment, armed with long clubs. They said they had been sent to order me before the council, and if I refused to come they were to drag me there. Everybody seemed to be on the qui vive. As quick as thought, the promises of President Brigham Young flashed through my mind; also the promise of Dr. Willard Richards, in which he told me, in the name of the Lord God of Israel, that though men should seek my life, yet I should return in safety to the bosom of the Saints, having done good and honor to myself and the Church and Kingdom of God. He also gave me instructions what to do; this was when starting on my mission. The next thought that came to my mind was: Have I forfeited those promises? The answer that came quickly from the Spirit was no; and this drove away all fear. Not a doubt was left in my mind.

Without hesitation I arose and walked out to the beach, where the people had assembled, the Saints following me. We passed by the log heap to the assemblage, at the head of which stood twelve or fifteen stout, athletic, young braves, with hair cut close. They were stripped naked to their breechclouts, and were oiled. They stood with folded arms, and certainly seemed formidable, although they were without weapons, for they had a fierce and savage look about them that must be seen to be realized in its effect.

As we came near, the man Tabate stepped out from the crowd and said, "All the Britons stand to the right hand with the sheep, and all the Mormons stand to the left hand where the goats are." Everyone responded to the order except two men from the Mormon party, who drew off to themselves and were neutral. At that, one faithful Mormon man named Rivae and his wife with an eight months old babe in her arms, stepped forward, well knowing what the sentence was to be. This brave brother said, "If you

burn this man," pointing to the writer, "you burn me first."
His heroic wife stepped forward, holding her babe at arm's
length, and shouted, "I am a Mormon, and this baby is a
Mormon, for 'nits make lice,' and you will have to burn all
of us, or Mormonism will grow again." I had told the
people the story of the massacre at Haun's Mill, Missouri,
in which some of the mob shot the children who had crept
for safety under the bellows in the blacksmith shop, the
murderers saying, as they butchered the innocents, 'Nits
will make lice"—Mormons in that instance.

Rivae and his wife was ordered to stand back, while
as a prisoner I was called to take a position in the space
between the two parties. As I obeyed the command, I
was confronted by Tabate, the spokesman or judge, who
had been the chief promoter of all the trouble from the beginning. Said he: "Iatobo, you have caused the people of
our land to sin by having them to travel more than a Sabbath day's journey on the Sabbath. You have also taught
the people that God is a material God, and that is not law-
ful to teach in our land." To this I answered, "Show me
where the teaching is wrong from the Bible." At the
same time I opened the Bible. A strong and determined
voice told me to shut the book, and put it up, for that was
the law of God, and the decision of the landholders and
authorities was that I should be burned to death, and thus
they would rid the land of Mormonism.

Pointing to the left and rear of the prisoner, to the log
heap, which was then at the zenith of its burning, with
haughty demeanor and in an exulting voice, Tabate said,
"Look there at that fire. It is made to consume the flesh
off of your bones." In that moment the Spirit of the Lord
rested mightily upon me, and I felt as though I could run
through a troop and leap over a wall. "In the name of
Israel's God," I said, "I defy ten of your best men, yea, the
host of you, for I serve that God who delivered Daniel from

FIRE PREPARED TO ROAST THE MISSIONARY—SENTENCED TO DEATH.

the den of lions, and the three Hebrew children from the fiery furnace!"

Dear reader, it is impossible for me to describe the power, the cool resignation, the unshaken confidence, and the might that overshadowed my soul and body, that thrilled through every fibre of my existence. For there was absolutely not one particle of fear or tremor in my whole being. But I did feel thankful for that great and marvelous deliverance, because in the very moment that I defied the host the spirit of division rested upon the judge who had passed the sentence, his counselors, and the executioners, insomuch that the counselors faced the executioners, and they grappled with each other in a sharp tussle. From that ensued a fight, until the whole people were mixed up in it.

Even two of our old tottering Mormons, Tautene and Hauty, came in with their clubs, and were so enraged that they actually champed their teeth together till the froth filled the corners of their mouths, as I have seen it with mad dogs. Both of them had been great warriors in their time, and could boast of having eaten human flesh, but at this time they were so old and feeble that I took each of them by the arms and forced them from the fight into the house, where I had ordered all the Mormons to go. I told them to stay in the house or I would excommunicate them from the Church. As they seemed to be almost ungovernable, I gave Fute, a priest and a stout man, a club, and told him to keep them in the house if he had to knock them down to do it, while I went back to the battleground, picked up my Bible and hat, and returned to find my party reconciled to their fate, and feeling more like rejoicing than fighting. In an effort to free himself from her clinging embrace Hauty had struck his wife with a club. This was before I had got hold of him. She was trying to keep him out of the melee. The woman was very lame for weeks after receiving the blow.

During all this time our enemies quarreled and fought with clubs and stones, pulled hair and screamed. They did not cease fighting till sundown. Then, with many sore heads, and more sore limbs, they dispersed, and I doubt very much if the majority of them knew what they had been fighting for. After they left, a feeling of quiet and safety pervaded the village, especially in and about our residence, such as we had not before known on the island, and for weeks everything was strangely peaceful. People who once seemed surly and defiant, now had a tame and subdued expression in their countenances, and appeared to prefer passing by unnoticed rather than otherwise.

Some two months later, I was traveling alone in the timber, and at a short turn in the road I chanced to meet one of the old counselors who decided that I should be burned. We were close together before we saw each other. At sight of me he turned and ran as hard as he could, and I, without any particular object in view, gave chase and ran him down. I seized him by the neck, and asked why he ran from me and why he was afraid of me. Said he: "Your God is a God of power, and I was afraid to meet His servant." I inquired how he knew that my God was a God of power, and why they had not burned me when they had decided to do so. He answered: "At the moment that you defied us there was a brilliant light, or pillar of fire, bore down close over your head. It was as bright as the sun. We remembered reading in the Bible about Elijah calling fire down from heaven so that it consumed the captains and their fifties, and we thought that you had prayed to your God of power, and that He had sent that fire to burn us and our people if we harmed you. The young men did not see the light. They were going to burn you, and we tried to stop them. So we got into a fight. Now we all know that you are a true servant of God, and we do not like to meet you, out of fear."

From what I was able to learn, that feeling was shared by the whole community, and I was treated with great respect ever afterwards. I felt freer and safer when alone than ever before. Indeed, there never was another council meeting called to devise a way to get rid of the Mormons from that island, while I remained there. But for all that, the islanders did not want to learn the Gospel. Yet ever afterward, when they feasted I was always remembered with a very liberal portion of the very best they had. I do not remember baptizing another soul there after that event. There I remained, and part of the time I fished, also hunted the wild chickens that abounded in the mountains—fowls of the common Dominique variety, which had grown wild in the fastnesses of the hills, and could fly equal to the sagehen or prairie chicken.

CHAPTER XXXIII.

LONG TIME WITHOUT NEWS FROM HOME—LETTER FROM ELDER B. F. GROUARD—RELEASED FROM MY MISSIONARY LABORS IN THE ISLANDS—LITTLE OPPORTUNITY TO LEAVE RAIVAVAI—NATIVES BUILD A SCHOONER—FAST AND PRAY TO LEARN WHETHER I SHOULD SAIL ON THE VESSEL—THE ANSWER—SAIL FOR RAPIA—DRIVEN BACK TO RAIVAVAI—MAKE A NEW START—ARRIVE AT RAPIA — RIDICULOUS IDEA OF THE PEOPLE CONCERNING A MORMON ELDER—I AM FORBIDDEN TO GO ASHORE, ON PAIN OF DEATH—FEELING IS MODIFIED SOMEWHAT, AND I GO ASHORE—BATTLE BETWEEN THE NATIVES—AN OLD MAN GIVES ME FOOD—ATTEND A MEETING, GET PERMISSION TO SPEAK A FEW WORDS AND AM ORDERED FROM THE ISLAND—INCREASE OF SENTIMENT OF TOLERATION—INVITED TO SUPPER AT THE GOVERNOR'S—STRANGE CUSTOM OF WOMEN WAITING ON MEN—RATHER THAN FOLLOW IT, I SUBMIT TO BEING CALLED A HEATHEN.

WHEN I had spent seven months alone on the island of Raivavai, without any news from the outer world or perhaps it would be more proper to say inner world—

for this island and Rapia are as near out of the world as any portion of it can be—I began to wonder when I could hear some tidings of the brethren on the other islands. I had not had an opportunity to leave Raivavai in all the time that I had been there; nor did I have the slightest idea when it would be possible for me to return to the land of my nativity, for the natives told me that within their memory there had been seven years at a time when they had not so much as 'seen a sail, and it was not infrequent for from one to three years to pass without a vessel calling. Therefore it will not be thought strange when I say that the time became very' monotonous.

Here is an extract from a letter received just before I did leave the island; it was from Elder B. F. Grouard, counselor to President Pratt in the presidency of the mission, and bears date of Papeete, Tahiti, April 18, 1852:

"DEAR BROTHER JAMES:—I embrace the present opportunity of writing you a line, perhaps for the last time before leaving for California, though I hope we may be able to arrange matters so that you will be permitted to come here and make one of our party across. The governor is now absent, down at Raiatea, consequently nothing can be done about your case until he returns.   *   *   *   *

"Wednesday, 21st.—Mr. Kelly has sent for you on his own responsibility. You must be careful and not go on shore on the protectorate islands, but be sure and come, or rather, he has authorized me to send for you.

"I have the honor to be, your brother in Christ, and fellow laborer in the Gospel,   B. F. GROUARD."

From this it will be seen that I was released from further labors in that mission. I also was without any means in sight to get away from the land that had been so fruitful of troubles to me. It is true that the natives had a schooner of twenty or twenty-five tons burden in course of construc-

tion, but they were so uncertain and tardy in their movements that there was really no dependence to be placed in
anything of the kind that they undertook. Indeed, it was
doubtful whether they would complete the vessel at all,
though six or eight weeks was ample time in which to finish it. Besides, they were liable to get into a quarrel that
would cause delay for many months. Again, so frail was
the boat that it did not seem that it ever could be safe to go
to sea. Nearly every stave and brace was made from the
bark of the buru tree, and twisted by hand. The anchor was
a chunk of wood with old scraps of iron spiked on to it, and
for a chain the same kind of material was used as for the
stays and braces. The galley was only a square box of
two and a half feet, filled with soil and tied down to the deck
with a bark rope; and as to the helm, it had to be held by
hand, taking two or three men to manage it, especially in
rough weather. The compass was no better than a tin plate;
in fact, it could not be of any service whatever—and the
sails were almost rotten. But at last the boat was launched,
and leaked so badly that it did not seem possible to make
it of service; but the natives persevered and baled it out,
and it was soaked up until they considered it safe.

This boat being built, it seemed to offer a possible
means for me to see white men's land again. There was
no one for me to advise with, the very men who had planned
my destruction being the owners and masters of the craft.
The voyage they anticipated taking was said by them to be
seven hundred miles, to the island of Rapia, and from thence
a like distance to Tahiti, in all fourteen hundred miles. The
food and fresh water supply was also very uncertain. The
water had to be carried in large gourds and cocoanuts. Nor
was this all that had to be considered. In those parts there
are dense fogs and rainstorms, for days together, so that
navigation is very hazardous where there is only the sun,
moon, and stars to depend upon, and these obscured.

The reader will perceive the gravity of the situation that confronted the writer when he came to decide what to do.   As the time drew near for the boat's departure, I retired to a lonely place in the woods, and there fasted and prayed for three days, fasting all the time and going to my retreat to pray as often in the three days as I thought proper.   This was done in order to ascertain from the divine Source whether or not I should take the risk of going on that vessel at that time.   The answer came plain and distinct to my understanding, though not in words to the natural senses, yet to my entire satisfaction that all would be well if I went.   From that moment I hungered and thirsted, but had not done so before in all the time that I had fasted.

Accordingly, on September 22, 1852, I engaged passage on the Raivavai schooner, bound for Rapia.   On the 23rd I went aboard, and we sailed out, but some of the rigging gave way, and we were bound to return for repairs. On the 24th we tried again, passing out of the harbor with a light breeze, at 5 o'clock a. m.   There were sixty-two souls on board, all seasick.   On the 26th and 27th there was a dead calm.   At daylight on the 28th we found ourselves on the opposite side of the island and very near it, surrounded by hundreds of great whales.   Our navigators were so confused that they did not know their own island until they went ashore. Again the rigging gave way, and we had to put into port to repair it and to replenish our food supply.

On October 4th we sailed once more, and with a strong and fair wind on the 9th we reached the island of Rapia, which has a high and abrupt coast with a good harbor, but a very narrow passage thereto, in which we were hailed by a fisherman who inquired about the white man on board. When the crew told him it was a Mormon Elder, he hastened to the shore, ran to the village and told the people that a Mormon Elder was on the schooner.   The people had never seen a Mormon, but had heard the most ridiculous stories about us. They became excited, and frightened as well, for they had heard that Mormons had cloven feet and shells on their backs, and were some kind of mongrel between man and beast. They also had been told that the Mormons were so lustful that it was very difficult for the females to escape from them. This being the only information the people had about the Latter-day Saints, it was no wonder that the men armed themselves with muskets and fish spears, and came to the landing or lay in ambush, the females keeping at a respectful distance, while the more brave and fearless ventured to come on board, inspect the "animal," and forbid him to set his foot on shore on pain of death. Strange as this statement of affairs may appear, it is nevertheless true.

At length a number of the people came on board and spied around as if to discover the peculiar features of a Mormon Elder, and they, with my friends, thought that possibly it was safe for me to go ashore; accordingly I went in the first canoe. As we neared the landing, six or seven men, some with muskets and some with fishing spears, rose up out of the brush and tall grass, and peeked and pried, as they afterwards said, to discern the cloven foot. As they could not discover the deformities which they had expected to find, they said, "Why, he looks like any other white man or minister; we do not want to kill him." There were others who, however, acted very surly, and would not speak nor shake hands, but told my friends that I must leave their island or I would be killed. Finally we were permitted to go up to the village, where the people all ran together to see the stranger. None dared invite him into their houses, so he took his seat out on a log, while they feasted. His friends joined with the feasting parties, thinking it would be better for him if they were sociable with the people and acquainted them with the supposed monster's customs and habits, as also with what he had been teaching the people.

Two weeks before we landed, the inhabitants of this village had had a battle with the people of another village across the island, and some of both parties had been killed, while others were yet suffering from their wounds. This, I suppose, had something to do with the spirit of murder and bloodshed that hung so thickly around the place. When the people finished feasting, one old man brought me some food on a banana leaf, and then slipped away as if he did not wish anybody to see him. To me it seemed a case of root hog, or die, or at least it was to eat or starve, so the kind offer was thankfully received. I found the admonition of Paul, wherein he said, eat what is set before you, and ask no questions, for conscience, sake appropriate in this case.

The bell was soon rung for meeting, and the people quickly came together. I met with them, and at the conclusion of their services asked the privilege of acquainting them with my business in their country; for myself and native friends were the first Mormons who had ever been there, and to save the necessity of anyone else coming I felt it my bounden duty to offer them the Gospel, as it has to be preached in every land and to every people. I succeeded in saying a few words, and received for my pains an order from the presiding priest to go out of the house and leave the island.

Although many of the people seemed to sanction the course of the priest, there were a few who did not seem to favor it; but to save trouble I left the house. The people then began to discuss the order and to question its justice, as we had been mild and made no display of obstinacy. At last they concluded that the Mormon was not quite so bad as he had been represented, and that he might come into the governor's and have supper at a table which the Protestant ministers had furnished for their own accommodation, and where they had left some dishes and a chair; so I was comfortably seated at the table and the food brought on. Quite a handsome young girl of about sixteen stood by the table, and as soon as a blessing was asked, she, with her fingers, tore the roasted chicken to pieces, stripped the flesh from off the bones, and held this to my mouth, saying, "There!"

I drew back a little, as that was so strange a custom that I did not appreciate it. The girl was quite dark complexioned, and some one observed, "She is so dark that he thinks she is dirty. Let her get some soap and wash before him, and then see if he will eat." As the people seemed so strange in their actions, I thought there was some trick to be played, so I waited until she had washed her hands and, in obedience to orders, stepped up, saying that her hands were clean, "Look, that is my color, and not dirt." Still I felt dubious about taking the bait. Then she was told to step back, and another young lady was called for. This one was quite fair, with rather light brown or auburn hair. They said "Now he will eat, for he will think she is white," but I still refused the courtesy. Then some one who was standing by said, "Let him feed himself, like a heathen." At this the master of ceremonies said, "Why do you not eat?" I tried to explain to them that it seemed to me to be wrong to require so much of the females—that they should prepare the food and then stand or sit by and put it into a man's mouth. "Well," said he, "she was the first to sin, and she ought to wait on the man."

At this an old man who lay flat on his stomach with the Bible before him, opened the book to where Paul said that when he was in Rome he did as the Romans did. The old man had his hair bushed, and, apparently, the very brand of heathenism in his face. I would have thought as much of looking on a brush heap or in a muskrat house for intelligence as to have anticipated anything smart from him. He said, "My friend, do you believe in the Bible?" I said, "Yes, and it is good to do as it says." "Then," said he, "you are a liar; for Paul said that when he was in Rome he did as the Romans did, and now you are in Rapia you will not do as the Rapians do; for it is our way for the women to put the food into our mouths. That is the way we do in this land."

Sure enough, I learned that this was true; for when the meal is ready it is brought into the room in baskets, and the male portion of the household get down on their hands and knees, while the females pick the bones from the fish, pork or poultry, as the case may be, and with their fingers put the flesh into their masters' mouths. To conclude with, the woman dips her hand into a dish of water, and wipes his mouth. Then he moves away, and the wife and daughter take the scraps, or what may be left. It is considered as great a shame on that island for a man to put food into his mouth as it is in China for a Mongolian to have his queue cut off. But to me it seemed so ridiculous that my stay there was too short to make it seem even human. I did not adopt the custom, preferring to be called a heathen by those who did practice it.

CHAPTER XXXIV.

AS I felt the great need of reform among the people
of Rapia, I tried again to get the privilege of preaching to them in their house, but found them unyielding on
that point.   There were three native brethren and their
wives who had come with me.   I was impressed that we
ought to make yet another trial to leave our testimony with
the islanders, so we went out by the side of their meeting
house, which was a frame building set up on blocks some
eighteen inches or two feet from the ground, the dirt floor
being thatched with dry grass.   We stood within ten feet
of the house and commenced to sing.   Before we were
ready to read our text, it seemed that everybody in the village had come around, but not in the ordinary way.   They
crowded into the meeting house and some filled the win-
dows, while others lay down and poked their heads out
under the sills of the house; still others got down on their
hands and knees some five or six rods off and crawled

along through the shrubbery, taking hold of the brush as they drew near, lying flat down and drawing themselves along, taking sticks and poking the weeds aside so they could get a better view. With this most singular congregation before us, and the most perfect order (for it seemed as if there was not a whisper,) we read a chapter in the Bible—the third of Matthew, I believe—then preached on faith, repentance, and baptism for the remission of sins. At the dismissal of our services the whole assembly withdrew, and after that I had lots of food, such as it was.

We held seven meetings on that little fragment of terra firma, and visited the king in the west village. We found the royal personage at home, sitting Indian fashion on his couch, half naked. He appeared to be a man of unusually strong character, very surly, and did not want to talk. When I attempted to tell him the object of my mission to his country, his neck swelled out, and he began blowing through his nostrils like a mad bull. He said, "You leave my country." By this time my native friends discovered that danger was gathering around us, and told me that we must not delay one moment, but must get away as quickly as possible, for that village had suffered defeat at the hands of the people of the other village, and we could not be friendly with the king and his followers if we were to the others.

We got away, and afterwards it developed that my friends had foreseen a peril that I had not fully understood, for when the king said we had better get away from his country, that was his ultimatum, and if we had remained longer every one of us would have been slain, as the people were preparing for the slaughter.

On our retreat I observed a castor oil bean tree loaded with beans. Its trunk was as large as a man's body. I began to inspect it when my friends called out, "Hurry up, or we will every one be killed," so we hastened to more friendly and hospitable parts, where we came across a large gourd, or calabash vine, and a watermelon patch. Never having seen anything of the kind on any other island where I had been, my inquisitive propensities were set to work ascertaining how those things came there. Were they a spontaneous growth? If not, where did they come from, since this little island is so remote from all others, and the natives tell me that white men seldom visit them? I inquired of the people where they got the seed of the vegetables named. "Why," said they, "our forefathers brought them here."

"Where did they come from?"

The reply was, "From the rising of the sun."

On hearing this, I asked from what country, and was answered, "We do not know. It was a big land, so big they did not know its boundary. It was a land of food, and of great forests of big trees, and great fresh waters that were filled with fish."

I next inquired, "How came they to leave such a good land?" The response was in these words: "We do not know, only they said they got lost in the fog, and were several days without seeing the sun. Then the strong winds came and blew them over here, and their vessel was wrecked on this island. They never could get back to the lands of their forefathers, so they stayed here. They increased so fast that all could not live on this land, so they made canoes and tried to get back, but the winds were against them, that they were carried away to the west, and for a long time those left here supposed the others were lost in the sea; but after a time it was learned that there were other lands where the sun goes down. Then our people made canoes and went to them, and we think that is the way these islands became peopled, for they are the same kind of people as ourselves."

"Have you any other knowledge of your forefathers?"

"No, we do not know anything but that which the fathers have said. They used to say that if they could get back to their fatherland they could find metal to make fish spears and hooks with. When the first white men's ship came in sight we tried to go to it, thinking we could get some fishing tackle therefrom. We thought that vessel must have come from our fathers' land. But the wind was so strong we could not get to the ship, and it was a long time before another one came. Finally we reached one, and got such things as our fathers had told us about."

Read the Book of Mormon, page 427, 63d chapter, 5th to 9th verses. Was the ship that Hagoth built the same that was wrecked on the island of Rapia, South Pacific Ocean, about 25° south latitude, and, as near as I can find out from French charts, time reckoned from Paris, France, in longitude 140 west?

The reader may form his own conclusions, as I return to my narrative of our stay on the island. When we had returned from our visit to the surly king, one man by the name of Mesearee opened his house for us to hold meeting in, but very few attended with us.

October 17th, the bark *John Williams* called with one Mr. Platt, a Protestant minister, on board. This clergyman was a man of fine address. He came ashore and preached, then sprinkled all the infant children of the village. Though very pleasant, he refused to talk with me in the Tahitian language, saying that if we did so on the Scriptures it would cause a split among the people. I insisted that he show the natives the scripture for his mode of baptism, but he declined to do that, and boarded his vessel and sailed away.

October 27, 1852, we sailed for Tahiti. On the 29th we encountered a very heavy storm, so severe that we lost all of our sails, and had to lash two of our strong men on deck with slack rope so that they might fasten down the

hatch and companion ways. The rest of us had to go below, for the sea was lashed into a foamy mass as white as
snow. It did not seem possible for us to survive the terrible ordeal. As in almost all similar cases, the wicked will
pray—that is in times of great danger, if at no other time
—so the natives who went below, some fifty-nine in number, divided themselves into three praying parties. One of
these occupied the bow, one stationed itself amidships, and
one was in the stern of the vessel. Then a man in one
party would pray at the top of his voice, and so on with
each party in turn. Thus they prayed, passing the word
back and forth, as long as the sea raged in its fury.

In all of our travels together, those in charge of the
vessel had never honored me with a request to attend prayers, or once called me to ask a blessing, but now, in our
great peril, one of the old priests found his way in the
dense darkness to my berth, and said: "Iatobo, you pray
to your God of power, to spare us, that we may not die in
this great sea." I told him no, for I had done my praying
on land, before I had boarded the schooner, and now I had
all that I could do to hold myself in the berth, that I might
not be thrown out and killed. He returned with a grunt,
and commanded the rest to pray. These conditions continued for six or seven hours, when the wind abated, and
the little schooner pitched and rolled as if she would go to
the bottom.

November 1, 1852, we sighted a reef called Herehe-
retue. On the 9th we came in view of Metia, and on the
10th we went into the harbor of Papeete, Tahiti. It was
on the 11th when, through the intervention of Mr. Kelly,
American consul, I got permission to land. The same gentleman gave me an introduction to one Charles Hill, a carpenter, who was rather a backslider from the Mormon
Church. Still, he was very friendly, and said that if I
would assist him in carpenter work he would board and

lodge me until I could get a passage home. Mr. Kelly counseled me not to be alone anywhere, as a watch would be kept over me every minute I was on the island. He said he would not be responsible if I preached or traveled out of the town, as I was liable to be shot the moment that I was found alone. Said he, "The French are more bitter towards you than ever. They seem to think you would turn everything upside down if you were allowed to run at large. I have never seen them so excited over anything as they are about you. They are actually afraid of you, for fear that if you were permitted to go among the people again they would revolt at once, and there would be another war." He also said that he would arrange matters so that I could go with Mr. Hill to and from his work, and if we kept close together, he thought it all safe, as Mr. Hill was well known; but that I had better stop in his office till he could see the governor, and I could go out to Mr. Hill's in the evening with him, as he lived in the suburbs of the town. Mr. Kelly also told me there had been more trouble at Anaa, and a number of our people from there were in prison on Tahiti; and further, that I was held responsible for all the trouble on that island.

It having been arranged for me to stop with Mr. Hill, he called for me in the evening, and next morning I went to work with him at his business. In the meantime the news of my arrival on Tahiti spread very fast, and the sons of the prisoners from Anaa, who had followed their parents in disguise, and could visit the prisoners one at a time, put pencil and paper into their hands on the sly, so that they could write to me. Five or six of the young men dressed themselves as the regular "toughs" of the town, and met Mr. Hill and me, one of them bearing a note in his hand. When they got near us they began to dance and sing in a very rude manner, acting as if they would not give any of the road to us. Then they pushed the one

17

with the note against me, and as he passed it into my hand the rest circled clear around so as to obscure me from two gen d' armes who followed us day and night. Then the young men would shout and laugh as if they had done it to annoy me in particular. Thus I received letters from the natives. The young men would meet us again, and I would pass to them the answers, while they would appear to the looker-on to be running against me purposely, to insult and annoy me. Sometimes I would try to show my displeasure by scolding at them. In this way a regular correspondence was carried on between the unfortunate prisoners and myself, during my stay. In that manner I learned that there were twenty-three of them in prison, there being ten Elders, five Priests, four Teachers and four Deacons. On the 12th there were eight more prisoners brought from the island of Anaa, six brethren and two sisters. All of the thirty-one were put to work on the steep side of a mountain, to make a road up to a fort. The hillside was so steep that some of them fell and were hurt quite seriously. Sometimes the prisoners were beaten by the guards that attended them. Their provisions were very poor, and they had not even enough of that.

I will again mention my former persecutors of the island of Raivavai, with whom I traveled to Tahiti, for they came to me in great trouble, and said their schooner had been so badly damaged in the storm we had been in that the French had condemned it, and would not allow them to go to sea again. They were four hundred miles from home, without money, provisions or friends. They very humbly asked my advice, which I gave freely, telling them to state their case to the French authorities, and these would be bound to find a way to have them returned home and give them support until they did so. This pleased them very much; they seemed to appreciate the counsel of one whom they had sat in judgment and helped to pass sentence upon, ordering him to be burned. Doubtless some of them had aided in gathering the fuel to make the fire for the burning. I condoled with them as much as the conditions would admit of; and when I came to part with them they seemed to feel, and in fact said, that I had been a true friend to them. They wept as though they were my near relatives. Thus returning good for evil brought blessings.

CHAPTER XXXV.

WATCHED CLOSELY BY GEN D' ARMES — EXPERIENCE WHEN AT PRAYER—TAKE DINNER WITH REV. MR. HOWE—DINING WITH A CATHOLIC BISHOP—IMPATIENCE OF THE GOVERNOR—LEAVE TAHITI ON THE ABYSSINIA—CURIOSITY OF PASSENGERS AND SAILORS—DIFFICULTY IN GETTING OUT OF THE HARBOR—HEAR OF MORE TROUBLE AT ANAA—CAPTAIN'S COMMENT ON MORMON BOOKS—A WATERSPOUT— CROSSING THE EQUATOR— ENCOUNTER A TERRIBLE STORM—A TIDAL WAVE—SHIP SPRINGS A LEAK—PANIC ON BOARD -ALL HANDS TO THE PUMPS—STOPPING A LEAK—FAIR WEATHER AGAIN.

SO far as my own conduct was concerned, now that I was again on the island of Tahiti, I continued with Mr. Hill. Two gen d' armes followed us or hung around where we were at work all day, and at night tramped about the house where we lived. At daylight the night guards disappeared in the brush. One morning I stepped three or four rods into the brush, for my morning devotions, and as I was engaged with my eyes closed I heard a rustling in the leaves. Supposing it was the hogs that ran around there, I paid no attention until I was through, when I saw two officers standing within fifteen feet of and in front of me, gazing straight into my face. They were heavily armed, but did not interfere with me, so I returned to the house, while they mounted the fence and sat there till we went to work, when they followed us up as usual.

During this time I met with Mr. Howe, the presiding official of the Protestant mission on the islands. He appeared to feel very sympathetic toward me, and invited me to take dinner with him and his good old lady. I accepted the invitation, and he made me a present of a Tahitian Bible, also of a Tahitian and English dictionary. He is the same Mr. Howe spoken of before, when he was so radically opposed to me, but now he seemed charitable and kind. After I left his house, and was passing along in sight of the Catholic bishop's office, the bishop sent a servant after me, inviting me in to dine and wine. Accordingly, I called, finding him a very polite gentleman. He met me at the door of his library, took me by the hand and courteously led me to a seat, then set out some wine, saying he was very sorry that he had but one glass of wine in the room, though he set out two glasses, but poured all the wine into one, which he presented to me. At that moment the saying of the Lord Jesus came to my mind, to be harmless as doves but wise as serpents. I adopted as much French politeness as I was capable of, divided the wine into the two glasses, presented him the one with the most wine in, telling him that I could not think of drinking alone—that he must join me or I should decline his very kind offer. I thought that if he could stand to drink the largest half of the wine, I could afford to try the least half, and as I preferred him to drink his first, I delayed until he had swallowed it, when I drank to his health. We had a sociable chat, and he insisted on my stopping to supper, when he would have plenty of wine. I told him I could not, as my attendants, the gen d' armes, were waiting patiently for me. He next presented me two books, telling me that they would show how the priesthood had descended from Peter down to the present pope. The books being in the French language, were of no use to me, so I bade him good-bye.

I learned from Mr. Kelly that the governor was impatient at my stay on the island, so I disposed of everythnig that I could spare, raised sixty dollars thereby, and prepared to sail on the English ship *Abyssinia*, from Sydney, Australia, and commanded by Captain George Gordon.

November 24, 1852, I boarded the *Abyssinia*, paying sixty dollars steerage passage to San Francisco, California. When I got on the deck, the seamen and some of the passengers crowded around me, and stared at me as if I had been a wild beast. When I saluted them with, "Gentlemen, how are you?" they looked at each other as much as to say, "Shall we return the compliment?" At last one of the sailors took off his hat, made a bow, and said, "Please sir, can you speak English?" I answered, "Yes, sir, a little." The next question was, "And are you a Mormon Elder?" My reply was, "Yes," and was followed with, "Well, pardon me, but I thought a Mormon Elder had a cloven foot and a shell on his back, and I expected that you would be brought aboard in a case, as I have been told that the Mormons were a kind of half beast, fierce, and wild."

Some of the others said that they had had the same ideas. A third party exclaimed, "What d——d lies they have told us! We have been anxious to see this Elder ever since we heard there was one coming on board, and we thought to see you brought in a big cage. We cannot see any difference in you and common men." So much for wild and slanderous stories afloat in those days and in that part of the world.

Shortly the vessel was got under way, but just as we entered the passage the wind slackened so that we came very near being crushed against the reef. Five boats from a French warship came to our aid, as we had cast anchor to save ourselves, and the Frenchmen towed us back to a safe location, where we lay until the 26th.

We tried it again on the 27th, and as we passed out of the harbor we went close to the French warship, which was weighing anchor. On the deck stood the Catholic bishop, who held up his cross and made signs. He said there was trouble in Anaa again, and he was going there.

After we sailed, the captain of the *Abyssinia* asked me to lend him some books on Mormonism. I let him take the Book of Mormon and the Doctrine and Covenants. He returned them on the 29th, saying, "I believe the books and your prayers have made me sick." He did not trouble me any more about Mormonism, yet treated me with proper respect, as a rule.

There were several male and female passengers on board, a portion of the latter being of the lewd class, judging from their actions; and the former were not much better. I loaned all the books that I had to passengers and seamen. Nearly all on board treated me in a courteous manner.

On November 30th a waterspout passed close to our ship, causing much excitement. Its roar was frightful, as it carried a very great column of water up into the air, and spread it out into the clouds like a whirlwind on land, but on so much larger scale as to be a dread to seamen.

December 1st we sighted what the captain called Flint's Island. It was large and high, and appeared to be inhabited. On the 10th we crossed the equator, where the seamen had some sport at the expense of several of the passengers who had not crossed it before. They made preparations for Neptune, and told many stories of his pranks with those who dared cross his path without paying penance, or treating the ship's crew.

On the 20th we encountered a terrific storm, which carried away most of our sail, and left us badly damaged.

On Christmas day we had something like a tidal wave in a calm sea. The wave was so great that it swept away the main topgallant sail and the jib boom. Two seamen were carried below for dead. The ship sprung a leak in the bow, and the peril became so great that all the seamen and the male passengers were called to lend a hand. It being in the night, the consternation was so intense that passengers were on the deck in their night clothes, screaming. Some shouted to pray, and others did pray with all the fervor at their command, especially when the carpenter, reporting that the vessel was parting in her beams, called for men to turn the windlass, and for kettles of hot tar, blankets, calking, chisels, and anything to make repairs. As the wind began to freshen, the boat headed before it, without any regard to course. The next order was, "Down with the hatches!"

"Aye, aye, sir."

"Then sound her."

"Aye, sir."

"How is she?"

"Gaining water, sir."

It was hurry to the pumps, and the carpenter was asked, "How is she?"

"All right, sir."

"Heave away at the windlass! Keep the pumps going!"

The carpenter had been pinning timber across the breach, and with windlass power preventing if possible the seam from spreading any more until he could make it safe. Blankets were dipped in hot tar and driven into the parting. With these efforts and by keeping the pumps going steadily for eight hours, the boat was partly freed from the rolling sea, and at length was patched up and put on her course. The captain then said that his greatest fear had been that, as his cargo was coal, the friction of the fuel and the water coming in below would cause the cargo to take fire. When we got righted and on our course, we had light winds, and cold and wet weather until the voyage was ended.

CHAPTER XXXVI.

ARRIVE AT SAN FRANCISCO—A WRECKED SHIP—THE ABYSSINIA CON-DEMNED—GATHERING WRECKAGE—DRUNKEN SAILORS—MY TRUNK HELD FOR HOSPITAL FEES—GO ASHORE, WHERE ALL IS CHANGED AND STRANGE—MY DILAPIDATED APPEARANCE—SEEK GUIDANCE OF THE LORD—WANDER ALMOST IN DESPAIR—MEET AN OLD FRIEND—FIND A HOME—MY TRUNK RELEASED—MEET ELDERS GOING ON MISSIONS—WELL TREATED BY SAINTS AND STRANG-ERS—PROVIDENCES OF THE LORD—OUTWARD-BOUND ELDERS ENTRUST MONEY TO ME FOR THEIR FAMILIES—ENGAGE TO CARRY MAIL TO LOS ANGELES—ON A STEAMER FOR SAN PEDRO—TAKEN SEVERELY ILL.

ON January 8th, 1853, we passed into the bay of San Francisco, where we came close to a big New York clipper ship, fast on a rock in the passage. While we were looking at the vessel, the tide came in and lifted it up; then it dropped back and was smashed as if it were only a match-box. Luckily, the ship had been there long enough to be surrounded by boats sufficient to save the passengers, and perhaps their baggage.

We soon dropped anchor from our dismantled bark, which, as I afterwards learned, was condemned as being unseaworthy, and never was allowed to go to sea again. The seamen on our vessel went to picking up the wreckage from the clipper ship. They chanced to catch a barrel of whisky, when the captain ordered it to be carried below. That made the sailors desperate. They seized an ax, crushed the barrel head in, and each seaman dipped with his cup. Within fifteen minutes they were wild with drunkenness. They armed themselves with axes, hand-spikes, belaying pins, marlinspikes, and any and everything they could lay hold of. Then the officers, and some of the passengers who had incurred their displeasure, were made to hunt hiding places below in doublequick time. That condition did not last long, however, before a compromise was effected, the captain took his position again, and the men went to landing passengers and baggage. I got my trunk ready to depart, when the captain demanded five dollars of me, for hospital fees, he said. As I had not so much as one dollar, I had to leave my trunk and go ashore, very sick and cold.

When I reached the streets I found things so changed from when I was there before that I felt lost in the throng of people. It seemed to me that everyone was seeking his own gain, regardless of his fellow-men. It was push, ram, jam, on all sides. I had worn my clothes pretty well out, my hat had been so crushed that my hair was showing in the crown, and my shoe soles were worn very nearly off.

In this condition I asked the Lord, in silent prayer, to show me what I should do. The Spirit said, "Go up the street." I was then on California Street. I obeyed the whisperings, until I got near the top of the street. Without any consolation the thought came, What shall I do? The still, small Voice said, "Go up the street," and I obeyed again.

At last, almost despairing of everything, wholly sick and tired, suffering from lack of some refreshment, and feeling that there was no relief for me, I saw a man start across the street above me, and from the same side. When he neared the center of the street, he stopped and seemed to be looking at me. As I advanced, he turned around, and walked back two or three steps. By this time I started across toward him, and he came to meet me. It was Redick N. Allred, of the Mormon Battalion.

We did not recognize each other until we went to shake hands. He said, "How are you?" I answered, "Tired, sick, and hungry." "Well," said he, "come back across the street with me, to a lunch stand, and we will have something to eat." Soon the inner man was comforted, when Brother Allred told me there were thirty-six Elders in San Francisco, bound to foreign lands on missions. He led me to some of my old friends, and I found John Layton, whom I had been acquainted with on the Society Islands. He told me that if I would I could come and stop with him, and chop the wood and do the marketing; for his wife, being an islander, could not talk English well. I accepted the kind offer, and thus was provided with a home.

I also met with Major Jefferson Hunt. We saw a Captain King, took supper with him, and told him that the captain of the vessel I had come on had retained my trunk because I had not five dollars to pay the hospital fees. Brother Badlam gave me the money to get my trunk, and Captain King gave me a note to a custom officer. I obtained my trunk after I had paid the captain of the *Abyssinia* the money, and I followed him up to the custom house, to the officer there, to whom I showed Captain King's note. The officer gave the sea captain a look, then said something to him, and without a word more he returned me the money.

I next visited the Elders, and attended meetings with them. They had arrived several days before me, and had sold their teams in the southern part of California. They had also taken up some collections among the Saints. Brother John M. Horner having been very liberal to them, a number of them rendered me assistance.

One day, as I was passing Widow Ivins', she called to me, and ran out to meet me, saying, "Here is ten dollars that a lady gave me to hand to you, and here is thirty dollars more that she wishes you to convey to that body of

Elders that is in town, to help them on their missions." I asked the name of the lady, and the reply was, "I am not at liberty to disclose her name." She said the lady was not a Mormon, but had attended our meetings, and had stated that she was unworthy to be personally known to us; so I never learned who she was.

At one time, when I was walking along the street alone, I was met by a stranger, who offered to shake hands with me. As we grasped hands, he pushed a five-dollar gold piece into mine. I said, "What does this mean?" He replied, "None of your d——d business. Take it, and bless yourself with it. I have money due me, and if I am successful in collecting it, I will see you again." At that he dashed away in the busy throng, and I never saw him more, that I am aware of.

On a still further occasion, I was met by an entire stranger, who put a dollar in my hand and said, "Come, let us have some good cider and cake." I begged to be excused, but he would not listen to it; I had to go with him anyhow. We stepped to a lunch stand, where he said, "Let this man have what he calls for; I want to catch that man," and away he went. The proprietor asked what I would have, and I told him I would await the return of my friend. He said, "Never mind him, he is all right; he may not be back again till tomorrow morning." Then he insisted on my order, so I took some crackers and cider; but I never saw my friend again. Thus it seemed to me that great and wondrous were the mysterious providences of the Lord, for I had landed in San Francisco on the 8th of January, 1853, and by the 26th I had seventy-five dollars handed to me, much of it by entire strangers whom I had never seen before, nor have I seen them since. It seems mysterious to me how my way opened up and my necessities were met.

The Elders outward bound treated me very kindly.

They fitted themselves out for their several destinations, paid their passage, and then had some fifteen hundred dollars to send to their families, with their photographs and some small parcels, all of which they entrusted to me, with three small trunks, to take to San Bernardino. Of the money seven hundred and fifty dollars in gold was put into a belt and girded around my body; the balance was in drafts or checks.

In the meantime, some of the Elders had met with Mr. Holliday, overland mail contractor. As he had not perfected his arrangements for regular mail service, he made some inquiries of the Elders about sending mail sacks by chance carrier to Los Angeles. They referred him to me, as they thought there would be something in it for me. He called, and I agreed to take charge of three sacks if he would deliver them on the steamer *Sea Bird*, on the morning of the 29th. On that date he sent the sacks just as we were putting off. He told me the pay would be all right when the sacks were delivered.

I had paid thirty-five dollars for my passage to San Pedro, and we steamed out. On the morning of the 30th we landed at Monterey, and lay there till 4 p. m. During that time I had a severe chill, followed by a very high fever, which held on till next morning, when a heavier chill came on, like the ague, followed by fever. I had made my bed down on some nail kegs that were on deck; for the boat was so crowded with passengers of all classes that there was no possible chance for comfort. It semed that everyone was seeking his own convenience, regardless of his neighbor.

CHAPTER XXXVII.

ON the voyage down from San Francisco I grew so desperately sick that I lost my reasoning powers, becoming so delirious that afterwards I could only remember removing my coat and vest and turning into bed, on the nail kegs, with my trunks and the mail sacks about me. The next thing that I recall was in the after part of the day, February 1st, 1853, when I began to regain consciousness. There was an old Spanish gentleman and his good old "mahara" (wife) rubbing my hands and feet, while a big crowd of the passengers stood around. My first thought was: What does this mean—who am I—where did I come from—where am I going—how did I come here, and why are these strangers so interested in me as to be rubbing my hands? The next thing, the old gentleman brought me some refreshments, with a cup of coffee; and when I finally returned to consciousness I inquired what had been the matter. I was told that I had been a very sick man, but was much better, and would soon be well. When the crowd were satisfied that the worst was past they dispersed, but the old gentleman and lady sat near, as if to anticipate any favor I might need. Doubtless the good old couple have been gathered home to their fathers long ere this writing. If so, peace to their ashes; may they in no wise lose their reward, for they administered to the suffering stranger, although they were foreigners, while my own countrymen passed rudely by.

With consciousness returned, I remembered the money that I had in charge. I felt about my body, and to my surprise and mortification the belt was gone. The next thought I had was that I had been robbed by some one on board, and I wondered what could be done to regain the property, or, if it could not be recovered, how could I make amends to the poor women and children whom their husbands and fathers had sent it to? How could I prove my innocence to them? By this time the mental sufferings had overcome the physical pain, and in despair I drew the blankets close about me. In so doing I felt the belt of money lying at my back, under cover. The buckle had been ripped or cut off, most likely the latter, for, as I learned afterwards, in some way it was noised around that I had money.

The reaction of the mental faculties was too much for my weak state, and I almost swooned away; but when I fully recovered from the shock to my nerves, I rolled the belt snugly up, and raised on my knees with my blankets so drawn about my shoulders as to cover the front part of the trunk. Then I placed the belt inside, at the same time taking some article out, so as to divert the observers' attention from my real purpose; I then laid down, suffering with a terrible fever, and put in one night more of great wretch-edness.

About 3 or 4 p. m. next day, February 2nd, we landed at San Pedro. There was a great rush for the shore, and for the four or five vehicles that were in waiting. The most of the passengers seemed to be without baggage, save a roll of blankets or a satchel, and as the the writer had so much and was sick, he was the last person to land. Every vehicle was gone, and all the passengers were out of sight before he got his baggage ashore. When this did come, it was thrown on the beach just above high water mark.

At that early date there was not a hotel, boarding-house, or restaurant anywhere in sight from the landing. One wall of an old adobe warehouse stood near by, and the only thing, for the writer to do was to seek what shelter that wall afforded. Thither he dragged his effects, then dropped down on his bedding exhausted. He lay there until he had excited the curiosity of a Spaniard and his wife who were some distance away. They came down and asked what was the matter, and as I did not know, I could not tell them. They saw that my face was swollen and they seemed afraid to come close, but inquired what I wished, and if they could do anything for me. I asked for milk and bread, which they supplied, and left me to my fate for the night.

The experiences of that terrible night baffle the writ-er's powers of description. Suffice it to say, he passed it alone, with the heavy mist of the briny deep resting upon him, while the fever and thirst seemed to be consuming his body.

At last the morning light came through a dense fog; but by 8 or 9 o'clock that had partly passed away. Some freight teams came down from Los Angeles, and the sufferer felt somewhat encouraged to think there was a prospect of his reaching civilization at the place where he had helped to rear the first liberty pole which was to bear aloft the Stars and Stripes on the Pacific coast. He accosted the freighters, feeling assured that he would not be denied a passage, as he was prepared to pay for this accommodation. The first man said no; he had all that he could haul. The second teamster said no, he was not doing a passenger business. The third said, "I don't know. It is too d—d bad to leave you here sick. I guess I can take you. Throw on your things if you can, and hurry about it." When the writer made an effort to do as invited, the freighter lent him a hand, and when the baggage was aboard the teamster said, "Come, get on here. It's a poor place for a sick man, away up on a goods box, among the bows, but it's your only chance with me. Up there!" and away we went on our journey twenty-one miles to Los Angeles, where we arrived about 8 p. m.

Near the center of the city, on the sidewalk at a street corner, my effects were dumped. I wandered around to find shelter, and at last reached Jesse D. Hunter's place. Hunter had been captain of Company B in the Mormon Battalion, and I thought I could do no better than stop with him, though I did not meet anything very inviting. I was coldly granted the privilege of dragging my blankets into the kitchen, and of bunking down on the dirt floor, after a light supper of bread and milk, the first food I had had since the night before. But I was too ill to do better, and Mr. Hunter was so cool and indifferent that I was glad to leave his place next morning without any further accommodations.

I started out alone, and turned so sick and dizzy that I had to lie down in the street on my blankets. While there I was approached by Daniel Clark and James Bailey from San Bernardino. They asked if my name was Brown, and if I was a returning missionary. I told them yes. They said they had heard of me, and that I had the smallpox, so they had been searching the town for me, and happening to see me lie down in the street, they became satisfied they had found the object of their search. Each of them threw me ten dollars in gold, and went in search of a room or place where I could be cared for. Failing in finding that, they called on the mayor, who started the marshal out to hunt a place. When Clark and Bailey had done all they could—and they were as kind as they could be—they had the mail sacks delivered, but did not find the pay that was to be all right on delivery. Then they went home to San Bernardino, while I did the best I could to find shelter, but my face was so terribly swollen that every door was shut against me; and when the news spread that there was a man around the streets with the smallpox, I could have the sidewalk to myself wherever I went.

At last I found Dr. Jones' office open, but dark and with no one in it. I dragged my bedding through the office to the bedroom, where I spread my blankets and turned in, leaving the door open and lights burning. When anyone came to the door I would shout "Smallpox!" and it was amusing to hear the people run.

About 11 p. m. the doctor came, and I shouted "Smallpox!" Said he: "Who is here?" I answered, "The man whom you said had the smallpox." He responded, "All right, but I would not have had it happen for five hundred dollars. Be quiet, you have done just right. But how did you get in?"

"Why, the door was open," I replied, and he said: "I never did such a thing before in my life. It must have been done on purpose for you, for it was not fit for you to be out." The doctor then held his breath, stepped in over me, took up his bed, and walked away.

CHAPTER XXXVIII.

CITY MARSHAL AND DOCTOR COME TO REMOVE ME—TAKEN TO A
DESERTED HOUSE, WHICH HAD BEEN USED AS A SHEEPFOLD
—BEDDED IN SHEEP MANURE—AN INDIAN NURSE WHO BECOMES
FRIGHTENED—SPANISH NURSE SENT TO ME—IN A BOAT WITH
PATIENT JOB—MY FEVER INCREASES—ATTACKED BY ROBBERS
—RELIEVED BY CITY MARSHAL WITH POSSE—MARSHAL TAKES
THE MONEY I HAVE IN MY CARE, FOR SAFE KEEPING—SPANISH
NURSE SCARED OFF—QUEER SAILOR NURSE—HE DRINKS WHISKY,
SINGS AND DANCES—HIS THOUGHTFUL CARE OF ME—VISITED BY
MY COUSIN—KINDNESS OF SAN BERNARDINO SAINTS—RECOVER-
ING FROM MY ILLNESS—MY CLOTHING BURNED—HEAVY EX-
PENSE BILL AGAINST ME—TELL THE CITY MARSHAL OF MY
ARRIVAL IN CALIFORNIA AS A UNITED STATES SOLDIER IN THE
MEXICAN WAR—KINDNESS OF THE MARSHAL—LOS ANGELES
ASSUMES THE BILL FOR MEDICAL ATTENTION GIVEN ME—START
FOR SAN BERNARDINO—EXHAUSTED ON THE JOURNEY—ALMOST
DIE OF THIRST—RELIEVED BY A PARTY OF SPANISH LADIES
—KINDNESS OF SPANISH FAMILIES—ARRIVE AT SAN BERNARDINO
AND MEET FRIENDS AND RELATIVES.

EARLY next morning, the marshal and doctor were
there with suitable refreshments, and when the patient had made a feint at eating they told him they had
secured a room if he could put up with it. Sheep had been
kept in it, and it was smoked very black, but they assured
him that the conditions were favorable to recovery from the
disease. Then they took him by his arms and assisted him
into an old cart that they had standing at the door; they had
an Indian to lead the horse.

The patient could not see a particle only as he held his
eyes open with his fingers. He told them of his trunk, which
had been left all this time where the freighter had dumped
it when the writer came into town. The trunk was brought,
and the Indian led out, the marshal and doctor bringing up
the rear.

When we passed the suburbs, we turned to the right, to an old deserted adobe house of two rooms. The front yard had been used as a sheepfold. The doors had been broken down, and the sheep had had free access to the rooms, until the sheep manure was some five or six inches deep on the dirt floor. The rooms were very poorly lighted at best; and to add to the darkness, the sheepherders had camped in them till the whole of the inside of the rooms was smoked as black as a stove. The doctor said it was the best they could do, adding: "It is too d——d bad to put you in such a place, but if you will put up with it, it will be the very best thing for you in the end. The sheepy smell, and the darkness, with some ointment that I will give you, will prevent your being marked; whereas, if you were kept in a light, clean room, you have got the disease so bad that you would be marked all over. Then again you have been so badly exposed that you must put up with the treatment in order to recover properly, lest something else follows."

I told him that my condition was such that I was compelled to submit to any treatment they saw fit to give. Then they got some tools, removed the dry, hard packed manure, and placed my mattress down on the dirt floor, so that when the covering was spread ready for me it was just level with the manure on the front, the foot, head and back being against the walls.

Having turned in, I opened my eyes with my fingers, and found myself in twilight, with an Indian man for a nurse. The marshal and doctor left, saying that I should be cared for. Then the nurse went off, and soon returned with a custard in a coffee basin; this he said was worth fifty cents. He brought it, and an iron spoon to eat the custard, but when I opened my eyes in such an unnatural way, they appeared so badly bloodshot that the nurse took fright and ran away, leaving me to my fate until 5 or 6 o'clock p. m.

Then an old Spaniard, who was very badly pox-marked, came and said he had been engaged as a nurse, as the Indian was so frightened at the disease that he would not return. The Spaniard seemed to comprehend the conditions. He got a Spanish roll of bread and a pint of milk for fifty cents, then straightened up the bed and left for the night. Next morning he was on hand to attend to my wants.

This was on February 6, 1853. The smallpox began to appear in pustules, or rather boils; for it so resembled the latter that I began to think of patient old Job. I was sore from the crown of my head to the soles of my feet, and yet it was only blisters that day, comparatively speaking.

The Spanish nurse seemed to understand his business, for as I would roll and toss, the old gentleman would tuck the bedclothes about me, saying, "Must not let the air to you. Must keep warm, and have warm drink, and have the bowels moderately easy." Then he would apply the ointment, and be as cheerful as possible, doing all that he could to divert my mind from my sufferings.

Night came on and the blisters enlarged; I became very sick at the stomach, and the kind old nurse stayed by me till daylight on the 7th. The fever still raged fiercely Night again came, and the nurse got alarmed at seeing some six or seven rough men, armed, approaching the house. He hastily gathered his arms full of cobblestones, ran in and piled them on the edge of the bed, and cried out, "Can you fight? The robbers are coming. Murder! murder!" At that I raised in bed, opened my eyes in the new way, and took up a cobble rock, the nurse standing by the bed shouting "Murder!"

The next moment three ruffians appeared at the partition door, in the house, while another presented himself at the window, near the head of the bed. So far as I could see, they were armed with revolvers and bowie knives.

There must have been two or three men at the outside door.

The shock came so suddenly that I had no time to get thoroughly scared until I heard men running around the northwest corner of the house. The latter noise was by the marshal and a posse which he had summoned hastily, for a party had been in the saloon and had heard the ruffians say, "Let's go and rob that man who has got the smallpox, for he has got money." It must be that some of the party had been the ones who had ripped the belt off of me while on shipboard, where they had been disturbed before they had time to slip it away. Thus they had learned about the money, and when they got to drinking and gambling, they probably had decided on robbing the smallpox man to make a raise, but had talked too loud for the success of their plan. The marshal acted so promptly that they were foiled in their plot, for when they heard him and his posse coming, and the nurse shouting "Murder!" they fled to the southeast and passed over into a dark, deep, brushy ravine, out of sight, just as the marshal and party gained the south side of the building. The officer said he saw them, but had not time to shoot before they disappeared in the brush and darkness.

The marshal came into the house and informed me of the plot and how he came to hear of it. He said, "Now, if you have any money or valuable papers, you had better send for some trusty friend to come and take care of them. I will send for anyone that you will name." I told him I did not know of a better friend than the one who had come to my relief, and if he, the marshal, would take care of the valuables, I would be much obliged. He said he would take charge of them and have them deposited for safekeeping till I wanted them. I then handed out my memorandum book, with the names of the men who sent the money, the amounts, and the names of those to whom it was sent.

Then, my eyes being propped open, I poured the money on to a handkerchief they had spread over my lap. As the money was mostly in gold ten and twenty dollar pieces, in fifty dollar packages, it was easily and quickly counted, and found to tally with the memoranda. Then the drafts and checks were counted, and all put together in the belt—some fifteen hundred dollars—and handed over to the marshal, with Dr. Jones as witness.

When the gold was being counted out, some of the would-be robbers appeared at the window, and doubtless saw that the marshal was taking charge of the valuables, by which action their plot fell through, and I was not troubled any more. But the experience was enough for the Spanish nurse, for the robbers undoubtedly were Spaniards or "greasers," and if they could take revenge on him they would do it. Some of the marshal's posse stayed till they felt satisfied the danger was all over, then they, with the nurse, left, and next day sent to me an old badly pox-marked sailor for an attendant. He came in with a bottle of whisky that he said was a hundred years old.

The first thing the new nurse said was, "Hello, old chum! What are you doing there? Come, and have a drink with me." The next breath he said, "No, no, for I know it would not do for you. I will drink for you. So here goes." He then took a liberal draught, and wanted to know what he could do for my comfort. On being told there was nothing I wanted just then, he said, "Let me sing you a song," and he sang a very comical ditty. Then he said, "I'll dance a jig for you," and at it he went. In the performance ·he kicked the dry manure pretty nearly all over me and my bed, for he was "three sheets in the wind and the fourth fluttering" (three-fourths drunk, or more.)

When he saw what he had done, he dropped on his knees and begged pardon, making the most humble apology. Said he, "Never mind, old chum, just lay over to starboard, and I will make it all right." He brushed and brushed away, then said, "Now to larboard, and I will fix you all right." So he pounded away, talking all the time in his sailor phrases. Finally he partially sobered up, and it would have been hard to find a more thoughtful and attentive nurse. From that time on he stayed with me, told many interesting sea stories, and sang love songs.

On February 10th my cousin, John M. Brown, who was passing through that part of the country, came to the door and called. "Is that you, James?" At the same time he threw a ten dollar gold piece on the bed; but not having had the smallpox, he dare not come in. We had not met before in eight years. At that date I was suffering intensely, if not the worst that I had done, for I was down so weak that I could not help myself at all.

On the 11th, W. G. Sherwood, of San Bernardino, came in, saying that the Saints had raised some money for me, and had sent him to take care of me until I was able to come out to them. Brothers D. Clark and J. Bailey had told President Seeley of my condition. I felt indeed very thankful for the favors shown me.

On the 14th the smallpox had nearly died away, and by the 19th I was considered out of all danger, with prudence. On the 20th, the doctor and marshal came and ordered all of my bedding and a good suit of clothes that I had on when taken down, boots, hat, and all, piled in the yard, and there burned. They said my expenses had been five dollars per day for the house, because of the disease and being close to where the landlord and his family lived. The nurses also had to be paid the same amount per day. I told them I had been out on a long mission at my own expense, and now had so little money that it would cost me every dollar that I had to meet the loss of my clothes and bedding, so it was impossible for me to settle such a bill, one hundred and forty dollars. I had paid for every article

I had used except a little medicine the doctor had furnished.

The marshal and doctor said they understood that I had come into the country as a soldier in the time of the Mexican war. I told them that I had helped to build the fort that overlooked the town, and that I went to San Bernardino canyon and helped get down the first liberty pole that ever bore the Stars and Stripes on this western coast. At this they asked a number of questions, as if to satisfy themselves whether or not I had told them the truth, and when they became convinced the marshal said: "Mr. Brown, do not make any trouble, for we will see that you do not have to pay that bill; you are worthy of all the care that you have had, and more too. Los Angeles will pay that, and you are free to go on your way. We are pleased to have made your acquaintance, and that you have recovered so well; for your case has been a very remarkable one, to have had the disease so badly and after being exposed as you were, to have recovered so soon, with scarce a mark left on you. It has been a most wonderful case, and we congratulate you on your safe recovery, and wish you success on your journey to Salt Lake." Of course I could not feel otherwise than very grateful to those two gentlemen for their kind attention and largeness of soul. Then we bade each other good-bye and I am not conscious that we have ever met since that day.

Brother Sherwood and I stored my trunk, put our other effects on his poor old stallion, went down town and got my money and some provisions and a bottle of old whisky, and were amused to see so many people run from the smallpox, while others stood afar off and gazed. Finally, on February 21st, we set out for San Bernardino, eighty miles, on foot, one leading and the other punching the old horse, which was so weak that he stumbled wherever the road was a little rough. We only got ten miles that day.

On the 22nd we proceeded on our journey another ten miles, when it was impossible for me to go any further. I was thoroughly exhausted, and had to lie down or drop. We were ten miles from water, and so thirsty that it seemed that I must die on that arid plain.   Brother Sherwood, however, proved equal to the emergency.   He got me on to a pair of blankets, led the old horse up so as to cast a shadow over me, then hastened to soak a piece of bread in some old whisky.   He gave me the bread, saying it would slake my thirst, and stimulate me.   Strange as it seemed to me, it did so, and in a short time I was able to rise alone, and sit up.

We had not been there a great while when we saw a party of Spanish ladies coming in on another road, that appeared to unite with the one we were on; so by an effort we gained the junction just as they did.   They stopped their cart, and asked if we would have some wine.   We said we preferred water, and they gave us both.   Seeing that I was very ill, they invited me to ride with them, making room so that I had a place between the two on the front seat and rested my head and shoulders on the laps of the two on the rear seat, while they bathed my head with water, and urged me to take a little more wine.   It did seem that if it had not been for this most unexpected kindness I should have died of thirst and exhaustion before we could have reached any other source of support.

Brother Sherwood followed in the rear to where the ladies lived, but before he came up I was helped on to a bed in a cool room, and had some refreshments, with a cup of chocolate.   Oh, how thankful I was to those blessed Spanish "senoritas!"   When their husbands came in, they shook hands and seemed to be pleased that their wives had dealt so kindly with the strange American.   Brother Sherwood soon arrived, and they unpacked his horse and took care of it, while the women supplied him with water to bathe his hands and face, and with refreshments.   Then he and I retired early.

Next morning, February 23, we were served with chocolate and tortias (pancakes) before we were out of bed. Our hosts had only a humble home, but so kind were they in their attentions to us that it aroused suspicions of a large bill to pay, but when we asked them the amount they shrugged their shoulders Spanish fashion, and with a pleasant smile said, in Spanish, "Nothing; friendship; no more." As we bade them good-bye they said they would be pleased for me to allow them to have the little smallpox scab that was on my nose, if we thought it would not leave a mark, so they and Brother Sherwood removed it, and thought it would not leave any pit; therefore I allowed him to remove it and leave it with them.   Still it did leave its mark till this day.

We proceeded on to a ranch where we met with a fourth cousin of mine, John Garner, who kindly offered me a seat in his wagon.   He was loaded and could not start till late, but we could reach his place before midnight, and Brother Sherwood could push on; for when we started Sherwood would not be able to keep up.   I accepted his proposition, and we reached his home at 11 o'clock p. m.

On the 24th I went to what they called at that time, I believe, Fort San Bernardino.   There I found many warm-hearted friends, and a number of relatives, among them John M. and Alexander Brown, my cousins.   I made my home with the latter, who, with his wife, was very kind to me.   I also visited many old acquaintances.   My trunk I sent for by Sidney Tanner, and he brought it from Los Angeles free of charge.

CHAPTER XXXIX.

ON February 27th, I was called on by President Seeley of the branch of the Church at San Bernardino, to give a report of my mission, and I did so before the congregation. On March 9th, I prepared to come home with John and Alexander Brown, to Salt Lake City, but for some reason they gave up the idea of traveling at that time, and I had to await another opportunity. Then we looked about the country, thinking that we would make some improvements, if we did not meet with a better chance to come to Utah.

About this time there was a great amount of sickness in the place, and Elder Thomas Whitaker, from the islands, and I had numerous calls to administer to the sick. Many seemed to be possessed of evil spirits; certainly, if they had lived in Mary Magdalene's day it would have been said of them that they had seven devils in them; for the actions were the same as in those days, and the evil spirits would not come out except through fasting and prayer. Consequently, President Seeley ordered a fast and a prayer meeting for the Saints. It was very well attended, and good results followed. Many people were healed of the diseases afflicting them. One incident I will mention: There lived in the town a man named John Brown; he had a Spanish wife and one or two children. One evening, Major Jefferson Hunt's wife called on me to come as quickly as possible, for Mr. Brown's child looked as if it were dying. I went in, and found the mother and child in bed together. The little one acted as if it were choking to death, and was fighting for breath; it gnashed its teeth and frothed at the mouth. I anointed it with consecrated oil, and as there was no other Elder handy I administered to the child, when every symptom of its trouble left it immediately, but seized on the mother. She raved, frothed and foamed at the mouth, gnashed her teeth, cramped, and seemed so ill that she could not live five minutes. Sister Hunt anointed her with oil, and I administered to her. She was healed that moment. An Indian woman was sitting there sewing, and the same power that had afflicted the child and its mother took hold of the Indian woman. By this time another sister had stepped in, and she and Sister Hunt raised the Indian woman up, for she had fallen over. They called on me to lay hands on her, but I did not feel to do so at once. I told them to wet her face and rub her hands. They did so, and she grew worse every minute, until I administered to her, by laying my hands upon her and praying, rebuking the evil spirits, commanding them in the name of the Lord to come out of her and to depart from her and from that house, and from the houses and homes of the Saints, and to get hence to their own home, and trouble us no more. That moment the evil spirits left, and did not return again. The three persons who were afflicted were perfectly well next morning, and I never heard of their being afflicted afterwards.

There had been a number of cases where persons had been similarly affected, and some of them were not healed until they had been baptized seven times in succession, when tney were permanently cured. Indeed, there were very many remarkable cases of healing in San Bernardino about that time.

On April 15th, my cousin, John M. Brown, learned that a man named Lamper was going to start with the mail to Salt Lake City, and had only four men with him. As that was too small a number to be safe, it was ascertained that if he could have three or four more he would like it very much. He told John M. Brown that if he would raise two or three other men, he would wait at the mouth of the Cajon Pass for them.

As my cousin had never had any experience with pack animals, he told me that if I would go with him and help with the stock and packs, for that service he would furnish everything needed en route, he knowing that I had had experience in that line, and in the handling of wild horses and mules.

I accepted the offer, so we made ready, and were off on the 19th of April. We overtook the party in waiting at the place agreed upon. The animal provided for my saddle mule was wild, large and strong, and given to jumping stiff-legged, or bucking, as it is called. It was a hard animal to handle, and was successful in dumping its rider three times in the fore part of the journey, to the amusement of his five comrades. We had nineteen head of animals, and traveled at the rate of fifty miles per day, for the first half of the journey, because our route led us through a hostile Indian country.

We stood regular turns of guard, and all went well till the last day before we came to the Muddy. That day we saw danger signs, of Indians. I will say now, my friendly reader, if ever you travel in an Indian country, and come to fresh Indian tracks, yet do not see an Indian, then you may be sure that some red man wants a few horses and some plunder, if, indeed, he does not want a scalp or two to hang to his bridle-bit or surcingle. That was our danger sign, plenty of fresh Indian tracks, where they had rolled large boulders into the narrow passes in the road, or gorges where the road passed through. This satisfied us that we were in danger of an unpleasant surprise, so we examined every firelock, made sure there was powder in every tube, good waterproof caps on, ammunition handy, packs securely bound, saddles well girt, and every man prepared to act promptly in case of an attack.

At this time we were crossing from the Las Vegas to the Muddy. I think the distance without water was sixty-five miles, so there was no alternative for us but to press forward to the Muddy River, were we arrived in safety about 4 a. m., watered our stock, and got a hasty meal, giving our animals a very short time for rest and to feed.

At daylight we began to saddle up for another start. Just as we were ready to mount, a large, stout Indian raised up out of the willows within bow-shot, and hallooed. He had his bows and arrows in hand. At that my cousin John leveled his gun on the red man, when I seized it and forbade anyone to shoot, as others of the party had made ready for the worst. At that moment the Indian held out his hand and came toward us, as if to shake hands. Every man of the party but myself was ready and anxious to open fire on the Indian, but I stood between him and them until they had mounted. I told them if there was one shot fired every one of us would be killed. The Indian said to me that he wished to be friendly. Then I mounted and the party started, and at the same time twenty-five or thirty Indians, all well armed, raised up out of the brush within easy pistol range. My party again drew their guns, when I told them to hold on, for the Indians were friendly, and their object was merely to beg some food; but some of my party were hard to control.

As my companions trotted up, I fell back with the Indians, who talked, and I began to understand them, although I had not been among them one day. It was given me to understand them, and I told my companions that I did so. I told them further, that I would stand between them and the Indians, if they would not shoot. One said, "How do you know that they are friendly if you have never been among them before? They are following us up. Send them away, if you know so much about their friendship."

The Indians told me that when the sun got to such a position, pointing to where it would be at about 9 o'clock a. m., we would come to a large camp of Mormons and non-Mormons, with their families; that they had horses, mules and horned stock, and wagons, also some sheep and goats. There was a lot of Mexicans camped with them, and these had pack-mules. This, and more, was told me in the Indian dialect, and was as plain to my understanding as if it had been spoken in my native tongue; yet my party were slow to believe, and some of them cursed the Indians, saying that if the black rascals were friendly, why did they not go back, instead of following us up. Being fearful that our party could not be restrained much longer, I halted and talked with the Indians, telling them I was afraid my friends would shoot them unless they fell back, and ceased to follow up so closely. The Indians replied that I would soon learn that what they had said was true, as they did not talk two ways.

Just then we saw a Mexican come dashing down the hillside towards us. When he came to us and shook hands, then confirmed what the Indians had told me, my cousin John said, "I believe Jim does understand the Indians, for he understands the Spanish language, and the Spaniards have told him just what the Indians have said. I believe he is half Indian, or he would not be so friendly with and understand them so well."

Soon we came to a raise, from which we could see the camps, just as they had been described to us minutely in the morning, by the Indians, who followed us up to the camps, and with pride pointed out to us everything they had spoken of, saying, "We do not lie." I believe that our party had become satisfied that the Indians had made the signs seen on the road the day before, and then had laid in ambush to intimidate us, that they might get something to eat, for they were very closely run for food; again, it may have been that they meant more serious things and were deterred therefrom by learning of the approach of the company we found in camp.

At any rate we felt safer to lay by with the camp one day, and rest ourselves and stock; then we proceeded over a big dry bench to the Rio Virgen, then up that river and across another high plateau to Beaver Dam. From there we crossed another high rolling country of some forty miles or more, to Santa Clara. When we got half way across we saw a signal smoke, apparently on the Santa Clara where the road comes to that stream, or perhaps a little above. Feeling conscious of our weakness, we watched the smoke with no little concern, and as I had had considerably more acquaintance with the red men than any others of the party, I told them that from the way the fire was managed there was mischief ahead, and we must prepare for the worst.   Our animals were thirsty and well jaded, yet there was no choice for us but to brave the danger ahead.   Then the examination of firelocks and the cinching of saddles was in order.   That matter, however, was delayed so long as we felt safe.

When the preparation was made, and the smoke had grown denser, we advanced and saw that the streak of fire was in the narrows of the canyon.   It extended from cliff to cliff, and evidently was made in a scheme of plunder or massacre, most likely both.   Under the circumstances, we were compelled to run the gauntlet, so it was hastily decided for me to lead the way, I agreeing to do this if the party would obey my orders, and not fire until I did, or gave the command to them.   If I gave the warwhoop they were to do the same.   The first order was to draw weapons for action, then charge with all possible speed.   Away we went, and as we neared the flames we chose the most open spot, or that which seemed freest of fire.   Although there was a continuous stream of flames clear across the canyon, some places were freer than others.   We chose the place where the least fire was, the flames there being not more than two or two and a half feet high.   If the timber in the canyon had been larger, it might have afforded the Indians a better opportunity, but instead of secreting themselves in the bottom of the ravine, they had chosen the cliffs on either side.

Just before we reached the fire, we urged our animals up to the best speed, and, raising as big a warwhoop as we were capable of, and brandishing our firearms in the most threatening manner, we dashed through.   At the same time, the Indians showed themselves in the cliffs with drawn bows, trying to take aim through the timber.   They answered our whoop or yell, and gave chase, but they being on foot, and our animals having become thoroughly frightened at the sudden change that had taken place and with the evergoading spurs of their riders, rushed on ahead. Though very thirsty, our animals never attempted to drink, although we crossed the stream a number of times. For fully five miles we never slackened our speed, the Indians keeping in sight of us for fully that distance, when they gave up the chase. Then our stock and ourselves quenched our thirst, and we continued on at as good a speed as was consistent with our conditions. Finally we met Apostles Amasa M. Lyman and C. C. Rich, with two or three wagons and twelve or fourteen men, mostly mounted. As it was camp time, we made a joint camp, and had no more trouble. If an arrow had been shot at us, we did not know it, though there may have been a hundred or more. We did not think it advisable to try to ascertain, as we felt that our scalps were more precious than this information, or than money or horseflesh. It was distance between us and the scalping-knife of the red men that we were hunting for just then.

We stood double guard that night, and all passed off peacefully. Next morning, each party proceeded on its way in peace, we to Cedar Fort, or city, where we arrived May 5th, and met with many friends. We attended meeting with the people, I was called on to give an account of my mission, and did so.

On May 6th, we proceeded to Parowan, and as it was considered safe from there on, my counsin John M. Brown and I stopped there with friends we had not seen for years. The rest of the party, having the mail in charge, went ahead, and we tarried one week, being royally treated. I preached two or three times. We resumed the journey on the 15th. In passing along, I preached in most of the towns where we stayed over night.

When we came to Lehi, I commenced to settle with the people whom I had money for, then went on to Little

Cottonwood and settled with more, then to Big Cottonwood, where I found still others for whom I had money.

On May 22nd we arrived in Salt Lake City, and stopped with our uncle, Alexander Stephens. On the 23rd, I called at President Brigham Young's office and reported myself and mission. He received me very kindly, and welcomed me home again. I also met Brothers H. C. Kimball and Jedediah M. Grant, a number of the Twelve Apostles, and other prominent men. All were very courteous, and expressed pleasure at my safe return.

On the 24th and 25th, I called and settled with all I had money, checks, or drafts for, and I found them all well, and much pleased to get the needed relief, financially. On the 26th, as I desired to go to Ogden City, I called at President Young's office to bid him good-bye. He kindly invited me to come to the stand in the Tabernacle on June 7th, to preach. I did so, though it delayed me in my intended visit to my friends and relatives in Ogden City. When I filled that call, I was honorably released from further labors in the missionary field at that time. My mission had occupied three years and eight months, and cost me every dollar that I had when I started out. I was then worth fifteen hundred dollars in good property, which I spent; but I never regretted it. The experience that I had gained I counted worth much more than the money expended.

CHAPTER XL.

ON June 9, 1853, I started to Ogden City, afoot and alone. On the 10th, I paid out the last quarter of a dollar that I had to the ferryman, to set me across the Weber River, at East Weber. From there I crossed the hills to my Uncle John Stephens', and found him and his family well and pleased to see me. I reciprocated the pleasure, had dinner and a short visit, then went on to Ogden City, where I again met with Cousin John M. Brown and his father's family, and our two aunts, Polly and Nancy Brown; as also more relatives and former friends, all of whom treated me with much kindness, and as if the lost had been found.

The first Sabbath after my arrival in Ogden, I was called on to give a report of my mission, and to preach. By doing this, there was a great spirit of inquiry excited about the Society Islands and their inhabitants. I found that scarce one in a thousand of the people had the remotest idea of affairs on the islands I had been to. The questions asked and the answers given were about like this:

Q.   Where are the islands?

A.   In the South Pacific Ocean.

Q.   What are they like?

A.   The spur of a mountain in a vast plain.

Q.   What are the chief products?

A.   Cocoanuts, oranges, lemons, limes, citrus fruits, arrowroot, sweet potatoes or yams (a species of potato that takes about eighteen months to mature), coffee, cotton, chili pepper, corn, rice, tobacco, sugarcane; a root called taro grows in the swamps and somewhat resembles the Indian turnip that grows in the Middle States, and on the islands is cultivated for food, being one of the most staple products; breadfruit grows in great abundance; there is a fruit called viapple and another called doava, neither of which is of much importance. There are also pineapples, bananas, and a fruit called feii which grows on a plant like the banana, and is one of the best and most generally used fruits there.

Q.   Is the soil rich?

A.   Yes; but this is limited to small strips along the coasts and the water courses.

Q.   What kind of a climate is it?

A.   Very hot. Papeete, the capital of Tahiti, is in seventeen degrees thirty-two minutes south latitude, and one hundred and forty-four degrees thirty-four minutes west longitude, computed from Greenwich, and if it were not for the frequent rains, southerly breezes, and the constant trade winds, it would be almost impossible for human beings to live there.

Q. What kinds of timber grow there?

A. Various kinds of scrubby timber not known in our country, chief of which is hutu or tamana, an excellent timber for shipbuilding, and for fine furniture; there is also sandal wood, the heart being of great value, as it is used for perfume, and decorating musical instruments, work-boxes, etc.

Q. Having given a brief description of the islands composing the Society group, the Tubuoi and Tubuoimono archipelago, and of their principal products, the next question was: What kind of people inhabit them?

A. They are very large in stature, are brave, and formerly were very warlike. Their complexion is like that of the American Indian, and their habits are much the same. They are hospitable to a fault. In their heathenish days, they were idol-worshipers and very devout. Originally, their government was patriarchal, but as they increased it became tribal, then confederate. A district of country called monteina would combine for war purposes, and finally would become a monarchy. Thus they had their kings and queens, and began to have royalty. As to other matters, there are no native animals, but of fowls there are such as sea birds, and the common wild duck; also of reptiles, a small, harmless, greenish lizard. The greatest insect pests are the nimble flea and the common mosquito, in numberless quantities. Many years ago the people had the smallpox, and as it was a strange disease to them, and they were without the knowledge of how to treat it, they died by hundreds, if not by thousands. As soon as they learned that it was contagious, the people fled to the mountains, and there hid away until their swine and chickens went wild, in which state these increased, producing the wild boar and wild chickens, which are frequently

A TYPICAL TAHITIAN WITH HIS BURDEN OF BREAD FRUIT AND FEII.

hunted by the people, and which, but for the rugged fastnesses of the mountains, soon would become extinct.

I will leave that subject now and return to my own experiences after getting home. I turned my hand to farm labor, and anything I could get to do until the 6th of September. Then Major Moore, having received orders from Governor Young to raise a company of men and send them north to Fort Hall, to protect or assist a company there on some business, called me to take charge of that company. When we were within three hours of starting, the order to go was countermanded, and I continued to work for two dollars per day until the 8th of October, when, at a general conference, I was called, with several others, to take a mission to the Indian tribes east of the Salt Lake valley.

Elder Orson Hyde was chosen to lead the company to somewhere in the region of the Green River, select a place, and there build an outpost from which to operate as peacemakers among the Indians, to preach civilization to them, to try and teach them how to cultivate the soil, to instruct them in the arts and sciences if possible, and by that means prevent trouble for our frontier settlements and emigrant companies. We were to identify our interests with theirs, even to marrying among them, if we would be permitted to take the young daughters of the chief and leading men, and have them dressed like civilized people, and educated. It was thought that by forming that kind of an alliance we could have more power to do them good, and keep peace among the adjacent tribes as also with our own people.

It was known that there were wicked and cruel white men among the Indians, working up the spirit of robbery and murder among the savage tribes, and against the Mormon people. Our missionary call was to take our lives in our hands, as true patriots, and head off, and operate as far as possible against the wicked plots of white men who were trying to carry their plans to success through the Indians, and possibly set the savages on the war path, that the government might send troops out, and thus make a better market for the schemers' herds of cattle and horses.

From the October conference I returned to Ogden City, settled what little business I had, and prepared for the mission, going to Salt Lake City on the 18th, ready for the work assigned me. There I reported myself, but the majority of the men who had been called at the same time that I was were not ready until the 1st of November, when we met in the Council House, and there effected an organization.

It was in the evening, about 8 o'clock, when we met. There were thirty-nine men who reported themselves ready to start next morning, November 2nd. Elders Orson Hyde, Parley P. Pratt and Ezra T. Benson, of the Twelve Apostles, were present, and organized the company by appointing Elders John Nebeker president and captain, John Harvey first counselor and lieutenant and James S. Brown second counselor and lieutenant. The captain and lieutenants were so that we might act in a military capacity if necessity required it, and the president and counselors were for ecclesiastical affairs. The officers were blessed and set apart by the three Apostles named. The Apostles told the members of the company that they would be blessed equally with the officers if they would be prayerful, do their duty, and hearken to and be united with their officers. We were also told that some of us might have to take Indian wives.

On November 2nd twenty wagons, with one hundred and ten head of cattle, horses and mules, were ready for a start. To each man there was three hundred pounds of flour, seventy-five pounds of seed wheat, and forty pounds of seed potatoes. Each man fitted himself up with such other provisions and seed as he chose or could do. We

started out at 1 o'clock p. m., and that night camped in
Emigration Canyon.

We crossed the Little Mountain on November 3rd.
Having to double teams, we made slow headway, and only
got to within four miles of the Big Mountain. On the 5th,
we crossed that, and camped at its eastern base. The road
was very bad, so that we made but few miles on the 6th,
and camped in the foothills, where our stock was attacked
about 3 o'clock a. m. by a pack of big gray wolves, which
were so savage that every man had to be called out to fight
them. The night was very dark, and we fired guns, built
fires in a circle around the stock, and stayed with them till
daylight. Yet, with all that, some of the milch cows had
part of their udders torn off, while others were badly
gashed as by a sharp knife. By hard work we succeeded
in preventing the wolves killing any of our animals, and
then got an early start on the morning of the 7th.

As we were heavily loaded, and the roads very rough,
we did not reach Fort Bridger until November 15th. At
that place there were twelve or fifteen rough mountain
men. They seemed to be very surly and suspicious of us,
and the spirit of murder and death appeared to be lurking in
their minds. Many of our party could feel that terrible
influence and made remarks about it. It was not long till
we were informed by some of the party at the fort that
two men there had fought a duel the night before with
butcher knives, and both were killed. The others of the
party had dug a hole and had thrown both men into it as
they had fallen and died—clasped in each other's arms.
Thus the gloom and cloud of death that we had felt so
plainly was partially explained. We passed one and a half
miles above the fort, and camped on Black's Fork. That
night it snowed about six inches.

We learned from the men at Fort Bridger that fifteen
or twenty mountain men had moved over on to Henry's

Fork, and that the Ute Indians were coming over there to winter. That was the place we were heading for, and some of the roughest men of the mountains were claiming that as their country. Our information now being that there was a well-organized band of from seventy-five to a hundred desperadoes in the vicinity of Green River, at the very point that we had hoped to occupy with our little company, the situation was serious; and with snow on the ground, to decide what to do was an important matter. We broke camp and passed over the divide to Smith's Fork. There the Spirit seemed to forbid us going any farther, and we held a short consultation, which resulted in the appointment of a committee of five, of which the writer was one.

This committee followed up the creek to a point where the water comes down through the foothills, and there, between the forks of the stream, selected a spot for winter quarters, and to build a blockhouse. Then they returned and made their report, which was accepted by the captain and his men. The camp was moved to the chosen ground on November 27th. We at once pitted our potatoes, the committee named being retained to draft and superintend the erection of the blockhouse. The writer made the plans of the blockhouse, which was built with four wings, or rooms, of equal size; these, uniting at the corners, formed a center room, which was built two stories high. All the rooms were provided with port holes, the center being used for storage, and the upper for a guardhouse, from which the country around could be overlooked. The plan being accepted, every man went to work with a will, and in two weeks the house was ready for occupancy. This was not an hour too soon, for the weather was very cold and threatening.

On the 26th, Captain Isaac Bullock came in with fifty-three men and twenty-five wagons. When they joined us our company was ninety-two strong, all well armed; and when our blockhouse was completed we felt safer than ever. The work of building was continued until all were comfortably housed in log cabins, and a heavy log corral was constructed for our stock in case of an emergency.

We had not been settled down long, when some of the mountaineers paid us a visit and applauded our energy and enterprise. Notwithstanding that, we could easily discern a feeling of envy on their part. In consequence, we did not feel any too safe, especially when the snow became deep between our friends and ourselves, for we frequently heard that the Ute Indians, then a very warlike and hostile tribe, were threatening to come upon us from the east, by an open country. Under the circumstances, we could see the wisdom of our military organization; and as we had to have a regular guard, we found that we must have a sergeant thereof; accordingly, the author was elected to fill that position, and as we had several beef cattle and other provisions in common, a commissary or quartermaster was necessary, and the sergeant was called to fill that position also. We further perfected our organization by electing a captain for every ten men. We were also instructed to keep our firearms in perfect order, and to have our powder dry, that we might be prepared for any emergency. Thus provided for, we continued to get out fencing timber, and exploring parties were sent out, which acted as scouts, and we learned the resources of the country, and sought out every advantage.

It was on December 8 when Apostle Orson Hyde came into camp. He preached to us that evening, and gave many words of encouragement. On the 9th he examined our work and defenses. He was highly pleased with the country, and applauded our choice of location; in fact, he seemed generally well pleased with what we had done. He preached again, and gave us much cheer and sound instructions. We prepared our mail in answer to the one he had brought us, and on the 10th he set out on his return trip, every one feeling blessed by his visit.

In our religious and social arrangements, we held regular meetings, had lectures on different subjects, organized a debating society, and had readings. On December 26, F. M. Perkins and a party returned from Salt Lake City, bringing much interesting news, and also supplies of food. On the 28th, the weather was so cold that we had to abandon outdoor work.

Wolves became troublesome to our stock, so we put strychnine and set traps for the wild beasts, which killed several head of cattle and one of the strongest horses in our band. The wolves were very numerous, and when they band, as they do sometimes, and did then, it is almost impossible for any kind of stock to escape without some loss. Yet, with rifle, trap and poison, we kept about even with our ravenous enemies.

January 1, 1854, the weather was fine. On the 5th cold and storms came, and we also heard more threatening news from the Ute Indians; but this did not alarm us much, though it prompted us to increased diligence in looking after our stock. There was some dissatisfaction about guard duty, as some thought there was too much of it to suit them, and felt that others should stand two hours to their one; but that was soon settled and we continued our studies in the Shoshone Indian dialect, having Elisha B. Ward, an old mountaineer and trapper, and his Indian wife, Sally, to assist us. Then there was an Indian family of four who got starved out and came to us for help. We took them in, fed them, and gave them a room to themselves. Then Sally's brother, Indian John, and his wife, Madam, came, so that we took them in and fed them. This condition afforded us increased facilities for studying the Shoshone dialect, which we carefully availed ourselves of.

About this time, Louis Tromley, a Frenchman, stabbed Samuel Callwell. The affair took place near Fort Bridger. Callwell was said to be at the head of the gang of desperadoes who plied their vocation from Bridger to Green River, and back on the emigrant route to Laramie; he was a large, trim built man, about six feet six inches tall, and very daring. But after a bowie knife was plunged into his vitals he did not survive long, dying in about twenty-four hours from the time he received the fatal wound. Tromley was one of Callwell's band, and made his escape. It was thought by some that if his victim had lived he would have made trouble for us, but this quarrel gave the gang something else to do.

We continued our labors and studies; yet with all the opportunities at hand, there were only about six of us out of the ninety-two that made even fair progress in learning the Indian tongue. On February 7, we received more mail. About the 22nd we lost many of our cattle from starvation and cold. Deep snows fell, and drifted so that our houses were completely buried, and from the south side we could walk right up on top of our cabins, while on the north the snow drifted to the tops of the doors, and packed so hard in one night that it had to be cut out with the spade, the large chunks being laid back on the floor until we could get out far enough to clear the houses. This condition continued for many days. On March 8, the wind blew fearfully, and the snow drifted so deep that we had to break snow roads, and then drive our poor cattle and horses from point to point where the snow had been blown off, leaving the grass bare. In this way many of our animals were saved.

On the 12th of March, a party of fifteen or twenty Shoshone Indians came and pitched camp close to the blockhouse. They were very hungry, and we divided bread with them, that being the only kind of food we had left; and in turn their presence afforded us better opportunity to study their language and customs, a knowledge of the latter being essential to the successful interpreter. On March 18, more hungry Indians came. They appeared almost starved, and they begged until they became a nuisance; yet we divided with them, and ran ourselves short before our store could be replenished. On the 27th we turned out on a general hunt for antelope; at this time we were living on bread and water. Our hunt failed, as it was probable the starving Indians had killed or run off all the game from that part of the country. On the 29th the weather was still blustery, with heavy snow. We cleared the blockhouse, and had a jolly dance, to drive dull care away. There being no ladies to join with us, we christened it the bachelor's dance.

April 1st came, and we cleared the snow and ice from our houses. On the 5th we received another mail from Salt Lake City, and on the 6th we hoisted the first liberty pole that was raised in Green River County to spread the Stars and Stripes of the United States of America to the mountain breeze. On the 17th there was continuous snow and rain, making very disagreeable weather. Committees were appointed to select and stake off the farm land, the writer being on one of the committees. We also placed out picket guards and chose men to herd our stock, and corral them at night. On the 18th we started the plows, marking to each mess their portion, as the committee had been directed to do. From the 23rd to the 26th we had cold, snowy weather.

On the 28th President Nebeker and C. Merkley started for Salt Lake City, and on May 1st D. R. Perkins and some others left for their homes. The rest of the company continued to plow and plant. On the 7th it snowed, and on the 8th Apostle Orson Hyde came with twenty-five new men, bringing us a fresh supply of provisions. This supply was very much appreciated, for we were, and had been for some weeks, living on bread alone. The new company also brought our mail. I had eleven letters, all containing good news from home.

Elder Hyde preached to us on the evening of the 9th, and we had good cheer; everyone seemed to be encouraged. We also held a council meeting to select Elders to go to the Indian camps, and learn as near as possible the feeling of the red men, and their movements, and to carry out the object of our mission. In that meeting, Elder Hyde called on the council for four or five Elders to volunteer to go east and hunt up the Indian camps. There were seven volunteered, namely, E. B. Ward, Isaac Bullock, John Harvey, J. Arnold, W. S. Muir, James S. Brown and one other whose name I have lost. Elder Hyde said that E. B. Ward, Isaac Bullock, and James S. Brown were three accepted from that list, while James Davis was taken for the fourth. The persons named were then sustained by the vote of the council, without a dissenting voice. Elder Hyde gave us some instructions, and said the party would start in one week from that day, or as much sooner as they chose.

The council meeting then adjourned, and Judge W. I. Appleby organized the county of Green River by appointing the officers therefor, Mr. Appleby having been duly commissioned as judge, and authorized to act in the capacity in which he did.

CHAPTER XLI.

SET APART BY ELDER HYDE FOR OUR SPECIAL MISSION—BLESSING
CONFERRED ON THE WRITER—DISCONTENT IN CAMP—UNITY
AGAIN PREVAILS—START ON OUR JOURNEY—WARNED AT GREEN
RIVER TO GO NO FARTHER—NOT DETERRED FROM PERFORMING
OUR MISSION — PROCEED ON OUR JOURNEY — FUTILE CHASE
AFTER BUFFALO — SCARCITY OF WATER — A WELCOME SNOW
STORM—REACH THE CAMP OF WASHAKIE, THE SHOSHONE CHIEF
—RECEIVED WITH CAUTION—TELL THE CHIEF THE OBJECT OF
OUR VISIT—GIVE HIM BREAD AND SUGAR—BOILED BUFFALO FOR
AN EPICURE—INDIAN POWWOW CALLED—PROCEEDINGS AT THE
COUNCIL -OBJECTION TO ONE OF OUR PROPOSITIONS, WHICH WE
WERE NOT ANNOYED AT — RECITAL OF HOW GOVERNMENT
AGENTS SOUGHT TO SUPPLANT WASHAKIE AS CHIEF—WASHAKIE
A GREAT ORATOR.

ANOTHER meeting was held on the 10th of May, and
Elder Hyde preached again. Then he called on those
who had been selected for the mission, told us to be wise as
serpents and harmless as doves, to be cautious and do all
the good that we could to the red men, and said that God
would bless us. He also said, "I do not know which to
appoint for the leader, Brother Brown or Brother Bullock.
They are both good men, but as Brother Bullock is the
eldest, he may have more experience." He then blessed
us, and promised me in my blessing that angels should go
before me, the visions of the Lord should be open to my
view, and no weapon that was raised against me should
prosper, but that I should go forth in the power and demon-
stration of the Lord God, and be mighty in gathering Israel.
Then he further instructed the party, and turned again to
me, pronouncing more blessings in line with those he had
given. Elder Hyde then started on his return trip home, and

20

we prepared ourselves as speedily as consistent for our expedition into a country mostly unknown to us.

April 11th and 12th were blustery, and there was snow. A reaction of spirit took place among the brethren of the camp, or probably it would be more proper to say that another spirit came upon the camp—a spirit of great discontent. For a time it seemed as if it would break up. the mission, but finally it was overcome, and all went well again.

On the 13th of April we set out on our journey, and went to Green River the first day, through rain and sleet part of the time. At Green River we found about thirty of the roughest kind of mountain men, engaged in drinking, gambling and carousing. Some Frenchmen, Mexicans or "Greasers," Indians, half-breeds, and some Americans of a low class, associated there, and insisted on us dining with them, and were very hospitable. They warned us not to venture any farther in the direction that we were going, saying that if we did so we would not return alive—that there would not be a "grease spot" left of us. This statement corresponded with what we had heard before, yet it did not deter us. There were in the crowd, Joshua Terry, also four Spaniards from the west, bound for Taos, New Mexico. They joined us, and we crossed the river, which was so deep that it was all that we possibly could do to ford it. The venture was harder than we expected it to be, but we succeeded, and struck out for the head of Bitter Creek, via Pilot Butte, making all the distance consistent with the condition of our animals. When we reached Bitter Creek, we followed up to the head, then bore to the southeast, crossing a high, dry country, for two days without water, then came in sight of a small herd of buffalo.

The Mexicans, with Ward and Davis, gave chase to the herd, while Bullock and I kept on our course with the pack animals, guided across the plains by mountain peaks and openings in the range of mountains. The hunters did not rejoin us until the latter part of the next day. They succeeded in killing one poor buffalo bull, and were so thirsty that they opened the tripe and drank the liquid it contained, to save their lives, for they were so far gone as not to be able to bring any portion of the carcass to camp. That day we came across a shallow pool of water, where we rested a short time.

We had been told that by crossing the country in the direction we were going we would be sure to strike the Indian trail leading in toward the headwaters of the Platte River; consequently we continued on till we came to the main divide between the waters of the east and the west. There Joshua Terry and the Spaniards parted with us, and we kept along on the divide, or summit of the Rocky Mountains, between the Platte and the Rio Grande, while they passed over. That night we camped on the divide, and had a snowstorm on us, in which we were fortunate, as by that means we obtained water for ourselves and animals. The next day we struck the trail of a few Indians, and by following it up five or six miles reached another trail which it ran into. This we continued to follow until 3 p. m., when we came to the camp of Washakie, the Shoshone Indian chief.

The first Indian we met would not speak when we accosted him. He shook his head, and pointed to the chief's lodge. That spirit of "mum" seemed to pervade the entire camp, and when we rode up in front of the chief's lodge, that Indian dignitary came out, bowed, and shook hands with each one of us, but without uttering a word. By gestures he invited us to dismount, come in, sit down, and tell the truth regarding our errand to his camp, but no lies. Then he had some clean, nice robes spread for us. At the same time his women folks came out, taking our horses by the bits. We dismounted, and took seats as invited. The chief and ourselves were all "mum" until the horses had been unsaddled, and everything belonging to us had been put under the bottom of the lodge, just to the rear of where we sat.

These proceedings being over, the chief said: "Who are you, from where do you come, and what is your errand to my country?" Then, by gestures, he said, "Tell me the truth; do not tell me any lies, nor talk any crooked talk." Here he paused, and, by motions, invited us to reply.

We told him we were Mormons, from the Salt Lake country, sent by the big Mormon captain, to make the acquaintance of him and his people, that we might talk and be friendly with them, as we wished them to be friendly with us and with all good people, as also with all the Indian tribes, for we all had one Peap (father), and it was not pleasing to Him to see His children nabitink (fight). We said the Great Father had told our chief many things about all the Indian tribes, and one part of our business was to learn better the Indian dialects, manners and customs, so that we could tell the Indians what the Great Spirit had told our big captain about them. Another part was to warn them that it would not be many snows before the game of their country would be killed off or disappear, and we wished to tell them, and to show them how to till the earth, and raise stock, and build houses, like the white man did, so that when the game was all gone their wives and children would not starve to death. We said that some of us might want to come out into his country and marry some of their good daughters and rear families by them. We would educate them, so they could read some good books that we had, and from them they could learn more about the Great Father, or Spirit.

Washakie sat and listened very attentively until we were through, when he said, "Wait a while. My little children are very hungry for some of the white man's food, and they want some sugar."

At that we gave him all the bread and sugar we had. He passed it to his wife, who in turn distributed it to the hungry little ones. Then, without another word, the chief walked out, but soon returned. His wife then set a camp kettle partly filled with buffalo beef that had been partially dried.

If I should tell the stranger to Indian customs how it was seasoned, I doubt not he would say, "I could not eat of such food. I know I should starve to death first." But stop, my friend, do not be too positive about that. These Indians have a custom among them that when they kill a buffalo they skin it, leaving the carcass on the hide; then they slice the flesh in long strips, remove the bones, turn the contents of the tripe over the meat, thoroughly knead or mix it all through the beef, and, with a slight shake, hang the meat on a horse rope or lay it on some sticks for a few hours; then they put it into a camp kettle and boil it, when it is ready for their guests. Such was part of the life on the great western plains in 1854.

Supper over, the council of the camp began to file in; the pipe was lit, and a rude figure of some of the planets ets drawn in the ashes of the fire that occupied the center of the lodge. Then the old man sitting on the left of the chief held the pipe, we having been seated on the right of the chief. The latter commenced, and told the story of our visit, from the time we came into the lodge up to that moment. It was told without interruption, and then the pipe was started on its way, following the course of the sun. Every man except the one holding the pipe put his hand over his mouth, and sat perfectly silent and still. The one with the pipe took from one to three long draws, allowing the smoke from the last one to escape gradually through his nostrils, at the same time passing the pipe with his right hand to the next person; then, if he had anything to say, he did it in as few words as possible, and put his hand over his mouth, thus signifying that he had no more to say. Occasionally some old man, when he took the pipe, made some signs above and in front of him, struck himself on the breast and offered a few words of prayer. Thus the pipe was whiffed by all the Indians of the council, and was then passed into the hands of the white men, who, in turn, took a whiff as a vow of peace and friendship. Then the pipe went to the chief, who glanced around the circle, and, as every man's hand was over his mouth, the chief summed up the subject in a few words, but always to the point. There being no appeal from this decision, it is usual at the conclusion of councils for some one present to walk through the camp and cry aloud that portion intended for the public, or if it is an order for the whole camp, they get it in the same way. This crier was called the high ranger of the camp.

In our case, the only objection that was raised to our proposition was when we suggested that some of us might want to take some of the young Indian women for wives. One old and wise counselor said, "No, for we have not got daughters enough for our own men, and we cannot afford to give our daughters to the white man, but we are willing to give him an Indian girl for a white girl. I cannot see why a white man wants an Indian girl. They are dirty, ugly, stubborn and cross, and it is a strange idea for white men to want such wives. But I can see why an Indian wants a white woman." Then the old man drew a graphic picture of the contrast he was making, and we gave up that point without pursuing our suit farther. Chief Washakie, however, said the white men might look around, and if any one of us found a girl that would go with him, it would be all right, but the Indians must have the same privilege among the white men. With this the council ended.

At that time Washakie told us that only a few snows before then he was chief of all the Shoshones, and the

Indians acknowledged him as such, but he was called to Fort Laramie, to have a talk with the agents of the big father at Washington, and to receive blankets and many other things. There the agents called a quiet, unobtrusive man, who never had been a chief, nor was in the line of chiefs, and designated him as head of the Shoshones, telling the Indians they must have him as chief, and respect him as such, and that they, the agents, would recognize him in that position, and through him they would do all government business. Then the agents passed out a great quantity of blankets and other Indian goods, through their appointed chief. In this act, the Indians saw that the agents had chosen a favorite of their own, so the red men called him "Tavendu-wets" (the white man's child), but never recognized him as chief.

That act of the government agents was the opening wedge to divide the Shoshone tribe into discontented factions, and thereby weaken it. Possibly that was the purpose in view, for before that the tribe was very powerful, with a chief at their head unexcelled for bravery, skill and far-sightedness. Chief Washakie was a bold, noble, hospitable, and honorable man. As an orator, I think he surpassed any man I ever met.

CHAPTER XLII.

THE morning after the council, Chief Washakie asked
us where we were going to from his camp. We said
we wished to go to White Man's Child's camp of Sho-

shones. Said he, "Maybe that is good, maybe not. I don't know. I hear there are bad men over there. I don't know." As there was no trail leading to that camp, we asked him to send a guide with us. He replied, "Maybe one go." Our horses having been brought up, we saddled them, and after a good friendly shake of the hand of the chief and of some of his council, we started to the southeast, with a young brave on the lead. When we had traveled about twenty miles, our guide disappeared over a ridge, but as we had come to a trail it did not matter to us so long as we could see pony tracks to follow. Still a feeling of mistrust lurked within us, as it had done all day. We discussed the matter, but could see no other way open than to press forward.

Soon we ascended a hill, from the top of which we could hear a drum, then many voices in a war song. As we rounded a little point of the hill we saw numerous lodges, and what appeared to be thousands of Indians. A large proportion of the latter were dancing and singing songs. About this time we felt a heavy feeling, and were certain that the spirit of murder was in the Indian camp. Everybody we met until we came to the chief's lodge looked as if they were going to war, judging by the expression of their eyes.

The chief came slowly out, coolly shook hands with us, ordered our stock taken care of, and a dish of boiled meat set before us. Then his family left the lodge, taking their effects, leaving only three robes for us. The sun was just setting, and the chief said we could occupy his lodge that night, as he was going away, being afraid to stop there, as there were men in camp that he could not control. Then he walked off and out of sight.

At this time three braves came by in their war paint, stepping along very lightly, and stripped and armed as if ready for a fight. They took a sharp glance at us, then passed on up the creek, to where the singing and dancing were going on. Then war whoops rent the air, and we were alone around the campfire.

There we were, surrounded by three hundred Indian lodges, and between fifteen hundred and two thousand Indians, principally Shoshones, though there were Cheyennes and Arapahoes mixed with them, for trading purposes, we supposed. It was dark, our horses had been taken away, we knew not where, and we were between four and five hundred miles from any source of protection, so far as we knew. The chief had confessed his inability to control some men in his camp, and had acknowledged that he was afraid to stop in his own lodge, he and his family seeking safer quarters. We were also without food, and the shadow of death seemed to hover over and close around us, while the war song and dance were heard plainly. We had also learned that L. B. Ryan, successor to Samuel Callwell as chief of the organized band of desperadoes, was at that time beating up and organizing a war party to carry on his nefarious work of robbery, and that he had sworn vengeance on the first Mormons that he met. We believed that he was the uncontrollable power that the chief had referred to.

Under these circumstances, it was a grave question as to what we could do for the best. Escape by flight was impossible, and as for attempting to fight three hundred to one, that was folly. Then what should we do? Put our trust in God, and go to bed, and if we were killed we wouldn't have to fall. This was our conclusion, so we attended prayers, and retired about 8 o'clock.

Soon the drum and some kind of whistle were heard drawing closer to us. In a few minutes our outdoor fire was surrounded by L. B. Ryan and seven young warriors, all well armed with Colt's revolvers. The Indians had bows

and arrows in hand, ready for action.   Thei paleface companion undoubtedly was the leader.

After a brief pause, Ryan came into the lodge and
squatted down just opposite to where Bullock and I lay.
He picked up a stick of wood, and with a cutlass chipped
off pieces and stirred up the coals, starting a bright light.
Then he said, "Gentlemen, where do you hail from, and
what is your business here?"

Mr. Bullock being spokesman, informed him that we
were from Utah, and our business in part was to get acquainted with the Indians, to ascertain the openings for
trade, and to look out the resources of the country.

Ryan continued, "Gentlemen, if you have got any
papers for me, bring them out.   I have been robbed by the
Mormons of my bottom dollar, and by the eternal gods I
am going to have revenge."

He then smote the billet of wood a heavy blow, at
which signal the seven braves filed into the lodge, and
squatted in order, with bows tightly corded, and arrows in
hand.   Ward, Davis, and I, were fully prepared to meet
the attack as best we could.   Bullock having the talking to
do, was not so well prepared, until I rubbed his ribs with
my bowie knife handle, when he got ready as quickly as
possible.   There were eight against four, all inside of one
Indian lodge, watching for the signal from Ryan, and we
would have acted promptly on his signal, or that of one of
his braves, and without doubt would have got our share of
the game, in exchanging lead for arrows.   It is possible that
Ryan took the same view, for he suddenly rose up and
walked out, the warriors following him.   They closed the
lodge door behind them, thus giving us the opportunity to
consult, while they held their council and danced around the
fire and sang.

We hastily concluded that if they entered again it would
be to massacre our party, and that if they began to come in

we would fire on them the moment they opened the deer-skin door. I, being in the most convenient position, was to give the first shot, presuming that Ryan would be in the lead, and we would be sure to dispose of him in that way. Meanwhile, all the rest would fire into the war party, whose shadows could be seen through the lodge, as they were between it and a big outdoor fire. The next move on our part was for Davis, who lay most convenient to the back part of the lodge, to make with his knife as large an opening as possible in the lodge, that we might escape through it into the creek that passed near by, the banks of which were only six or eight feet high. Our decision was that the moment we left the lodge every man was to try and if possible make his escape, no matter what the conditions might be, so that if either one of us could get away, and tell where he last saw the rest, it might be some satisfaction to our friends and relatives. Then each man took the most easy position to act his part, made ready his firelock, and held it with finger on the trigger.

Just then the party outside came around in their dance circle, straight for the lodge door, Ryan in the lead. They sang and danced right up to the door, but did not lift it. Next they circled around the lodge, and with their scalping knives, or some other sharp instruments, slit the lodge in a number of places. Then, as they came around to the front, they gave a war whoop, and passed up the creek in the direction whence they came. Thus we still lived, and were spared the awful necessity of snedding man's blood, even in self-defense, thanks be to God for His protection and mercies. Still the clouds hung so low, and so thickly around, that we could not feel safe in an attempt to leave camp.

Next morning the chief sent us some boiled buffalo beef, and called and talked a few moments. He impressed us with the fact that the danger was not yet over, and that we were safer in his lodge and camp than we would be out

A WAR PARTY OF SHOSHONES DANCING AROUND THEIR PRISONERS WHILE IN THE CHIEF'S LODGE.

of it, so we contented ourselves as best we could by loitering around, while the drum and the whistling reeds of the war party, and the wild shouts, continued all day. At last night came, and we turned in, as we had done the evening before, with all our clothes, arms and boots on.

Nothing occurred that night to mar our peace, but the ever threatening din of the drum and the savage yell of the red man. Again the morning light broke over us, and our scalps were still in place, but the very elements seemed to say, "Stay in camp." The Spirit whispered to every one of us the same thing. We were a unit, and therefore lingered in the place, closely watching every move.

Finally the chief came, and our horses were brought. This was at about 1 o'clock p. m. Then, as plainly as ever we saw the clouds in the firmament break and scatter, we felt the clouds of death begin to part. We waited no longer; our horses were saddled, packs were put in place, and the chief gave us a slight indication, letting us understand that it was a good time to move. At that moment Ryan and his allies came up, apparently changed in their behavior. Ryan inquired of us by what route we intended to return. Mr. Bullock said we expected to go to Washakie's camp, and thence back by the same route we had come on. Immediately the chief stepped away into the brush, we mounted, and saying good-bye, started down the creek.

A few moments later, as we rounded a bend, the chief popped out of the brush just in front of and so as to meet us. Without seeming to notice us in the least, he said, "Do not go the way you said you would, for there are men in my camp that I cannot control." Brother Bullock did not catch the idea, but the other three of us did. We understood his action as well as his words. Soon we came to where we had got to decide which course we would take. Brother Bullock was determined to keep his word, and go by the route that he had told Ryan he would do, but the three others were a unit in insisting on taking another way. We told him we understood perfectly the chief, that if we went by that route we would be ambushed, and every soul of us would be killed. Still Brother Bullock insisted on keeping his word with the Indians; and more, he had promised Washakie that he would return by his camp. Then Ward and Davis came straight out and said they knew that meant death, and they would not follow on that trail; so they started off another way.

At this juncture I said: "Brother Bullock, I never deserted my file-leader in my life, and I will not do it now. I will follow you to the death, for I am certain that path leads there, and if you persist in going that way I will follow, and will claim my blood at your hands, for the others, the three of us, see alike." Then Ward and Davis turned and said that on the same conditions as those I had named they would go with Brother Bullock; but the latter said the price was too great, and he would go with us, but he very much regretted breaking his word with the red man.

Every minute was precious at that time. We were well satisfied that Ryan would not shrink to do from ambush what he had hesitated to do in the chief's lodge, and that if he could strike our trail he would do it to the death; so we made the best speed consistent with the conditions surrounding us.

As we were passing up the long slope of the mountain, and while yet almost in sight of the camp, a small, dense, black cloud arose in the south. It passed in our rear and over the Indian camp, and torrents of rain seemed to fall there, while we were caught only in the storm's edge. Thus our tracks were completely obliterated. Soon we came into a trail leading along our way, and followed it to quite a bold running creek. As the rain had ceased where we were, to further elude our enemies we followed up in the bed of the creek until we came to a rocky ridge which led us up among the cliffs, where it would be difficult for any one to follow us and make much headway. While there among the rocks, Ward and Davis saw an old mountain sheep, which they pursued and captured, but he fell in a place so difficult of access, and night coming on, that it was impossible to get but a small portion of him. Bullock and I kept on our course, and were overtaken by our companions just at dark.

We pushed on as quickly as possible, for the rain was coming on in torrents. At last the night became so densely dark that we could only keep together by the noise of our camp equipage, and by talking. It was impossible to see where we were going, so we camped in a sag. It rained so hard that it was with much work that we started a fire, and then it was quite as difficult to keep it going till we could frizzle a morsel of the old ram; so each bolted his rations half raw, and having hobbled our animals securely, we rolled ourselves in half-wet blankets and laid down on the ground, which already had been soaked to the consistency of mud, and we wallowed there until next morning. Then two of us brought up and saddled horses, while the other two frizzled a little more of the ram, which was bolted, as before, for it was too tough to chew in a way anything like satisfactory. We then wrung our blankets, for they were full of water, as in the place where we had laid down the water was half shoetop deep.

By sunrise we were mounted, feeling satisfied that our track of the day before had been covered up, and thirty miles of our flight was behind us. The country was high and barren, but we avoided conspicuous points, and traveled the most secluded way, ever on the alert to catch the first sight of an enemy, or of any kind of game, for our portion of flesh of the ram of the Rockies had disappeared.

In the after part of the day the sun shone. This was

while we were crossing the head of an open flat, in a dry country, with a dry gully coursing down through it. This gully was fringed with an abundant growth of sagebrush, and as we looked down the flat we saw some animals coming out from a bend in the gully. We ascertained to our delight that there were seven buffaloes. Our decision was to spare no efforts in an endeavor to secure one of the animals, for this was a rare chance, as the Indians had hunted every bit of game that it was possible for them to do in that part of the country.

To accomplish our most desirable object at this particular time, Ward, Davis and I secured our horses, leaving Bullock to guard them and the pack mules. The three of us made our way down the gulch, and as the wind came to us from the buffaloes, there was no danger of them scenting us. Thus we secured an excellent position, and waiting a few minutes for them to feed to within about sixty yards of us, we decided on the one that had the sleekest coat, thinking he would be the best beef; for all were very poor old bulls, and we did not wish to injure more than we needed to keep us from starvation. We all took deliberate aim, and three rifles rang out as one. The only result visible to us was that the game wheeled, and ran directly on the back track, leaving us without even a hope of buffalo meat until we followed on their trail seventy or eighty rods. There we found where one animal had cast his cud, and later we saw some blood splattered about. All felt sure we had hit the buffalo, for each knew how his rifle shot, and said he never drew a nicer bead on an animal in his life. Then Ward and Davis got their horses and gave chase, as the game had run almost parallel with our route toward the notch in the mountains for which we were aiming.

Bullock and I kept on the course our party had marked out to travel, but before we reached the mountain pass we were heading for, night and rain came on, and we had to

camp in an open greasewood plain.   Coming to a very deep
wash that had good feed in it, we concluded to hobble
our animals in the wash.   It was difficult to get our stock
in, as the banks were very steep, but at last we succeeded
in getting them down, and felt that they were tolerably safe
for the night, with some watching.   We gathered a little
greasewood, for there was no other fuel, and tried to get a
fire started in the rain and darkness.

During this time, Bullock began to have cramps, in the
stomach and bowels, and then in his limbs, and soon he was
taken with a heavy chill.   It seemed that he would die, in
spite of all that I could do for him.   I rubbed him, prayed
for him, and put him in a pack of wet blankets, for we had
no other, and were without any earthly comfort for such
an emergency.   At last I caught some rain in the frying-
pan, then got hold of our cracker sack, in which was about
two tablespoonfuls of crumbs and dust that had rubbed off
the crackers.   I heated the water, put the crumbs in, and
brought the mixture to a boil, stirring it so that it appeared
something like gruel, and gave it to the sick man, who
became easier.   Then I went out, feeling my way, to see
what had become of our stock, and got so far off in the
darkness that I had great difficulty in finding my way back
to my sick companion, but after much anxiety and bother
I found him suffering intensely.   I set to work rubbing
him and encouraging him the best I could.   I spent the
entire night in attending to him and watching the stock.

Morning came, and still the hunters were unheard of.
At one time I almost despaired of the sick man's life, and
thought, if he died, what could I do with him, so far away
from help.   I could not take him home, neither could I put
him out of reach of wild beasts, for I had no spade,
pickaxe or shovel; nor was there timber in sight to cremate
him.   I had not a mouthful of food, and what had become
of our partners, Ward and Davis, I could not tell.   Then

came the reaction of the spirit, and the thought that I must do the best that I could. It would not do to despair. I must pray for the patient, pack up, and get out of that place.

The patient seemed to rally with the dawn of day, and by sunrise we were on our way, and entered the canyon we had been heading for. We saw no signs of our friends until we reached their camp in the canyon, for it had rained so heavily as to obliterate the horse tracks. As they had gone on, we were not quite sure that it was their camp and tracks, and the canyon afforded excellent opportunity for ambush. But we were there and must go through. The sick man held up with wonderful fortitude, though suffering greatly. About 2 p. m. we sighted our comrades, the buffalo hunters. They mistook us for enemies and fled, until they found a convenient place to hide themselves and horses, and where they watched until they saw the gleaming of the sunlight upon our rifle barrels. Then they recognized us, and as we came up we had a warm greeting.

Being together once more we hid our animals among the cedars, and selected our camp with care, as it was night. Our hunters had been successful, after a chase of ten miles, in getting the buffalo; they had a hard and hazardous fight with the wounded animal, and it took them till after dark before they could get what buffalo meat they could carry on their horses. They also had a very severe night of it; but the lost were found, and with plenty of buffalo meat in camp we were thankful.

We broiled and ate, boiled and ate and ate raw liver, and marrow out of the bones; for be known that men in the condition we were, with severe hunger, do not always realize how much they have eaten until they eat too much. So it was with us. When we were through with the meal, we prepared to "jerk" the remainder of the beef, but before that was done my three companions were attacked with vomiting and purging; then followed chills and cramps, and for about four or five hours it seemed they might all die. I could not say which would go first, and the previous night's experience was reiterated. I confess that I had been guilty of as much folly and unreason as they, but being more robust than the others, I could endure more than they; but I had the very same kind of an attack as they did, before the journey was over.

When morning came, a sicker and a harder looking lot of men seldom is seen in the mountains. Yet we must travel, so passed through that canyon out onto an open plain, leaving the creek to the south of us. In the afternoon we came to a smooth clay grade, on which were fresh horse and moccasin tracks, and four large capital letters, in English; I think they were N, W, H and E. We concluded they had been marked out with a sharp stick, but not in a manner intelligible to us, so we were suspicious and cautiously pushed on to a place of shelter and rest.

It was on the 1st day of June that we reached the Middle Ferry on Green River, Green River County, Utah. There we met with W. I. Appleby, probate judge, Hosea Stout, prosecuting attorney, William Hickman, sheriff, Captain Hawley, the ferryman, and his family and some others. They did not have to be told what we most needed, but supplied with liberal hand our necessities, for all were aware that the object of our mission had been to protect just such as they, and the innocent immigrants, and their property, from not only the raids of the red men, but also from the more wicked and baser white brigands.

We rested at Green River until the 4th of June, when my fellow missionaries left for Fort Supply. I remained as interpreter, and to fill our appointment with Chief Washakie, who was to be at the ferry by July 15.

CHAPTER XLIII.

A S I had become a fairly good interpreter, the ferry company proposed to pay my board at Green River while I stayed, as there was no one else there who could converse with the Indians. The country was new and wild, and while there were some very good people, the road was lined with California immigrants and drovers, many of them of a very rough class, to say the best of them. They would camp a day or two on the river, and drink, gamble and fight; then the traders and rough mountain men, half-caste Indians, French and Spaniards, were numerous; there were also blacksmith and repair shops, whisky saloons, gambling tables, and sometimes there would be a perfect jam of wagons and cattle, and two or three hundred men. There were quarrels and fights, and often men would be shot or stabbed. As the court had been organized only about two months, it was almost impossible for the sheriff or any other officer to serve a writ or order of court, unless he had a posse to back him. Sometimes the ferryman at the Upper Ferry would be run off his post, and a company of mountain men would run the ferry and take the money, and it would require every man that was on the side of law and order to back the officer. In this situation I, though a missionary, was summoned to take charge of a posse of men to assist the sheriff in making arrests.

One time there came a man with four thousand head of cattle. He crossed the river, passed down about four miles and camped under a steep sand bluff. He had missed a calf, and sent a man back for it. A small party of Indians, passing along that way, had picked up the animal and carried it off, supposing that the drovers had abandoned it. The man who had been sent for the calf, not finding it, rode up to the ferry and demanded the animal of the boatmen. These told him they did not have his calf, whereupon he swore at them, called them liars and thieves, and threatened to kill them, at the same time leveling his double-barreled shotgun at them.

Judge Appleby happened to be standing within a few feet of the boatmen, and heard the whole conversation. He ordered the sheriff to take the man, dead or alive. The sheriff summoned me to his aid, and we started at once for the culprit. When we got to within four rods of him he called out, "Do you want anything of me, gentlemen?" The sheriff said, "Yes; I am the sheriff, and you are my prisoner." The man being on horseback, defied the sheriff and fled. We fired two shots in the air, thinking he would surrender, but he did not, and the sheriff pressed into service the horses of two immigrants near by, and he and I pursued the fugitive, following him about four miles, where we suddenly came upon his camp of twenty-four men, armed with double-barrelled shotguns.

The man having had considerably the start of us, had time to get the camp rallied and ready for action, telling them that two men had shot at and were then in hot pursuit of him. We were not aware of his camp being there until we reached the brow of the bluff; then our only chance was to ride boldly down into the camp, which we did, the sheriff shouting, "Hold on, gentlemen! I am the sheriff of this county." The captain of the camp, being a cool-headed and fearless man, said to his men, "Hold on, boys, wait for the word."

The moment we got into camp we dismounted, and I presume that at least a dozen guns were leveled at us, their holders being greatly excited, and swearing death to us if we dared to lay a finger on the fugitive, or on any other person in the camp. The captain, however, said, "Hold on, boys! Let's hear what these men have to say." Then the sheriff said the man (pointing to the culprit) had committed an offense against the law, in threatening the lives of the boatmen, and leveling his gun as if to carry out the threat, and the sheriff had been ordered by the judge to arrest him, but he had defied the officer and fled. "But," said the captain, "you shot at him." To this the sheriff replied, "We called on him to halt, and as he refused to obey, a couple of shots were fired over his head to make him stop, but he did not do so, and we followed him to your camp. I now demand him of you as his captain."

At this the captain declared that the sheriff had shot at his man and had scared him almost to death. He pointed to the man, who was shaking as if he had a treble shock of the ague, and continued that before the sheriff should take him every drop of blood in the camp should be shed. The men brawled out, "Hear! Hear!" when the sheriff said, "All right, Captain. You may get away with us two, but we have between seventy-five and one hundred men just over the hills here, and in less than twenty-four hours we will have you and every man in your camp, and your stock will have to foot the bill."

Thereupon the captain made response that he would come and answer for his man, but the sheriff could not take him. Thus the matter was compromised subject to the court's approval. The captain promised to be at the judge's within two hours, and was there. So the whole matter was settled without bloodshed.

This incident is only an illustration of what had to be met every few days, in which men would refuse to yield to the law until they had to do so or die, and many were the times that we had to force them down with the revolver, when, if we had not had "the drop" on them they would not have yielded. We met men face to face, with deadly weapons, and if it had not been for the cunning and the cool head of "Bill" Hickman, as he was commonly called, blood would have been shed more than once when it was avoided. I speak of "Bill" Hickman as I found him in the short time I was with him. In his official capacity he was cunning, and was always ready to support the law while I was with him on Green River.

One day about 10 o'clock a. m., a herd of four hundred head of cattle came up, and the owners ferried their wagons across the river. Then they tried to swim their cattle over but could not do so. I stood by and watched their futile efforts until I observed the reason the cattle would not go across. Then I attempted to tell the captain that he could not swim his stock with the sun shining in their faces. The captain being one of those self-sufficient men often met with, rather snubbed me, saying, "I have handled cattle before today." I turned away, remarking that he never would get his cattle across in that manner, and saying that I could put every head over at the first attempt.

Some one repeated to the "boss" what I had said, and asked him why he did not get that mountaineer to help, as he understood the business better than anyone else on the river. "Well," he said, "we will make another try, and if we do not succeed, we will see what he can do." The trial was another failure. Then he came to me and said, "Cap., what will you charge me to swim those cattle, and insure me against loss?" I answered, "You have wearied your cattle and fooled them so much that it will be more trouble now than at first, but if you will drive your stock out on that 'bottom' and call your men away from them, I will swim them and insure every hoof, for twenty-five cents a head." Said he, "I will do it, for it will cost fifty cents a head to cross them in the boat. So you will take charge of them on the 'bottom?'"

"Yes," said I, "so you do not let them scatter too much."

The river was booming, but I knew of a place where the bank was three or four feet higher than the water, and where the stream ran swiftly, setting across to where the cattle would reach a gradual slope. I then went to a camp of Indians near by, and hired four of them to assist me. They stripped and mounted their ponies with their robes about them. One went between the cattle and the river, so as to lead, and the others circled around the stock and got them all headed toward the place designated for them to take to the water. Then they caused the cattle to increase their speed until they were on the gallop, when the Indians gave a few yells and shook their robes, the man in the lead leaped his horse into the river, and every hoof took to the water, and were across safe and sound within thirty minutes from the time they started. The captain paid without objecting, and would have me go over and take supper with him and his family. He said, "Aside from having my cattle across safe and sound, I have the worth of my money in valuable experience." Next day he was back over the river, and would tell of the incident and say to the drovers he met with, "There is that mountaineer. I am —— if he can't beat any man swimming cattle that I ever saw." And others would tell the drovers the same story.

Now, my friendly reader, I will tell you the secret of swimming horses and cattle across a river. It is: Find a place (which you always can do) somewhere in the bends of the watercourse, where you can swim your stock from the sun, and where they take to the water the deeper the better, even if you have to make them jump from the banks. The swifter the current the better; then they are not so likely to injure one another in jumping. Again, see that the outcoming place is on a grade, and the water is shallow. Then have some good swimmer, on horseback, take the lead; push your stock to a lively gait, and success is assured. I had charge of swimming ten thousand head of cattle across Green River, in the months of June and July, 1854, and never lost a hoof, yet forced hundreds of them over banks eight to ten feet high, into the water. In such case, the water must be deep, or we might have sustained damage. I have found, as a rule, that nearly all men who have much money or property think that they know it all, and are hard to convince. But some of the drovers learned by object lessons, and almost all of them thought they could swim their own cattle; and so they could have done, if they had known the correct plan, or had made the effort after sundown or before sunrise.

About the time set for his arrival, Washakie, the great Shoshone chieftain, came in with seven of his braves, and quietly walked around. First, he inspected the boat and its fixtures, or tackle; then he went to the brewery, the bakery, store, court room, whisky saloon, blacksmith shops, card tables, saw much money changing hands, and observed that money would purchase about anything the white man had.

When the chief had had a friendly visit all around, he went to the office of Captain Hawley, the ferryman. There he saw the captain taking and handling considerable money, among the precious metal being two or three fifty-dollar gold slugs. He asked for one of these, but the captain laughed at him, and offered him a silver dollar.

This action offended Washakie, who walked away, and by some means got hold of some intoxicants. Then he began to think what was going on in the land of his forefathers, and came to me and said: "This is my country, and my people's country. My fathers lived here, and drank water from this river, while our ponies grazed on these bottoms. Our mothers gathered the dry wood from this land. The buffalo and elk came here to drink water and eat grass; but now they have been killed or driven back out of our land. The grass is all eaten off by the white man's horses and cattle, and the dry wood has been burned; and sometimes, when our young men have been hunting, and got tired and hungry, they have come to the white man's camp, and have been ordered to get out, and they are slapped, or kicked, and called 'd——d Injuns.' Then our young men get heap mad, and say that when they have the advantage of the white man, as they have often, they will take revenge upon him. Sometimes they have been so abused that they have threatened to kill all the white men they meet in our land. But I have always been a friend to the white man, and have told my people never to moisten our land with his blood; and to this day the white man can not show in all our country where the Shoshone has killed one of his people, though we can point to many abuses we have patiently suffered from him. Now I can see that he only loves himself; he loves his own flesh, and he does not think of us; he loves heap money; he has a big bag full of it; he got it on my land, and would not give me a little piece. I am mad, and you heap my good friend, and I will tell you what I am going to do. Every white man, woman or child, that I find on this side of that water," pointing to the river, "at sunrise tomorrow I will wipe them out" (rubbing his hands together). He went on: "You heap my friend; you stay here all right; you tell them to leave my land. If they are on the other side of my water, all right, me no kill them, they go home to their own country, no come back to my land. Tomorrow morning when the sun come up, you see me. My warriors come, heap damn mad, and wipe them all out, no one leave."

"Good-by, you tell him, chief, he mad!" was Washakie's parting exclamation, as he mounted his horse and rode away to his camp on the Big Sandy, some fifteen miles back from the Green River.

CHAPTER XLIV.

CONSTERNATION AT WASHAKIE'S DECLARATION—PEOPLE HURRY ACROSS THE RIVER—THE WRITER IS ASKED TO ATTEMPT A RECONCILIATION—NIGHT TOO DARK TO TRAVEL—CHIEF WASHAKIE AND BRAVES APPEAR AT SUNRISE—THE CHIEF NOTES THAT THE PEOPLE ARE TERROR-STRICKEN, AND DECIDES THAT HE WILL BE THEIR FRIEND—TROUBLOUS EXPLOITS OF MOUNTAIN MEN—SHERIFF'S PLAN OF ARREST—HOW THE SCHEME WORKED—DESPERADOES FREED BY THE COURT—CHASING AN OFFENDER—SURROUNDED BY HIS ASSOCIATES—COOLNESS AND PLUCK OF THE SHERIFF WIN—READY TO RETURN HOME—A TRYING EXPERIENCE.

AS might have been expected, I lost no time in apprising the people of the Indian threat, and the white population promptly complied with the order to move; so that by daylight there was little of value on that side of the river. There was great consternation among the people, and Captain Hawley was quite willing to send a fifty-dollar slug to the chief; but it was late in the evening, and no one to go but myself. There was no telling how much liquor there might be in the Indian camp, so it was not a pleasant job for either friend or foe to approach the savages on such a dark night as that was. Although I had Washakie's promise of friendship, I knew that when the Indians were drunk they were not good company, and I did not care to expose myself to unnecessary danger.

Individually I had nothing at stake, but there were others who had their families and thousands of dollars' worth of property at the mercy of the enraged red men. In this crisis, when I was asked if I would take the risk, and what amount I would give my service for, I said I would undertake to go that night and attempt a reconciliation, and charge fifty dollars, if they would provide me with a good horse. That they agreed to do. The night was so dark, however, that it was impossible to get hold of a horse, so we had to move all of value that could be taken across the river. We also made every preparation for defense that was possible during the night.

Next morning, true to his promise, Chief Washakie, with fifteen well armed men, came up, just at sunrise. I went out to meet him, and found him perfectly sober and friendly, as also his men. The chief rode up and glanced at the desolate appearance of everything, and saw that the women and children were greatly frightened. His companions sat on their horses and looked across the river. Finally the noble chief said, referring to those who had left their homes, "Tell them to come back. We will not hurt them. We will be good friends."

Thus ended the big scare, and the people returned. But there was another stir to come; for in a few days the ferryman from the Upper Ferry, ten miles above the Middle Ferry, told Judge Appleby that a party of rough mountaineers had driven him off, threatening his life if he did not leave immediately. They had taken charge of the ferry, and were running it and pocketing the money. There were twenty-eight of them, determined "cut-throats," a part of the desperado band I have referred to before. The judge ordered the sheriff to summon every available man, and go at once and ascertain who the leaders were, then arrest them and bring them before the court. There were only fourteen men obtainable for the posse, and this number included the ferryman. The sheriff delegated me to take charge of the posse and go up on the east side of the river, ahead of him and the ferryman, who would come up on the west side some time after, so as not to create any unnecessary suspicion. He instructed us to be sociable with the outlaws, treat and be treated, and join in any game that might be engaged in. Said he, "We will get them drunk and divided among themselves, and then I think we can manage them."

The plan was laid, and every man being well armed, we set out on our hazardous mission. We had with us one man who could drink an enormous amount of whisky and yet not get drunk, for he would turn around and put his finger down his throat and vomit up the liquor before it would affect him much. He said, "Boys, I can make a dozen of them drunk, and keep straight myself." He was asked how he would go about it, and replied, "Well, I will offer to drink more whisky than any man on the river, and we will drink by measure; then I will slip out and throw it up. To hide the trick you must push me out of doors roughly, as if mad. At other times jam me up in a corner, so I can throw up. Thus I will have half of them so drunk that anyone of you can handle half a dozen of them at once." His statement of his ability to drink and empty his stomach of it being corroborated, he was assigned that part of the strategy. Then another man, who had been a soldier in the Mexican war, said, "Well, if you will get them drunk, I will win the money from their own party to buy the whisky, for I know just how to do it." He was given that part, for whisky was fifty cents a drink.

When we had perfected arrangements as far as possible, we rode up, dismounting as if we had just happened to call and knew nothing of the trouble. Each man took his part, and played it well. To our surprise, we found their leader, L. B. Ryan, apparently in a drunken stupor; he was the same person I had met in the Shoshone Indian camp, five or six weeks before. As he and the sheriff had been on good terms, they drank together and appeared to be quite friendly; but the ferryman and one of the band of outlaws got into a fight, and revolvers and bowie knives were drawn. Twenty-five or thirty of the mountain men, with deadly weapons flourishing, rushed into the saloon in front of which the fight began. One man slashed the other with a knife, and one of them fired two shots, but some bystander knocked the weapon up, so it did no harm. The prompt action of the sheriff and his supports, together with the aid of a number of immigrants, stopped the row. If it had not been for that, a dozen men might have been slain in as many minutes. Some of the men were of the most desperate character, and swore and made terrible threats of what they would do.

At last the combatants drank together, while a number of others got so intoxicated they could scarcely stand alone. Then the sheriff called Ryan to one side and quietly arrested him, placing him under ten thousand dollars bonds for his appearance in court on a certain date. The ferryman and some of the more moderate of the outlaws compromised their difficulties, and business settled down to a normal condition. We went back to the Middle Ferry, and the sheriff made his returns on the official papers.

At the time appointed for Ryan to appear in court, he was there, with seven young, well-armed warriors and a number of his band, who sauntered around the court room. Ryan was so desperate and so well supported by his clique that the court was glad to let him down and out as easily as possible; for it was evident that the court must do that or die. So Ryan and his gang returned to their haunts more triumphant than otherwise.

So we had to deal with desperate men every day or two, and it was seldom indeed that we could effect an arrest without a determined show of arms. Yet, we were not compelled to use them. The offenders must see that we had them, and had the nerve to use them, before they would yield. In one instance I was ordered by the sheriff to take a man who had broken from the officer. The man was running, and I followed, revolver in hand. As the fugitive ran, he drew his weapon and wheeled around. I was so near as to place my revolver uncomfortably close to his face before he could raise his weapon. He saw at once that I had the "drop" on him, as we used to say, and delivered his revolver to me. The next moment the sheriff and posse had their backs together and weapons raised, while twenty-four armed men appeared on the scene and demanded the man. But when they looked into the muzzles of fourteen Colt's revolvers with bright, shining, waterproof caps exposed, and the sheriff called out in a firm and decisive voice, "I am the sheriff of Green River County, and have a writ for this man," they paused, though some of them swore the officers could not take the man from camp, and advanced in a threatening manner. Then the sheriff commanded, "Halt! The first man that advances another step, or raises his weapon, is a dead man. Stand! I, as sheriff, give you fair warning." At that some of the more cautious said, "Hold on, boys! We must not oppose an officer," and all concluded they must give up the man and submit to the law for that time. The offense of the accused was shooting the ferryman's dog, while the latter was eating something under the table, and while the ferryman's wife and daughter were standing at the table washing dishes; and when the ferryman remonstrated at such conduct, threatening to shoot him. Ultimately the matter was compromised, the culprit and his friends paying the costs.

On the 7th of July, I began preparations to return to Fort Supply, as my real missionary labors seemed to have come to an end in that part, and I was glad of it. From May 13 to July 8, 1854, had been one of the most hazardous, soul-trying, disagreeable experiences of my life, for the short period it occupied. I have written a very brief synopsis of it in the foregoing account; for it might seem impossible to the person of ordinary experience for so many thrilling incidents as I had witnessed to happen in so short a time.

CHAPTER XLV.

GO TO FORT SUPPLY—START BACK TO GREEN RIVER AND MEET O. P. ROCKWELL AT FORT BRIDGER—HE BRINGS ME A TRADER'S LICENSE, ALSO GOODS TO TRADE TO THE INDIANS—BEING LATE IN THE SEASON, WE STORE THE GOODS, AND GO TO SALT LAKE CITY—RECEIVE THE APPROVAL OF GOVERNOR YOUNG—MOVE TO OGDEN—ACCOMPANY GOVERNOR YOUNG AS INTERPRETER—MY HORSE STOLEN—CALLED ON A MISSION TO THE SHOSHONES—ON GOING TO SALT LAKE CITY, I AM RELEASED—ORDERED TO TAKE PART IN DISARMING INDIANS AT OGDEN—A DIFFICULT JOB —CHASE TO MOUND FORT—HAND-TO-HAND STRUGGLE WITH A POWERFUL SAVAGE—INDIANS DISARMED, BUT SULLEN—CHIEF'S BROTHER OFFERS ALL HIS POSSESSIONS FOR HIS GUN—PRECAU- TIONS TAKEN TO FEED THE INDIANS THAT WINTER—TEACH THE INDIAN LANGUAGE IN SCHOOL—PROSPER IN BUSINESS.

ON July 9, I started for Fort Supply, arriving there on the 11th, where I found all well. On the 14th I began a journey back to Green River, but met Porter Rockwell at Fort Bridger. He had a license from Governor Brigham Young for me to trade with the Indians; also some two or three thousand dollars' worth of Indian goods for me to market. At that time there was no opportunity to trade, as the Indians had disposed of their robes,

22

pelts and furs for the season, so we sent the goods to Fort Supply and had them stored there.

I accompanied Rockwell to Salt Lake City, arriving there on July 19. We reported conditions to the governor, who received us very kindly, and approved of what we had done. On August 15 I went to Ogden City and on the 28th accompanied Governor Young, as interpreter, to Chief Catalos' camp of Shoshones, four miles north of Ogden. This large camp of Indians had some grievances to settle, and particularly desired to ask favors and get a better understanding with the white men through their big chief. The Indians claimed that they were friendly to the whites, and wanted the latter to be friendly to them; they also wished to have trade brought to them. The governor gave them a liberal present of assorted Indian goods, talked friendship, and told them he would leave other goods with me to trade. He also advised them to be good people, and to live at peace with all men, for we had the same great Father. Governor Young told them it would be good for them to settle down like the white man, and learn of him how to cultivate the land as he did, so that when the game was all gone they could live and have something to eat and to feed their families on. The Indians said this was "heap good talk," and their hearts felt good; so we parted with them in the best of feelings, notwithstanding that some of their bad Indians had stolen my only horse from where I had picketed him on the bottoms. I did not learn the facts in the case in time to get redress, and all the consolation I could obtain was that the thief did not know it was my animal—"heap no good Indian steal your horse."

I returned to Ogden City, and there continued to trade with the Indians as they came, until October 10, on which date I received a letter from Elder Orson Hyde, stating that Governor Young wished me to go on a mission among the Shoshones that winter. I answered the call, but when

I got to Salt Lake City, on the way, it had been learned that the Indians had gone out so far into the buffalo country that it was not advisable for me to follow them; so I returned to Ogden and continued to visit and trade with the Indians, and got up my winter's wood.

On November 20 Wm. Hickman, L. B. Ryan and D. Huntington came up from Salt Lake City with an order to Major Moore and the citizens of Weber County to disarm Chief Little Soldier and his band of Indians, and distribute them among the families in Weber County where the people were best able to feed and clothe them for the winter, and set them to work; for they had become very troublesome to the citizens of that county, by killing cattle, burning fences, and intimidating isolated families. On the 30th the major called on me to go with his party to the Indian camp at West Weber. I did so, and with considerable talking we got the Indians to accompany us to Ogden City. Still, they felt very warlike and stubborn, being unwilling to give up their arms.

In the midst of the parley, the three men from Salt Lake City returned to that place, and the Indians were allowed to go with their arms across the Ogden River and camp among the willows near Mound Fort. On December 1st we went after them, finding them so hostile that we had to make a show of arms before they would submit to our proposition of distributing them among the whites, but when we brought a squad of armed men they very reluctantly and sullenly complied, so we marched them back to Ogden City, to a location on Main Street, near where the old tithing office stood. Almost every man that had side arms was called to mingle among the Indians, so that each man could command a warrior by disarming him by force if he refused to surrender his arms at the command of the major, which command I was required to repeat in the Indian dialect. At the word, each man was to take hold of an Indian's gun, and I was to tell the aborigines to surrender; but there was not a man who obeyed the order, for what reason I do not know. I then went through the crowd of Indians and took every weapon with my own hands. The white men took them from me, and they were stored in the tithing office, a guard being placed over them.

Just then a young Indian was observed on horseback, going northward as fast as his horse could carry him. Some one said, "There goes that Indian boy to warn a camp over by Bingham Fort!" Major Moore had one of the fastest animals in the county; he ordered me to "take her and beat the boy into camp, or run her to death. Don't spare horseflesh. Call out the citizens and disarm every Indian you find."

I obeyed the order, and found a small party of Indians camped in the center of what was called Bingham Fort. Just as the Indian boy reached the camp, I entered the east gate of the square, and rode to the west gate, shouting to the people, "To arms! To arms! Turn out, every man, and help to disarm the Indians!" Men turned out quickly and surrounded the camp. I succeeded in reaching the west gate just in time to wheel and grab a big Ute's gun as he was trying to pass me. He held to it firmly, and both struggled with a death-like grip. We looked each other squarely in the eyes, with a determined expression. At last his eyes dropped, and his gun was in my possession. He was full of wrath and a desire for vengeance. I found him to be one of the strongest men I had ever grappled with anywhere.

I next turned to the camp and disarmed all the Indians in it, placed their weapons under guard and sent them to Ogden, then vainly tried to talk the red men into reconciliation. I next returned to Ogden, and there found the whites and Indians on the streets, the latter as discontented as ever. The major and I tried to [pacify them, but they were very stubborn and sullen. At last the chief's brother said, "Here are my wife, my children, my horses and everything that I have. Take it all and keep it, only give me back my gun and let me go free. I will cast all the rest away. There is my child," pointing to a little three-year-old, "take it." The little innocent held up its hands and cried for the father to take it, but he frowned and looked at it as with a feeling of disgust, saying, "Go away. You are not mine, for I have thrown you away, and will not have you any more."

This spirit was but a reflex of that which animated the whole band; "for," said they, "we are only squaws now. We cannot hunt or defend our families. We are not anybody now." But finally, though very sullenly, they went home with the whites and pitched their tents in the back yards. To us it did seem hard to have them feel so bad, but they had no means of support for the winter, the citizens could not afford to have their stock killed off and their fences burned, and it was the better policy to feed the Indians and have them under control. They could husk corn, chop wood, help do chores, and be more comfortable than if left to roam; but for all that, they were deprived of that broad liberty to which they and their fathers before them had been accustomed, therefore they felt it most keenly. As I was the only white man who could talk much with them, I was kept pretty busy laboring with them.

In the evening of December 3rd the Indians had a letter from Governor Young. I read and interpreted it to them. Then for the first time they seemed reconciled to their situation. Their chief was filled with the spirit of approval of the course that had been taken with them, and he preached it long and strong. After that, the Indians and the citizens got along very well together, and I continued teaching and preaching to the former.

December 5th I took up school and taught the Indian language, or rather the Shoshone dialect. I had about thirty male adults attending. Brother George W. Hill, who afterwards became the noted Shoshone interpreter in Weber County, was one of them.

I was very much prospered that winter, purchased a city lot and quarter of another on Main Street, fenced the lot, closed my trading with the Indians, and settled with D. H. Wells for the goods I had had.

CHAPTER XLVI.

ANOTHER MISSION TO THE INDIANS— START FOR THE SHOSHONE CAMP — DIFFICULTIES OF TRAVEL — NEAR THE CROWS AND BLACKFEET—A DREAM GIVES WARNING OF DANGER—DISCOVER A LARGE BODY OF INDIANS—NO OPPORTUNITY OF ESCAPE— RIDE INTO THE CAMP OF A HUNTING AND WAR PARTY –MEET CHIEF WASHAKIE—A DAY'S MARCH—SITUATION CRITICAL—HOLD A COUNCIL—PRESENT THE BOOK OF MORMON—ALL BUT WASHAKIE SPEAK AGAINST US AND THE BOOK — AWAITING THE CHIEF'S DECISION.

AT a general conference held in Salt Lake City, April 6, 1855, I was again called to go east among the Indians, to labor with and for them. I was appointed by President Brigham Young to take the presidency of the mission among the Shoshones. At this call I hastened to provide as comfortably as possible for my family, and to fit myself for the mission assigned me.

I set out on May 8, 1855, in company with four other Elders, going east via Salt Lake City. I drove one of the two teams, to pay for the hauling of my baggage, as I had no team of my own. On the 10th we reached Salt Lake City, and left the same day. On the 11th we overtook another wagon and two of our fellow-missionaries. We arrived at Fort Supply on the 17th, having had a pleasant trip. We found seven Elders planting the crop. On the 18th we joined them in the work of plowing and seeding, and repairing the stockade and fences. On the 29th, eight of us fitted up a four-horse team and wagon and six saddle horses and started for the Shoshone camps, which we had heard were on the headwaters of either the Green or the Snake River. On June 1st we came to a tributary of the Green River, called the Fontenelle. There we rested one day, then moved camp up to the mouth of the canyon.

On the 3rd of June, E. B. Ward, Joshua Terry and I crossed over the divide between the Green and Snake Rivers, leaving Elder George W. Boyd in charge of camp. The three of us went along the western slope, passing one lodge of friendly Indians. On the 5th we came to Siveadus' camp of twenty lodges. He and his people were very cool towards us, so we proceeded to a stream called Piney, and up that to the top of the divide, from where we could see to the head waters of the Wind River. Having been told that Washakie and his camp were somewhere on the head-waters of Horse Creek, we made for that point, traveling over snowdrifts that we supposed were fifty feet deep. The descent was very steep, and in some places rather danger-ous. That night our coffee basins, that were left standing half or two-thirds full of water, had become frozen solid; and the weather seemed seasonable for Christmas.

We suffered much with cold until 10 o'clock a. m., on the 7th of June. We turned northeast, and came onto Horse Creek, camping just below its mouth, under a high, steep bluff, in a fine grove of cottonwoods. Everything seemed deathly still. We were in the borders of the Crow and Blackfeet Indians' country, with jaded horses, so that if we were discovered it would be impossible to escape. We began to feel a little concern for our scalps, for we were aware that both the Crows and the Blackfeet were hostile. We gathered our wood, taking care that no branch or anything connected with our fire would make much blaze or smoke, lest by it we should be discovered. Everything being placed in the best possible position for flight or fight, as might seem best if emergency should arise, we rested there that night; and something told us we should not go farther north, but that south should be our course in the morning.

Early the following morning, about 3 o'clock, I dreamed that I saw a large band of Indians come down and pitch camp on the creek above us. I was so forcibly impressed that I awoke the other two men, and told them I felt confident that the dream was true, and that we would prove it at daylight. They agreed with me, so I told them to make as dark a fire as was possible, and to get breakfast, while I would go on the high bluff that overlooked camp and the country adjacent, where I would watch everything that moved, and if there were friends or foes in the country we would see them or their lights before they should see ours. We all arose at once, the others preparing the meal and saddling the horses ready for a hasty move, while I went up on the bluff and there kept a sharp lookout until the dawn. At the first streaks of daylight I saw a blue smoke creeping up through the willows, perhaps a mile and a half above me, then another and another, until it was plain there was a camp of Indians just where I had dreamed they were. Soon the tops of lodges appeared, then a band of ponies was driven up. By this time it was fairly daylight.

I reported to the others what I had seen, and we took breakfast. By the time the sun cast his earliest rays over the landscape, we were in the saddle. Then came the question, what shall we do? To flee was folly, for it was not likely that we would escape the ever vigilant eye of the red man, in an open country like that was. We decided to ride out boldly on the open bench, and go straight to their camp. No sooner had we done so than we were discovered, and some twenty or more warriors started to encircle us, but we rode direct for the camp without showing any concern.

Soon we were completely surrounded by a score of armed warriors in full costume of war paint; as these closed in their circle, they saluted us with a war-whoop. Some had "green" scalps hanging from their bridle bits, while others had them suspended from their surcingles. As the warriors drew nearer to us it became evident that they were of the Shoshone tribe, but we could not recognize any one of them, and they did not appear to recognize us. When we spoke to them and offered to shake hands, they shook their heads and pointed us to the camp, while they proudly escorted us there, some going before us and clearing the way up to the lodge of Washakie, their chief, who, with some of his leading men, stood waiting to receive us. As we rode up, Washakie and his associates stepped forward, and in a very friendly manner shook hands. By gestures they said, "We are moving camp, and you will go and camp with us tonight. Then we will hear what you have to say. We fell in with a war party of Crows and Blackfeet yesterday, and defeated them, and now we are fleeing to a safe place for our women and children, lest they get reinforcements and come upon us and our families;" then with a motion, the chief said, "Forward," and soon the whole band was on the move.

We estimated that the Indians numbered about three thousand all told, and there was a pony for every soul; they were well supplied with rifles, Colt's revolvers, bows, arrows, shields and some cutlasses, and large, heavy knives. They were excellently mounted, and their discipline could not well be improved for the country they were passing

over and the force they were most likely to fall in with.
Their flanking party was so arranged as to act as a front
guard, and at the same time drive all the game into a circle
and thence into a second circle, so that everything, down to
the smallest chipmunk and squirrel, was bagged. This was
over a strip of country about eight miles by thirty; and the
pack of sagehens and squirrels that was brought into camp
was astonishing. The old and middle-aged men formed the
rear guard, while the whole female portion of the camp
drove the pack animals. The chief and his most confiden-
tial advisers rode just in front of these, and we were called
to be a part of the escort.

When all was on the move, the camp made quite a
formidable appearance. It looked to us as if the shrubbery
on our way had changed suddenly into a moving army,
what with people and ponies all moving up hill and down,
over the rolling country, to the south, between the high
Snake and Wind River ranges of the great Rocky Mountains. We thought of ancient Israel, of the Ten Tribes coming from the north country, and of the promises that had
been made to the Indians by the prophets of their forefathers.

To us this was a great day of thought and meditation, for
at times it seemed to us that we could see the opening glories
of a better day, and could almost declare, "Now is the dawn
of the day of Israel," for we had a letter from that modern
Moses, President Brigham Young, to read and interpret to
the red men, and also the Book of Mormon to introduce to
them that very evening, for the first time; and the question
uppermost in our minds was as to whether they would receive it or not, for there were many hard looking countenances in the throng, and we could see plainly from their
frowns that they were not at all friendly to us.

When we had traveled till about 3 o'clock p. m., camp
was made in a lovely valley. The chief's lodge was first

pitched, clean robes spread, and we were invited to take seats thereon. Our horses, packs and all, were taken charge of by the women of the camp, just where we dismounted, and we had no more to do with our animals until we had use for them next day.

A little fire having been built in the center of the lodge, the councilors began to file into their places, each very quietly shaking hands with us, some of them very coldly. When all was quiet, the chief said, by gesture, "Now tell us what you have to say. Tell it straight, and no crooked talk, for we do not want any lies, but the truth." It seemed to us that they were ready for square work, so, with as few words as possible, we told Washakie we had a letter from the big Mormon captain to him and his people. Then he said, "Tell us what it says," and between the three of us we could tell him every word.

I am sorry that I have not at hand the full text of the letter, but it was a very friendly document, and, so far as I can now remember, told them that President Young had sent us to Washakie and his people as their friends, that we were truthful and good men, who would tell them many good things about how to live in peace with all people; that President Young and the Mormon people were true friends to the Indian race, and wished them to be our friends, that we might live in peace with each other, for it would not be many years before all the game would be killed off or driven out of the country, and the white men would want to come and settle in the land; that if the Indians would settle down and build houses like the white man, and cultivate the land as the white man did, when the game was gone they and their families would have something to eat. President Young proposed to furnish seed and tools, and some good men to show and help the Indians to put in their crops. The letter further said that after a while, when we understood each other better, we would tell them about their forefathers, and about God; that we had a book that told a great many things regarding the Great Spirit's dealings with their forefathers, and what He would do for them and their children. Then we presented the Book of Mormon to Washakie, while his lefthand man filled the pipe and drew a rude figure of the sun, in the ashes of the smouldering fire; he also muttered a few unintelligible words, smote his chest with his hand, took a whiff or two from the pipe, passed it to the next man on his left, and reached for the book; he opened it and said it was no good for them—that it was only good for the white man.

In that same order the pipe and book passed around the circle twenty-one times, and each time the Indian made a new figure in the ashes, each representing a different planet. During the whole time only one man spoke at once. One said, "This book is of no use to us. If the Mormon captain has nothing better to send than this, we had better send it, his letter, and these men, back to him, and tell him that they are no good to us, that we want powder, lead and caps, sugar, coffee, flour, paints, knives, and blankets, for those we can use. Send these men away to their own land."

Another of the council, when it came to his turn, said, "We have no use for this book. If the paper were all cut out and thrown away, we could sew up the ends and put a strap on it, and it would do for the white man's money bag; but we have no use for it, for we have no money to put in it." He could not understand what good it was to the Shoshone, and said, "Let the white man take it and go home, and come back with something that we can eat, or use to hunt with."

These were the sentiments expressed by the members of the council. But Washakie had not yet spoken, and we anxiously awaited his decision.

CHAPTER XLVII.

WASHAKIE'S BOLD ATTITUDE—TELLS HIS COUNCILORS THEY ARE FOOLS
—SAYS THE WHITE MEN, WHO ARE WISE, HAVE BOOKS—TELLS
THE TRADITION OF HOW THE INDIANS FELL INTO DARKNESS—
GREAT SPIRIT ANGRY AT THE RED MAN—ADVOCATES THAT THE
INDIANS LIVE LIKE WHITE PEOPLE—HIS POWERFUL SPEECH
GAINS THE DAY FOR US—SHOSHONE TRADITION—WE START HOME
—A HUNGRY TRIP—RETURN TO THE INDIANS, FINDING THEM
SULLEN—FOURTH OF JULY CELEBRATION AT FORT SUPPLY—
RETURN HOME.

THE book passed around the entire circle without a solitary friend, and came back to our hands. The chief reached for it, and when he got hold of the volume he looked at and opened it, turned leaf after leaf as readily as though he had been accustomed to books, then straightened to his full height as he sat there, and looked around the circle. "Are you all done talking?" he asked. Seeing every man with his hand on his mouth, he spoke: "You are all fools; you are blind, and cannot see; you have no ears, for you do not hear; you are fools, for you do not understand. These men are our friends. The great Mormon captain has talked with our Father above the clouds, and He told the Mormon captain to send these good men here to tell us the truth, and not a lie. They have not got forked tongues. They talk straight, with one tongue, and tell us that after a few more snows the buffalo will be gone, and if we do not learn some other way to get something to eat, we will starve to death. Now, we know that is the truth, for this country was once covered with buffalo, elk, deer and antelope, and we had plenty to eat, and also robes for bedding, and to make lodges. But now, since the white man has made a road across our land, and has killed off our game, we are hungry, and there is nothing for us to eat. Our women and children cry for food, and we have no meat to give them. The time was when our Father who lives above the clouds loved our fathers who lived long ago, and His face was bright, and He talked with our fathers. His face shone upon them, and their skins were white like the white man's. Then they were wise, and wrote books, and the Great Father talked good to them; but after a while our people would not hear Him, and they quarreled and stole and fought, until the Great Father got mad, because His children would not hear Him talk. Then He turned His face away from them, and His back to them, and that caused a shade to come over them, and that is why our skin is black and our minds dark." Stripping up his shirt sleeve, he continued: "That darkness came because the Great Father's back was towards us, and now we cannot see as the white man sees. We can make a bow and arrows, but the white man's mind is strong and light." Picking up a Colt's revolver, he went on: "The white man can make this, and a little thing that he carries in his pocket, so that he can tell where the sun is on a dark day, and when it is night he can tell when it will come daylight. This is because the face of the Father is towards him, and His back is towards us. But after a while the Great Father will quit being mad, and will turn His face towards us. Then our skin will be light." Here the chief showed his bare arm again, and said: "Then our mind will be strong like the white man's, and we can make and use things like he does."

The chief next drew a strong contrast between the Indian's way of living and the white man's, telling his people that the mode of the white man was far preferable to that of the Indian. He also told them that the Great Father had directed "the big Mormon captain to send these men to us, to talk good talk, and they have talked good, and made our hearts feel very glad, and we feel that it is good for them to come and shake hands. They are our friends, and we will be their friends. Their horses may drink our water, and eat our grass, and they may sleep in peace in our land. We will build houses by their houses, and they will teach us to till the soil as they do. Then, when the snow comes and the game is fat, we can leave our families by the Mormons, and go and hunt, and not be afraid of our families being disturbed by other Indians, or by anybody else, for the Mormons are a good people. Let these three good men go, and find a good place for us to live, close by where they live; and after a while we will come, and they will show us how to build houses, for they are our good and true friends, and we wish they would go home, and bring some blankets, powder and lead, knives, paints, beads, flour, sugar and coffee, to trade for our furs, pelts and robes."

Washakie spoke thus with great power and wisdom, while his wise old councilors sat with their heads bowed, and their hands over their mouths, only grunting assent to the strong points of his powerful speech, of which this account is only a brief synopsis.

No vote was taken, but seemingly every man gave his assent to the chief's decision, by a grunt of approval. Then each man quietly withdrew, and a kettle of boiled antelope meat was set before us. The chief had a separate dish put before him. Then we retired for the night.

The camp was almost destitute of food, notwithstanding the squirrels and sagehens that had been taken the day before. The whole camp was hungry, and the last morsel of our provisions was gone, so next morning, June 9th, we left camp, having a very scant breakfast of meat; but we had introduced the Book of Mormon, and had had the pleasure of having it received favorably by Washakie, the great Shoshone chief, and his council, as the history of their

forefathers. The chief said the wolves had written that
book when they were men, but had since been turned into
wolves; that being an ancient tradition among the Shoshones.

We rode hard all day the day that we left the Shoshone
camp, and at sundown camped by a mountain leek spring,
without a bite to eat. Nor had we had anything to eat at
dinner time; so we made our supper of mountain leeks.
Next morning, the 10th, we had leeks for breakfast, and
at sunrise we were in the saddle, and on our way back to
where we had left the other brethren. I was on the lead,
with a double-barreled shotgun before me. We had not
gone very far before a blue mountain pheasant flew up from
under my horse's head, and lit in the trail a few yards in
front. I shot it so quickly that I never thought of my horse
being frightened. Another man jumped from his saddle, and had the bird skinned before the blood had stopped
flowing, while the other built a fire. The pheasant was
broiled and eaten before the animal heat could have gone
out of it, if it had been left where it was shot. Then we
traveled all that our horses could bear until 3 o'clock p. m.,
when we came to a flock of sagehens. As I was still on
the lead, I shot three of them before the rest fled. We
broiled one of them, and soon devoured it, as we had the
other bird, then continued our journey till evening.

As we traveled along by a small stream of water, I saw
a fish about eighteen inches long, and almost as quick as
thought shot at and stunned it, so that it turned up at the top
of the water long enough for an Indian boy who was traveling with us to shoot an arrow through it. With the arrow
sticking through it, the fish shot up to where the creek
widened out, and I, thinking the water only knee-deep,
plunged in up to my hips. I caught the fish, we broiled it
for supper, and ate it as we had done the birds and leeks—
without salt or pepper.

On the 11th we had a bird for breakfast, and traveled till afternoon, counting that we had journeyed about one hundred and twenty-five miles, and reached our camp, where we found all well.   The boys soon spread a white man's meal before us, and each of us did our part without a grumble.   Then we made a short drive, and on the 12th pushed forward on our way to Fort Supply, reaching that place on the 14th.   We found all well, and in good spirits.

June 15th we loaded two wagons with a large assortment of Indian goods, as we had agreed to meet the Indians with the merchandise, in twenty days, on the Labarg, a tributary of Green River.   On the 20th we reached that stream and as there were no Indians there I sent Joshua Terry, E. Barney Ward, and my cousin James M. Brown, to inform the red men that we were on time as agreed.   It seemed that after we left them they had quarreled and divided into three parties, and came very near fighting among themselves.   They were therefore very different in spirit to when we left them.   At last they began to come and lodge in three distinct camps around our wagons.

On the 28th, all the Indians were very sullen and did not seem to be the same people they were a few days before.   Knowing something of their nature, we turned out about seventy-five dollars' worth of provisions and other goods as a present.   Still that did not seem to satisfy them; they wanted all we had.   Finally I told them that we had done as we had agreed to do, and if they wished to trade we were ready.   They continued to manifest a very mean spirit, and we were not able to sell more than five hundred dollars' worth of goods out of a stock of three thousand dollars.

On June 30th we left three of our party with the Indians, while the rest of us returned to Fort Supply with our stock of goods.   The Indians felt very bad because we had not given them all we had.   It was July 4th when we arrived at the fort, and found the brethren there celebrating the glorious Independence Day.   I was quite ill, but the brethren insisted on my taking the lead of the ceremonies. That being my birthday, I accepted the offer, and we had a very enjoyable time.

From July 5th to the 18th we continued our farm labors.   Then E. B. Ward and three or four other men, including myself, set out on a little exploring trip among the hills. We crossed over to Henry's Fork, then returned to Smith's Fork, where we selected a place for the Indians to settle when they saw fit.   Having thus completed our obligations to them, we returned to the fort, and continued our labors until August 1st, when we had a recruit of twelve men sent to us, under command of John Phelps.   About August 3rd or 4th I rebaptized all the Elders, and baptized three of the first Shoshone women that ever came into the Church. Their names were Mary, Sally Ward, and Corger.   I also baptized a young Indian man named Corsetsy.   From the 5th to the 7th, the Indians came and went, attended our meetings regularly, and felt very friendly and somewhat inquisitive.   We gave them a few presents.   They said they were well pleased to have us locate in their country, and were satisfied with the places we had selected for them to settle and live upon as we did.   On the 7th of August, Joshua Terry and I started for Salt Lake City, each with an ox team and two wagons loaded with furs, pelts and robes. We arrived in the city on the 11th, and reported our success to Governor Young, who was pleased with our efforts. We also settled for the goods we had had of him.

On the 13th I started for Ogden City, and reached there the next day, meeting my wife and firstborn child, a daughter, who was born August 10th.

CHAPTER XLVIII.

AFFAIRS AT HOME—START FOR FORT SUPPLY—ILLNESS OF MYSELF
AND FAMILY—GIFT OF HEALING—TROUBLE WITH INDIANS AT
FORT SUPPLY—TURBULENT RED MEN—I HELP ONE OFF MY BED—
THEY PERSIST IN TAKING OR DESTROYING OUR PROPERTY—WE
STOP THEM—ONE ATTEMPTS TO KILL ME—INDIANS RETIRE FROM
THE FORT—ALMOST A CONFLICT—I CHECK THE WHITE MEN FROM
SHOOTING—INDIANS WITHDRAW—WE SEND TO GOVERNOR YOUNG
FOR ASSISTANCE—OUR STOCK AND GUARDS DRIVEN IN—INDIAN
AGENT APPEARS WITH ANNUITIES—THE SAVAGES SUBMIT—
WE GUARD DAY AND NIGHT—INDIANS MORE PEACEFUL—RE-
INFORCEMENTS ARRIVE FROM THE GOVERNOR—MATTERS QUIET
DOWN.

AUGUST 14, 1855, I went to Salt Lake City, and on
September 3rd returned home.   On the 5th my family were taken sick with cholera morbus.

Notwithstanding this sickness, I started on my return
to Fort Supply, for it was the faith of myself and family
that if I went to my mission they would be healed.   Just as
I mounted my horse to start out, my uncle, Captain James
Brown, came along and said, "Jimmie, are you going off
and leaving your family sick?"

I told him, "Yes, sir."

Said he, "You are cold-hearted, and I would not do it."

When I told him that they with me believed that if I
would go to my missionary labors they would be healed
sooner than if I should neglect my duties in that line, he,
with uplifted hands, said, "Jim, you're right.   Go ahead,
and God bless you.   Your family shall be healed, and not
suffer.   I will go in and pray for them."   He did so, and I
afterwards learned that they were healed the same hour
that I proceeded on my journey.   I did not see them again

till December 20th, when they told me that they had not been sick one day after I left.

Although when I started out I was very ill myself with the same trouble, and had to call at a friend's and get a dose of painkiller, and take a rest for an hour or two before I could proceed on my way to Salt Lake City, yet on the 13th I started for Fort Supply, and overtook the two wagons which had preceded me the day before. I travelled with them until the 17th, then left them and went on horseback forty-five miles to the fort. I was very sick for five days, so that I had to keep my bed part of the time. I found all well and the wheat harvest ready for the laborers, a heavy frost having injured the crops considerably. On Friday, September 28th, I sent four men to invite Washakie to the fort, and on the 29th we learned that Chief Tibunduets (white man's child) had just returned with his band from Salt Lake City. October 1st I sent Isaac Bullock and Amenzo Baker to visit him. They found him and all of his band feeling very bad and revengeful.

October 10th Tibunduets and his band threw down our fencing and came charging up through our field, riding over wheat shocks, and singing war songs. At the same time the warriors from a camp above came into the fort with their weapons in their hands. Our men tried to be friendly and talked peace to them, but it was not what they wanted. They said they were "heap mad," for when they were in Salt Lake City the big Mormon captain had written with blood on their children, and a number of these had died while they were among the Mormons. These Indians refused the seats offered them, but jumped on the beds and behaved very saucily, saying they wanted pay for the death of their children who had died on the Mormon lands. Of course, we could not afford to give presents of that kind, and their demands were rejected.

Three of the hostile Indians went to my room, and

one engaging me in conversation, the other two jumped on my bed and stretched themselves full length on it. My cousin James M. Brown called my attention to their rude actions, and I turned around and told them to get off my bed, but they answered with a contemptuous laugh. I told them a second time, and they sneered again. I stepped to the side of the bed and told them the third time, and as they refused, I jerked one of them off the bed so quickly that it surprised him, and the other one thought he preferred to get off without that kind of help, and did so quickly.

Tibunduets made heavy demands on us, which we could not comply with. We told him that we were not prepared to do his bidding, and he replied, "You're a wolf and a liar, and you will steal." Then the Indians turned their horses into our fields among our shocks of wheat and oats, while their women went to digging and sacking our potatoes, the Indians throwing down our fences in many places and ordering our men out of the fields. They told us to leave their lands, and continued their insults until I sent some men out to order their women out of the potato patch. The squaws only laughed at our men, who returned and reported the results. Then I went out myself, and as I passed a brush fence, I caught up a piece of brush and started towards the potato diggers, who screamed and ran away before I got near enough to use the stick.

I returned to the house and soon was followed by two young braves, who rode up in front of the door and called for the captain. I answered in person, when the braves said, "You heap fight squaw, you no fight Injun." They continued their insulting words and threats of violence, until at last I ordered them out of the fort, upon which one of them drew his bow and pointed his arrow at me, within three feet of my breast. At that one of my men pushed the horse's head between me and the arrow. At the same time Amenzo Baker handed me a Colt's revolver, and another man covered the Indian with a revolver.

At that movement the Indians started for the big gate, and as there was quite a number of warriors inside the fort I called my men out with their guns, for the Indians seemed determined on bloodshed. They rushed outside, and the white men followed them to where a young chief sat on his horse, just outside of the gate. There must have been a signal given to the camp above, for the warriors came running with their rifles in hand, until seventy-five to one hundred warriors were on the ground, while there were only about forty white men. Everybody wanted to say something, and in the confusion that followed some ten or twelve men leveled their guns to shoot, being in such close quarters that they struck each other as they brought their weapons into position.

At that moment I sprang under the guns and held some of them up, and forbade the men to shoot. This act seemed to please the young chief, and he commanded his men to desist. I ordered my men back and into their bastions, and to bar the gate. This done, I took a position in the watchtower, where I talked with their chief through a porthole, and told him that we were in a position to do them harm, but did not wish to do so, yet they must withdraw in peace and not molest our property, for we should defend it and ourselves to the best of our ability. I said that if they would withdraw peacefully we would not interfere with them, but to that they would not agree. After considerable parleying, however, they did withdraw to their camp among the cottonwood timber and willows on the creek, and built large fires, around which they danced and sang war songs the greater part of the night, while we made every possible preparation for defense.

As captain of the fort, I wrote a despatch to the governor and superintendent of Indian affairs, stating the facts.

Then we covered with blankets a slab bridge that had to be crossed near the gates, to deaden the sound of the horse's feet as he went out, and a clever young man by the name of Benjamin Roberts speeded away with the note to Salt Lake City.

On the 11th all was quiet. A few Indian lodges remained near our fort, and the women and children were around them as usual, so Isaac Bullock and I went down to learn what the situation was. We found some of them friendly, while others were very sulky. The main part of the Indian camp had gone down the creek, and we thought it safe to turn our stock out under a mounted guard, with one man in the watchtower to keep a lookout. About 2 p. m. the man at the watchtower sounded an alarm, saying he saw a great dust in the north; and a few minutes later he shouted that a large body of horsemen was in sight, coming rapidly from the north, while our horse guards were coming with our band of horses, hastening with all speed to the fort. Immediately every man was called to take a position for prompt action. I occupied a commanding place, giving instructions to the men not to shoot without my order, and then not unless they felt sure of making every shot tell. They were told to see that every tube was filled with powder, "for here they come," said I; "keep cool boys, for it is a close race with our men and horses."

It was a question of which would reach the fort first, they or the Indians. The race was so close that the guards with our band just succeeded in getting in with the animals in time to close the gates against the Indian ponies, whose riders called out, "Open the gates!" They were answered with a positive "No! not until you give up your arms." They had three mountain men in their party of over one hundred warriors, who shouted that they would be responsible if we would let them in, for the Indian agent, George

Armstrong, was a short distance in the rear, with two wagons loaded with goods for the Indians.

As I had not been advised of the agent's approach from any other source, I still refused them admittance. Soon the agent's wagons were in sight, and some of his party came up and told the Indians they would have to give up their arms before they could enter the fort, for the captain was determined not to allow them in with their arms. At last they submitted, and the gate was opened just wide enough for one man to pass through. I stepped outside, the Indians handed their arms to me, I passed them to the other men, and they placed them on a part of a wagon sheet. Then the weapons were bound up strongly and taken away and put in my room, and a guard placed over them. The Indians were then told that they could enter the fort and pass directly into the blockhouse, but would not be permitted to wander around in the fort.

About this time the agent's wagons rolled up and were hastily unloaded. Then a friendly smoke took place, and a short council, in which the Indians agreed that they would withdraw in peace and go to their hunting grounds, and would not molest us any more. They said we might remain on their lands let our stock eat grass and drink water in peace; that we might cultivate the lands and use what timber we wanted, and that they would be our friends, and we their friends. The goods the agent had for the Indians were then turned over to them.

On the 13th the red men brought in a report that the Sioux Indians had killed one of Jack Robinson's beeves. This they did to screen themselves, for it was they and not the Sioux who had killed the animal. The agent gave them a beef ox, and they moved down the creek. On the 14th the agent and party returned home, and we kept up a guard day and night to prevent being surprised by the renegades of the Indian camps; for we had evidence of their treachery. We had given them back their arms, and when they obtained all we had for them they said the white man was "heap good, Shoshone no kay nabatint Mormon." (Shoshones do not want to fight Mormons.)   They packed and left, feeling quite pleased.

General R. T. Burton with a party of twenty-five men were met at Fort Bridger on the 16th, by myself and a small party. On the 17th I went with them to Fort Supply, while they concluded to send out a scout to ascertain whether the Indians really had crossed the Green River or not, thinking that if they did we could be satisfied that all was right. When our scouts returned and reported that all had crossed the river and gone farther on, General Burton and command returned home, while myself and men did up our fall work at Fort Supply.

CHAPTER XLIX.

START HOME FROM FORT SUPPLY—CAMP ALONE AT NEEDLE ROCK—
AWAKENED BY MY HORSE—SURROUNDED BY WOLVES—FLASH
POWDER ALL NIGHT TO KEEP OFF THE WILD BEASTS—REACH
HOME—SUPPLIES SHORT—HARDSHIPS OF A GRASSHOPPER YEAR—
GETTING MY CATTLE OUT OF A CANYON—PERILS OF BEING
CAUGHT IN THE SNOW—GREAT SUFFERING—BREAKING A SNOW
ROAD—BUSINESS AFFAIRS.

THE writer left Fort Supply December 14, 1855, and started for his home in Ogden City on horseback and alone, having placed Isaac Bullock in charge of affairs at the fort. The first night out I camped at a place called Needle Rock, just east of Yellow Creek. There I selected a spot where the feed was good, picketed out my horse,

set my saddle over the picket pin, and spread my blankets
so as to lay my head on the saddle, lest the coyotes should
cut my riata and turn loose the horse.

As I was alone and yet in an Indian country, I did not
make a fire, but ate a cold lunch, rolled up in my blankets,
and soon dropped to sleep, to be awakened by my horse
snorting and kicking. The animal brushed his nose on my
head before I was sufficiently awake to understand what
he meant by his actions; but no sooner was I aroused than
I found that he was surrounded by a pack of large, grey
wolves which were growling and snapping at his heels and
at each other. The night was so dark that I could plainly
see the fierce eyes of my ravenous enemies shining in the
darkness all around me.

I had a good Colt's revolver, but having heard that if
wolves smelled blood when they were gathered in such
a pack they would attack man or beast, I reserved my fire.
I remembered having heard that these wild beasts were
afraid of the flash and smell of burning powder, so I spread
some gunpowder on the leathers of my saddle, and with
flint and steel struck fire, and in that way flashed powder
by intervals all night. The wolves would run off, but return in a short time, as if determined to have flesh. My
horse was too weak to attempt to flee, and as for myself I had
become so chilled and benumbed that it was with some difficulty that I could keep up the flashes till daylight, at which
time the pack of wolves went away, leaving horse and
rider to resume their sufficiently hazardous journey without
such unwelcome company.

I crossed over to the head of Echo Canyon, where I
found a yoke of oxen that some emigrants had left to die.
As the animals had got rested up, I thought I could drive
them in and save their lives, but had to abandon them in
Round Valley, Weber Canyon. Then, on a poor, jaded

SURROUNDED BY A PACK OF HUNGRY WOLVES.

horse, I pursued my way, arriving at home about 9. p. m. on December 20th.

I found all well, but winter supplies of food so short that I sold the only respectable suit of clothes I had for breadstuff. I had about worn out all the rest of my clothing when I was in the Indian country, so that I had but one old flannel shirt left, and that I had made out of two old ones. I had one pair of buckskin pants, a rough beaver cap and a pair of moccasins.

It will be remembered by the early residents of Utah that the year 1855 was a grasshopper year, as well as a season of great drought, and therefore one of the hardest years that many of the people had ever experienced, both for man and beast. Hundreds of horses and cattle starved to death, and many of the people barely escaped the same sad fate. I could do no better than to let my horses go out on the range to die of starvation and cold, and turn my hand to anything I could get to do to earn an honest dollar.

Soon after arriving home I was called to devote a portion of my time in traveling from settlement to settlement, and preaching to the people; also in visiting the Indian camps along the Weber River and preaching and talking to them, for it was a terrible winter for the Indians. Before entering upon these duties, however, I returned to where I had left my cattle to rest for a few days, and where the feed was tolerably good. When I started out it commenced to storm and by the time I reached the cattle the snow was eighteen inches deep.

Before I could get out of the canyon with the animals the snow was two and a half feet deep. My horse gave out, and I had to travel on foot, breaking the trail and leading the horse a few rods, then going back and driving up the cattle. I continued these efforts until myself and stock were exhausted. When I tried to start a fire, my matches were all wet. I had left my rifle and shotpouch at home, and in the pouch were my faithful flint and steel, which had never failed me. But for the snow, the night was total darkness. At last I reached a clump of cottonwood trees, and for a time I thought I would die of exhaustion and thirst. I knew that if I ceased to exert myself I would chill to death. Finally it occurred to my mind to tear off a piece of my shirt, roll it up, hold it in one hand, and with my revolver shoot through it and start a fire. I found a large sagebrush, and from it gathered the dry bark. This I wrapped around the roll of shirt, then fired a shot through it, and in that way succeeded in starting a flame. As there was plenty of wood handy, I built and kept up a large fire during the night. The river banks were so steep that it was impossible in the darkness to get water to drink. I was driven almost frantic by thirst, but finally thought to take off my heavy leggings, place them in a position so that they would form a kind of basin, and cover them with snow, so the fire would melt it to water in the leather bowl. In that way I obtained water and quenched my terrible thirst. My blankets and everything I had on had been soaked thoroughly with the melting snow, but I succeeded in drying all during the night.

The dawn of day was welcome indeed, but my troubles were not yet over, for I found my animals standing in snow to their necks, and they would not move out of their tracks only as I broke an opening around and urged them on. The snow was so wet and heavy that it was an awful task to break a road and get those animals through for the first five miles. After that the snow was not so deep, and with a very great effort and hazard of life I succeeded in reaching Ogden, as thankful as I ever was in my life to get home —to "home, sweet home."

Being once more with my family and friends, I got up my winter wood and visited the people as a teacher. In the spring I finished a two-roomed house that I had under way on Main Street. I then moved into it, preparatory to going to Fort Supply again, but was honorably released by President Young from further missionary labors in that part. I rented land, put in corn and potatoes, and spent the fore part of the summer at farm labor. Having acquired a fourth interest in three ferries on Green River, I arranged with my three partners, Isaac Bullock, Louis Robinson and W. Hickman, so that I did not have to go there, as my health was not very good; hence I remained at Ogden.

CHAPTER L.

CALLED ON A MISSION TO DEEP CREEK INDIANS—SHORT TIME FOR THE JOURNEY—PREPARE FOR THE TRIP—JOURNEY IN THE DESERT—HORSES STOLEN—TRAVEL ON FOOT—SAVED FROM PERISHING WITH THIRST—MEET THE INDIANS—COULD UNDERSTAND AND SPEAK TO THEM—INDIAN AGENT'S OFFER—I ACT AS INTERPRETER—PREACH TO THE INDIANS—ON THE RETURN TRIP—VISIT GOVERNOR YOUNG WITH A DELEGATION OF BANNOCK INDIANS.

ON August 22, 1856, I received a letter from President Young, calling me to take a mission of thirty days, west across the desert, to Deep Creek, to the Indians in that region. As I did not understand fully the object of the mission, I thought there was some mistake in the letter, since the distance that had to be traveled out and back would be about five hundred miles and I was to preach to a tribe of Indians I had never seen, much less being able to speak their dialect, and do it all with only thirty days' rations. To me it was, to say the least, a singular call; so I went to Salt Lake City August 23rd, to find out that the letter meant just what it said, no less; only that Geo. W. Armstrong, an Indian agent from Provo, was going out to distribute some goods among the Indians, and it would be a good time to send a few missionaries to preach to the red men.

From Salt Lake City I returned to Ogden and purchased a splendid mare of widow Ruth Stuart, on credit, promising to pay when I could.   On the 27th I joined Mr. Armstrong and twenty-five other men in Salt Lake City, fitting up for the journey, some as guards to the agent and some as missionaries.   Among those I remember were Seth M. Blair, Oliver Huntington, Ormus Bates, John Whitney, J. Cooley, Harrison Sagers, Harrison Sevier, and Peter Conover; there were others whose names I do not now recall.

The company left the city on August 29th, and traveled through Tooele, Rush Valley, and over Johnson's Pass into Skull Valley.   With five others of the party, however, I went around by what is now called Dugway, and met the rest of the company at the springs in Skull Valley.

On September 2nd, we reached Granite Rock, sometimes called Granite Mountain, as it stands out in the midst of the desert.   There the company camped at some alkali springs, where, with cup and bucket, it took all night to dip water for the stock.   Next morning we found that the Indians had stolen all the team horses, eight head, so the agent called on the men to volunteer their saddle horses to take his wagons across the desert.   Among the rest, I let my horse go, and eight of us set out on foot to cross the desert, while some went after the stolen stock.   Other horsemen pushed across to water, and the teams brought up the rear.

The route was brushy and rocky, in some places there was heavy sand, in other parts stiff alkali mud, and much of the time without a sign of a road.   The writer was taken very sick with a severe bowel complaint and was compelled to turn to one side, so I fell behind my fellow footmen. The teams lagged in the sand and mud till long after dark. I became so weak and faint that I could not travel any longer, and I laid down on the damp ground, so tired and thirsty that it seemed impossible for me to live until morning without relief. When I had laid down for some time, I heard my bunkmate, Doc. Woodward, shout that he had found water and filled his canteen, and was coming back hunting the missed and needy one. When he got near enough for me to answer him, I did so, and with a drink I was somewhat revived. I was helped on my friend's horse, and we proceeded on for about five miles to camp and water. One of the party gave me a brandy toddy, spread my blankets, and I turned in, a very grateful sufferer. I was given a cup of coffee, after which I felt very much relieved, and by morning was ready to resume the journey, the wagons having come up about 11 p. m. Next morning, September 4th, we moved up five or six miles, to what was called Fish Springs. There we found a number of Indians, and the party pitched camp for a few days.

When the animals had been cared for and fires built, the Indians gathered around in considerable numbers. As they were talking among themselves, the writer understood and commenced to speak with them in their own dialect, at which they were surprised and said one to another, "Who is this man, that talks our talk? He has never been in our country before." I was no less astonished myself; and I call the reader's attention now to the peculiar feature of a man being called to fit himself out with provisions to last him thirty days, travel out in the desert two hundred and fifty or three hundred miles, and preach to a tribe of Indians in whose country he had never been and whom he had never seen before. Yet when the agent's interpreters failed to get the Indians to understand, the agent asked if I could talk with them. I told him I had never seen these

Indians before that hour, "but," said I, "I understand them, and you see they understand me." "Yes," said the agent, but I do not see how it is that you can talk with them. I have two men employed as interpreters, but they cannot make the Indians understand. Now if you can make them comprehend what I wish to tell them, I will pay you three dollars per day from the time that you left home until you return there."

"I do not know whether I can do your talking or not," was my response to this proposition. "I came here to preach to this people, and I have power given me to do it in their own tongue. But I do not know whether I will be permitted to speak for you or not; if I am, I will talk for you." "All right," said Mr. Armstrong, "have them form a circle in front of my wagons, and tell them who I am, and what the great father at Washington has sent me here for; that I have brought them clothing and blankets as a present from the great father at Washington, and that he expects them to be good people and live in peace with each other, and also with other people, and if they will do so the great father will send good men to bring more goods to them."

When I told them what the agent wanted, they at once formed a circle as desired, to the satisfaction of all present. Then the agent distributed the goods, to the great pleasure of the Indians. He talked very kindly to them and gave them much good advice. I interpreted what he said, and then continued to preach to them, telling them about the Book of Mormon and their forefathers, and many other things of interest to them. I seemed to have perfect liberty of speech as I desired it, in their dialect, and they listened attentively to all I had to say.

The next day Seth M. Blair, Peter Conover, Ormus Bates and myself and four or five other men that belonged to the missionary part of the camp, employed an Indian guide to travel south around the head of Deep Creek, to see

24

what natural advantages there were for settlements, but we failed to find anything inviting until we came to Deep Creek, where the country seemed quite suitable for stock raising. About the 11th of September the party returned to the agent's camp, where we again met with many of the Indians, who wished us to stop and live with them as their friends, adding, "If you will not stop with us, then tell the big Mormon captain to send some good Mormon men that will tell the truth and show us how to make clothes like the white man."

It was the next day, I think, that the party started back to Salt Lake City, the agent having secured his team horses. We traveled north of Granite Rock, and around the point of the mountain to the lake, thence along the shore to Grantsville. We tarried one day with Mr. Cooley, and partook of the hospitality of himself and family.

After our visit to the Deep Creek Indians, some of them claimed to have received dreams and visions, in which heavenly messengers appeared and told them to go into Tooele and call on the Bishops, who would tell them what to do, and for them to obey the Bishops. Accordingly, scores of them went to Grantsville and related their story, when they were told to believe in Christ and repent and be baptized. Many of them obeyed this advice, and then a missionary was sent out and located among them.

With our one day's rest at Grantsville, the party continued on to Salt Lake City, where Mr. Armstrong paid me ninety dollars in cash for my services as interpreter. I returned home and paid the ninety dollars on the mare I had purchased on credit for the mission. My labors as a missionary, however, were still called for, and I visited all the settlements in Weber County, also the Indian camps, and acted as a presiding teacher in Ogden City, often being called to arbitrate differences between the white people and Indians.   About that time Snag, the Bannock Indian chief, and twelve of his prominent men called on me to accompany them to Salt Lake City to see President Brigham Young on some business. They said they wished a friendly talk, and to tell some of their grievances and ask some favors of him.   The latter constituted the greater part of their business.   I accompanied them to President Young's residence, where he received them kindly, furnishing them with necessary supplies of food and fuel.   Next day, after they had had a very friendly talk with the President, he gave orders to the Bishops in the northern settlements to supply the Indians' wants as far as practicable, as it was cheaper to feed than to fight them.   Then after all the complaints of the Bannocks had been satisfactorily adjusted, we left, they for their homes in the north near Fort Hall, the writer for Ogden, where I continued my labors.

CHAPTER LI.

UTAH MILITIA ORGANIZED—ELECTED CAPTAIN OF A COMPANY—HEAR OF JOHNSTON'S ARMY—SCOUTING PARTY SENT OUT—I AM CHOSEN AS GUIDE—TRAVEL TO THE BEAR LAKE COUNTRY—COLD NIGHTS AND LITTLE FOOD—COMPLAINT IN THE PARTY—PROVE THAT I AM RIGHT—REACH LOST CREEK—SOME OF THE MEN OBJECT TO DOUBLE GUARD—A DISCOVERY THAT REMOVES ALL OBJECTIONS—STRIKE THE TRAIL OF HORSEMEN—PREPARE FOR ACTION—TAKE A CAMP BY SURPRISE—THE MEN ARE FRIENDS—ARRIVE AT OGDEN—CALLED TO GO ON AN IMPORTANT ERRAND—TUSSLE WITH AN INDIAN—FAIL IN GETTING DESIRED INFORMATION, AND RETURN TO OGDEN.

IN the spring of 1857 I rented some land and put in a crop. Soon after this an order came from Governor Young to the Weber County officials to organize the militia of the county, which was done. I was elected captain of the first company of infantry in the Weber militia district. The company consisted of captain, commissioned and non-commissioned officers, and one hundred men of the rank and file. Chauncey W. West, then the Bishop of Weber County, was commissioned general of the district. He appointed days for drill, and four companies came together in Ogden City for that service.

At that time we had not learned of threatened danger from any source except occasional Indian raids; but no sooner had we got properly organized and ready for self-defense than news came from the east to Governor Young that an invading army was coming, with hostile threats against the citizens of Utah.

As the governor had not been officially notified of the approach of United States troops, his official oath bound him to repel any invading forces. He accordingly sent out scouts to ascertain the movements of the troops referred to, and soon learned that there was a well equipped army of nearly ten thousand men on their way west, with the avowed purpose, it was said, of destroying the Mormon Church and people.

Some time in August General West called out twelve or fifteen men as a scouting party, to go over in the Bear Lake country, along the emigrant road, and from there to the head of Lost Creek and down the Weber River. He had heard of a party going up Lost Creek, and over to the Bear Lake country. General West appointed Major Monroe to take charge of the party, of which the writer was called to be one, as I had been acquainted with mountain travel and understood the Indian language. General West told the major to make no move of importance without consulting me as to the journey.

The party proceeded to the divide between North Ogden and Ogden Valley, where we halted and the major privately told me that he was not accustomed to journeys of that kind, and wished me to lead the party through, for I had more experience than he had. I declined the responsibility, but the major said: "I will be responsible if you will lead," so I headed out to Blacksmith Fork and thence to Bear Lake, and around the east side thereof to the river. We crossed to the California road near the present site of Montpelier, thence back east to the road where Cokeville settlement is now located. As we failed to learn anything of importance, we returned back over the river and struck out for the head of Lost Creek, where it was supposed that we would fall in with the scouts from the approaching army.

The nights began to be cold, and the food supply was getting low. The horses were somewhat jaded, the route very rough, and the most of the party were young and in-experienced. They began to complain and said that no-body had ever traveled in so rough a country as that, and it was all foolishness to be wearing ourselves out in that way. They said the writer did not know himself where he was going, and I had no business to be on the lead, as that was Major Monroe's place. The major, however, promptly told the party that I was in the proper place. Finally I called a halt and told the party that I knew that we were going just right and had been on a trail all day, but they did not know it. They asked, "Where is your trail?" and I again told them that we were on it. They laughed at me when I said, "I can prove it to you, and even tell you the color of the horses that have passed this way." But they thought me a fool to talk thus, so I told one of the young men to jump down and remove the leaves from a root of a tree that stood near by a steep bank, as it was plain to the practiced eye that an old trail passed there, and when the leaves were removed he would find that the bark had been bruised at the roots of the tree by the hoofs of passing horses. He found the trail and the bark off the tree roots, as I had said. I told the men to look on the tree about the height of a pony's side, and they would find hair that would tell them the color of the ponies that had passed there. They found bay and white horses' hair. Next I said to them, "Look on the point of that snag which projects over the trail." They did so, and found a duplicate of the hair they had found on the tree. Then they said that I could prove anything I pleased, and they would not dispute with me any more.

The party passed on down Lost Creek, to a point where the country was more open. When camping time came we turned into a little creek bottom and put out the stock. I remarked to the major that I felt as though we should put on a double guard that night. This was more than some of the boys thought they could stand. Several said that I would run the party to death, but that they would not submit to any extra guard. Others said there was no use for any guard, for nobody but Brown would ever lead a party there; but just then some one hallooed, and we found, on looking, that no one was missing from camp. One said it was a coyote, another that it was an owl. Again the cry was heard distinctly, and no doubt remained of its being a human voice. Then the order was given to get up the stock, ready for whatever might come. The horses were soon picketed near camp, and every man thought it was proper to put on a double guard that night, some of the boys remarking that Brown was not such a fool as they had thought.

Things settled down for the night, and next morning the party started out. We had gone less than a mile when we saw fresh horse tracks made by shod horses, and the droppings looked so new that I directed a young man to ascertain if they were warm. The novel way in which the young man performed that task created some merriment for the moment. Then the party continued on a short distance, when we saw a smoke just over the creek bank ahead. Every man was ready to obey orders, and all dismounted at command and tightened up their saddle girths.

Then came the order to see that every tube was filled with dry powder, and each man was assigned his position for action.

The party was instructed not to halt without orders, and not to let a horse put his head down to drink. If perchance we saw a blanket, a handkerchief, or any camp equipage, we were to pass it unnoticed; if brush or any obstructions were observed, we might be certain that all such signs meant ambuscade. We then advanced cautiously and found evidence of a party about our own number, lying encamped at the fire. We pressed forward on the trail, and found several bushes lapped across it, so that we felt certain we would soon fall in with those ahead, whom we felt sure could be none other than a scouting party from Johnston's army. We prepared for the worst, and as we were moving on double-quick time we saw a man running towards a grove of cottonwood trees, from a point of the mountain. Next we saw the horses of a party of scouts, the top of whose tent was soon discovered.

Quickly capturing the horses, we charged on the tent and surrounded it, taking the men by surprise. As they began to file out of their tent, our party leveled their rifles and called on them to surrender. Just at that moment one of the surprised party recognized one of our men, so that we only required them to acknowledge that they were "dropped on," a phrase used in those times to express the condition. We were not long in ascertaining that the party was a scout from Davis County, in pursuit of the same reported detachment we had been sent to intercept. But neither of us had seen or heard anything of the party that was supposed to be in the region of country we had been over. Without much delay, our party hastened home to Ogden City, and joined our regiment, finding much excitement and hearing many rumors.

It seemed that there was no rest for me, for in a day

or two General West called on me to visit the camp of James and Ben Simons, who lived about twenty miles up the Weber River. The men named were Cherokee Indians who, it was said, were in possession of some important information which the general wanted to get. He told me to learn what I could from the Simonses, as they were friendly.

When I got to the mouth of the canyon I chanced to meet Ben Simons coming from Salt Lake City. It was evident the Indian had been drinking, and as soon as I met him he drew his Colt's revolver and said, "Hold on there!" threatening to kill me if I was Uncle Sam's man. I succeeded in riding close alongside of him, grabbed his pistol and held the muzzle away from me. I tried to persuade him not to shoot, for we must be good friends. He yelled again that if I were a Mormon I must fight his old uncle or he would kill me. He was a powerful man, and I had all that I could do to keep the pistol turned from me.

For ten miles I had to tussle with that Indian, and at times thought I would have to shoot him in self-defense; but after the most disagreeable and hazardous ten miles' ride of my whole life, we came to Gordon Beckstead's ranch. Simons regarded Beckstead as his friend. The latter persuaded the warrior to dismount and have a drink of whisky with him, and let me go my way, for I was a good friend to both of them.

I went to James Simons' camp but failed to get the information desired. Simons was very friendly, and said that if he heard anything of interest he would be pleased to let us know it at once. I then returned to my regiment, which was ordered into camp the next day. We bivouacked on the east bench in Ogden City.

CHAPTER LII.

THE first night in camp at Ogden, General West and
his adjutant, D. Gamble, called at my tent, and told
me I was wanted to take charge of a scouting party to go
over in the Bear Lake country, and start by sunrise next
morning. They directed me to choose the men I would
like to have accompany me, and they should be released to
go home and prepare. I made a list of five young, active
men, who met me next morning at sunrise, having received
their orders. We proceeded to the emigrant road across
the Bear River, about fifteen miles above the lake. There
we met with some emigrants, but could not learn anything
from them, so we crossed back to the foot hills, and there
camped in a secluded place, where we could overlook the
emigrant road. Next morning at 4 o'clock I awoke from a
dream, in which I had seen two hundred and fifty cavalrymen come and pitch camp just across the river from where
we were; then I saw two hundred and fifty more come and
reinforce the first detachment; I also saw their baggage

and artillery wagons. I was impressed so forcibly with the
dream that I called my comrades and told them to prepare
for a move, while I went up one of the high points and
watched developments. At daybreak I saw the camp of
the first two hundred and fifty men, saw them form in line
for roll call, and a mounted guard drive their horses across
the river towards our camp.

The main object of our scout was to learn if the army
or any portion of it was coming down Bear River and into
Salt Lake Valley from the north, and if we saw any troops
on that route to communicate the information to headquarters at the earliest moment possible, so that our forces
could meet them at the best places on the route, and repulse
them. That that end might be served I sent two of my
men with a dispatch to General West, and as soon as the
messengers had gone out of call I again went on the hill.
Everything was ready to move as developments might indicate, and just as the first party was saddling its horses I
saw the second two hundred and fifty come up and join the
first party. Then the five hundred cavalrymen proceeded
down the river, just as I had seen them in my dream. This
necessitated a second dispatch and two more of my men,
leaving me only one, with whom I followed up the troops
till they camped. It rained and snowed alternately all that
day and night. My comrade, James Davis, and I went
after dark within the lines of the troops, but did not learn
of their intentions. Davis was taken with something like a
congestive chill, and we were forced to retreat into the hills,
where we camped for the night. Davis was so bad that I
worked in the storm all night with him and prayed for him;
at last he was healed and we set out on our way home at
daylight.

About 8 a. m. the writer came down sick, just the
same as my friend had been, only I also suffered with pleurisy in the right side. I could ride no further, so we camped

in the snow, where it was about eight inches deep. Snow was still falling as it can only in the mountain country. Our clothes were wet as could be, and our blankets were in the same condition. The only food we had was the crumbs and dust from some crackers.

Davis succeeded in making a fire, but by that time I had cramped so that I could not speak. Davis, supposing I was dying, started out to a quakingasp grove to get some poles to make an Indian litter or drag, on which he thought to take my body home. As he went he felt he ought to have faith and pray for his comrade, as he had been prayed for the night before; so he fell on his knees and prayed, as he afterwards said, as he never had done before. Then something said to him, "Go back and put your hands on him and pray again, and he will be healed;" and it was even so.

We then traveled some fifteen miles, when the sun shone. We partly dried our blankets by a fire and the sun, and continued our journey for some ten miles, when I had a second attack of illness, which was so severe that I thought I had better die alone in the mountains than to allow the enemy to gain the advantage in the country. Consequently, I told Davis to make my horse fast by the trail and spread my blankets, that I might lie down. This done, I directed him not to spare horseflesh, but take the news to our friends as soon as it was possible. Davis did not want to leave me in that plight, but was urged to go. He started reluctantly, and in tears.

For a time it seemed that I had rendered my last services to family and friends, as I lay down by an Indian trail, sixty miles from any white man's habitation. While I was pondering the situation, a magpie came flying down over me, and said "quack," then alighted on a willow near by, in plain sight. Next came a raven, which gave its "croak," as it settled down near me, and it seemed as though it had found prey. Being aware of the habits of these carrion birds, I wrapped my head in blankets, to prevent the birds from picking out my eyes, if the worst came to me; yet I knew that my body could not be protected from the wild beasts that roamed in the mountains, such as the bear, wolf, wolverine, panther or mountain lion, wild cat and lynx, some of which, if not all these various kinds, would be tugging at my carcass inside of twenty-four hours.

Then the birds circled over me, as if to say, "We want an eye," or some fragment of my body. I felt that my time was nigh, and unless the providence of God interposed, I would go the way of all the earth before the rising of the sun. I was chilled to the very bone, and cramped so that it was impossible for me to build a fire. It did not seem possible for me to survive until my companion could ride sixty miles and send relief.

While I pondered the situation, four young men who had been sent with fresh horses and food supplies came up, they having met Davis, who sent them on with all speed. I think the eldest of them was not over seventeen years old. They soon built a fire and prepared much needed refreshments, and I was greatly benefited by that special providence of God, as it certainly seemed to me to be. While I partook of the food, the young men saddled my horse, rolled up my blankets, and we rode eight or ten miles that night, and camped while the rain came down in torrents. The boys soon provided me with shelter by sticking willows in the ground and winding the tops together and spreading blankets over, so that it afforded a little protection for me, and I was soon wrapped in wet blankets.

The next thing was to start a fire. Every match had got wet, and the boys thought it impossible to make a fire, so they asked me what they should do. I told them to get some cotton out of a quilt if they could find a dry spot in it, then put a small priming of powder in a rifle and ram down the cotton on the powder; in the next place, go to the heaviest topped sagebrush they could find, and carefully reach under and strip the dry bark off the main stalk of sagebrush, and in that way get a tinder, then come to my shelter and hold the bark loosely over the muzzle of the gun and fire it off. They got a light, but they had too much powder and it blew the fire out. They tried repeatedly without satisfactory results, and the case was becoming desperate, as darkness was coming on. Two of them got under cover with me, and I finally succeeded in measuring the powder to them. Then they started a flame, and as wood was plenty they made a rousing fire.

In the meantime I took to cramping and suffered so severely that one of the boys remarked, "Brother Brown will die. O what shall we do?" Another said, "Let us pray." Then one led in prayer, and he prayed mightily. As soon as he was through, one said, "Let us go in and lay hands on him," and in a moment they all gathered around me, placed their hands on my head, and prayed from their hearts. The cramping ceased and never returned as severe as it was before; yet I suffered greatly from the pain in my side. The writer regrets very much that he cannot recall the names of those young lads. I believe they were all sent from Willard City, Box Elder County. God bless them, whoever they are. Their action showed them to be young heroes, with great faith in God; and but for them I would have died that fearful night.

Next morning, the party was up, and off we went down Blacksmith's Fork Canyon and across to Wellsville, where I was taken in by Bishop Peter Maughan and his good wife, who did all they could to relieve my sufferings. The Bishop also saw that the boys were well taken care of.

The following morning Samuel Obray drove up with

a light, covered wagon, and a good team, and I was helped into the wagon. Sister Maughan had provided a large canteen full of composition tea. She came to the wagon, and without thinking of anything else, she placed it partly under the side where I had the pleurisy pain. Then the team started for Brigham City, and before we had gone five miles the pain had disappeared from my side, thanks to the Bishop and Sister Maughan for their special kindness, and S. Obray. The latter delivered me into the hands of Colonel Smith in Brigham City, where I was cared for until next day, and then the colonel forwarded me to my home in Ogden City, where I recovered after suffering from a severe cold and cough for a few days.

During my absence the regiment had gone to Echo Canyon, and there was scarcely an able-bodied man to be found in the city. The women and children were cutting and hauling wood, and doing all the outdoor work as best they could. A great deal of sickness was brought on by exposure and hardships. At a Sabbath meeting a general vote of thanks was given the writer for his efforts for the general good of the people and his self-sacrifice.

About this time there was a very worthy young man named Yough, who died, and I was called on to take the part of sexton and bury the deceased, as well as some small children that had died. Meanwhile, there were four prisoners brought in from the north; they were supposed to be spies. I was called on to be one of the guards to take them to Salt Lake City, where they were turned over to the military authorities. Then I returned home, to learn that the troops my scouts and I had seen on Bear River were General R. T. Burton's battalion of Utah cavalry, which had been sent out to intercept a detachment of Johnston's army which had been discovered in that direction, but had returned to the main body, which went into winter quarters at Fort Bridger. Then the Utah militia was withdrawn from Echo Canyon.

I was next called to take up my missionary labors in Weber County. From 1856 to 1859 I baptized and rebaptized four hundred persons, and visited with the catechism from house to house. In that work I spent the winter of 1857-8.

CHAPTER LIII.

MORMONS ABANDON THEIR HOMES AND MOVE SOUTH—PREPARE FOR THE WORST—GO TO PAYSON—AFFAIRS BEING SETTLED, RETURN TO OGDEN—CALLED TO GO EAST AS A MISSIONARY—JOURNEY ACROSS THE PLAINS—MEET MY PARENTS IN IOWA—PREACHING AND TRAVELING—MY FATHER'S TESTIMONY—MISSIONARY LABORS —CALLED TO MISSOURI—SENT TO BRING A HERD OF CATTLE— RETURN TO MY PARENTS' HOME—BID FAREWELL TO THEM— PURCHASING CATTLE.

SOME time in May, 1858, as I remember, an order came from President Brigham Young for everybody living north of Utah County to move south and leave their homes prepared for burning; for it had been decided that if Johnston's army came in, as it had threatened to do, with hostile intentions, the people would lay waste the country and fight to the bitter end. I do not remember that there was a dissenting voice from this determination.

Everybody moved out to the south, myself and family going to Payson, one hundred miles from Ogden. There we made a camp, and I cut wild hay and hauled it for a livelihood, that being the only employment I could find.

In the latter part of July, when peace had been re-established, I returned home and made hasty preparations for my family for the winter, as I had been called by President Brigham Young to accompany General Horace S. Eldredge to Florence, Nebraska, with a company consisting of twenty men who were going on business and partly as missionaries. I belonged to the latter class. I went into the western part of Iowa, being assigned to that field of labor, while the others went to their several destinations.

The company was to have moved out on the 1st of September, so I. A. Canfield and I, fitted with a four-mule team and light wagon, were in Salt Lake City ready to start at the appointed time; but the rest of the party would not or could not be ready for ten or twelve days, so we returned home and stayed until the 11th. We then went to Salt Lake City and waited until the 14th, and, as the party was still tardy, we moved out to the top of the Little Mountain, and there camped. From that place we proceeded to the Weber River, where we were overtaken by John Neff and Dusten Arna, who were to join the party when it came up. As their teams were not in the best of plight for the journey, we traveled together to Ham's Fork, where we stopped on the 19th, and waited for those yet in the rear to come up. About 8 o'clock that evening H. S. Eldredge, Jos. W. Young and Horton Haight reached our camp.

On the 20th, the company having got together, proceeded on the way to the Sweetwater. On the 26th we reached the Platte River, where I was taken very sick with hemorrhoids of the bowels. With that exception, all moved smoothly. On the 28th we passed Fort Laramie, and my health began to improve, though I had been brought almost to death's door, and the company was detained one afternoon in consequence. After that I improved, and the company made rapid headway. October 3rd two deserters from Fort Laramie passed the party. They had stolen two horses and a mule from the government, and, as I remember it, made good their escape.

Nothing happened out of the ordinary until October

19th, when the party arrived at Florence, Nebraska, on the Missouri River. From that point each went to his field of labor or to his business, as planned beforehand. Canfield and I crossed the river to L. O. Littlefield's, in Crescent City, and stayed over night with him and his family, and on the 20th proceeded on our way to Calhoun, Harrison County, Iowa, where my father lived with his family. We were soon overtaken by Clayton Webb and B. H. Dennis, my brothers-in-law. I accepted a seat in their buggy and they took me to my father's home.

I had not seen father for eleven years. I was an entire stranger to every one of the family, who kept a hotel. I went in and ate with strangers, and did not make myself known until after all the evening work was done. Then, after I was satisfied that they had not the remotest idea of my identity, I told them who I was. It was some time before they could realize that what I said was true. To them it seemed that the dead had come to life, and the long lost had been found, for they had all given up hope of ever seeing me again. It was not difficult for me to recognize my father and mother, but my elder brother and sister were dead, and the younger ones had all grown out of memory.

When I had visited with them a few days, I preached several times in the public schoolhouse, and then traveled and preached. On one occasion I had a walk and talk with my father alone. We talked of my absence, and he said, "James, I had given up all hopes of ever seeing your face again, but thanks be to God I have that privilege. You always have stood up for the faith and have been a man through thick and thin for your religion." Then he said, "Oh that I had the faith that I once had, and felt as I have felt! I would be a happy man if I had the spirit that you have, and that I once had." He burst into a flood of tears, and exclaimed, "Oh, my God, I am in the dark and I do not know that I shall ever feel as I once felt. Then I could divide the last loaf, yes, the last morsel of food that I had with a Mormon. Talk about heaven! The true spirit of Mormonism is heaven. I thank God that you have kept the faith, though you have had a hard time of it." Then he added, "James, stick to it and never give it up; for if there is any salvation for me or any of my family it will be through you, for you are the Joseph of my family, and I have known it since before you were born." He then seemed as humble as a little child, and continued: "James, be faithful in the work, but as for me or any of my family going to Utah, I don't think we will ever go."

I told him he could do no better than to go with his entire family and renew their covenants, for the good Spirit was for all who would seek it in the proper way. At last father said that he did not know what they should do yet, the weather being wet and cold.

We returned into the house and I stayed with the family the first month, preaching in the public schoolhouse every Sabbath. Then my brother Willis and I traveled around from place to place, and preached everywhere we found an opportunity, first to Raglan Township, and then to the northeast, forty miles into Shelby County. We preached several times in Garden Grove schoolhouse, and went from there to a small town called Monteno, thence to Pottawatomie County. We preached to a full hall in Council Bluffs City, then went out on Mosquito Creek, in what was called the Garner settlement. Thus we continued to travel and preach from place to place and bear our testimonies, as health and opportunity permitted.

In January, 1859, I preached my cousin Ira Johnson's funeral sermon; he had been accidentally shot and killed while out with a surveying party in that region of country. The same day I baptized six persons and confirmed them; this was at my father's house, and from that time my father seemed quite changed in his feelings. He said it was all that he could do to keep out of the water, and stated that he had never felt better in his life than he did on that occasion. Said he, "James, I want you to preach all the time."

On April 7th I received a letter from General Horace S. Eldredge, asking me to come down to Platte County, Missouri, and receive one hundred and seventy-seven head of work oxen that he had contracted for with Mr. Lampton and Mr. Thompson, cattle merchants. Having also received the written contract for the cattle, I started on the 8th, and on the 9th I took passage on the steamboat *Satan*, which lay at the Council Bluffs landing. I paid ten dollars for passage to Parkville, Platte County, Missouri. The boat called at all important towns and landings. Nothing out of the ordinary happened except that we were driven under a high sandbank in a short bend of the river, by a powerful wind storm, and in trying to extricate the boat, the side-wheel next the shore threw the water with such force against the bank as to cause it to cave in onto the boat, so that the guards and wheelhouse were carried away.

I landed at Parkville on April 13th, stopped over night, and on the 14th proceeded eight miles to Mr. Thompson's. On the 15th I went with him to his partner in the contract, Mr. Lampton. The men General Eldredge promised in his letter on the 15th to send to help drive and care for the cattle, did not arrive until the 27th, when Eldredge came with five men. He furnished money to pay the expenses, and gave instructions, then returned to St. Louis. On the 28th, 29th and 30th, myself and party received and branded one hundred and seventy-seven head of work oxen and two valuable mules.

We started for the north on May 1st, traveling through Rochester, Marysvale, Lindon and Sydney, keeping from the river and on the high, rolling prairies, through what was called the Platte purchase in Missouri. We arrived in Council Bluffs on May 15th, and went from there to Florence, Nebraska, where I delivered up the drove of cattle and span of mules, on the 16th, to Bishop Frederick Kesler, who was General Eldredge's agent. We lost but one head from among the cattle, although we had an exceedingly stormy and muddy time of it most of the way, having to swim several streams that had been swollen by the heavy rains, so that the journey was taken with great hardships, and danger as well.

I went to my father's home on the 17th, in Calhoun County, Iowa, settled with my father, who was very kind to me and my brother Willis, helping us to two yoke of oxen to cross the plains with. We bade farewell to the parental home and to the family on the 27th. Father accompanied us to Council Bluffs and paid our expenses until the 30th, when we parted with him. We crossed the river at Omaha, and moved up to Florence, where we went into a camp or rendezvous and waited for others to come to make a company strong enough to cross the plains.

The company had its camp some three miles northwest of Florence, where General Eldredge, the Church agent, and Elder George Q. Cannon, agent for the European emigration, both called on me to go out into Nebraska and also to cross into Iowa and purchase work cattle for them. Each furnished me with five hundred dollars in gold then, and as it was the time that hundreds of gold hunters were returning from Pike's Peak, I had great success in my purchases, spending a thousand dollars some days in the purchase of cattle, buying whole teams as they stood on the road, sometimes wagons, equipage and provisions. I would hire a trusty man to drive them up to Florence, and then I would replenish my pockets and go on again. For ten days I traveled early and late, and did thousands of dollars' worth of business for the Church and emigration.

CHAPTER LIV.

GIVEN CHARGE OF A COMPANY TO CROSS THE PLAINS TO UTAH—
COMPOSITION OF THE CAMP—START WEST—PERFORM BAP-
TISMS—MEET A WAR PARTY OF SIOUX INDIANS—PLACE WHERE
A. W. BABBITT WAS KILLED—MEET MORE INDIANS—HOW
TROUBLE WAS AVOIDED—CAMP LIFE AND DUTIES—ENTER SALT
LAKE VALLEY—COMPANY GREETED BY THE CHURCH AUTHOR-
ITIES—REPORT TO PRESIDENT YOUNG AND AM RELEASED—
TRADE AT CAMP FLOYD—EXPERIENCE WITH A THIEF—GO
TO WORK ON THE OGDEN CANYON ROAD—HARDSHIPS EN-
DURED.

ON Sunday, June 12th, Elders Eldredge and Cannon visited the camp and held meeting, then organized the company, naming James S. Brown for president and captain, the selection being unanimously sustained. George L. Farrell was made sergeant of the guard, William Wright chaplain, and John Gordon secretary. A captain was appointed over each ten wagons, namely: first, Wm. Steel; second, W. Williams; third, Christopher Funk; fourth, Newbury; fifth, Kent; sixth, Giddens. These names were suggested by Messrs. Eldredge and Cannon, and were unanimously sustained by the company of three hundred and fifty-three souls. The outfit consisted of fifty-nine wagons and one hundred and four yoke of oxen, eleven horses, thirty-five cows, and forty-one head of young cattle that were driven loose. We had provisions for seventy-five days.

On June 13th, 1859, the company set out for Salt Lake City, Utah. There were nine different nationalities of people represented, namely: English, Irish, Scotch, Welsh, Danish, Swedish, Norwegians and Icelanders; we also had some Americans from the Eastern, Middle and Southern States, all mixed together. Many of them had never driven an ox one mile in their lives, and the result was almost like herding a train on the plains. If it had not been for G. L. Farrell, James Hickson, Samuel Garnet and Willis Brown, all excellent ox teamsters, besides some five or six others that were quite handy, we would doubtless have had most destructive stampedes. As it was, the company did not have any serious mishaps. In a few days the train became regulated and we had more system and order in travel. For the first five or six days of the journey the stock seemed in danger of being destroyed by flies and mosquitoes, and the people suffered much from the same cause. On the 18th we passed Captain Rowley with the handcart company.

On June 19th the camp stopped on the Loup Fork, a tributary of the Platte River. There was a small town there called Columbus. On the 20th the company moved up the river and camped on a small stream, Looking Glass Creek. That afternoon I baptized and rebaptized eighty souls, and other Elders confirmed them, while some men of the company bridged the stream. On the 21st we proceeded to Genoa Ferry, where we were joined by Captain Walding's company of thirty-seven souls and ten more wagons, thus increasing my company to three hundred and ninety persons and sixty-nine wagons, with cattle and other property in proportion. At that place we chartered the ferry boat from J. Johnston and did the work ourselves. We paid seventy-five cents a wagon, and it took fifteen hours' hard labor to cross. The stock all swam safely over, and the company camped on the west bank. The handcart company came up that night about 10 o'clock. On the 23rd our company proceeded up the river.

We met with a company of Sioux Indians on the 24th. These formed a line of battle across the road ahead of the company, and sent two men to meet us. I was traveling in advance of the company, and although I had never been among the Sioux Indians in my life for an hour, nor had I ever been where I had an opportunity to study their language, I had not the slightest difficulty in talking to them, or they to me.   Consequently I learned at once that these Indians were on the war path, and were hunting the Omahas and Poncas.   They were hungry and said they must have food from the company; so they were told to form a line parallel with the road, and to keep one-fourth of a mile back, so as not to stampede the train or frighten the women and children.   They were allowed to send two men on foot to spread blankets where the company could put such food as we had to share.

Meanwhile I gave orders to the sergeant of the guard, G. L. Farrell, and the several captains to draw up in close order, have every teamster in his place, and all the women and children in the wagons, and for each man to have his gun where he could lay his hand on it without a moment's delay.   Each family was to place some food on the blankets by the roadside.   Not one team was to stop without orders. The wagons were to be corralled as quickly as possible, if they must be, at the first signal from the captain to do so; for the Indians appeared very warlike in their paint and feathers.

When the red men learned that it was a company of Mormons they had met, they readily complied with the captain's terms, and a number rode up and shook hands with him.   As the company passed their lines of not more than one hundred and fifty warriors, there came fourteen buffalo in sight, quite close, and attention was turned to them so much that the Indians took what the company had placed on their blankets and we passed on without further interruption.

It was about this date that the teamsters had become acquainted with their teams and the latter acquainted with their drivers, so that things began to work more orderly than before. The camp was called together every evening for prayers, and for instructions for the next day.

About the 26th the company started across from the Loup Fork to Wood River. That night the stock took fright and gave some trouble before they were recovered; but the next morning the company resumed its journey, leaving Wood Birdno to pursue two valuable young fillies, one his own and the other belonging to Captain Brown. Mr. Birdno did not overtake the company till the fifth day.

One evening the company camped on a tributary of the Platte River, where Almon W. Babbitt was killed by the Sioux Indians some eighteen months or two years before. The company crossed the stream and camped just opposite where that terrible tragedy occurred, and just as the cattle were being unyoked the Sioux Indinas flocked into camp, all well-armed warriors. I saw that it was quite possible that they meant mischief, as there were no Indian families in sight; so I called to the company to continue their camp duties as if nothing unusual had happened, but for every man to see to his firearms quietly and be ready to use them if an emergency should arise. Then I turned to the chief, and it being again given to me to talk and understand the Indians, I asked what their visit meant, if it was peace that they go with me to the middle of the corral of wagons and smoke the pipe of peace and have a friendly talk, as myself and people were Mormons and friends to the Indians, and that I wished them to be good friends to me and my people.

The chief readily responded, and called his peace council of smokers to the center of the corral, where they seated themselves in a circle. I took a seat to the right hand of the chief and then the smoking and talking commenced. The chief assured me that their visit was a friendly one, and to trade with the emigrants. I inquired of him why, if their visit meant peace, they all came so well armed. He answered

that his people had just pitched camp a short distance back
in the hills, and not knowing who we were had come down
before laying down their arms.

By this time it seemed that there were about three
Indians to one white person in the camp.   I told the chief
that it was getting too late to trade, my people were all busy
in camp duties, and I was going to send our stock to where
there was good feed for them.   It was my custom, I said,
to send armed men to watch over them, and the guards
always had orders to shoot any wild beast that might disturb them, and if anybody were to come among the stock
in the night, we thought them to be thieves and our enemies.
If they attempted to drive off our stock, the guards had
orders to shoot, and our camp guards also were ordered to
shoot any thief that might come prowling around camp at
night.   I said that, as we did not desire to do the Indians
any harm, we wished the chief and his men to go to their
camp, as it was now too late to trade.   But in the morning,
when the sun shone on our wagon covers, not when it
shone on the mountain tops in the west, but when it shone
on our tents and wagon covers, they could leave their arms
behind and come down with their robes, pelts and furs, and
we would trade with them as friends; but he was not to
allow any of his men to visit our camp or stock at night.

The chief said that was heap good talk, and ordered
his people to return to their own camp.   They promptly
obeyed, to the great relief of the company, which had been
very nervous, as scarcely one of them except myself had
ever witnessed such a sight before.

Next morning, between daylight and sunrise, the Indians appeared on the brow of the hill northeast of camp.
There seemed to be hundreds of them formed in a long line
and making a very formidable array.   Just as the sunlight
shone on the tents and wagon covers they made a descent
on us that sent a thrill through every heart in camp, until

it was seen that they had left their weapons of war behind, and had brought only articles of trade. They came into the center of the corral, the people gathered with what they had to trade, and for a while a great bargaining was carried on. For once I had more than I could do in assisting them to understand each other, and see that there was no disturbance or wrong done in the great zeal of both parties.

The trading was over without any trouble, there was a hearty shaking of hands, and the company resumed its journey up the river, passing and being repassed by numerous companies moving west to Pike's Peak and to Utah, California, or Oregon. There were gold seekers, freighters, and a host of families of emigrants; and as the company advanced to the west we met many people going to the east. They were traveling all ways, with ox, horse and mule teams, as well as by pack trains of horses and mules; while some were floating down the Platte River in small row boats.

I have omitted many dates, but feel that I must say that some time in July we came up with Captain Horton Haight, who started two weeks ahead of us, with a Church train of seventy-five wagons of freight. Both trains passed Fort Laramie that same day. Mine camped seven miles above the fort on the river, where we laid over the next day, and had our wagons unloaded and thoroughly cleaned from the dust and dirt; then they were reloaded so as to balance their loading anew. All sick cattle were doctored, while the female portion of camp washed and did considerable baking. The next day we proceeded on to the Black Hills, in good spirits, the people generally well and encouraged. The road then began to be rough and gravelly, so that the cattle began to get sore-footed, and that changed the tone of feelings of some of the people.

We went on in peace over hills and dales to the Sweetwater, thence up that stream to what was called the last crossing, where we stopped one day, and again overhauled our load, doctored sick cattle, baked, etc. From there we crossed the summit of the great Rocky Mountains to Pacific Springs, so called because their waters flow down the Pacific slope. From that point we traveled over very sandy plains and saleratus deserts, to the Little Sandy, then to what was called the Big Sandy, and thence to Green River, the last hundred miles being the most soul-trying of the whole journey, owing to being sandy and poisonous to the stock. We traveled day and night, all that the cattle could endure, and in fact more than many of the people did endure without much complaint and fault-finding.

After a day's rest on the Green River, however, and being told that there was no more such country to cross, the train entered on the last one hundred and fifty miles of the journey, crossing over to Ham's Fork, then to Fort Bridger on Black's Fork, and on to the two Muddys and to Quaking Asp Ridge, the highest point crossed by the emigrant road. From there we went down into Echo Canyon, then to Weber River, crossed it and over the foothills to East Canyon Creek and to the foot of the Big Mountain, where we met Apostles John Taylor and F. D. Richards. A halt was called to listen to the hearty welcome and words of cheer from the Apostles. Then the company passed over the Big Mountain to the foot of the Little Mountain, where we camped. Many of the people were sick from eating chokecherries and wild berries found along the roadside.

Next day we proceeded to the top of Little Mountain. When I saw the last wagon on the summit, I left the sergeant, G. L. Farrell, in charge, and went ahead to report the approach of my company and their condition, as there were one hundred or more without food for their supper. I called first on General H. S. Eldredge, and took dinner with him. He received me very kindly, and accompanied me to President Brigham Young's office. The President wel-

comed us as cordially as a father could. After he had inquired and was told the condition of the company, he sent
word to Bishop Edward Hunter to have the tithing yard
cleared for the cattle, to have cooked food for all who needed
it, and to have the company camp in Union Square.

When steps had been taken to carry out these orders,
I called at my father-in-law's in the Fourteenth Ward, where
I learned that my family were well. Then I went back, met
the company on the bench east of the city, and conducted it
down to the square, where we found Bishop Hunter and a
number of other Bishops and people of the several wards,
with an abundance of cooked food for supper and breakfast
for the whole company. Several of the Twelve Apostles
were on the ground to bid the company a hearty welcome,
and delivered short addresses of good cheer. This was
August 29, 1859.

Next morning, the 30th, Orson Hyde, Orson Pratt,
Wilford Woodruff, Ezra T. Benson, Charles C. Rich and
Erastus Snow of the Twelve Apostles, Bishop Hunter and
other prominent officers of the Church, came to the camp,
called the people together, and again bade the Saints welcome to our mountain home. They advised the people
where to go, and what to do to support themselves for the
winter.

It was while yet on the Union Square that Apostle
Charles C. Rich told me that he and others had been called
to take a mission to England, leaving home in the spring,
and that they would like me to go with them; he thought I
had better shape my affairs so that I would be ready for the
call.

During the day the people found shelter and friends,
and I reported to the *Deseret News* office and to President
Young, who told me I was honorably released from any
further responsibility for the company.

On our journey across the plains we had two deaths in

the company, and five births, and had lost twenty-five head of cattle—a very small percentage compared with losses in general.

After the interview with President Young, I followed up my brother Willis, who had gone ahead with our team. We stopped that night at Charles C. Rich's, twelve miles north of Salt Lake City, and on September 1st reached my home in Ogden City, where we found all well and pleased to meet us again.

At Ogden many friends and relatives called to see us. In a day or two after our arrival, we went to cutting bulrushes along the slough on the bottom lands, with a scythe, that being the only chance for us to winter our stock. In a short time we purchased a wagon load of butter and eggs, and took it to Camp Floyd, forty miles southwest of Salt Lake City. We made a good profit on that load, then made a second trip and had stolen from us one of our mules worth one hundred and fifty dollars.

As we could not get a trace of the mule, Willis returned to the city to get another animal, so we could move our wagon. About 12 o'clock one night, while he was gone and I was sleeping alone in the wagon, the moon shining bright and clear, a thief cut the hind end of the wagon cover open, and drew out one of the quilts. As he was taking the second I awoke and caught him in the act. I asked what he was doing there, and was told it was none of my business, but to get out of his wagon, or he would send an officer after me. At the same time he put his hand on an old fashioned United States holster pistol that he had in his belt, then staggered off, feigning drunkenness. I saw that he went into a corner where he could not pass out, so I hastened and called the landlord, Mr. Kinney, a man about sixty years old, and told him what had happened. Said he, "If he went in there he cannot get through that way." He peeped into a dark corner, where the buildings were so close that a man could not squeeze through. "Here he is; come out, you thief," said he, and the midnight marauder made a break to pass. The old gentleman struck at him as he went by, and the next instant I had him by the throat. By that time the thief had got his pistol disengaged from his belt, but before he could turn it towards me I caught it from his grasp, threw him heavily on the ground, and held him there till Mr. Kinney brought an officer.

Meanwhile we were surrounded by half a dozen gamblers. one of whom said to the thief, "What are you doing down there, Rainbow?" A second ordered him to get up. They all seemed to know him, but all were strangers to me. I had passed the pistol to the old landlady, who brought it out, offered it to the officers, and told them she saw the thief try to shoot me when I snatched it and passed it to her. At that the thief swore the weapon was not his, but mine, and that I had drawn it to shoot him. Then the officers told me to keep the pistol, and they let the thief go to a saloon in a gambling house, where he treated the crowd, and told them that he had an engagement for a woman to meet him there that night, but he found a man instead, and that was all there was of it. At that the officers liberated him, and I concluded that I had got into a den of thieves. so disposed of my load and left for home as soon as I could. All the profit that we had made in the first trip was lost in the second, for we never recovered the mule.

The weather being cold, we threw up that business and took a contract amounting to two hundred and fifty dollars on the Ogden Canyon road, and in the bitter cold weather of winter worked till the job was completed. That work finished, we took another contract to get out timber for the first county jail in Weber County, and continued to work in the canyon until April 1st. The winter had been so long and severe that we sold part of our wearing apparel and bed clothes for hay to keep life in our animals.

CHAPTER LV.

CALLED ON A MISSION TO GREAT BRITAIN—PREPARE TO DEPART— START WITHOUT PURSE OR SCRIP—JOURNEY TO SALT LAKE CITY —SET APART FOR THE MISSION—BEGIN THE JOURNEY EASTWARD —ORGANIZATION OF THE COMPANY—MY POST AS CHAPLAIN— OVERTAKEN BY APOSTLES A. M. LYMAN AND C. C. RICH—TRAVEL- ING THROUGH THE MOUNTAINS—SNOWSTORMS AND WIND—FOR- AGE IS SCARCE—MEETINGS WITH THE INDIANS—CAPTAIN REY- NOLDS' EXPLORING PARTY—ARMY DESERTERS IN OUR CAMP— MAIL FROM HOME—EMIGRANTS WESTWARD BOUND—DISSATISFAC- TION IN CAMP—FEELING ABOUT APOSTLES LYMAN AND RICH—I RESIGN AS CAPTAIN, BUT AM ELECTED AGAIN, AND FINALLY RE- SUME COMMAND—MAIL ROBBERY—MORE DISAGREEABLE STORMS —MEET A HANDCART COMPANY, AND APOSTLE GEORGE Q. CAN- NON—REACH THE MISSOURI RIVER—VISIT MY FATHER AND HIS FAMILY—GO TO ST. JOSEPH, MISSOURI—MY FIRST VIEW OF A RAILWAY TRAIN—AT MY OLD HOME IN BROWN COUNTY, ILLINOIS —JOURNEY EASTWARD BY RAIL—ARRIVE IN NEW YORK FOR THE FIRST TIME—FIND FRIENDS.

SOME time in February of this year (1860), I received a letter from President Brigham Young, informing me that I had been selected to accompany Apostles Amasa M. Lyman and Charles C. Rich on a mission to Great Britain, starting in April. The letter authorized me to call on Bishop Chauncey W. West, to have my city and five-acre lots fenced and cultivated by labor tithing, for the benefit of my family; also for the Bishop to furnish my family, from time to time, with such necessary articles as they needed and could not otherwise obtain. I called on the Bishop as authorized, and showed him the letter, but the work he was called on for never was done, and my family suffered in consequence.

I settled my business and prepared for the mission, and in April attended conference in Salt Lake City, where my name was presented and sustained with those of many others called to perform missions. On the 19th of April, I blessed my family and bade farewell to them till I should be released from the duty which now rested upon me of preaching the Gospel among the inhabitants of the British Isles. I had a ham and a few articles of food, a light change of clothing, and my rifle. These I put in the wagon of H. Hanson, who was starting to Salt Lake City, on his way to fill a mission in Denmark. Then, with my shot-pouch and a new pair of boots across my shoulder, I began my journey from Ogden, intending to hunt up a yoke of cattle I had on the range, and drive them to Salt Lake City. Not a dollar of money did I have—I was entirely without purse or scrip. I found my cattle, drove them to Salt Lake City, turned them over to my father-in-law, Nathan Tanner, to pay a debt I was owing and to obtain some flour for food on my journey, and I was ready on April 20th, the date appointed, to leave on my mission. But some of the others were not ready, and the departure was postponed to April 25th.

On the last named date, we gathered at the Church historian's office in Salt Lake City, to be set apart and receive instructions for our missions. President Brigham Young there gave us counsel never to be forgotten, and our hearts rejoiced therein. Each of us received a certificate of our missionary appointment, signed by the First Presidency, Brigham Young, Heber C. Kimball, and Daniel H. Wells. We were then instructed to meet next day, the 26th, at the mouth of Parley's Canyon, and to proceed therefrom under command of Joseph W. Young, our baggage being hauled by teams owned by the Church that were going to Florence, Nebraska.

President Young had designated me to take charge of

one of the teams, with permission to leave it when Apostles Lyman and Rich overtook us, which they expected to do in three or four days. Thus I had in my care four yoke of oxen and a large government wagon; and, in company with several others, went to President Young's mill south of the city. We took on from a thousand to twelve hundred pounds of flour to each wagon, and proceeded to the place of rendezvous, where there were gathered thirty wagons, with about forty missionaries and the Beebe and Buzzard families, who were going back to their farms in Iowa.

On April 17th, Presidents Young and Wells came out and organized the company, appointing Joseph W. Young as captain, and John Woolley as sergeant of the guard. Myself and two others were selected as chaplains. The company was instructed as to necessary duties in crossing the plains, and we started. Our route was up Parley's Canyon, then down Silver Creek to the Weber River, thence up to the mouth of Chalk Creek. At the Spriggs coal pit a number of us visited the mine, the tunnels of which went straight into the mountain side. Then we proceeded across to Bear River, and followed along the Big Muddy. The Beebe and Buzzard families and E. D. Woolley and company continued on by way of Fort Bridger, while the rest of us made a road across the bend of the Muddy.

Apostles A. M. Lyman and C. C. Rich overtook us on May 4th, and we all camped together that night. Walter M. Gibson and I were transferred to Samuel White's wagon, and on the 5th we bade farewell to Joseph W. Young's company, taking an early leave of them, and proceeded to Ham's Fork, on which we camped for the night. There I was made captain of the company, with John Tobin as sergeant of the guard, and W. H. Dame as

26

chaplain. Guards were placed out to take care of the stock. That night there was quite a snowstorm.

Next morning, the weather was cold and disagreeable. We made our way to Green River, where we met some people who had apostatized from the Church, and were going back to St. Louis; we also met some Shoshone Indians who were friendly. We camped on the Big Sandy that night, and had quite a hunt for our animals, which strayed off because there was so little grass. But we recovered all of them.

On May 10th we came to Pacific Springs, where we met Buzzard, Beebe, Woolley and company, and received them into our company without any change in organization. That day we crossed over the South Pass and the Sweetwater River, and camped on Willow Creek. Next day we went through a number of snowdrifts, passed over the Rocky Ridge and to the Sweetwater; following along the river. That night we met a party of Shoshone Indians returning from a fight with the Crow Indians. The following morning, the 12th, we missed part of our animals, and were detained till 11 o'clock securing them again. We then moved forward on our journey, and on the 13th, at the second crossing of the Sweetwater, encountered a severe snowstorm.

From then till the 18th the wind was very high, and the weather disagreeable. Grass was very scarce. On the 14th we met a band of Arapahoe Indians on a buffalo hunt, and on the 15th met Captain Reynolds with a party of explorers. We afterwards heard that the entire party were killed by Blackfeet Indians, on the headwaters of the Missouri River. On the 18th, as we were traveling down the Platte River, Sergeant Min, with a small party of soldiers from Fort Laramie, searched the wagons in our company for three deserters from Camp Floyd. There were two of them in our camp. They had come to us in

Parley's Canyon, saying they had been discharged. One of them, George Kelly, showed his discharge papers, but he had re-enlisted, and deserted after receiving his bounty. The other was a servant who had stolen a gold watch. His name was Alexander Demster. Both were taken to Fort Laramie.

On May 20th we arrived within seven miles of Fort Laramie, where we rested our animals and attended to necessary work for proceeding farther. We also built a raft and went across to the fort for our mail, getting a few letters. There was none for me. We wrote to our families, and on the 22nd again moved forward. This time we had two other discharged soldiers with us; one of them had a wife and child. I had changed from Samuel White's wagon to D. Savage's, and drove his six-mule team most of the way. From the 23rd on we met many people bound for California, Oregon, or the Pike's Peak gold mines.

We passed Chimney Rock on May 25th, and rested that evening at a fair camping ground. There had been some dissatisfaction on the part of owners of teams because the grass had been short and the animals were not doing well. Fault was found with the camping places, and as Apostles Lyman and Rich often had been consulted and had suggested the location for camp, these prominent members of our company felt that if there were any blame in making the choice it belonged to them. So the Apostles asked forgiveness for what they had done, and promised they would have no more to do with directing the journeyings of the company. When I found that I was deprived of the counsel of such men, I resigned my office as captain. John Tobin also resigned as sergeant of the guard. That night was passed with the camp in a disorganized state, and next morning there was no one to lead out with orders to proceed. The team owners and others found themselves well puzzled, and began to realize the mistake that had been made.   By advice of Apostle C. C. Rich, I called the company together, but none knew what to do.   Finally, Elder Rich suggested that they elect as captain someone they would not find so much fault with.   The vote was for me, and at the request of Elder Rich I again assumed command, and we moved on. John Brown was selected as sergeant of the guard.

At Ash Hollow we learned that the St. Joseph and Great Salt Lake mail coach had been robbed on Greasewood Creek, by Shoshone Indians, and that the mail carriers had been killed. We were detained at Ash Hollow several hours on the 27th, by the severe illness of A. Beebe's wife. For several days thereafter there were high winds, and showers, making the roads very disagreeable, so that it took us till May 31st to reach Buffalo Creek, where we saw some buffalo. The next night we camped ten miles above Fort Kearney. On June 2nd we called at Dr. Henry's ranch for dinner, and seven miles further on reached the place where Joseph E. Johnson and his brother had located, and were publishing a paper called the *Mountain Echo*. At this point Nephi Johnson and Daniel Babbitt left us, as they had reached the end of their journey. We continued on four miles further, and camped.

Proceeding on our journey, we reached and crossed the Elkhorn River on June 6th, and that night met and camped with a company of Latter-day Saints crossing the plains with handcarts. The company was in good spirits, and glad to see us, and we spent the evening in singing the songs of Zion. Just as we had gone to bed, Apostle George Q. Cannon, who had charge of the Church emigration that year, came up, in company with Horton Haight and others, and we were glad to arise and shake hands with him. He was a particular friend and brother with whom several of us had traveled many miles and spent many pleasant hours. After a long talk Elder Cannon turned in with me for sleep.

On the morning of June 7th, the members of the hand-cart company were called together, and Apostles Lyman and Rich gave them some good instructions. Then we bade them good-bye, and proceeded to Florence, where we met many warm-hearted Saints from Europe. On the 8th, I procured a span of mules from Horton Haight, and a carriage from George Q. Cannon, and accompanied by J. C. Rich, crossed the Missouri River to Calhoun, Harrison County, Iowa, where we met with my father and his family. They were well, and greatly pleased to see me. We visited with my relatives till the 11th, when J. C. Rich and I parted at Crescent City, while I returned to Florence, where my father visited me on the 12th, and invited Apostles Lyman and Rich and myself to take dinner at the finest hotel in the town, which we did. My father promised me there that if he lived and was able to sell his property, he would accompany me to Utah when I returned from my mission.

On June 15th, I went to Omaha in company with J. C. Rich, F. M. Lyman, and R. McBride, where we were joined next day by A. M. Lyman, C. C. Rich, G. Q. Cannon, and John Tobin. We took passage on the steamboat *Omaha* for St. Joseph, Missouri, where we landed on the morning of the 18th. That day while strolling through the city with Francis M. Lyman, I first saw a locomotive and railway train in motion. It was to us a grand sight, and we viewed it with admiration and satisfaction. At 6 a. m., on the 19th, we boarded the train, C. C. Rich, J. C. Rich and John Tobin going to St Louis, and the rest of us to Quincy, Illinois, where I left the party and went to Versailles, Brown County. There I received a hearty welcome from relatives and friends.

I remained in that locality five days, until the 24th, visiting uncles, brother-in-law, cousins, and other relatives, and also the farm on which I was reared. At Versailles, on the evening of the 21st, I lectured, by request, on my travels and experiences. The schoolroom being too small to accommodate the people, the Methodist church was procured, and was well filled, many of the audience being my old schoolmates. They were glad to meet me, as I was to meet them.

I stayed that night with Joseph F. Vandeventer, and next day, in company with him and his brother Thomas, visited my father's old farm, then owned by William Knox. There were many changes about the place. The cemetery was fenced into a pasture, and I was unable to find my brother's grave. The fruit trees in the orchard were well grown, and I was given some good apples and the best cider I ever tasted, made from fruit from trees I had set out with my own hands.

That day's walk brought to my recollection my youthful days, my hunts through the woods and my adventures, my toilsome labors in grubbing underbrush and clearing the land, threshing wheat in the hot, autumn sun, feeding stock in the cold winter, my cold fingers, benumbed body, and frozen toes—once shedding my toenails through frost, and peeling the skin off my feet—in short, I was reminded of much toil on the part of my parents, brothers and sisters and myself, and of many days of sickness with fever and ague. We returned to Versailles, and next evening, the 23rd, after more visiting, I consented to preach, and was given good attention by a large congregation. On the 24th, I went down to the river landing at the mouth of Crooked Creek, with my uncle and Joseph F. Vandeventer, but learning that the boats were uncertain, I resolved to go to Meridotia and there take train for New York, in order to meet Elder C. C. Rich. To do this, it was necessary for me to borrow twenty dollars, which I did of Mr. Vandeventer. At 9 o'clock that evening I was on my way, on the Quincy and Toledo line, passing through the great Wabash valley. After several changes of cars, and crossing North River on a ferry boat, I landed in New York City on June 26th, without knowing a soul that lived there.

I walked up to Broadway, and took a Sixth Avenue omnibus to Twenty-third Street, where I found the residence of Brother Jonas Croxall, and introduced myself to his wife, as he was not at home. I had eaten but two meals since I got into the cars at Meridotia, and they cost me seventy-five cents. I had ridden over one thousand miles on the cars from Illinois, and had ninety-five cents when I reached the end of the journey. My supper that night was provided at Brother Croxall's. About 11 o'clock in the evening Brothers Croxall and A. M. Lyman came in, they having been on a visit together at Brother Schettler's.

CHAPTER LVI.

VISIT VARIOUS PLACES OF INTEREST IN NEW YORK AND VICINITY— ARRIVAL OF THE GREAT EASTERN—PREACH AT WILLIAMSBURG— NEW YORK'S CELEBRATION OF THE FOURTH—MY THIRTY-SECOND BIRTHDAY—SECURE PASSPORTS AND OCEAN PASSAGE—CROWDED IN THE STEERAGE—FOGGY AND WET WEATHER—VIEW OF THE IRISH COAST—FLEET OF BRITISH WARSHIPS—LAND IN LIVERPOOL —ASSIGNED TO BIRMINGHAM CONFERENCE—IN BIRMINGHAM— LISTEN TO AN ANTI-MORMON LECTURE—VISITING FROM HOUSE TO HOUSE AS A MORMON MISSIONARY—PLACES OF INTEREST—TRANS- FERRED TO NOTTINGHAM CONFERENCE—PREACHING AND VISIT- ING—MISSION TRAVELS—GO TO LONDON--SEE NOTABLE PLACES-- NEWS OF MY DAUGHTER'S DEATH--BIRTH OF ANOTHER DAUGHTER—RETURN TO NOTTINGHAM.

THE 27th of June was spent with Apostle A. M. Lyman and J. Croxall, walking about the city of New York. That day F. M. Lyman and Reuben McBride arrived, and next day Apostle Lyman and his son Francis M. left for Boston. With Reuben McBride, I visited the various departments of the place where J. Croxall and his son worked. We then crossed East River with Thomas Miller, and strolled through Williamsburg. We were introduced to a Brother Stone and family, with whom we stayed all night. On the 29th we were made acquainted with many Latter-day Saints in Williamsburg, then crossed over to Brooklyn, where we went through the navy yard and other places; at the first named place we went on board the old ship of war *North Carolina*. That day we heard the salutes fired for the *Great Eastern*, as she steamed up the wharf in New York The ocean monster was hailed with joy and enthusiasm. She had been sighted at sea the evening before.

In New York City, on the 30th, we visited Barnum's museum, Castle Garden, the postoffice, and had a view of the *Great Eastern*. I received a letter from my family reporting all well. The 1st of July was Sunday, and we met with the Latter-day Saints in Williamsburg. The speakers at the meetings that day were Apostle C. C. Rich, Elder Walter Gibson and myself. I crossed over to New York that night, and the remainder of our stay in the city was the guest of Bernard A. Schettler, who treated me very kindly. During the next few days we visited many factories, ships and places of interest, and wrote letters home. On the 4th, which was my thirty-second birthday anniversary, there was a grand celebration. The militia of New York City paraded, passing the George Washington monument in review. There was a grand fireworks display in the evening; and in the afternoon we witnessed the aeronaut, Mr. Wise, ascend out of sight with a balloon. On the 9th we sent to Washington for our passports. W. H. Dame and I were appointed on the 12th to take the money of our party, secure berths on the steamship *Edinburgh*, of the Blackball line between New York and Liverpool, and to purchase articles necessary for the journey across the Atlantic Ocean. We attended to this duty on the 13th.

July 14th, our party, thirteen in number, went on board, and at 12 o'clock noon, the vessel left the landing. We paid twenty-five dollars each for steerage passage. There were nearly three hundred passengers, and the berths were all taken up, so our lot was rather hard. Being very much crowded for room as well, it was plain that our part of the voyage was not to be very pleasant; but we were on board and had to make the best of it.

By the 18th we were off the banks of Newfoundland, in a dense, damp fog, that obscured the sun and made it impossible to see more than a few rods from the ship. The steam siren kept up a constant whistling, to warn other vessels of our location and approach. The fog lasted till the 23rd, when it lighted up, but the weather was cloudy, with some rain. On the 24th a vessel bore in sight.

Next day we had headwinds, and the sun shone for a short time. We came in sight of the southwest coast of Ireland, and at the cry of "Land!" every countenance brightened. All were on deck to catch a glimpse of the welcome scene. As this proceeding was going on, we heard the cry, "Sail ho!" and in a short time there came into full view a fleet of her majesty Queen Victoria's warships, eleven in number. They were steaming along the coast to the south and in advance of us. Suddenly they changed their course and came to meet us. When they drew near, their signal flags were hoisted on the masts, making a beautiful and imposing appearance.

That night at 11 o'clock we ran into Queenstown, the harbor of Cork, Ireland. There some passengers for Ireland, and mail were taken off, and we headed for the coast of England, coming in sight of Wales the next day.

Early on the morning of the 27th we were on the muddy, dark waters of the Mersey, and soon landed in Liverpool, where the dank, smoky, mildewed walls looked to us as if they had stood for a thousand years. To our

eyes the city had a very dismal and forbidding appearance.

After the usual custom house inspection, we sent our
baggage to the Latter-day Saints' office at 42 Islington,
and walked there ourselves, a distance of a mile and a half.
At the office we met Elder N. V. Jones and others, who
received us very kindly. The following day we were
appointed to our various missionary fields, J. C. Rich and I
being assigned to Birmingham pastorate. That afternoon
Elder Rich and I paid a visit to Birkenhead, across the
river Mersey, and met with some of the Saints.

Sunday, July 29th, we all attended meeting with
the Liverpool Saints, in their assembly room on Great
George's Street. Next day, Elder Rich and I took train
for Birmingham, passing through a tunnel a mile and a half
long on the route. Arriving at New Street station, Birmingham, we hailed a cab and were taken to No. 163 Burton Place, Spring Hill. There we had expected to find
Elder Charles W. Penrose, but he was not at home. His
sister-in-law met us, and seemed surprised at our call. I
told her who we were, and we received a rather mistrustful
invitation to come in; but after questioning us some she
became satisfied of our identity, and provided us with something to eat.

Later, F. G. Blake, who was traveling Elder in that
place, came in, and we took a walk with him, meeting
Elder Penrose. We all went to West Bromwich that evening, and heard one Mr. Bird, an old apostate from Utah,
lecture against the Mormons. He was doing this for
money, and the large hall was full of people. He made
many false accusations against the Latter-day Saints, which
were loudly applauded by his ignorant hearers. After the
lecture we returned to Birmingham, and stayed all night at
Elder Penrose's.

To us, Birmingham seemed as dark, smokey and mildewed as did Liverpool; but it was well located. The place was one of the busiest manufacturing centers of the world. The railway lines passing through do not obstruct or occupy the streets; on one of the roads, which is built on a series of arches, the cars run level with the chimneys on three-story houses; and other roads pass beneath the city, running under large houses. The New Street station was one of the best and most commodious I have ever seen; indeed it is now one of the largest in the world, occupying eleven acres, with a fine iron and glass roof eleven hundred feet long.

After visiting from house to house with the Saints on August 1st, we preached that evening in the Oxford Street Hall. Next day our visiting continued, and we found a dull spirit among the people. Trade was very bad, and the working people were extremely poor. Many of them were unable to give us a good meal of victuals unless they suffered themselves in consequence; yet they seemed very kind to us, but sluggish in spirit. That night we preached in Hockley Chapel, Farm Street.

On the 3rd we visited the different markets in the city; on the 4th met Elders A. M. Lyman, C. C. Rich and N. V. Jones; and on the 5th were with the Saints in conference in the Odd Fellows' Hall, where large congregations assembled. The presidents of the branches in the Birmingham conference made favorable reports, and the Gospel was preached by Apostles Lyman and Rich and others of the Elders. That night J. C. Rich and I stayed at Brother Acock's. It did not seem possible to get the people into the notion of going to bed before midnight; that seeming to be the custom in the English cities.

The Gillott steel and gold pen factory was the object of an interesting visit by J. C. Rich, F. G. Blake and myself on August 6th. We passed through the factory, and saw the work from rolling the large bars of steel down to finishing the pen ready for use; there were four hundred persons employed in the factory. That evening the Elders met in council, and J. C. Rich and I were appointed to labor in the Nottingham pastorate. Next day, in company with several others, I visited the grave of Elder James H. Flanagan, who died while on a mission; his body was interred in the old Birmingham cemetery. In the evening we had a pleasant sociable at the home of Brother Smith, and next day J. C. Rich and I took the train for Nottingham, where we were met at the station by Elder Edward Reid, president of the conference, and were conducted to No. 24 Promenade, Robinhood Street, where the wife of Elder David John had dinner waiting for us. We next went to Radcliffe Chapel, where we met with a goodly number of Saints, and preached to them. Elder David John presided over the Nottingham pastorate. The day after reaching the town I took a severe cold, and had to lay by the next day.

We found Nottingham a very different place to Liverpool and Birmingham. The town and adjacent country were not so smoky and unhealthful. The town had about one hundred and eighty thousand inhabitants, and was the center of the silk and cotton lace and hosiery industries.

On Sunday, August 12th, Elders A. M. Lyman and N. V. Jones (who had come from Liverpool) and I preached to the Saints; on the 13th J. C. Rich and I went to visit G. Wright, at the request of his niece who lived in Utah; his home was at Fisherton, on the river Trent, and after an unwelcome greeting there we returned to Nottingham. Next day we went to Mansfield with Elder James Payne, passing through the place where Robin Hood roamed. That evening we preached to the Saints, then spent the next two days preaching in different villages. At Pixton, on the 16th, we visited a coal pit.

Leicester, the county seat of Leicestershire, and center

of the boot and shoe trade, was our destination on August 19th. We preached there that night, and on Monday visited the museum. The rest of the week we spent in visiting and preaching in several villages, then returned to Nottingham. At Loughborough, on the 22nd, our meeting was disturbed by several rude young men, who laughed and asked questions in an offensive manner. A stone was hurled through the window at me, while I was preaching. It passed just in front of me, but no one was hit. The meeting was dismissed in confusion.

On the 26th, we went to Derby for a couple of days. My health continued to be very poor during this period of my travels. Burton-on-Trent, a place noted for the brewing of malt liquors, was visited on the 28th, and that night I preached at Branston, then stayed at the house of a chimney-sweep named Doman. He had been in the Church nineteen years. Next day we preached in the pottery district, then returned to Derby, where, on the 31st, we went through Fox & Company's shot factory, going to the top of the tower, two hundred and twenty steps. That evening we went to a theatre.

During the first part of September, I traveled and preached, visiting Nottingham, Derby, Belper and several adjacent villages. I attended the Derby races on the 6th; there were about twenty thousand people in attendance. On the 12th, I left Nottingham for London in company with Brothers J. C. Rich and Blackburn, and Sister Cook and daughter, going via the Midland railway. From St. Pancras station we went to Brother John Cook's, at No. 30 Florence Street, Cross Street, Islington, London, where I made my home during my stay in the metropolis. There we met with Elders John Brown, F. M. Lyman, and John Gleason.

I remained in London and vicinity until October 3rd. During our stay at the national capital we visited many in-

teresting places, among them being the tunnel under the
Thames, which is reached by a flight of one hundred steps,
is four hundred yards from end to end, and while we were
passing through there were some fifteen to twenty ships
lying above it, and steamboats passing over it up and down
the river. We visited the British hospitals for invalided
soldiers and sailors, and went from there to Greenwich,
whence is measured longitude east and west, and where we
also saw the standard weights and measures of Great
Britain.

The British Museum; the King's Library; Westmin-
ster Abbey, where Great Britain's rulers are anointed and
crowned by the archbishops of the Church of England;
the Parliament buildings, wherein are the House of Lords
and House of Commons, with the throne and the woolsack;
Buckingham Palace, the city residence of Queen Victoria;
St. Paul's Cathedral, which was undergoing repairs;
National Gallery; Cattle Market; Zoological Gardens, with
the giraffe, the hippopotamus, the rhinoceros and all manner of beasts and birds; South Kensington Museum; Hyde
Park; White Tower of London, where are the block and
ax used in beheading Queen Anne Boleyn and Mary,
Queen of Scots. also the royal regalia, and much other
material of historic value; London Bridge, with its vast
traffic; Crystal Palace with its tower four hundred and
twelve steps to the top, from which can be seen six counties
of England; Anatomical Museum ; Madame Tussaud's
Bazar; the Dockyards, and the rich residence portion of
London, all were visited by us, and were very interesting
and entertaining.

On September 13th we attended a tea party of the
Saints near King's Cross station. Several times I preached
to congregations, both on the Surrey side of the Thames,
and on the north side. On the 14th, Elders A. M. Lyman
and N. V. Jones came from Scotland to London. I received

a letter from home on the 25th, Tuesday, bringing the sad intelligence of the death of Deseret Ann, my second daughter, also of the birth to her mother, my wife Rebecca, of a daughter. I wrote an answer to that letter the same day. During the time I was in London I had a severe cold and my health was far from good. I returned to Nottingham on October 3rd, via the Great Northern railway, and resumed my missionary labors in that conference.

CHAPTER LVII.

AGAIN AT MISSIONARY LABORS—BAPTISMS—BECOME QUITE ILL—APPOINTED PRESIDENT OF THE NOTTINGHAM DISTRICT, EMBRACING THREE CONFERENCES—VISITED BY APOSTLES A. M. LYMAN, C. C. RICH AND OTHERS—SETTLING DIFFERENCES AMONG CHURCH MEMBERS—ATTEND A PHRENOLOGICAL LECTURE—GET A CHART —GO TO LIVERPOOL—IN CONFERENCE AT NOTTINGHAM—MY PASTORATE ENLARGED—WITNESS A MILITARY REVIEW—MORE BAPTISMS—VISIT SHEFFIELD—FIXING MY NAME—POVERTY IN NOTTINGHAM—INVITED TO TAKE A TRIP TO PARIS—GO TO LONDON— HAVE TO GIVE UP THE VISIT TO FRANCE—IN POOR HEALTH— RETURN TO NOTTINGHAM—SEE PROFESSOR BLONDIN.

THE month of October was occupied in traveling and preaching in the district where I was assigned to labor as a missionary. In fulfilling this calling I visited, besides the town of Nottingham, which was headquarters, Derby, Leicester, Burton-on-Trent, Radcliffe, Arnold, Hucknall, Mansfield, Pixton, Ilkiston, Woodhouse, Wirksworth, Mount St. Bernard, Tutbury and other places, preaching in some of them several times. On October 23, I visited the Mount Saint Bernard monastery, and a reformatory for incorrigible boys. The first named was a Catholic institution.

November was occupied similarly to October, and in

addition to most of the places visited in the last named month, I was at Belper, Carlton, Coalville and other small towns. On the 11th I baptized three young women, Annie Simpson, Harriet Cadman and Eliza Bates. The weather turning cold and stormy, my health was not very good. Apostle C. C. Rich came on the 24th and on the 28th we went to Sutton, where I had to stop for several days, I was so ill.

The month of December had some very cold and stormy weather, but my health was somewhat improved. I continued in my missionary district, going to several new places. I was invited by Sisters Underwood and Burrows to take dinner on Christmas. Mr. Burrows was a policeman, and was not a member of the Church. I stayed with him at his home on Christmas night. The next evening we had a meeting in Radcliffe, at which an unpleasant spirit was displayed by some. I advised the Saints to fast and pray to get the Spirit of the Lord. Brother John was offended with this advice, and remonstrated, and when the meeting was dismissed there was a feeling of dissatisfaction among the people. On the 30th of December I was appointed to the presidency of the Nottingham pastorate, embracing the Nottingham, Derby and Leicester conferences of the Church. I was quite ill at this time, with the mumps. My appointmemt came from Apostles A. M. Lyman, C. C. Rich and George Q. Cannon, the presidency of the European mission of the Church of Jesus Christ of Latter-day Saints.

The opening of the year 1861 found me quite ill, and for the first few days of January I was confined to my bed most of the time. On the 6th we held conference in Nottingham, and on the evening before, Elders A. M. Lyman, C. C. Rich, G. Gates, J. Gleason, C. Welsh, A. Orme and H. Druce came to meet with us. We had a good time at the conference. Elders A. M. Lyman and C. C. Rich stayed with us till the 11th, and I visited part of the time with them, going to various villages in the neighborhood, where they preached.   During the remainder of the month I traveled and preached and attended to the conference books and business generally.   Brother David John came to me on the 28th, being very sorry for the unpleasant remarks he had made, and we settled matters satisfactorily to both, parting with the best of feelings.   The next day he and his family moved to South Wales.   My health continued to be quite poor.   On the 30th I took a shock from an electric battery, hoping it would do me some good.

My health was not much improved during the month of February; but I continued my missionary visits and other duties, writing to my father and family, and endeavoring to carry the Gospel message wherever I could.   On the 13th, at the urgent request of Sister Mary Wilson, I visited her parents and sick sister at Newark, being kindly received and invited to call again.   From the 19th to the 23rd, Elder C. C. Rich paid a visit to the conference and preached to the people.

On March 2nd I attended a meeting called at Pinxton to settle a difficulty among some of the members of the Church.   It had continued about three years, but after a long meeting we succeeded in arranging matters, and three of the parties concerned agreed to repent and be baptized. My visits to the various branches continued.   On the 6th I baptized Wm. Burton, Miss Cadman and Miss Betts.   On the 12th I was associated in the confirmation of twelve persons who had been baptized by Elder J. C. Rich the evening before.   On the 25th of this month I attended one of the Fowler and Wells lectures on phrenology, and was so interested that on the 28th I obtained a phrenological chart of myself.

I attended a tea party on April 1st, about two hundred persons being present.   The evening was spent pleas-

27

antly, in singing, reciting and speech-making and partaking of lunch. The next day I baptized seven persons at Nottingham. In the course of my missionary duties, I called a meeting of the Mansfield branch on April 9, to settle a difficulty of long standing. I released from performing any Church official duties all who held the Priesthood, because of continual jarring and contention among them. On the 18th I went with some emigrating Saints to Liverpool, to assist them, settling their business and getting their tickets.

At Liverpool, on the 19th, I accompanied Apostle C. C. Rich on a search among the docks for a ship that could be chartered, but we were not successful in finding one. The next day the Saints went on board the ship *Underwriter*, which had been chartered previously for this company, and I assisted those who had come with me to get settled on the vessel. The next day, Sunday, the presidency of the mission went on the ship, where the company was organized with Elder Milo Andrus as president, Elders H. Duncan and C. W. Penrose as counselors, and John Cook as steward. The migrating Saints were also given appropriate instructions by Apostles Lyman, Rich and Cannon. Next day the vessel sailed, and on the following day, Tuesday, I returned to my missionary duties at Nottingham and vicinity. On the 29th, the day after holding a conference at Nottingham, I baptized six persons.

In the early part of May—the 5th—conference was held in Leicester, Apostle C. C. Rich being in attendance. He remained till the 9th, preaching to the people in different places. On the 17th I received a letter from Apostle George Q. Cannon, informing me that my district had been enlarged, the Lincolnshire conference being detached from Elder Joseph F. Smith's district and added to mine, so there were four conferences in my pastorate. On the 20th I baptized one man and two women who had been cut off the Church, but desired to return. Next day I was a spectator, with about forty thousand other people, at a review of the Nottingham Rifles, before the Duke of Newcastle, at Nottingham Forest. On the 25th Apostle G. Q. Cannon came from Liverpool, held meetings, and attended to business in conference.

On June 2nd I attended to three more baptisms, and on the 6th was at the Sheffield conference, which was in charge of Elder Joseph F. Smith. During my stay there I visited a large manufactory of steel and iron ware, and called on the Norfolk giant, but he was too ill to be seen. On the 13th I returned to Nottingham, traveling as far as Grantham with Apostles Lyman and Rich, who went on to London. The remainder of the month was occupied in my general duties. It was in this month that I wrote to the *Millennial Star*, explaining how my name was James Brown, and then because of others of the same name I became known as James Brown 2nd, then James Brown 3rd, and had concluded to take my mother's maiden name, Stephens, so that thereafter I would have an initial to distinguish me, and be known as James S. Brown.

At Nottingham, on June 6, many poor people marched through the streets, asking and singing for food, or money to buy it. The next day after meeting, I was presented by Sister Elizabeth Wilson with a small anchor, cross and heart she had made out of a stone she had picked up on the beach at Folkestone, England. On the 8th I received a letter from Apostle C. C. Rich, inviting Elder J. C. Rich and myself to meet him and Apostle A. M. Lyman in London on the 14th, to take a trip to Paris, France. Accordingly, I arranged the conference business, and we were in London on the date named, attending conference.

Our contemplated visit to France had to be given up, however, as the Apostles were called to Scotland to attend to some matters there. We visited many places of interest in London, such as the Anatomical Museum, the Polytechnic

Institute, Crystal Palace, Bank of England, the Fire Monument, the Docks, Tower of London, St. Paul's Cathedral, Smithfield Market, the Mint, Windsor Castle, and Eton College. On the 17th, at Crystal Palace, we heard the chorus of three thousand five hundred children. At Eton College we found the students inclined to be impudent, throwing pebbles at passers-by and staring rudely at them.

During the latter part of my stay in London I was quite ill, and had to remain indoors part of the time, once being in all day. I returned to Nottingham on the 24th, where the only thing of particular interest outside of my missionary duties that I observed during that month was on the 30th, when I went out to the park and saw Professor Blondin perform on the tight rope.

CHAPTER LVIII.

PROLONGED ILLNESS—ATTEND TO MY DUTIES WITH DIFFICULTY—LET-
TER TELLING OF THE BATTLE OF BULL'S RUN—WITNESS AN EXE-
CUTION BY HANGING—VISIT FROM GEORGE Q. CANNON, JOSEPH
F. SMITH AND OTHERS—DEATH OF THE PRINCE CONSORT—GO TO
BIRMINGHAM—CONFERENCE OF THE PRIESTHOOD IN THE BRIT-
ISH MISSION—LARGE MEETING IN ODD FELLOWS' HALL, BIRMING-
HAM—AGAIN AT NOTTINGHAM—VISIT LIVERPOOL—CONSULT A
PHYSICIAN, BUT GET LITTLE RELIEF—SEE THE LIVERPOOL
GRAND NATIONAL RACES—DEPRAVITY AMONG POORER CLASSES
IN LIVERPOOL—AGAIN AT NOTTINGHAM—RELEASED TO RETURN
HOME—BID THE PEOPLE FAREWELL—DISPLAY OF THEIR AFFEC-
TION FOR ME—REPORT OF MY LABORS PUBLISHED IN THE MIL-
LENNIAL STAR—ON BOARD SHIP—PLACED IN CHARGE OF THE
COMPANY—SAIL FOR AMERICA—DRIVEN BY HEADWINDS ALONG
THE COASTS OF THE ISLE OF MAN, WALES, IRELAND AND SCOT-
LAND — SEVERE SEASICKNESS — GET TO SEA—SLOW VOYAGE—
DEATHS AND BURIALS AT SEA—LAND AT NEW YORK—GUEST
OF HON. W. H. HOOPER—JOURNEY TO FLORENCE, NEBRASKA—
CAPTAIN AND GUIDE OF INDEPENDENT COMPANY—REACH SALT
LAKE CITY—REPORT TO PRESIDENT YOUNG—AGAIN AT HOME.

DURING the remainder of the year 1861 I was in very poor health, often having to stay in my room all day, and when I was able to get about, many times it was with great difficulty, as I was quite lame in my hips and shoulder. I tried various applications and simple remedies, but to little purpose. I moved around as best I could, however, and by determined efforts I was able to attend to my duties, visiting the Saints, and preaching the Gospel wherever opportunity offered, whether at indoor or outdoor meetings. Sometimes, when I was able to get to the meetings of the Saints, I was too ill to stand up and preach, but toward the latter part of the year my health improved a little.

The civil war in America was on. having begun after I

left; and on August 5th I received a letter telling of the battle of Bull's Run, near Manassas Junction, which was fought July 21, 1861, and in which the Union forces were defeated. On the 16th of August I went to the Derbyshire jail yard in Derby, and there saw a young man named George Smith executed by hanging. He had murdered his father. From thirty-five to forty thousand people witnessed the execution.

On the 1st of September Apostle George Q. Cannon was in Nottingham, attending conference, and we had large meetings and an excellent time. On October 1st Elder Joseph F. Smith and other missionaries came from Sheffield on a visit, and remained several days, spending the time among the Saints. At Nottingham we had a tea party in the Arboretum, at which about two hundred persons were present. I was visiting the Saints at Pinxton on December 14th, the day that Prince Albert, husband of Queen Victoria, died at Windsor Castle.

I started for Birmingham on the 31st of December to attend a conference of those in the British Mission who held the Holy Priesthood. This conference began on Wednesday, January 1, 1862, and was largely attended. We had a most enjoyable time in making reports of our experiences and in receiving instruction and testifying of the blessings of the Gospel. The meetings began at 10 a. m. and lasted till 2 p. m., then at 4 p. m. and lasted till 7 p. m. They continued through Wednesday, Thursday, Friday and Saturday, the presidency of the European Mission, Apostles A. M. Lyman, Charles C. Rich and George Q. Cannon, being in attendance and directing the meetings. On Sunday, the 5th, we met with the Saints in Odd Fellows"'Hall, the congregation numbering about fifteen hundred persons; an excellent feeling prevailed. Next day the Priesthood meetings were concluded, and on Tuesday I left Birmingham for Derby, in my own missionary district. On the 27th of

January I was in Nottingham, and baptized and confirmed Elizabeth Hardy.

My health again became quite bad, but I performed my duties, preaching, baptizing, visiting and conversing with the people on the subject of the Gospel, and attending to the business in my pastorate, until March 5th, when I took the train for Liverpool. There I consulted Apostles A. M. Lyman and G. Q. Cannon, and on the 7th Elder Cannon introduced me to Dr. Smith, who pronounced my ailment neuralgia, and prescribed turkish baths and the magnetic-electric machine. I remained in Liverpool till the 22nd, occasionally visiting, in company with some of the Elders, places of interest such as the new park and the botanical gardens. On March 11th we saw the Liverpool races at Aintree, a suburb. There were two plate races and the grand national steeple chase. At one hurdle a horse fell on his rider and the latter was picked up for dead, but he recovered; three other riders were unhorsed. About twenty thousand people were in attendance at these races. It was while in Liverpool, on March 18th, as I was walking through the northwest part of the town in company with Elder George J. Taylor, that I saw hundreds of people in the most degraded state in which I ever beheld human beings.

My health having improved a little, I returned to Nottingham on the 22nd, Apostle G. Q. Cannon's wife and child accompanying me. Mrs. Cannon had been very ill, and had been advised to go to Nottingham in the hope of the change benefiting her health. On reaching Nottingham, I there resumed my missionary labors. My health again began to fail, and early in April I received notice of my release to return home. On the 7th of April Sister Cannon went to Liverpool in company with her husband. I settled business of the conference and went to different branches and bade the Saints good-bye. They exhibited their affec-

tion for me by many words and acts of kindness. On April
13th I preached my farewell sermon in Nottingham, and it
was with mingled feelings of sorrow and joy that I bade
the Saints farewell—sorrow to leave them, and joy to see
the display of love toward me by both members of the
Church and numbers of people who were not members.
On Monday, April 14th, I went to Liverpool. The next
day I wrote the following, which was published in the *Millennial Star*:

"LIVERPOOL, April 15, 1862.

"*President Cannon:*

"DEAR BROTHER:—I take pleasure in writing to you
a brief report of my labors in the ministry of the Nottingham District. On the 7th of August, 1860, I was appointed
by the presidency here, namely: A. M. Lyman and C. C.
Rich, to labor as a traveling Elder in the aforementioned
district, where I continued my labors in company with
Elder Joseph C. Rich and under the pastoral charge of
Elder David John, until January 1st, 1861. I then received
an appointment to the presidency of the Nottingham District, composed of the Nottingham, Derby, Leicester and
Lincolnshire conferences, where I continued my labors until the 14th instant, when I arrived in Liverpool, having received your letter of release, with the privilege of returning
to our mountain home in Utah.

"I can truly say that I have taken much pleasure in my
field of labor, for I have seen my feeble exertions in connection with the Priesthood laboring with me crowned with
success. I have witnessed an increase of the good Spirit
among the Saints. We have not only witnessed these
symptoms of increase, but have added by baptism some
two hundred and fifty souls, besides many rebaptisms; and
many misunderstandings of the Saints have been corrected,
so that, with a few exceptions, the Saints are in fellowship
with one another.

"In that district, I think, there have been some four excommunicated and five disfellowshiped during the last twenty-one months; and with the present year's emigration, we have two hundred emigrated from that district. Suffice it to say, that the district is in a healthy condition. The Saints are feeling very well, and are full of the spirit to emigrate. Many strangers are becoming very much interested in our meetings, insomuch that some of them attend regularly; and on Sunday evening, the 13th, after I preached my farewell sermon in Nottingham, some four or five strangers, whom I have no recollection of ever seeing before,—shook hands with me, saying, 'God bless you,' and at the same time they did not forget to bless me themselves, thus exemplifying their faith by their works. I find the people in the midland counties to be a kind-hearted people; and when once you get the crust of tradition in which they are encased cracked, so as to feed them with the bread of eternal life, they generally receive it with great joy and gladness.

"Although I have not enjoyed very good health any of the time I have been in this country, I feel sometimes to regret leaving the mission, when I reflect upon the memory of so many warm throbbing hearts for Zion, whose circumstances are rather forbidding at present; yet I feel that if they would arouse with more energy and life, and be more faithful in reading the *Stars* and *Journals*, attend their meetings, and be more faithful in their duties, and not pore over their poverty so much, the time is not far distant when they will be able to accomplish that most desirable object of going to Zion.

"And now I beg to bid good-bye to the Saints of the Nottingham District, and say, may the God of Israel bless and preserve them, together with all the Saints and the honest in heart in all the world. And as I expect to leave this country on the 21st instant, I bid adieu to her majesty's dominions and to all her subjects. I have lifted up my voice and cried aloud, and spared not, till I feel that my skirts are clear, so far as this mission to the British nation is concerned.

"And now with kind regards to yourself, Presidents Lyman and Rich, my brethren and co-laborers in the ministry and the many faithful Saints under their watchcare, I bid all an affectionate farewell, praying God to bless and prosper every effort made to advance the interests of His kingdom.

"I subscribe myself your brother in the Gospel of Christ,
"JAMES S. BROWN."

I was variously engaged the next two days in preparing for the voyage, and in assisting others. On Saturday, the 19th, I went on board the ship *John J. Boyd*, on which we were to sail. That day a young man who resided at Nottingham and who had been courting Miss Mary Oakey, from the same district, came to Liverpool, and the young lady went out with him. They were never seen again by us. We supposed they had eloped.

On Monday, the 21st, I again went on board. Apostles A. M. Lyman, C. C. Rich and George Q. Cannon came on the vessel and organized the company of emigrating Saints, with the following presidency: James S. Brown, president; John Lindsay and J. C. Rich, counselors. The Apostles gave us much good instructions and bade us good-bye, after which we made a further temporary organization so as to call watches for the night; then, after prayer, we retired, it being about midnight. Next day the company was organized into nine wards, with a presiding teacher over each. There were on board six hundred and ninety-six emigrating Saints, and the crew, which made the total up to seven hundred and thirty-five souls.

At half-past seven o'clock on the 23rd we weighed

anchor, and the vessel was towed about twenty miles out to sea, and left, in a strong headwind. We beat about the Irish Channel all day, and about 4 p. m., drew so close to the Isle of Man that we could see the towns and distinguish the houses. Then we tacked about and sailed away along the coast of Wales. Nearly everybody on board was seasick, and one child, about five months old, in a family named Hardy, died. It was buried at sea on the 24th. Myself and counselors went among the people, waiting on them and cheering them.

Next day the heavy headwind continued, and the seasickness seemed very severe. I was affected myself, but still was able to help others. We went along between the Isle of Man and the coast of Ireland, and by the 26th, when the wind became lighter, we could see the coast of Ireland on our left and the Scottish hills on the right. We could also see the Irish houses, farms and roads quite plainly. It was noon on the 27th before we passed out of sight of land, the last we saw being a small island off the northwest coast of Ireland.

From that time on we experienced all kinds of weather, from a dead calm to a heavy gale. On the 1st of May the wind was so strong it carried away the jib-boom and foretop-gallant mast. On the 5th a little boy named Benjamin V. Williams died from a fall down the hatchway on May 1st. Taking all things together, however, we got along fairly well. Once we had to complain to the captain of rough treatment by the third mate and some of the sailors, and it was checked. On May 21st we sighted Sandy Hook, and on June 1st we cast anchor in the bay of New York. On the voyage we had had cases of measles and whoopingcough, and there were seven deaths in our company while we were at sea.

On landing in New York I received an invitation from Hon. Wm. H. Hooper for the Utah Elders to stay at the

Astor House at his expense. Eleven of us availed ourselves of the courtesy extended. On June 2nd the
emigrants were landed and we proceeded west via Niagara
Falls and the lakes to Detroit, then by way of Chicago,
Quincy and Hannibal to St. Joseph, Missouri. From that
point we went to Florence, Nebraska, by steamboat, and
there I turned over my charge to Joseph W. Young, who
was conducting affairs at that place.

I was next assigned to an independent company which
had its own outfit, and was selected as captain and guide.
The company consisted of two hundred and fifty souls, with
fifty wagons and teams. We left Florence in the latter part
of June, and arrived in Salt Lake City on September 23,
1862. I made my report to President Brigham Young, and
was honorably released. I stayed in the city till after the
October conference of the Church, then hastened home to
my family in Ogden City, finding them all well.

CHAPTER LIX.

SHORTLY atter my return from my mission to Europe,
President Brigham Young was in Ogden, and told me
he wished me to locate my family in Salt Lake City, preparatory to my going on another mission, if not a foreign,
a home mission; "for," said he, "I don't know of any
people on earth that need more preaching to than do the
Latter-day Saints at home. We send our Elders out to
preach and to gather the people from workshops and factories, then set those people down here in a new country

and leave them to do the best they can, without necessary experience; and the result is that many of them get discouraged and apostatize ; whereas, if the Elders would keep the harness on, and preach to and encourage them, they would stay and make good Latter-day Saints."

I moved to Salt Lake City according to President Young's advice, and was about eleven months in his employ. Then, by his appointment, I traveled through the Territory, preaching, and lecturing on my travels and experiences. The people in Utah were liberal, giving me much assistance, principally in the way of farm products.

In 1863 I purchased a lot from President Young, began the erection of a two-story adobe house, and moved into it in 1864. It was not completed, and in August I went into the mountains to get finishing lumber. On the night of the 20th of that month I was shot by a camp mate, in mistake for a bear. The young man who shot me was Alexander Gilbert. The bullet entered two-thirds of the way above my knee, on the inside of the left thigh, and shattered the bone into many fragments. The weapon was a United States yauger, and carried a half-ounce ball, which was broken to bits, and, with parts of my clothing, including two pieces of a brass suspender buckle, lodged in my limb.

The accident occurred in Alexander Canyon, about three miles above Wanship, Summit County, between 11 and 12 o'clock at night. There were four of us in camp at the time. The man who did the shooting ran and told George G. Snyder, who was soon at my side with a team and light spring wagon, and with some stimulants. He and my camp mates tenderly lifted me on the bed, and conveyed me to the home of my father-in-law, Nathan Tanner, in Wanship, where I was kindly cared for by him and his family, and my own family notified of the accident that had befallen me. My wound being of a most serious character, the best surgical attention procurable at the time was obtained.

The surgeon advised amputation, but I objected as long as there was any hope of saving the limb. I laid there till November, then was moved to my home in Salt Lake City. For nine months I laid on my back, unable to move from that position. During that time two surgical operations were performed, taking out parts of shattered bone and the bullet. I was reduced to a skeleton, and became so weak I could not feed myself or even lift a sheet of paper between my thumb and finger. After the second surgical operation, however, I began to improve, and in a few weeks could get around with a crutch and a cane.

As I grew stronger, I was able to work some in my nursery; and when, in the autumn of that year, 1865, the municipality opened the Warm Springs to the public I was given charge thereof, and remained in that position till the autumn of 1866. I was there at the time Dr. J. King Robinson, who had had a dispute with the city over the Warm Springs property, was killed, October 22, 1866. When I was brought from Wanship in November, 1864, after being shot, Dr. Robinson, as associate surgeon in my case, was the first one to do any cutting on my limb.

During the time after I was able to move around. subsequent to the months I had to lie in bed, my wounded limb gave me much trouble. Abscesses would form, causing me severe pain, then would burst, and when the pus was drained the flesh would heal again. But I was able to perform only light physical labor, so when, late in the autumn of 1866, business fell off at the Warm Springs, I was notified that, as I was unable to do all the work required and the bath house did not have sufficient patronage to pay two men's wages, my services were no longer required. While business was good I had purchased a hack, one of the first in the city, to convey passengers to and from the Warm Springs, the route being to the business part of town, but as traffic fell off I had to dispose of. the vehicle. Thus when I was thrown out of employment I was left without means of obtaining a livelihood for myself and family.

I had some specimens of the gold I had discovered near the southeastern boundary of California in 1849, when I was going on my first mission to the Society Islands. I showed the specimens to President Brigham Young, and in the spring of 1867, with a company which he had authorized me to select, started for the California border, our destination being a point in the desert known as Salt Springs. The company included Wood Birdno, Lemuel Steele, Dr. Hickman, Robert Egbert and seven others besides myself.

On reaching Los Vegas, we learned from white men, of whom there were about fifty there, that the Indians were on the warpath. Two of the savages had been killed by the white men, and their tribe was seeking revenge. The red men had challenged the white men to come out of their fort and fight; but the challenge was not accepted. We were warned that to continue the journey meant certain death, so I told my companions they were at liberty to return, but I proposed to go on. All of the company elected to do the same.

We proceeded very carefully, and in going along a narrow canyon we observed fresh Indian tracks. These were noticeable for about five miles, but in that distance we saw no Indians, though we momentarily expected them, and kept a sharp lookout. At last we discovered one Indian who claimed to be friendly, but he left us soon—an action which we accepted as an indication of trouble. In the afternoon we selected a camping place on an almost bare knoll, where it seemed impossible for a man to find shelter enough to hide himself. As I was very tired, my companions spread some quilts for me to lie down on. Scarce had they done so when a large Indian rose up from a little gully where he had been hidden. He was within shooting distance, and was well armed. As soon as we saw him, my companions seized their weapons, whereupon I shouted "Hold on!"

The Indian made a motion as if to express a wish to shake hands, and I threw my hand up and down again, in an involuntary movement, the meaning of which I did not know in Indian sign language. The stranger received it as a friendly invitation, and came forward and shook hands. Again, as on former occasions, I had the gift of the tongue or language which the Indians in this vicinity —near Williams' Ranch—spoke, though I had never heard it before. I talked to him, and learned that there were other Indians secreted close by. He called to them, and about fifteen rose up and came to camp. I was informed that white men had killed some of their number, and that one wounded Indian was lying a short distance away. This one I asked to be brought in and laid near my bed, which was done. Dr. Hickman examined his wounds, a shot through the cheek and one in the hip, which he said were not fatal.

I also directed a piece of wagon cover spread out, and told the Indians I wanted their weapons laid on that, which was done. Then some of our company rolled the wagon cover up and tied it, so the guns could not be got at readily if there were trouble. Then, when our guards had been set for the night, we laid down and slept in peace and safety. We made a bargain with the Indians to take care of our animals at a place where there was good grass, and they did so.

The next day we moved on and met no further trouble or danger. We reached our destination in due course, and examined the gold prospect, which was quite rich. But there was no water within twenty-five miles, and it was not

28

practicable to work the mines with the methods within our reach in those days. We had to give up and return home, our route of travel being by way of the Colorado River as far as Call's Fort, then by the settlements on the Muddy into Utah. I reported the trip and its results to President Young.

At that time there had arisen some excitement over gold discoveries on the Sweetwater, near South Pass. Fourteen years previous to that date I had related to President Young how the Indians had told me of gold in that locality. President Young showed me specimens that had been brought him from the new discovery, and told me to get a few men and see what I could do, as he believed it was a good opportunity for me. I did so, and in July, 1867, in company with Foster Curtis, Brower Pettit, Benjamin Brown and B. Y. Hampton, started for the Sweetwater.

Reaching our destination, we prospected for the precious metal. One day I went out alone, and at the base of a slope near the Teresa mine I discovered free gold. I dug a hole and worked at it, securing dirt that carried fifty to sixty cents per pan. It was a placer claim, and I decided that we would occupy it. While I was getting out some of the gold, S. Sharp Walker came along and saw it, and on going to camp told the men. I did not know this till after, but early next morning, before daylight, I overheard a man in the tent next to our wagon tell of a plan to seize the claim. A lot of men were there, Mormons and non-Mormons. I awoke my companions, and it was agreed that they should go and stake the claim, while I should get it recorded. This we did, and had the work accomplished before day was fairly on. I reached the claim, to which the others had preceded me, before those who intended to jump it arrived at the place, and when the latter came up I was prepared to defend it. One man said he had staked the claim before us, but as his statement was not true, we stood him off and retained possession.

Our party went to work, while I started to find my horses, which had strayed away. As I rode up on a knoll, I discovered a war party of seventy-five or eighty Indians, supposed to be Sioux. I had intended to dismount and fasten my saddle, but finding I was discovered and that about twenty-five of the Indians were closing in on me with horses much faster than I had, I started for camp with the loose saddle, skurrying over rocks and sagebrush. On the way back I found my horses and started them, and they ran directly into camp. In the ride my foot came out of the stirrup, and my lame limb dangled, beyond any power of mine to use it. Two Indians ran close up on me and one drew his bow with a fixed arrow. I straightened up, expecting to receive the missile in my back. Just then some of the men who were in our camp, and who had heard my shouts, came out and fired, and my pursuer turned to save himself, while I escaped injury.

At the camp all was excitement. One man, Corinth Lawrence, had been shot and scalped, his body being found some time after I came in. Isador Morris had had a narrow escape. That day there were two others killed on their way to camp. They were Anthony Showell, an eastern man, and Orson Taylor, from Springville, Utah. Showell was found and buried, but Taylor's body never was discovered, that I can recall. In the camp there were George Naylor, Gilbert Webb, Jesse West, John Pitts, Robert Watson, Jr., George Boyd and many others from Salt Lake City, as well as men who had come from various parts of the country. The man who had tried to jump the claim I had found assumed charge and got the camp together, intending to make a stand in the brush. I knew the danger of such a proceeding with seventy-five or eighty hostile Indian warriors near, so, with my companions, with-

drew to a better position; soon all the camp followed, and we prepared for defense. The intended claim-jumper, whose name I am unable to recall, was a partner of Corinth Lawrence, and requested me to take charge of the funeral of the dead man, which I did, and he was buried as carefully as we could do it. That day I suffered greatly with my lame limb, and an abscess burst and discharged freely.

Next morning we broke camp and returned home, for it was not safe to remain there, in a hostile Indian country. Later in the season, Brower Pettit and Foster Curtis returned to our claim, but it had been seized, and was held by parties from California. There was a great rush in of people, and the town of South Pass, or Atlantic City, was built. The next spring I went out with more men, but our claim could not be regained, so we had to give it up. The parties who seized it took many thousands of dollars out of it. The second year, however, the mining boom collapsed.

During the summer and autumn of this year, 1868, grading for the Union Pacific Railway was going on. I hauled coal from Coalville to Salt Lake City, and also hauled tithing produce from Ogden and Logan, taking produce for pay, so that my family was well supplied with provisions. On my last trip from Ogden I was caught in a snowstorm on the sandridge, took a congestive chill, and almost died on the way. When I reached home I was unable to get off my wagon. I was cared for by my family, but suffered greatly, and in addition to the suppuration in my thigh, the wound bled so as to endanger my life. Finally, on May 27, 1869, my left limb was amputated about four inches from the hip joint. The surgeons were Dr. W. F. Anderson, Dr. H. J. Richards and Dr. J. M. Bernhisel. Apostles Wilford Woodruff and George Q. Cannon were present also. The operation which I had objected to for nearly five years became necessary to save my life.

In a few weeks from the time of the amputation I was able to get out a little, and pruned a few trees. From that time on I worked, though it was under many difficulties. till I had pruned my nursery of ten thousand trees, and had given them necessary care. I was able to be present at the ceremonies at the entrance of the railway into Salt Lake City, January 10, 1870. During the succeeding two years I attended to my nursery, also traveled and lectured on my experiences and preached as a home missionary, from Paris, Idaho, on the north, to St. George, Utah, on the south. In the summer of 1871, while working in my orchard, I was overcome by heat, having a slight sunstroke, some of the effects of which have never left me. Still my health was better than before my limb was amputated, and with crutches I got along fairly well.

CHAPTER XL.

CALLED ON A MISSION TO THE UNITED STATES—JOURNEY EASTWARD
—VISIT RELATIVES EN ROUTE—REACH NEW YORK—MEASURED
FOR AN ARTIFICIAL LIMB—HOW IT WAS PAID FOR—VISIT AND
PREACH — MEET POOR ENCOURAGEMENT — GO TO BOSTON —
WORLD'S PEACE JUBILEE—BUNKER HILL—AGAIN AT NEW YORK
—RELEASED TO RETURN HOME—BACK IN UTAH—TRAVELING AND
PREACHING—SENT FOR BY PRESIDENT YOUNG—CALLED ON A
MISSION TO ARIZONA—DIRECTED TO FURNISH NAMES OF OTHERS
—SEND THE LIST—PRESIDENT YOUNG ADDS OTHER NAMES—SET
APART FOR OUR MISSION—DIFFICULT TO COLLECT MONEY DUE
ME—LEAVE MY FAMILY POORLY PROVIDED FOR BUT TRUSTING
IN THE LORD—PLACED IN CHARGE OF THE MISSION—LETTER OF
INSTRUCTIONS—START SOUTH—PEOPLE CONTRIBUTE LIBERALLY
—TRAVELING IN STORM—ARRIVE AT KANAB—IN ARIZONA—A
HARD JOURNEY—MARRIAGE OF MY DAUGHTER—REACH LEE'S
FERRY ON THE COLORADO—CROSSING THE RIVER—REACH MOAN-
COPPY WASH—DECIDE TO WINTER THERE—EXPLORE THE VICIN-
ITY—MEET FRIENDLY INDIANS—BUILDING A HOUSE—EXPLORING
THE LITTLE COLORADO—A DIFFICULT TRIP—DESCRIPTION OF
THE ROUTE—FIND A PLACE FOR ANOTHER SETTLEMENT—SAN
FRANCISCO MOUNTAINS—FINE FOREST GROWTH—CAUGHT IN DEEP
SNOW—THROUGH WITH A PERILOUS JOURNEY—DECIDE TO RE-
TURN TO SALT LAKE CITY AND REPORT—HEAVY SNOW—TRIP
HOMEWARD—CORDIALLY GREETED BY PRESIDENT YOUNG—WITH
MY FAMILY.

ON the 8th of April, 1872, at the general conference of
the Church in Salt Lake City, I was called on a mission to the eastern part of the United States, and hastened
to settle my business preparatory to my departure. At 5
p. m. on May 1st I left Salt Lake City, going by train to
Ogden, and then east. There were about twenty-five other
Elders in the company. My companion in the Pullman car
was Moroni Brown, of Ogden. On reaching Missouri
Valley Junction, Iowa, I stopped over with my brother-
in-law, B. H. Dennis. On May 4th, I went to Calhoun and

preached in the schoolhouse; returned to Missouri Valley Junction on the 6th, preaching in the courthouse. My father paid the expense of securing the last-named building.

I continued my journey on the 7th, going by way of Chicago, Philadelphia, Newark and Jersey City, to New York. There we met with Elder Wm. C. Staines, and on the 12th went with him to Brooklyn. On the 13th I was measured at Mr. Hudson's, 696 Broadway, New York, for an artificial limb. The way I came to do this was through Leonard Wines, of Salt Lake City. Mr. Wines and I had been good friends in our younger days. In later years he had made some money on the mail line west, and meeting me one day on the train the idea struck him that I ought to have an artificial leg. The result was that he and some friends whom he called on raised the necessary amount to pay for it, which sum he presented to me, telling of his purpose. Naturally I had a high appreciation of his kindness. It was on May 27th that I received the artificial limb.

We obtained lodgings with Brother Isaac Elkington and family, and visited and preached where we could. We met very little encouragement from the people. On June 13th we left for Boston on a steamer of the Neptune Line, going first to Providence, from which place we went by rail to Boston, and thence to Portsmouth, N. H. At the latter place I visited my father-in-law, Thomas Lester.

On the 17th of June we were at the World's Peace Jubilee, in Boston, and also visited Bunker Hill and mingled with the vast assemblage there. I paid a visit to the home of Thomas Lester, Jr., about fifteen miles out from Boston, on the 18th, and then returned to New York, where, on the 19th, we met President George A. Smith of the First Presidency of the Church. He told us we were at liberty to return home, as the antagonism was so great that there was no chance to preach the Gospel to the people at that time. That evening we filled an appointment at Paterson, N. J., staying at the home of W. Dover till the 23rd, when we returned to New York.

Having been released from our mission, owing to the indifference of the people, we started home the first of July. For some three years after my return I traveled and preached as I had done formerly, in southern Idaho, western Wyoming and northern Utah.

On Wednesday evening, September 29, 1875, on returning from a preaching tour in the northern part of Utah County, I was informed by my family that President Young had sent for me to do some interpreting in the Navajo language. I had met the Navajo Indians going away from his office, and as I knew my presence was not necessary then, and as I was quite ill with a nervous headache, I did not go up till next day.

Going to see President Young, I met him in front of his office, in his carriage. He said he had wanted me to talk with the Navajos, but I was too late, for they were gone, "but," said he, "I knew you had the spirit of it." He then drove off, and his private secretary, Elder George Reynolds, invited me into the office, saying the President wanted to see me particularly on missionary business. At this I went inside and waited. Soon the President came in and after speaking to some others who were waiting for him, came to me and said, "Oh, Brother James, that I could see you as I have seen you, strong and active! I should like to send you on a mission to those Indians, for you are just the man to go there with a few other good men. The Spirit of the Lord is upon them and they need a few men among them who will teach them the truth."

To this statement I replied that I was unable to endure hardships and exposure as I had done, for my health was very poor and I was not able to wait on myself in camp life. I stated, however, that what the Spirit of the Lord directed through him I was willing to try to do to the best of my ability; and added, "You know where to find me; I am just where I always have been, on hand."

President Young then said, "Bless your soul, the Spirit does and has dictated to me all the time to send you to take charge of a mission in that country. You are just the man for it, and if I had sent you before, we would have had a mission and settlements there now. I think that if we fit you up with a good spring wagon or carriage, and some good brethren to wait on you, that you can go. Just get a list of names of good men, and hand them to me—a list of men that will stand by you, but none of your babies. I want good men to go with you on this mission, so hand me a list of names."

When the conversation ended, I returned home, and after much thought and prayer for the guidance of the Lord, wrote the following names, my own at the head of the list: Daniel B. Roson, John C. Thompson, Seth B. Tanner, Morton P. Mortenson, Bengt Jenson, Hans Funk, Ernest Tietjens and John Davies. The latter got excused, and President Young added the following: Andrew L. Gibbons, Luther C. Burnham, Thales H. Haskell, Ira Hatch, Warren M. Johnson and William H. Gibbons. These were called on a mission October 9, 1875, at the general conference. On Monday, October 11th, we were set apart for our mission.

I found some difficulty in collecting debts due me, over a thousand dollars altogether, so that I could not get enough to fit me out comfortably nor to provide for my family. Still I was determined to go. When it came to parting from my family, it was hard to leave them, with only ten days' supply of fuel and less than fifty pounds of flour in the house, and not knowing where the next would come from. It seemed as if they could not endure the separation when they saw me fitted out so poorly. But I blessed them in the name of the Lord, and told them that if they would live their religion they would not suffer so much want when I was away as if I had stayed home. Then we separated sorrowfully, and on October 30th I went by train to Provo. Some of the company had preceded me a day or two. I had in the meantime received much personal instruction from President Young, and was given the following letter:

"SALT LAKE CITY, U. T., October 28, 1875.
"*Elder James S. Brown, Salt Lake City:*

"DEAR BROTHER:—You are hereby appointed to take charge of the mission about to go south and southeast of the Colorado River.

"It will become your duty to found settlements in suitable locations, where the brethren can congregate in cultivating the earth to bring forth substance for the families of the brethren who may feel disposed to join you.

"You will work in harmony with other brethren who are now in the south building up new locations, and will in all things seek the welfare of those associated with you, and the building up of the kingdom of God.

"In the formation of settlements, and in all circumstances that may arise on your mission, you will seek the wisdom of the Spirit of the Lord, and be guided by its whisperings in all things from day to day.

"The brethren with whom you are associated are counseled to act under your directions, that the spirit of union and concert of action may characterize all your movements. And we call upon all men unto whom you shall come to aid and assist you according to their ability in promoting so good and glorious a cause as settling this rugged new, country.

"We would counsel you, if you will do it, to sustain each other as brethren, and work together in the holy order that God has revealed.

"We pray God our Heavenly Father to bless and prosper you and to make you instrumental in accomplishing much good to those with whom you are called upon to associate, and to labor for on this mission, in the name of Jesus Christ. Amen.

"Your brethren in the Gospel,

"BRIGHAM YOUNG,

"DANIEL H. WELLS,

"First Presidency of the Church of Jesus Christ of Latter-day Saints."

From Provo I got a ride with a team to Spanish Fork, where, on Sunday, October 31st, I preached to the people, having great liberty of the Spirit. Then Bishop Snell asked the people for a contribution and they responded liberally, raising twenty-two sacks of flour, twenty-six bushels of potatoes, and thirteen dollars in money. That night I went on to Salem and preached, and also received a small donation from the people. I next went to Payson, where I preached on Monday evening, and where the people subscribed liberally, so that I had thirty-three dollars in currency, fifty sacks of flour, and twenty-six bushels of potatoes. Thus my words to my destitute family were fulfilled, and they were provided for as well as myself.

At Payson I met some of my missionary companions, and we moved on southward. Others joined us on the journey, and on November 9th we reached Salina, where we pitched our tent and I camped out for the first time on our trip. At Richfield we received contributions of provisions, and again at Panguitch. Much of our journey between these two places was in storm—rain and snow—and was far from comfortable. On the 18th we crossed the rim of the Great Basin. We reached Kanab on the 20th, where we were joined by the four brethren who had been called from the southern settlements.

I left Kanab on November 22nd, going to Navajo Wells. Before leaving Kanab I had telegraphed to President Young, written to my family, and arranged with Bishop L. John Nuttall to have our mail sent after us as soon as possible. At Navajo Wells I joined our party, and next day we went on to the Buckskin Mountains, making dry camp that night. On the 24th we reached House Rock Spring, where we were overtaken with letters from home. I had one from my eldest daughter, Lydia Jane, stating that she was to be married to Homer Manley Brown on November 22nd. It had been arranged before I left home that the wedding was to take place this month.

We traveled steadily on, the country being dry and forbidding. Our beef cattle having run off, Ira Hatch and Luther C. Burnham went to find them. Burnham brought them into camp at Badger Creek, on the 26th, but it was 2 o'clock on the morning of the 27th when Ira Hatch got in from his fruitless search. That day we went on to Lee's Ferry, on the Colorado River. We had sent two men ahead to arrange for us to be ferried over the river, but they reported that it was not possible to cross that night. I thought differently, and as it was Saturday, I determined to get over. Some of the party objected and some were willing, and this division delayed our crossing with the wagons till about 10 p. m.; but we were safely over the stream. Next day our animals were ferried over. At the ferry, Mrs. Lee was out of provisions, and we helped her to some, and also gave her ten dollars, of which I contributed two dollars. Next morning she sent me a Navajo blanket and a cotton handkerchief.

We left Lee's Crossing on November 29th, and continued over a dry, rough, difficult road till December 3rd, when we reached Moancoppy, the pleasantest spot we had seen since before arriving at Kanab. I was impressed to make this place winter quarters, and designated a site for a fort. We were all pleased to have a rest from traveling, as our feed had given out and our stock was sick with the epizootic. Near this place there were some old Indian farms and a few stone huts laid up without mortar, but all had been deserted. There were also some springs near by.

The morning after we had camped there, a small hunting party of Navajos came in, and after we had given them their breakfast they smoked their corn-husk cigarettes and departed. A. S. Gibbons, Ira Hatch and I examined the country around Moancoppy, and found a few ponds of water and a good place for a reservoir to catch the spring rains; we also discovered a fertile spot of a few acres, and two small springs. December 5th was Sunday. We held a meeting, and all our company, thirteen in number, expressed themselves as feeling well and zealous in our missions.

On Monday we explored the vicinity, but found nothing inviting outside the neighborhood of our camp, where we all were satisfied a missionary station should be built, as it was the best we could do. We went to work getting timber and doing other necessary work, my part being to guard against hostile Indians. T. H. Haskell and Ira Hatch, our interpreters, went to the Oriba Indian village, some fifty miles away. On their return they reported all was peaceful; they were accompanied by Chief Tuba and his wife Telassinimki, who were highly pleased to see their old Mormon friends.

On the 8th we laid out a house twenty by forty feet and twelve feet high, to be built of stone. Our beef cattle having become very wild, we had to kill them and cure the meat.

J. C. Thompson, Ira Hatch, S. B. Tanner, L. C. Burnham and I started on December 9th on an exploring trip up the Little Colorado River and around the San Francisco Mountains. When we had gone twelve miles, breaking the road through the canyon, we were glad to find some pools of water, and to rest for the night. Next day we came to the Little Colorado River from forty to fifty miles above its mouth. The river bottom was about half a mile wide, and the water very low. We continued up the river to the Black Falls, where the stream passes over a ledge of volcanic rock twelve or fourteen feet high. Four miles farther up it ran through a very narrow gorge, and we had to pass over the hills through deep sand, which our team found it very difficult to cross.

Fifteen miles farther on we came to Grand Falls, where the river runs over shelving rocks for eighty to a hundred feet. Higher up the stream the bottoms widened out, in some places to four miles, the timber was better and the stream was larger. We killed two antelope and dried the meat. Our forward journey continued to the old Beel trail, then on to Sunset Crossing and the old Prescott road. Seven miles above was a mail station, and there, at 9 o'clock on the night of Friday, December 17th, the mail carriers met, and we learned some general news from them. Next day we traveled fifteen miles farther, to where some Mexican herders were camped with about four thousand sheep. The water in the river had improved in quantity and quality, and the surroundings were such that we felt we could recommend it as a place for settlement. We were also impressed to return to Moancoppy, and started on that journey on the 19th. We changed our course and took more to the hill country, heading for the San Francisco Mountains.

The return trip was very hard. We saw plenty of timber—the finest forest growth I ever beheld. On December 24th, when crossing the divide between the San Francisco Mountains and Mount Hendrick, we encountered a terrific snowstorm, and had to camp for the night. Next day we continued on our way, making slow progress in the deep snow. We passed below the snow line on a very rough country, where sometimes, with brake set, it took the

four of us all we could do to keep the wagon right side up.
We were thankful to reach the river on the 28th and Moancoppy on the 29th.

At a brief consultation that day, it was decided that I
should return to Salt Lake City and report to President
Young the result of our explorations. Next day the band-
aging of my artificial leg gave way and T. H. Haskell repaired it. On New Year's Day, 1876, J. C. Thompson, W.
H. Gibbons and I set out for Kanab, where we arrived on
January 6th.

I requested Bishop Nuttall to forward me to Order-
ville, which he did. From there Bishop H. O. Spencer
took his team and conveyed me to Panguitch. We met a
heavy snowstorm on the road, the snow on the rim of the
Basin being up to the wagonbox. From Panguitch I was
forwarded to Monroe, where I telegraphed President Young
that I would be in the city by January 15th. I was advanced by team from there to the railroad, where a pass
sent by President Young was ready for me, and I arrived
in Salt Lake City and reported to him at 6 p. m. on the
14th. At the railway station I was met by my children and
the neighbors and two vehicles. If I had been President
Young's own son he could not have received me more
cordially than he did when I reached his office. After our
conversation I returned home, where my folks thought I
should have gone first; but they were overjoyed to see me,
as I was to see them, all in good health and well provided
for. We were highly gratified to realize that the Lord had
heard and answered our prayers.

CHAPTER LXI.

ATTEND MEETINGS WITH THE FIRST PRESIDENCY AND APOSTLES—MORE
MISSIONARIES CALLED TO ARIZONA—MANY INQUIRIES REGARDING
THE MISSION—OUTLINE THE ROUTE—PREPARATIONS FOR TRAVEL
—START SOUTH—AIDED BY CONTRIBUTIONS—REACH MOENCOPPY
—MEET LOT SMITH AND COMPANY—BAPTISMS—START FOR THE
LITTLE COLORADO RIVER—GUIDE MISSIONARY COMPANIES TO
THE PLACE WE HAD SELECTED FOR SETTLEMENT—LOT SMITH
REFUSES TO ACKNOWLEDGE MY APPOINTMENT FROM PRESIDENT
YOUNG AS PRESIDENT OF THE MISSION—HE ASSUMES LEADER-
SHIP AT THE NEW SETTLEMENT—I RETURN WITH MY PARTY TO
MOENCOPPY—OTHER COMPANIES OF MISSIONARY SETTLERS SUS-
TAIN MY PRESIDENCY—MY HEALTH IS POOR—SETTLERS DISCOUR-
AGED—CHEER THEM UP—WORK OF FRONTIER LIFE—SUCCOR A
COMPANY WHOSE WATER SUPPLY IS EXHAUSTED—TAKING UP
LAND—MAKE A LONG EXPLORING TRIP—INTRODUCE BOOK OF
MORMON TO NAVAJOS—RETURN TO MOENCOPPY—INDIANS DIS-
SATISFIED—GO TO SALT LAKE CITY WITH A DELEGATION OF NA-
VAJO CHIEFS—THEIR SUPPOSED GRIEVANCES SETTLED—TELL
PRESIDENT YOUNG I HAVE COME HOME TO STAY—HE SENDS ME
OUT AGAIN—DIRECTED TO PROCURE VOLUNTEERS—LETTER OF
INSTRUCTIONS—LECTURE, AND TAKE UP CONTRIBUTIONS—RE-
TURN HOME—MY FAMILY ILL—PROVIDE SUPPLIES FOR THEM—
CONDITIONS IMPROVE.

MY stay at home lasted till January 30, 1876. I attended several meetings with the First Presidency,
the Twelve Apostles, and other leading brethren in the
Church. They were consulting as to the best means of
colonizing that part of Arizona we had been exploring, and
two hundred missionaries were called to go there and settle
the country. Scores of visitors also came to my house to
inquire regarding my travels and the place where I had
been. I went over to Apostle John Taylor's house on invitation, and there George Goddard reported our conversation, as I was requested to outline the route to Arizona,

29

which outline was afterwards published in the Deseret News. During my stay I also made a brief visit to Ogden.

As the time drew near for me to start south again, President Young loaned me a team and light wagon to travel with. He also advised me to find a boy about sixteen years old to go with and wait on me. I was thinking of how I should follow this counsel, when John Reidhead, who was one of those called to the Arizona mission, came in and proffered his son—an offer I was pleased to accept. On Friday, January 28, Brother Reidhead and son started south with my team and baggage.

Early on the morning of Sunday, January 30, I took leave of my family, and went by train to Spanish Fork, making an appointment at Springville as I passed. I was met at the station at Spanish Fork, and conveyed to the meetinghouse, where I addressed the congregation. That evening I returned to Springville and filled the appointment there. Next morning I was met by Brother Reidhead and son, and proceeded to Payson. I had had raised for me, by subscription, a span of small mules, so I sent back President Young's team and harness, and went on my journey, preaching almost every evening in one or other town on the way. We were treated very kindly. Our route lay through Fillmore, Beaver, Parowan, Cedar City, Toquerville, and on to Kanab, which we reached February 23, finding Bishop Nuttall quite ill. We made our home at Bishop Levi Stewart's.

On March 2nd we set out from Kanab, and reached Moencoppy on the 8th, where we found all well. The building constructed by the settlers was so far completed as to protect us comfortably from storm and cold; and a dam had been constructed, with a water ditch three miles long, giving us quite a reservoir. Plowing also had been begun, though the weather was very disagreeable.

On the 11th, J. C. Thompson and A. S. Gibbons went

to meet Lot Smith and a company coming from Utah. On Sunday, the 12th, we held meeting, and a young man named Franklin D. Gillespie, who had fallen in with us, desired to be baptized into the Church, as did Ly and his wife, two of the Oriba Indians. The ordinance was attended to, and I also ordained the chief, Tuba, a Priest.

During the next three days I arranged affairs of the company, some of the men being directed to locate springs, to act as guides to the companies coming, attend to our mail, etc., and on the 15th, with S. B. Tanner, Ira Hatch, and J. B. Reidhead, set out with six mules and a light wagon to search a road for vehicles between Moencoppy and the Oriba village. Hans Funk and E. Tietjens, with a four-horse team, went to the top of the hill to haul water for our animals, and from there our party proceeded along the Indian trail three or four miles, then struck out over the trackless, sandy plain, to avoid rugged buttes and deep gulches that rendered the trail impracticable for wagons. We went on about fourteen miles, and camped in the sand; I was quite ill.

Next day we traveled about twenty-five miles in a southeasterly direction, over sandhills and up a long wash, to a divide, where we made dry camp. We met four hunting parties, and two of the hunters camped with us. The following morning we went on seven miles, to the pools of water where the Oribas were camped with their flocks of sheep and goats. Each flockmaster stood guard over his animals, for his turn to get at the pools. We passed on three miles to the Oriba village, located on the crest of a steep bluff. The houses were built close together, and there were about five hundred inhabitants. Those Indians obtained all their water from a well about a mile distant, and the carrying of the precious liquid was going on day and night, while the Indians were praying continually for more water.

Leaving the Oriba village, we proceeded onward over a rough and sandy country, reaching the Mohave Springs, where the Hopees water their stock, on the 18th. That night we experienced a fearful windstorm. On the 20th we came to the Little Colorado River, and on the 23rd arrived at the place selected on my first trip for a settlement. Between this time and my previous visit five houses had been built there, so our purpose was interfered with a little. Next day we chose a place for the pioneer camp, and S. B. Tanner and I started back to meet the company from Utah which was to occupy the locality as a settlement, and which had been following us closely. We met the newcomers that day, and returned to the site that had been chosen.

It was at this place that the first disagreement in the expedition occurred. Captains Smith, Lake and Allen had charge of three sections of the company. I invited them and others to a meeting to consult over what should be done, and there presented to them my letter of instructions from President Young and my appointment as president of the mission. Captain Lot Smith opposed my presidency, and Captains Lake and Allen failed to give me support. Things were not pleasant, and the meeting was dismissed. Next day matters in camp were in a rather confused condition.

The succeeding day was Sunday, March 26th. Lot Smith called a meeting, and invited me to speak. I recounted what we had done in searching out and selecting this place for settlement, and welcomed the company to it; I also gave information and instruction concerning the country. When I finished, Lot Smith assumed charge of the meeting, and paid no further attention to me. Next day I invited him, and also Major Ladd, to take a walk with me. They came, and I asked Brother Smith what he intended doing. He replied that he was going ahead independent of me. I told him he had insulted me and trampled upon my God-given right, through President Young, who had appointed me to preside over the Arizona mission, and if he would persist in doing wrong he must bear the responsibility. He was very defiant, so we separated. I called Brother G. Lake, who had informed me that Lot Smith seemed to think he was in charge of the companies but he (Lake) knew it was my place and would sustain me. I told him he had betrayed my confidence, for when it came to the test he had failed to keep his word. I advised him to think the matter over, and as I had decided to return at once to Moencoppy, our party bade good-bye to the newcomers, and we started. This was on March 27th.

On the 30th we reached the lower crossing of the river, and camped, the stream being too much swollen to cross. S. B. Tanner shot a deer, and by about five hours later he and the others brought in two more deer—a valuable addition to our stock of provisions. By Saturday, April 1st, the river had fallen, and other companies having come up, we crossed and held a meeting. Next day another meeting was convened, and I called David E. Fullmer to return with us, which he did. In a meeting held at the old Arizona camp on April 4th, at which there was a large number of those who had recently come from Utah, my letter of instructions from President Young was read, and the brethren unanimously sustained me as president of the mission. Our party continued the journey, and after much toil reached Moencoppy settlement on April 7th. I was quite ill at this time.

We continued the work necessary to establishing a settlement, but there were so many difficulties that some of our company, which had been increased by additions from Utah, began to feel discouraged. I admonished and cheered them, causing them to feel better. We also arranged for some of the company, in charge of S. B.

Tanner, to go up the Little Colorado River and secure twenty-three land claims for us. This party started on Monday, April 17th.   On the 22nd a Brother Phillips came from Moencoppy and said a small company had reached there without water, and that their teams were so exhausted that they could not travel longer than about noon.   We comprehended their suffering condition, gathered all the barrels and kegs we had, and filled them with water— about one hundred gallons—and Brothers Roson and Thompson went to their relief.   I then made out some notices to put up, giving instructions so that other companies should not be caught in the same predicament as this one had been.

From time to time our numbers were augmented by additions from Utah, many having come in and located at the places we had selected.   Among those who joined us at Moencoppy was my son-in-law, H. O. Fullmer, and my daughter, Rachel E.   On the 17th of May the members of our settlement proceeded up the river to where S. B. Tanner and party had taken up land for us.   There was some dissatisfaction in the company, but after prayerfully considering the situation all was made right.   Then, on May 19th, Brothers Tanner, Haskell and I started on an exploring trip.   We were gone till July 3rd, and traveled several hundred miles, going north and east through the country of the Navajos, the Moquis and the Zunis.   We saw the villages of each, and also many ancient ruins.   We passed over some good country, but much of it was very rough, and our trip was an arduous one.

While on this journey we were traveling along the Rio Perco, a tributary of the Rio Grande del Norte, when, on June 17th, as we were following a trail through a forest, an Indian stepped out from the edge of the undergrowth, held up his hand, and said: "Stop! Who are you, where do you come from, where are you going, and what is your business in the Navajo country?"

"We are Mormons from Utah," was our response, in Spanish, the language in which our interrogator had spoken.

"Stop your wagon under this tree," continued he, indicating a place, "and talk to us; for we hear the Mormons have the history of our forefathers. The Americans and Spaniards say you claim this, but we know they often speak falsely, and we wish to learn from your own lips whether you have such a record, and how you came by it. We want you to stop here till our people come together, and you can tell us the truth."

By this time another Indian had presented himself. We turned aside as ordered, and the first Navajo said to the newcomer: "Show these men where water is."

Seth B. Tanner and Thales H. Haskell unhitched our team, and led them to drink, the Indian going as guide. I was asked to get out of the wagon, and as I was doing so a large number of Indians appeared, coming from all directions. Almost before I realized it, there were two hundred and fifty to three hundred Navajos there, men, women and children. My chair was taken out of the wagon, a blanket was spread for me, and I sat down, the Indians sitting close around. Two chiefs, whom I learned were Juan San Juall and Jualito, sat as near to me as they could, and one of them said, "If you have the book of our forefathers, tell us about God and them, and how you came by the book."

I produced a copy of the Book of Mormon, told them it was a record of God's dealings with their forefathers, and explained to them how it was revealed to the Prophet Joseph Smith by an angel. As I proceeded to tell what was in the Book of Mormon, tears came to the eyes of many in the audience, and some of them spoke out, "We know that what you say is true, for the traditions of

our good old men who never told a lie agree with your
story. Our forefathers did talk with God, and they wrote;
and when they became wicked and went to war they hid
up their records, and we know not where they are."

At this point the chiefs and about ten other leading
men rose up and embraced me, saying, "Continue to tell us
of God and our forefathers, for it does our hearts good to
hear of them."

I talked on for a time, and when I was through,
Messrs. Tanner and Haskell, who had listened to what had
been going on, bore witness that what I had said was true.
We remained with the Indians for dinner, and they wanted
us to stay longer, but we felt that it was better to proceed on
our journey. This meeting, one of the most sudden and
singular in my experience, occurred in New Mexico, about
thirty miles north of the old mail route from Albuquerque
westward. When it was over we continued our journey
south and west, turned west to Fort Wingate, then on to
Fort Defiance, and through the Moquis villages to our
settlement.

On the day of our return to Moencoppy, July 3rd,
Brothers Roson and Thompson came to meet us with
barrels of water—a relief that we appreciated greatly. We
were highly pleased to learn that all was well in the settlement.

Soon after this I released two of the missionaries till
October 1st, to visit their families in Utah, and five others
till November 1st, for the same purpose. During July and
the early part of August we were engaged in tending and
gathering crops, and the work incident to establishing a
settlement, which was by no means easy. We also visited
and endeavored to keep on good terms with the Indians,
and for ourselves did so; but there were some of the Navajos who seemed bent on making trouble, and who com-
plained that the settlers on the Little Colorado had taken

some of their animals. Finally, on August 6th, we received word from the Indian council that a delegation of chiefs would meet with us in three days, to accompany some of us on a visit to the "Mormon Chief," to settle the alleged grievances. Ira Hatch and I set out that same evening to meet the delegation. I took very ill, and it was only through the best care and with great effort that I could travel, but we were determined not to disapppint the Indians. I received marked attention from Ira Hatch, also from J. D. Lee and wife at the Moenabbey, and in a few hours was able to move around again as usual. We met the Indians, and made the journey north, reaching Salt Lake City on the evening of August 22nd, the Indians being lodged at D. B. Huntington's for the night.

Next day President Young met the delegation in his schoolhouse, and talked over the supposed wrongs of the Mormon settlers to the Navajos—for they were only supposed, as it turned out. I acted as interpreter, using the Spanish language. Efforts had been made to find some other interpreter who could talk the Navajo dialect, but in vain. Everything was made satisfactory to the red men, who remained in Salt Lake City four days. At this time a delegation of Shoshones from Bear River came with George Hill as interpreter, and these met the Navajos and the two tribes "buried the hatchet." Then the Navajos received a few presents and returned to their homes.

I had a conversation with President Young, in which I told him I had come from Arizona not to return unless he ordered me to do so. A few days later he met me and said he had been thinking over my mission. He intended to press onward in settling Arizona and New Mexico, and as I knew what that country was, he thought I had better travel through Utah and lecture on the prospects of the work in the southern mission, and also call for volunteers to accompany me in returning to Arizona. He told me further that I was to take up collections among the Saints for the support of myself and family, and for an outfit for myself. In pursuance of these instructions he gave me a letter to the Bishops and other authorities. This document mentioned my missionary labors in Arizona, said I was directed to lecture among the Saints on the mission work and take up contributions, and counseled the authorities to render me assistance in harmony with the call made of me. It closed as follows:

"Brother Brown is also authorized to receive the names of those who are willing or desirous of helping to build up the Kingdom of God in that region. We learn that the brethren are discovering new and desirable valleys in the neighborhood of their present settlements, and elsewhere, and it is our intention to keep pushing out and onward as fast as prudence and the whisperings of the Spirit of the Lord shall dictate.

"We desire the active co-operation of our brethren in this important work, and shall be pleased to receive a goodly list of volunteers through Brother Brown, consisting of men who love the Gospel, have faith in the promises of the Father, and have the integrity, determination and zeal of true Latter-day Saints. We have no fear that too many will respond to this invitation, as the rich valleys south and east of the Colorado offer homes for hundreds of those who desire to extend the curtains of Zion in that direction.

"We are informed that some of the brethren entertain the idea that it is better to be called by the authorities to such missions than to volunteer. To such we will quote the saying of the Lord to the Prophet Joseph Smith, as contained in the Doctrine and Covenants: 'He that waiteth to be commanded in all things is a slothful servant.'

"Ever praying for the welfare of Israel, I remain your brother in the Gospel,

"BRIGHAM YOUNG."

This letter was dated September 16, 1876.

Soon afterward I went as directed, traveling and lecturing in northern Utah, with a visit to Almy, Wyoming; then worked my way southward in the various counties, to Richfield. I lectured sixty-five times, and secured about eighty volunteers, mostly from Sevier County. Ira Hatch came up with me and at Richfield we separated, he taking my team and going to Kanab, and I returning home to provide for my family and then rejoin him at the town last named. I found several of my family quite ill, and there had been one death—my Aunt Polly, who died on Christmas day, a few days before my arrival home.

The opening of the year 1877 found me with my family, who soon began to amend in health. I was also able to supply them fairly well with what they needed for sustenance during my absence, as the Bishops and Saints whom I had visited had been very kind and liberal, in response to the invitation of President Young to promote the interests of the southern mission by rendering assistance to me so I could proceed to that field of labor.

CHAPTER LXII.

MY stay at home was brief, and the 26th of January, 1877, found me again at Kanab, ready to proceed southward. Three days later the start was made, and on the morning of February 5th we reached Moencoppy. The people there were in poor spirits, and considerably dissatis- fied. During my absence they had sowed about fourteen acres of fall grain and had built eight log rooms. On my arrival, A. S. Gibbons made complaint against S. B. Tan- ner, for they had had a disagreement. Tanner was found to be in error, and made the matter right.

This trouble settled, the work of plowing and planting and setting out trees, was proceeded with. Friendly Nav- ajo and Oriba Indians visited us, and as the United Order was being preached to the Church at that time, I gave my views on the subject in an address at the Thursday even- ing meeting, March 8th. Again on Sunday, the 11th, I preached to the Saints, telling them plainly the wrong that was in their neglect of duty and disaffection. My remarks had quite a salutary effect, and matters moved more smoothly.

Shortly after midnight on the morning of March 23rd, the message was brought that our reservoir had given way. We hurried out, but had to wait till daylight before we could do effective work in repairing the dam. In the meantime the Indians were greatly excited because the water was injuring their crops, and we had to pacify the red men as best we could, and make good the damage. Two days after this my daughter, Mrs. Fullmer, became a mother, and I rendered her necessary care and attention.

On March 31st we received mail with the news of the result of the presidential election, when Hayes and Tilden were the candidates, also of Amasa M. Lyman's death, and of John D. Lee being sentenced to be shot. On April 4th we received tidings of Lee's execution.

Our time was well occupied now with the work around the settlement; I also engaged in studying the Navajo language, preparatory to an extended visit among those Indians. All went well till May 8th, when I learned that the Piute Indians intended to steal our animals. Chief Patnish was dead, and his people were angry. For the first time in the history of the mission, we called out a guard, gathered our animals and property, and provided against a raid on the part of the savages. We were assisted by some friendly Navajos. At our inspection we ascertained that we could fire eighty-five shots without stopping to reload. On the 17th, two Piute Indians came in and informed us that a council had been held to discuss the raid on us, but the vote was six to five against molesting us, and the council broke up in a fight. The five Indians who were in favor of attacking us started to seek the assistance of the Ute Indians, while the others came to our side. A week later we had a talk with some of the Piutes, and the threatened trouble was averted.

A funeral occurred in the settlement on May 27th—
that of Minty, the little daughter of W. J. Johnston. I
preached the funeral sermon. For some time previous to
and after this occasion my health was quite poor. On June
1st we had another Indian scare, and made ready for attack,
but the alarm was without sufficient cause.

Before this time several of our company had endeavored to learn the Navajo language, but met with little success; so I determined to study the Indian language and
customs myself, that I might be able to talk freely with the
red men. Accordingly, on June 4th, I went up the Moencoppy Wash to Chief Hustelso's camp, about twenty-five
miles. It was arranged that I should be left there alone,
except that Ira Hatch's eight-year old girl was to stay with
and wait on me. The Indian camp was located two or
three miles from where George A. Smith, Jr. was killed
some years before, probably by the same Indians.

H. O. Fullmer and Ira Hatch went with me, and eight
Navajos assisted in letting my wagon down into the Wash,
where I was left. The bed of the stream was perhaps
three thousand feet below the plain above on the north
side, while the cliffs on the south towered up almost per-
pendicularly about five thousand feet. The Indian camp
was in the deep recess, the descent into which was both
difficult and dangerous. A wagon could not be drawn
down or up by team, but for a thousand feet or so had to
be lowered from one cliff to another with ropes. In one
place the Indians had cut eighteen steps, to enable them to
get their animals up and down; and then occasionally a
horse would go over and be killed.

In this place the first night gave me a decidedly lonesome feeling. Chief Hustelso was friendly, but not so his
people, except a few old men. The young men were very
surly, and would not talk. Some of them were shooting
arrows, and I tried to be friendly and proposed to

shoot with them, but three of the young braves drew their bows on me, as if intending to kill me. I made no headway that night, and I realized the gloominess that had prevented my companions remaining there and learning to speak the Navajo tongue. The next day or two I was threatened and illtreated, the burrs taken off my wagon, and I was subjected to other annoyances. The little girl with me did fairly well, for, being a half-breed Indian herself, she affiliated with the Indian children without difficulty.

Then the Indians became less offensive in their conduct day by day, and I learned rapidly to converse with them, and began to experience kindness at their hands. Several strange Indians came from a considerable distance to see me, and on June 12th, about three hundred and fifty Navajos gathered around to hear me tell them of the Book of Mormon, its discovery and contents. Book in hand I related to them the story of the volume being the history of their forefathers. Some laughed at me and others asked most searching questions, which I was able to answer satisfactorily in their own dialect.

Then came the inquiry, "If it is our book, how did you get it? Did you steal it?" I was getting pretty well puzzled, owing to my imperfect acquaintance with the Navajo language. I told them that the book was obtained in the east, about so many days' journey off. But I could not explain to them that it was in a stone box in the Hill Cumorah, and that the writings were on gold plates, for I did not know what terms to use to convey my meaning. One Indian told me the book could not have lasted so long as I said, because paper would decay, he knew that. In order to learn what hill was, I made a small hill of sand, and by comparison with the mountains and much explanation I learned the word for hill.

I had noticed, almost up to the plateau above, some

slate rock; and after great difficulty I managed to climb and get several pieces of slate down, being aided by the little girl. Then I improvised a stone box, set it in the sand hill, placed the book therein, and thus ascertained how to say stone box, in Navajo, and explained that the record was deposited therein. I was almost beaten to tell of gold plates, for I did not know the words to use. At last I bethought me of a brass suspender buckle, and pointed out that what I was referring to was like that, but was not that; and a little piece was worth several silver dollars. Then one Indian recognized what I wanted to say, and gave me the word for gold, on the coins of which he had seen small letters. I was thus able to explain that the record was on plates of gold; but the way I learned to do it was one of the marvelous experiences of my life, and illustrates the difficulties I had to meet in learning the Navajo language.

When I reached the point of telling how the Book of Mormon plates were preserved and obtained, my audience was quite in touch with me, and they rejoiced and wept while I told them further of its contents. From that time no friendship was too great for me, and before my departure I spent a day, by invitation, viewing Indian sports. By June 20, I was through at Hustelso's camp and ready for a journey of exploration which had been planned.

On June 21st our exploring party, consisting of six persons, including my son-in-law and his wife and child, started on a trip, the general direction of travel being a little south of east. Our journey led us through some good country, and some that was very rough. We went a short distance into New Mexico, and obtained considerable knowledge of the country and its inhabitants, there being many Indian villages, houses and farms on the route we traveled. As we were crossing over a broad mesa, on June 27, after passing the Fort Defiance road, we met with a strange person among the people. This was a fullblood Indian girl seven or eight years of age, with white hair, blue eyes, and skin as fair as the fairest white person.

Next day we reached the camp of Pal Chil Clane, a Navajo chief at whose place a council had been appointed. From there a messenger was dispatched to Totoso-ne-Huste, the head chief of the Navajo nation. On the evening of the following day that chief arrived in the camp.

A consultation was held on June 29th with the chieftain, at which we informed him of our desire to settle the country, to teach the Indians the Gospel, and to aid in improving their general condition; we also told of the Book of Mormon, a record of the Indians' forefathers, which had been made known. The chief responded that it was a departure from his usual rule to come and see the white men. Before this, they always had come to him, or he had sent good men to meet the government agents and others. This also had been his custom with the Mormons up to that occasion. Among other things he said:

"When I heard that you had come, I quit work and came to see you. My heart is glad at the meeting with you, and that I see your wagon there, and the brush shade that your men have built. Stop here four days, and many of our best men will come and talk to you, for a great many of our people want to go and see the Mormons. We shall have a big talk and know what to do. We are glad that you come among us as friends, that you are making a road through our country, and that you have built houses at Moencoppy. We want to live with you in peace and let your animals eat grass in peace. But water is scarce in this country, there is barely enough for our numerous flocks and increasing people, and our good old men do not want your people to build any more houses by the springs; nor do we want you to bring flocks to eat the grass about the springs. We want to live by you as friends. I sent some good men with you last year, and they say you talked one talk all the time. The great Mormon father he talked straight all the time. I think that a good road to travel in. I have had two daughters prisoners among the Apaches for many years but have never left my home to search for them, for I love my home and my people, and I do not love to travel. I have sent good and true men to search for my children, and have appealed to the American captains in different places, yet my daughters have not been brought back. I am an old man now, and it is hard for me to travel long roads, but I wish to see the Mormons and my father their captain. I am inclined to go with you. I want twenty-five or thirty men to go with me, and one or two women, to see your women and learn how they do. I am much pleased to see you and your daughter and her baby. I want to see more of your people. The Americans and your people differ in religion. The Mormons say their captain talks with God (Pagocheda), and Americans say God does not talk to men. We do not know what to believe. When God talks to us, then we shall know. Until then we want to live as friends."

After our talk we separated, he promising to return in three days. He came, and I accompanied him to a Navajo religious feast, where I was introduced to thirteen chiefs and over two hundred other Navajo Indians. This was on July 2nd. It was decided that some of them would go to see the Mormons, and be at Moencoppy in thirty-eight days. Then we bade the Indians good-by, and proceeded on our journey, going over into New Mexico, and back to Moencoppy, where we arrived on July 15th. There were quite a number of Navajos, Piutes and Hopees there, and I had to talk with them and three Mexicans till quite late.

A week later, on July 22nd, I declined to administer the sacrament, owing to the feeling of dissatisfaction among the people. A. S. Gibbons and M. P. Mortensen circulated reports against me, that I had used provisions contributed to the mission, and I had a full investigation made; this

showed that the accusation was entirely wrong.   Other
meetings were held subsequently, and the ill feeling that had
arisen was dispensed with.   The mission affairs then proceeded smoothly again.

It was on the morning of August 8th that the Navajo
Indian delegation began to assemble for the journey north,
Totoso-ne-Huste among the number, and by the 10th all
were ready for the start.   The journey was a hard one much
of the way, but when we got among the settlements in Utah
we were well treated, and the Indians highly pleased.   We
reached Salt Lake City August 28, 1877.

The next day I visited President Young.   He was very
ill, and I merely called to see him.   The great pioneer and
prophet who had done so much for the opening up and
settlement of the Great West was on his deathbed.   The
magnificent work of his life was over.   In half an hour
after I left his room, the noble spirit passed from his body,
and he slept in death, awaiting the resurrection morn.

On the evening of August 29, the *Deseret News* published the following regarding the Navajo delegation and
myself:

"Indian Delegation.—Last   evening   Elder   James   S.
Brown arrived from the south with a delegation of Navajo
Indians, one of whom is a woman, the first female Navajo,
we believe, that has ever visited this part of the country.
Garanu Namunche, or Totoso-ne-Huste, the former being
his Spanish and the latter his Indian name, is at the head
of the party.   He is, in fact, the head chief of the Navajo
nation.   He is accompanied by two other leading men,
Honeco, brother of the former, and Esclepelehen, son of
the same.   In June last Elder Brown and a party of brethren visited the northeastern part of Arizona and the north-
western portion of New Mexico, and found a strong spirit
of inquiry among the Navajos relative to the Mormon people,
their methods of farming, manufacturing, and in relation to

their institutions generally. These inquiries were incited by the report of the Navajo delegation which visited this city a year ago, and these composing the one now here have come to see, hear and examine for themselves, that they may be witnesses of the same things. Brother Brown and party held a council with the Indians at the camp of Pal Chil Clane, about two hundred men of the tribe being present on the occasion, including Totoso-ne-Huste, the leading chief already mentioned. It was then that the latter proposed to pay the present visit. Manlete, or Pahada Pahadane, is the war chief of the nation, but in the estimation of the tribe is second in rank to Totoso-ne-Huste, although the whites, or "Americans," recognize the war chief as the head. The delegation are stopping at the house of Brother Brown, and have been visiting the leading places of interest in the city today. Elder Brown purposes taking them north to Bear River on Monday."

On August 30th, the Indians and I met Daniel H. Wells, who had been counselor to President Young in the First Presidency. At that interview President Wells told me I had performed a great and good work, and to ask me to return to Arizona was too much to require of me. I was therefore honorably released from that mission. Subsequently I received a formal release from President John Taylor, who succeeded to the presidency of the Church.

After the funeral of President Young, which was held on September 2nd, I accompanied the Indians as far south as Gunnison, Sanpete County, on their way home. There I bade them goodbye, and returned northward, to resume my missionary labors, traveling and lecturing among the settlements in Utah, southern Idaho, and western Wyoming. I also purchased a tract of eighty acres of land on the Redwood Road, in the western part of Salt Lake City, and worked on that in the spring and summer, traveling and preaching in the autumn and winter as President Young had directed me to do.

Thus my time was occupied till the spring of 1892 with the exception of the months of March, April and May, 1888. With a firm conviction that plurality of wives was a law of God, I had entered into that relationship honorably with a sincere purpose to follow the right. My family were united with me in accepting this union as of the highest, holiest, most sacred character in the sight of the Most High. I could not feel to cast aside my wives whom I had married under these conditions, and therefore, on March 12, 1888, I was sentenced to prison on a charge of unlawful cohabitation, the legal term applied to living with more than one wife, the law being specially directed at one of the religious practices of the Latter-day Saints. The judgment pronounced against me was three months' imprisonment in the penitentiary and to pay a fine of one hundred dollars and costs, which amounted in my case to twenty-seven dollars and fifty cents. I paid the fine and served the term, less the time allowed for good behavior, and was released May 28, 1888, having been in prison two months and sixteen days.

As was the case with other Mormons in my position, our offense was not looked upon even by non-Mormons acquainted with the circumstances as containing the element of crime; but our incarceration was in fact an imprisonment for conscience sake, that being the position in which the law found us. A term in the penitentiary under those conditions and at that time, while a severe hardship, especially upon one in my state of health, was by no means a moral disgrace, since those who had to endure it were of the better class of men, whose uprightness, honor, integrity and sincerity were beyond question in the community where their lives were an open book.

CHAPTER LXIII.

ON March 30, 1892, President Joseph F. Smith called
at my residence in Salt Lake City, and handed me a
letter written by an Elder who was on the island of Tahiti.
At the same time President Smith asked me how I would
like to take another mission to the Society Islands, in the
South Pacific Ocean. I told him I did not wish any man
to call me on a mission—that my health was not good, and
such a journey as he suggested was a big undertaking for
one in my condition. He replied that he would leave the
letter for me to read, and would call the next day to learn
what I thought of it. He came according to appointment,
and informed me that the First Presidency wanted me to
undertake the mission. I replied that when properly called
I was not afraid to go, as I had faith that God would not
require of any man more than he would have the ability to
do if he were faithful. The day following this conversation I visited the First Presidency and learned that they
were a unit in requesting me to go to the Society Islands.

From this time I began to settle my affairs to meet the

call. On April 8th, I was set apart for the mission, Elder Francis M. Lyman being mouth in the blessing. On the 15th, I went to Ogden on business, and while on the train met Apostle Lorenzo Snow, who told me he felt the spirit of prophecy. He said that the mission I was going on should be one of the greatest I had ever performed; that I would prosper therein and be blessed with more power and influence than ever before; that the Lord would be with me to sustain and comfort me, and that my family should be provided for. As he spoke I felt a thrill of testimony through my whole being. When he concluded he took from his pocket two five-dollar gold pieces, remarking that he had been a missionary himself, and insisted that I should take the money, keep it till I got in a close place, and then use it, which I did.

On April 22nd I received at President Woodruff's office a letter of appointment to preside over the Society Islands Mission, which included the Society and Tuamotu groups, comprising from eighty to one hundred islands and an area of about fifteen hundred square miles. About this time I had many visitors, a considerable number of whom expressed surprise at my being appointed to such a mission at my time of life and in my condition; for I was sixty-four years of age and walked on crutches and one foot, as I had to abandon my artificial limb in Arizona, owing to the intense pain it caused me. One man said that he would not go in my situation for ten thousand dollars. But these discouraging remarks did not raise a doubt in my mind of the propriety of the call.

On the 24th of April I was engaged in writing, when my children and grandchildren to the number of sixty-five burst in upon me in a surprise party. We had a happy time and I gave them a father's blessing. Then we repaired to the Seventeenth Ward meeting house, where members of the ward had assembled, and I preached a farewell sermon and took an affectionate leave of the people.

I sold some of my real estate to pay the expenses of my journey, and for my family; also received contributions in money from a number of friends; and on April 26th I started on my mission, accompanied by my son Elando. We stayed over night at Ogden, then continued on to San Francisco, arriving there April 28th. On April 30th we boarded the barkentine *City of Papeete*, which sailed the next day.

The sea voyage occupied the entire month of May, Tahiti coming into view on the evening of the 31st. Our fare, cabin, was seventy-five dollars each. The first few days out we had headwinds, and there was a goodly share of seasickness. On the 10th a native of Tahiti, named Manhele, commonly known as John Bull, became violently insane, and had to be restrained. On the 12th he freed himself and crawled out on the jib boom, from which he was about to plunge into the sea, when he was secured. It took five men to handle him. At five o'clock on the morning of the 15th it was discovered that the madman had made a fire by rubbing two sticks together. Fortunately he was detected in time to prevent the ship being set aflame. A few days after this occurrence his condition improved and continued so to the end of the voyage.

It was at the Marquesas Islands on May 26th, when we sailed into port, that I went ashore with the rest of the passengers, and met a native of Rapia, a very uninviting person in appearance. The people warned us to beware of him as he was a savage and had killed five men. He told me he had seen me forty years before on his native island, and related circumstances of the event that convinced me his statement was true.

The next man I spoke to ashore was John H. Rumrell of Boston, Massachusetts, who was taken prisoner by natives

MARQUESAS FIRE DANCERS.

on the Marquesas Islands in 1847, and in the following year was tattooed from the tip of his nose to just above his eyebrows, and back to his ear on the left side of his face; on the right side the tattooing went from the lower part of the nose back to the ear; while above the eyebrow, and reaching to the ear, was another strip. The ink was pricked in with human bone. He said that it was because of this tattooing that he would not return to his people. In his experience he had been without clothing for years. He had two sons and one daughter, and lived like the natives in every respect. He related how that on one occasion the natives had killed a white man and cooked and ate him, and at the same time they had killed a colored man, who was eaten raw, before the flesh was cold. Mr. Rumrell said he seldom heard from his relatives in Boston. He seemed almost oblivious to everything except what was immediately before him; he took as little interest in civilization as did the natives, and I have not found a lower class of people in the South Pacific than on the five of eleven Marquesas islands which were inhabited at the time of this visit.

The captain of our vessel informed me that the inhabitants of the group numbered about four thousand eight hundred souls, and that there were ten deaths among the natives to one birth, the chief cause of this mortality being the opium habit. The French governor was trying to prohibit the use of the drug, but so far had not been successful.

On the voyage down to the Marquesas we saw many flying fish, whales and other varieties of the finny tribe. On May 12th the sailors caught two sharks, and after cutting them up threw them overboard. We left the port of Taihai, in the Marquesas, on May 28th, and on the 31st sighted Tahiti, entering the harbor of Papeete on June 1st, after considerable trouble.

I remained on board till the afternoon. Mr. Dorence Atwater, formerly United States consul there, came on the vessel, and recognizing me told me he had an empty room that I was welcome to occupy with my friends until I could do better. I felt that this courtesy had been offered as an answer to my prayers to the Lord. I accepted the invitation and we went to the house he had been speaking of, from where we returned to the wharf, and he bade me good evening.

While resting myself a moment near a group of natives I spoke to them, when one came forward and asked why I was there. I replied that I had come to preach the Gospel. At this he called four of his companions and introduced them as Mormon missionaries of the Reorganized Church of Latter-day Saints, or followers of young Joseph Smith, the Prophet's son. I told them I did not belong to their organization, but to the true Church of Saints, the same as when I was on the islands before. They seemed surprised and confused, and after a pause inquired if I knew the Josephite missionaries that came from America. I answered that all the true Mormon missionaries came from Salt Lake City and vicinity. Then I asked if they knew where I could get a bed, and after consultation one of them said I could go with him. My baggage, however, was not through the custom house, and the captain suggested that I had better stay on board, so I went back to the vessel.

That evening Elders Joseph W. Damron and Wm. A. Seegmiller, missionaries from Utah, came on board and asked if there were any Latter-day Saints there. I introduced myself, then my son Elando, and Elder Thomas Jones. Elder Damron insisted that we go on shore with him for the night, which we did, and my son and I were comfortably located at the home of Tiniarau, where we remained some time. The other Elders went to a house about three miles distant, but next day moved to Mr. Atwater's place.   For some days I was very tired and in poor health, and remained at the house talking to people who called.

CHAPTER LXIV.

FIRST SABBATH IN TAHITI—MEET SEVERAL PERSONS WHOM I KNEW OVER FORTY YEARS BEFORE—HOW THEY REMEMBERED ME— SEEK PERMISSION TO HOLD PUBLIC MEETINGS—WIDOW OF MY OLD FRIEND, JOHN LAYTON, CALLS ON ME—OTHER FRIENDS— PREACH TO THE JOSEPHITES—GOVERNOR REFUSES TO PERMIT US TO HOLD PUBLIC MEETINGS—GET ADVICE OF THE UNITED STATES CONSUL—A LAWYER'S COUNSEL—JOSEPHITES TELL OF B. F. GROUARD—I EXPLAIN HOW HE HAD TURNED INTO THE WRONG PATH—THE CHURCH NEVER DISORGANIZED—MISSIONARY LABORS —GREETING A FRENCH ADMIRAL—EARLY MISSIONARIES TO TA- HITI—THEIR SEVERE EXPERIENCES—SIXTY-FOURTH ANNIVER- SARY OF MY BIRTH—LEARN OF MORMONS WHO WERE HANGED FOR HAVING KILLED A POLICEMAN IN THE TROUBLE WHEN I WAS ARRESTED ON MY FIRST MISSION TO THE ISLANDS—MEET A NATIVE OF PITCAIRN'S ISLAND—HIS STORY—VISIT TAUTILA— SEVERE VOYAGE—A BAPTISM—SAIL FOR TUBUOI—AMONG STRANG- ERS—CELEBRATION OF A FRENCH FETE DAY—DINE WITH THE GOVERNOR—PEOPLE BECOME LESS UNFRIENDLY TO US—BREAK- ING OF THE CLOUDS—BAPTIZE TWENTY-FOUR PERSONS—EN- COURAGING RESULTS OF MISSIONARY EFFORTS.

OUR first Sabbath in Tahiti (June 5, 1892,) we attend- ed the Josephite meeting.   The service was very brief, and the people seemed worried.   Next day several of the Josephites called on me, and after a lengthy conver- sation told me they knew I spoke the truth to them.   I was also visited by a number of friends who were young when I was on the islands before, but who remembered me. One who came from Anaa said he was present when I first landed on that island, and he knew of my labors and my having been arrested by the French.   He remembered me by my voice, and said the people who heard me then would know me in the same way, if they did not by seeing me. Many natives came and said they were glad to see and hear me, though they had been born since I left the country.

A Mr. Henry, a son of a former minister of the Church of England, called, and I loaned him a Voice of Warning. He invited me to spend the evening with himself and wife, but I had an appointment. I went next evening, however, and passed a very enjoyable time, as I did on several occasions afterwards. During that week I was visited by very many people. Mr. Atwater gave us the privilege of holding public meetings in his house, but we understood it was necessary to get the permission of the director and secretary of the interior for the province, so Mr. Atwater and I called. That official said we were to submit the application to the governor, and he would notify Mr. Atwater of the reply. On Saturday evening I talked on the market grounds to a large number of people, several of whom recognized me as having been on the island forty years before. That evening, at the wharf, I also met with an aged man from Anaa, who had known me on my former mission, and who said that if I would go there the people would follow my teachings.

On Sunday, the 12th, who should come to see me but Mrs. Layton, a native, the widow of my old friend John Layton. I had seen her in San Francisco. My own sister could not have been more pleased to see me, and I was very glad to meet her. She gave me the best history of my former friends on the islands that I was able to obtain. Next morning I took a short stroll, then returned to the house. The other Elders distributed tracts among the English-speaking residents of Papeete, and I received another call from Mrs. Layton, who brought her little granddaughters and also a man—the son of an old friend of mine

—who said that on my former visit to the island I had named him Iatobo, after my own Tahitian name.

It was while taking breakfast, on the 14th, with a Mr. Mervin, some of whose children had been blessed in the Church, that an old lady who came up, recognized me, and shook hands so persistently that it seemed as if she did not intend to let go, and did not do so for some minutes. She had seen the French officers take me away from Anaa. The old lady had known me on sight, though forty years had passed. The same day I met an aged man who also recognized me from having known me before. That same evening I was given the privilege of addressing the Josephite meeting and told them how and by whom the Gospel had been brought to them, and which was the true Church. I tendered my services to preach in their meeting house, but my offer was not accepted.

On the 16th I started with Elder Seegmiller to visit the old prison where I had been incarcerated by the French, but the distance being too great I had to give up the journey. Next day we received from the governor a reply to our application for permission to hold public meetings. Our request was denied, the reason assigned being that we believed in polygamy. We had no disposition to let the matter rest there, so we called on the United States consul for advice. He told us to make application in writing for permission to preach, and if refused to submit it to him. This we did on the 20th, and next day received an unfavorable answer. The governor asked what we taught, and we told him. We stated that we did not teach polygamy. The reason he then gave for refusing us the permission desired was that there were enough religions there and he did not want another established. Mr. Atwater suggested that we consult with Mr. Bonett, formerly director and secretary of the interior, and an able lawyer. We did so, and he informed us that it was not necessary to get permissiom to preach, but that we must notify the mayor or justice of the peace of the time and place of our meetings.

To return a few days: On Sunday, the 19th of June, we attended a Josephite meeting, where all were friendly but the presiding officer; yet after meeting he told us to come and eat, sent a half-caste to wait on us, and otherwise was quite attentive. After dinner we talked to the audience, who appeared well pleased. They said B. F. Grouard had set native songs to American tunes, and that he had also sent letters endorsing the Josephite church; he had been one of the first to preach the true Gospel to their fathers, as I had been, and they were confused at my coming, for they could not refute what I had said. I was under the necessity of telling them how that Grouard had turned into the wrong path—an action which they admitted was quite possible. After our talk this day we felt that we had done our full duty towards those Josephites in explaining to them the true condition of affairs.

On the afternoon of the 20th my old friend Mahana Toro called, but did not seem so friendly as in former times. He was about seventy years of age, and very much broken in health. He also had joined the Josephites under the misapprehension that they were of the same Church as I was. I told him the difference, that the Josephite organization was distinct, and was not the Church of Jesus Christ of Latter-day Saints, which never had been disorganized. He then seemed to feel more kindly towards me, and visited me on subsequent occasions, bringing gifts of oranges.

My health was very poor, and at times I was quite ill. I was able most of the time, however, to get around, and to preach to the people, either those who called on me, or those I had the privilege of visiting. My missionary companions were also energetic in their labors. Occasionally we had the opportunity to extend our acquaintance into prominent circles of society. For instance, on June 27th, we attended a select party in honor of the French admiral. There was a grand illumination. I also visited captains of vessels engaged in traffic between the islands, and had pleasant chats with them on the principles of the Gospel. I did not fail to talk to the natives whenever occasion offered, and this was frequent. On July 2nd, in the market square, a large crowd gathered around me as I preached, and most of them acknowledged the truth of the principles I taught. Then, lest the police stop me for raising an excitement, I changed to asking questions, as in conversation, so no offense could be taken by the officers.

I learned an interesting bit of missionary history on July 3rd. This day, I met Mr. J. S. Henry, who said his father was one of the first Christian missionaries on the islands, having come to Tahiti in 1797. They had a very hard time of it. For years their clothing was made of the bark of the bread-fruit tree, and they had gone barefooted for a long time, their shoes and clothing having worn out. They had been five years without receiving any supply from their society. My informant was born on the island. I loaned him a copy of the *Deseret News*, which contained sermons by President Wilford Woodruff and by Elder C. W. Penrose, who was editor of the paper at that time.

Monday, July 4, 1892, was the sixty-fourth anniversary of my birth, and I was spending it in far off Tahiti. I had but few callers that day, and consequently but few congratulations. I continued my efforts to make myself more proficient in the Tahitian language, and from day to day proceeded with the duties that rested on me. July 12th an aged man Tematu called on me, saying that he was from the island of Anaa, and had been my servant on the occasion of my former visit. He told me of the four members of the Church that were hanged by the French; for in the trouble then they had killed a policeman and had

wounded severely a Catholic priest. The names of the
executed men were Tefaitina, Reifara, Maru, Mafeuta and
Temutu.

Among the very aged people I met was one who
called on me on July 18, Timou, aged one hundred and
three years. I also met, at a blacksmith shop, on July 21st,
a native of Pitcairn's island, William Christenson. He was
a descendant of one of the mutineers of the British ship
Bounty. He told the story as follows: The *Bounty* sailed
from England in the year 1689, the company intending to
collect plants from the South Sea Islands. They called at
Tahiti, and made their collection, then got some natives
and their wives and some other women on board, and put
out to sea. Fletcher Christenson, first mate, and some of
the crew mutinied, getting control of the vessel. They put
the captain, whose name was Blythe, and those who
wished to go with him, into the best boat, supplied them
with such articles as they desired which were at hand, and
set them adrift. This party subsequently reached England,
while the first mate and crew ran the ship into a small bay
at Pitcairn's Island, where they wrecked the vessel, taking
the supplies on shore. All went well for a time, till the native
men became jealous of the white men and killed most of them.
Afterwards, at the instance of the remaining white men,
the women killed the native men who had escaped in the
former trouble, so there were left but two of the white men
and the women. These, and after them, their descendants,
lived on the island, which was but a few miles in circumference. The population increased to about four hundred
souls, when the British government moved them to Norfolk
Island. Some of them returned to Pitcairn's, and at that
time (1892) there were one hundred and thirty-six souls on
the island, every one belonging to the Seventh Day Ad-
ventists, and all speaking the English language. Mr.
Christenson said that the only names of the mutinous crew he

remembered besides those of the captain and his own pro-
genitor, were John Adams, ———— McKay, John Mills,
Isaac Brown and ———— Yindle. Christenson's story does
not harmonize precisely with the generally accepted history
of the affair, but I have given it as he related it.

For a considerable time we had endeavored to get
.passage for some of the Elders to the island of Tuamotu.
but were unsuccessful, so we divided Papeete into missionary districts, Elder Damron and my son Elando taking the
east side, and Elders Seegmiller and Jones the western district. During the latter part of July and the greater portion
of August, I was quite ill, and was troubled greatly with
neuralgia. On August 14th, we applied to the Josephites
for permission to speak in their house, but it was refused,
resulting in quite a discussion among the members of the
Josephite congregation, some of whom were quite friendly
to us. On the 23rd my son Elando and I left Papeete, by
invitation, for Tautila, going in a boat in which there were
four other men and a woman, the latter being a sister of
the owner of the craft. When we got off Haapape the
wind became so high that the men were obliged to row for
the shore, and we found refuge in the home of Terumana,
a native, who fed us on native food and gave each of us a
good bed.

We had to remain there till 11 p. m. on the 25th, when
we started to sea again, the night being pitch dark. The
woman made me as comfortable as was possible in the small
boat, and all went well for a time with the exception of seasickness. Then it came on to rain very hard, and we were
all wet. Early in the morning we ran into shore, and the
men in charge of the boat asked us to pray, which I did.
We then proceeded on our way with a cocoanut each for
breakfast, and at half-past eight p. m., on the 26th, reached
the mouth of a river on Tautila.

Our host was Mr. Hiotina, and his wife's name was

Teumere. She was an invalid, her frame almost a skeleton, but she was a very bright woman intellectually. Her memorizing of Scripture passages was truly a marvel. The next day after our arrival was Saturday, and many people came out of curiosity to see us. On Sunday, the 28th, about sixty people assembled, and our host requested us to hold religious services, which we did. While I was preaching on faith, repentance, and baptism, taking my text from the third chapter of Matthew, an old lady went over to my son, who was near the door, and requested baptism. This was the first application of the kind made to us on the island. The lady had been a member of the Church, but had become negligent. At 5 p. m. that day she was baptized by Elder Elando Brown, and I confirmed her a member of the Church, there being many people present, among them a Protestant minister.

We stayed on Tautila until September 9th, visiting among the people and preaching and talking to them, as opportunity afforded, though we could not get a house to preach in. On the 9th we returned to Papeete, the voyage being very rough and trying. I could hardly stand on my crutches when we landed, at 10 p. m.

On the 11th we arranged for four of us to go to Tubuoi, but the governor informed the captain that he could take but two white passengers, so on August 15th Elder Seegmiller and I left on a vessel bound for the island named. The voyage lasted till the 20th and was decidedly uncomfortable. We did not have sufficient food, there was no bedding, and the water on board was filthy. Worn and exhausted, we were glad to get ashore at Tapuai, where we were coldly greeted. We secured a comfortable lodging room, so far as appearances were concerned, and plenty of fleas for bed-fellows. Our room-mate was a young man named Alexander Drolett, interpreter for the French captain of a government schooner that was lying in the harbor.

There we met Tapuni, a native Josephite preacher who had been on the island about five months. He tried to be sociable, but was ill at ease, apparently being discomfited by our arrival. We found the people generally very distant, as if they did not wish us there. Mr. Drolett, however, was kind and sociable, and we had the privilege of explaining to him the nature of our calling on the islands.

September 22, 1892, was the one hundredth anniversary of the first French republic, and a feast and holiday had been proclaimed. Flags were hoisted, and the people gathered to the feast. We were among those invited, and were seated at the table with the captain of the French schooner and his interpreter, and the governor and his wife, also Tapuni. About ninety persons were at the feast. Dinner was served in French and native styles blended. This was followed by singing, and by dancing and contortions of the old heathen fashion, until I was worn out.

The following day the French schooner left, and Elder Seegmiller and I sent a letter to our brethren at Papeete. As we were in the house a policeman called and gazed at us for a time, then left without speaking. Next came the native governor, Tahuhuetoma, who entered without noticing me, but I slapped him on the shoulder and asked him if he had eyes, whereat he spoke, but had little to say. Then came a native, Tehaheatihi, from the village of Mahu, on the south side of the island. He was very friendly, and said he had joined the Josephites but had discovered his mistake. I was quite ill, so could not accept his invitation to accompany him to Mahu, except on the condition that he furnish a conveyance, which he promised to try to do. Our landlord, however, told us not to trouble, but to remain till Sunday, when we would all go to Mahu, and could speak to the people there. He said Tapuni was not pleased, but that made little difference.

Next day was Saturday, the 24th—the occasion of

greater kindness to us from the natives than previously; for two children aged ten and twelve years brought us some food, as did also the governor's wife. On Sunday further friendship was displayed, and the people came to ask us questions; but we were unable to go to Mahu, and were refused the privilege of speaking at the religious services in the place where we were. On Monday, however, we went to Mahu, where we met twelve to fifteen men, with whom we had a pleasant visit, talking to them quite freely.

During that week we met a number of people who exhibited a kindly feeling towards us in conversation. Some applied for baptism, but I advised them to wait. By the end of the week the clouds over the mission began to break. When Sunday came there was a religious feast, but we were not allowed to take part, so, with about five natives, held services of singing, prayer and conversation. Again in the afternoon we had a meeting at which about thirty persons were present, and I explained how the authority had continued in the Church from the Prophet Joseph to the present organization. At that meeting Elder Seegmiller spoke publicly in the native tongue for the first time. There were several applications for baptism, and on the following Tuesday, October 4th, Elder Seegmiller baptized twenty-four persons, whom I confirmed members of the Church. Thus the missionary work on the island was opened up again, with a fair start for prosperity.

CHAPTER LXV.

MIRACULOUS HEALING—MEET AND CONFOUND THE JOSEPHITES—
FURTHER MISSIONARY SUCCESS—MEET A NATIVE WHO WAS
PRESENT WHEN I WAS SENTENCED TO BE BURNED—ELDER
JOHN LAYTON'S GRAVE—ARRANGE TO RETURN TO TAHITI—
DISAPPOINTED—PREACH A FUNERAL SERMON—FORBIDDEN TO
HOLD PUBLIC MEETINGS—BLIND WOMAN ONE HUNDRED AND
TWENTY YEARS OLD—HER TESTIMONY—ADMINISTER TO HER
FOR HER EYESIGHT, AND SHE IS ENABLED TO SEE A LITTLE—
SHE PRAISES THE LORD—PREACHING AND BAPTIZING—SAIL FOR
PAPEETE—AN ODD CARGO—HARD VOYAGE—HELD BY A CALM—
LAND ON TAHITI—SAIL FOR AVAROA—ON A WELL-ORDERED
SCHOONER—CALL AT VARIOUS ISLANDS—LANCE A CARBUNCLE—
CHRISTMAS DAY AT SEA—WATERMELONS—A BEAUTIFUL RESI-
DENCE AND CORDIAL WELCOME—PERFORM THREE MARRIAGE
CEREMONIES—CONFERENCE OF SAINTS IN THE TUAMOTU ISLANDS
—MEET A NATIVE CHILEAN—VISIT VARIOUS PLACES—PUBLIC
WELCOME—FISHING—ON THE ISLAND OF ANAA—VISIT WHERE I
WAS IMPRISONED—GRAVES OF THOSE CONCERNED IN THE
TROUBLE THEN—WARRANT SERVED ON ME—SUMMONED TO THE
GOVERNMENT HOUSE — WARNED AGAINST CREATING A DIS-
TURBANCE.

IT was on October 6, 1892, that the first case of miraculous healing after our arrival occurred. We were becoming recipients of greater kindness from the natives, and
that day Roai, the oldest man on the island, was brought to
us, shaking violently with a chill. He appeared to be dying. Some cocoanut oil was brought—no other was obtainable—and we blessed it and anointed and blessed him, when
the chill immediately left him. He rested well, and next
morning was in his usual good health.

On the 7th there was quite an argument among the
people as to whether the Josephites or the Mormons should
have the meeting house. The decision was in our favor,
and we were also offered a house in the village of Taahuaia.

The Josephite preacher, Tapuni, wanted to hold joint meetings with us, as we both followed the same form of baptism; but we refused, as we could not make any alliance with him. We represented the true Church of Jesus Christ, while his organization was by persons who had been excommunicated, and had not divine authority.

When Sunday came we held three meetings, blessed fourteen children, and took dinner with the policeman. Next day, the 10th, we ordained Ote an Elder, and added nine persons to the Church by baptism. On the 11th we met a man—the fourth on the island—who was on the island of Raivavai when the natives had built a fire to burn me, and when I was delivered by the power of God. They claimed to have been present when I was sentenced, but denied taking any part in the proceedings.

Friday, October 14th, we bade the Saints of Mahu farewell (having, the day previous, ordained two Elders, two Priests, one Teacher and one Deacon) and went to Taahuaia, where the people were quite indifferent to us. From time to time, however, we were able to converse with some of them, and baptized several. On the 23rd, the governor gave us permission to hold meetings, and we began doing so. I visited the grave of Elder John Layton on the 24th, and on the 25th arranged to leave on a schooner for Tahiti. My health had been quite poor for some time. I did not go on the boat, however, for it was so heavily laden that there was no room, so it sailed on the 27th without me. Monday, October 31st, I preached the funeral sermon of a little girl.

On the 5th of November, the Josephite preacher and his wife called on me. In the evening a special meeting of the people was held, the purpose of which was kept secret from us. That night I dreamed I was on trial and the judge said he knew I was not guilty, but because of the demand of the people he would have to give judgment against me and assess a fine of twenty dollars, which the court would pay. I awoke and told · Elder Seegmiller the natives had made a decision against us, as we learned the next day, when the governor withdrew from us the privilege of holding meetings.

We went to Mataura on November 7th, to see a man possessed of a devil. The evil spirit was dumb, and for three years the man had not spoken to anyone, but sat or laid around. We also visited the school where there were about thirty students, and the teacher called one pupil to the blackboard, where the exercise in writing required of her was well done. Then we called on Tetuatehiapa, the oldest woman on the island. She was one hundred and twenty years of age, and had been blind for eight years. The people said she had insisted that she would live till the servants of God came from Salt Lake City. When told who we were she rejoiced greatly, and exclaimed, "I always said you would come again! The Lord has brought you, and has prolonged my life till you came. I rejoice exceedingly at the mercies of the Lord!" On November 8th, we baptized her with seven others, and on the 10th administered to her for her blindness by laying hands on her head and blessing her. When we had attended to the ordinance she stated that she could see a little, which was more than she had done for eight years. "God be praised for His mercies," she said.

Sunday, November 13th, I preached twice to large congregations at Mahu, where we arrived on the 11th. We also had a number of applicants for baptism, and on the 14th eight members were added to the Church by the ordinance, and we blessed two children. A Catholic priest called on us, and I had a pointed discussion with him on authority in the Church, and the true Gospel. We parted good friends, he promising to come again next day, but he did not do so; although he passed by the house, but never

loooked towards us.   On the 16th we added five more souls
to the Church by baptism.

Our missionary labors continued in different villages,
and on November 23 Elder Seegmiller baptized the school
teacher at Mataura, also two of the governor's daughters.   On the 21st the captain of a schooner that had
called at the island told us we could go to Tahiti on his vessel, starting on the 24th.   Elder Seegmiller aided me in
preparing for the voyage, and I bade farewell to the people,
who were very much attached to us.   I shook hands with
the governor, when his eyes filled with tears, he kissed me,
and was so full of emotion that it was difficult for him to
speak.   In due time the vessel sailed, Elder Seegmiller going on it to Mataura, three miles down the coast, where he
went ashore, as we had agreed, and I was alone so far as a
missionary companion was concerned.

At Mataura the French police justice and his wife, a
Marquesas woman, came aboard, and at 6 p. m. we weighed
anchor.   The schooner was very much crowded, the cargo
including four women, two children, fourteen men, three
horses, twenty hogs, one goat, one dog, about one hundred
chickens, eight or ten turkeys, eleven thousand cocoanuts,
and a lot of other things.   The most comfortable place I
could find was on the companion-way, where I sat, as I was
not able to use my crutches on the vessel.   The first night
out I found I could not sleep in my berth, as it was too
cramped and the tobacco smoke and foul air were too much
for me, so I camped on the companion-way with my blanket,
and was very seasick.   The next night I fared about the
same, and it was pretty hard on me; but the third night,
Saturday, I went below before the others did, and obtained
a fairly good night's rest.

Sunday, November 27, we sighted Tahiti, but a heavy
rain and calm held us back over Monday, Tuesday and
Wednesday.   On the last-named day the crew caught a

shark, and we had some of it boiled for supper. Thursday, December 1st, we landed at Papeete in a heavy rainstorm, and quite exhausted. I was met by my son Elando, and once on shore I was refreshed with palatable food and good news from my family. We spent our time the next fourteen days in missionary labors in Papeete, to the best advantage, and on the sixth baptized eight persons into the Church. My health was decidedly poor at this time.

We had arranged with Mr. Henry Marvin for passage on the schooner *Avaroa* to the Tuamotu islands, sailing on December 15th. We left on the date named and though we had some headwinds and calms, we had a good voyage; for the captain (a Hawaiian) and crew were agreeable, the vessel was kept clean and in perfect order, and the table was well supplied with a good variety of food. We sighted several islands, and on the 20th stopped at Niau, which has a population of one hundred, all members of the Josephite Church. Their presiding officer and a number of his people came on board and gave us six chickens and six baskets of cocoanuts as a token of friendship. I talked to them on the Gospel message I had to deliver as a missionary.

We went ashore on the island of Apatai on the 23rd, as Mr. Marvin had some business there. The people were rather indifferent to us as missionaries. I visited the governor, who said he had been my servant on the island of Anaa when I was there forty years before. He was very much afflicted with a carbuncle on the back of his head and neck, and could move about only by crawling on his hands and knees. I lanced his carbuncle, and he recovered.

Christmas Day, 1892, was spent on the schooner *Avaroa*, and we sought the coolest place we could find and ate watermelons, thinking of our mountain home and the loved ones in Utah. Next day we sailed into port at Taroa, and were met by Elder Joseph W. Damron and some native

Saints. I was welcomed to the home of Mr. Mapuhi, a seven-roomed frame house, built on pillars of coral stone and beautifully furnished in American fashion. The place seemed perfectly lovely, and a surprise for us in the way of a spring mattress to sleep on was doubly welcome. The following day was the 27th, and I had the privilege of preaching to a good audience.

The 28th of December was Wednesday, and the morning was marked by the receipt of an invitation to a triple wedding and feast to be held that afternoon at the government building. I attended and by request performed the marriage ceremony for the three couples. I also availed myself of the opportunity to address the assemblage briefly on the subjects of marriage and baptism for the dead. This day I had the unusual experience of standing in the door of the house where we were lodging and viewing a large school of whales pass by.

New Year's day, 1893, was the time for a conference of the Saints to be held on the island of Faiti, so preparations were made on December 29th for us to leave Taroa. On this date I met a native Chilean, who said he came from San Antonio, about thirty miles south of Valparaiso. When I heard this, it called to my mind a statement of Dr. J. M. Bernhisel, that he had learned from the Prophet Joseph Smith that that was near the place where Lehi and his colony, told of in the Book of Mormon, landed in America, on their journey from Jerusalem. In the afternoon we started, on Mapuhi's schooner, for Faiti, six boatloads of the Saints going along. Our vessel had twenty persons aboard. The wind was fair, and on Saturday, December 31st, we reached Faiti, landing about 9:30 a. m. Our reception was rather cool, as we were ushered into a large room, almost bare save a long table and a few chairs, and were left alone much of the time. However, we had good beds at night. In the morning, Sunday, January 1st, we held meeting, and I called for those who had known me on my former mission to stand up.   Seventeen persons arose to their feet, and stated that they remembered and recognized me.   Our meetings at conference were well attended. The presiding officer of the Church in the Tuamotu islands was a blind man, and he asked me a number of questions to satisfy himself that I was the same one who had been there forty years before with Elders Pratt and Grouard.   I baptized him at that time.   When he was fully convinced he remarked that if I had not come he would not have received the young missionaries, referring to Elders Damron, Jones, and my son Elando.

It was January 4th before the people gave us the public reception that was customary.   At the ceremony an aged man related how they had prayed that I might come back to them again, to teach them the true Gospel.   That day the French gen d' armes made some charges of irregularity against the owner of our boat, saying the captain had not the proper papers.   It was generally understood, however, that the trouble originated with the Catholic priest.   Matters were finally settled.   Next morning I went fishing with our landlord and caught six nice rock cod, where the sea was ten fathoms deep.   The water was so clear that through a glass we could see the bottom, with the myriad beauties and great variety of fish at that place.   The anchor of the canoe got fast in a coral reef, and our host dived down and released it.

We continued to hold meetings all the week to give the people a correct understanding of our mission; then, on January 9th, my son Elando and I sailed for the island of Anaa, arriving there at noon that day, and being warmly welcomed by the people of Tuuhora, where we landed.

On the 11th, I walked over the ground where I had been held a prisoner by the French government, and visited the cemetery where was the grave of the policeman who had been killed in an affray subsequent to my departure. On the afternoon of the 13th, I visited the graves of those who were hanged by the French government for their part in the tragedy. Upon my return from the cemetery, a warrant was served on me by a policeman. It was in both French and English, the English translation reading as follows:

"*Monsieur Jacob, Ministre Mormon:*

"The gen d' arme chief of port at Anaa invites Mr. Jacob (James), Mormon minister at Tuuhora, to come to the government house at Tuuhora (Fare Hau), to listen to a communication which he desires him to hear.

"Cy. Cours,

"The Gen d' arme Chief of Post.

"Tuuhora, 13th January, 1893."

Of course I responded to this invitation from the chief of police, so with my son Elando reported as requested, to listen to an order made by the governor of the Tuamotu group of islands. The chief of police warned us particularly that if we caused the slightest disturbance among the people over the meeting house, or otherwise, it might result seriously to me. This was repeated six times, in an emphatic tone of voice. The officer refused utterly to hear anything from us, saying, "I follow out my instructions. You must not step your foot inside of the meeting house at Temeraia, nor the house here."

Finding it was useless for us to say anything, we bade the chief of police and the interpreter (Mr. Burns, an Englishman) good-bye, and left them to their stench of strong drink.

CHAPTER LXVI.

PREACHING AND VISITING—PEARL FISHING—PLACE OF MY ARREST IN 1851
—ACCIDENT TO A YOUNG MAN—INCIDENT WITH THE GOVERNOR
OF ANAA—SEE A LEPER—CAPTURE OF AN EEL—CONFERENCE ON
ANAA—TIME OF DEDICATION OF SALT LAKE TEMPLE—SPECIALLY
INTERESTING MEETINGS—NEW ELDERS FROM UTAH—START BACK
TO TAHITI—ANOTHER FUNERAL SERMON—MEET THE FRENCH
GOVERNOR OF THE TUAMOTU ISLANDS—HIS CORDIAL GREET-
ING—ARRIVE AT PAPEETE—APPOINTMENTS FOR THE NEW MIS-
SIONARIES—FAIL TO GET A PASSAGE TO TUBUOI—MY HEALTH
VERY POOR—LEARN OF THE DEDICATION OF THE SALT LAKE
TEMPLE—ELDERS UNANIMOUS IN THE DECISION THAT I SHOULD
RETURN HOME BECAUSE OF MY ILLNESS—I DEMUR—CONCLUDE
TO GO—TROUBLE ON ANAA—MY SIXTY-FIFTH BIRTHDAY—NOTABLE
KINDNESS OF A NATIVE CHILD—SAIL FROM PAPEETE—DIFFI-
CULTY IN LANDING FROM SMALL BOATS—IN THE SOCIETY
ISLANDS—REACH SAN FRANCISCO—ARRIVE IN SALT LAKE CITY
—REPORT THE SUCCESSFUL OPENING OF THE SOCIETY ISLANDS
MISSION.

AFTER the severe warning from the governor, we returned to our missionary labors, preaching to the
people as we could find opportunity. The Sunday following this occurrence (January 15th) we had three well-at-
tended meetings in a private meeting house, and on Monday
we went in a boat to Putuahara, a town of two thousand
people on my first visit but now dwindled down to a place
with less than sixty inhabitants. All the ablebodied men
were away, engaged in pearl-fishing. This is the place
where the people killed the French policeman and severely beat the Catholic priest, as already stated.

We conversed with and preached to the inhabitants
until the 25th, when we went to Otopipi, but returned that
same day, as our friends there were absent from home.
Our missionary work in Putuahara continued till February

4th, when we again went to Otopipi. Next day being
Sunday I had the privilege of preaching to a large congregation. There were thirty-one native members of the
Church present. Many of the people in attendance were
Catholics, and my remarks raised quite a discussion among
them, some of them being for and others against me.
Early on Monday, according to previous arrangement, we
sailed around to Temeraia, receiving a hearty welcome
there.

At this place we met the granddaughter of John Hawkins, once an Elder in this mission and now a Josephite. I
also visited the spot where I had been arrested in the year
1851. The house had been cleared away since then, and
an old wrecked boat occupied the site. We held meetings
and had a large attendance, though the weather was intensely hot and oppressive, and my health quite poor.

On February 17th a young man named Temia fell
thirty-five feet from a tree and broke his arm in three places,
the bones coming through his skin in one place. With
such hot weather, and no surgical or medical attendance
available, it looked as though his chances for recovery
seemed slight. We visited him again on the 28th, and his
case looked even more serious. We administered to him,
and he ultimately recovered. Towards the latter part of
the month the people began to feel more friendly to us,
and received us more cordially than at first.

While we were in meeting on March 1st, the governor passed, and as he was averse to recognizing us then as
previously, I called to him and asked the reason. His reply was that it was not wise to do so. I continued to talk
with him, and he became more sociable, confessing that it
was the darkness of his heart that had caused him to act
so improperly. I advised him to repent of his sins and ask
the Lord to give him light, and he felt better. Two days
after this I beheld the unusual sight of a leper, as one

passed the house—a painful picture to behold. The third day a man and his wife were baptized into the Church. A visit to Tuuhora was made on March 6th, and on the return voyage, while diving for pearls, an eel was discovered under a rock in deep water. It took quite a fight to capture it, but it was a fine one—about four feet long. We went to Putuahara on March 13, and during the remainder of the month continued our missionary labors, meeting with no unusual experiences.

On March 31st, Elders Damron and Jones came from Fakariva, and native members of the Church began to arrive in preparation for our conference, which was set for April 6th, 1893. At 7 o'clock that morning we assembled in conference, being the same actual time when the Saints were meeting for the dedication of the Temple in Salt Lake City, Utah—10 a. m. at the latter place. I explained to the Saints in conference the nature and importance of the event just named. Elder Damron also spoke on temple building, and after the close of our meeting we went to the seashore, where we held a short service, and my son Elando baptized five persons into the Church. We also ordained three native Elders and appointed two of them to preside over branches of the Church. The conference continued till Sunday evening, and all in attendance had a most enjoyable time.

We had received word on Saturday that eight Elders had arrived at Papeete from Utah, and at the close of conference we decided that we had better return to Tahiti as soon as possible. Next morning we bade farewell to the weeping Saints, and set sail for Tuuhora. From there we took passage for Taroa. On April 12th, we stopped at Apatai, where I went ashore and met a number of people whom I had baptized on my former mission. They did not display much of a hospitable feeling, as none invited me to their houses.

Taroa was reached on April 16th, and the hearty welcome there was highly appreciated after a voyage which had been very unpleasant to me, as I had been quite ill. We were met by Messrs. Marvin and Mapuhi, and escorted to the latter's fine residence. It being Sunday, we attended meetings. My son Elando was also called on, on on April 21st, to preach the funeral sermon over a young man who had died of consumption.

On the morning of April 27th, the schooner *Avaroa* came into port, having on board the French governor of the Tuamotu group, also the native governor of Taroa. We had a friendly chat with them, the Frenchman saying he had been in Salt Lake City. He invited me to visit him when I went to Fakariva again. Next day the people assembled to pay their respects to the governor, and we also had another pleasant chat with him.

We started from Taroa on Monday, May 1st, on the *Avaroa*, but as the vessel was going out to sea she struck on a rock which disabled the rudder, and it took till evening to repair it. Then we sailed for Fakariva, reaching there the following afternoon. The French governor went ashore, and later we did the same. Next morning we took breakfast with him, being invited to come again whenever we were on the island. That afternoon we sailed for Tahiti, reaching Papeete harbor on Saturday, May 6th, and meeting there Elders Edward Sudbury, Frank Goff, Frank Cutler, Eugene M. Cannon, Carl J. Larsen, Thomas L. Woodbury, Fred C. Rossiter and Jesse M. Fox, all from Utah.

At a meeting of the missionaries held on May 13th, Elders Carl J. Larsen and Thomas L. Woodbury were appointed to go to the Tuamotu islands, Elders Frank Goff and Jesse M. Fox to Tubuoi, with my son Elando and myself and the others remaining on Tahiti for a short time. Through Mr. Marvin we engaged passage on a French man-of-war going to Tubuoi, the captain giving his per-

mission. But after we had packed our trunks and purchased our provisions for the journey, the captain suggested
that we had better get a permit from the governor. We
tried to do so, but that official responded with an abrupt
"No." So we had to await another opportunity.

For some time previous to this date my health had
been poorer than usual, and it grew worse, so that it was
with difficulty I attended to missionary labors and to conducting the mission affairs. I continued at work, however,
the best I could, and my fellow-missionaries were devoted
to their duties. Some of them were in the best of health,
but others were not so fortunate; indeed, one of them, Edward Sudbury, was under the necessity of returning home
shortly after the date of which I write. On May 25th we
received mail telling us of the dedication of the Temple in
Salt Lake City, and the notable events connected therewith.

I had tried to get a hall in which to hold meetings for
the European residents of Papeete, my last efforts in that
line being on June 13th, but I was unsuccessful, so we had
to do without, and endeavor to reach them and the natives
in other ways. On June 25th we held a council meeting of
all the Elders on Tahiti, eight in number, at which methods
for the best conduct of the mission were considered.
Among other events of the meeting was the unanimous expression by my fellow-missionaries of the opinion that my
state of health was such that I should go home. A motion that I do so was put and carried, all but myself voting
in favor of my going by the next mail steamer, which
sailed July 8th. I thought that if conditions improved before
that time, I would be at liberty to remain longer in the
mission field. Elder Sudbury was also in such health that
he was booked to start home at the same time, and my
son Elando was selected to accompany us, and give me the
attention I needed.

32

My health showing no signs of improvement, passage was secured on the brig Galilee, bound for San Francisco. On June 27th we had seen two persons from Anaa, who informed us there was trouble there, the missionaries not obtaining their rights to preach. I gave such advice as I felt would be safe to follow, and Elder J. W. Damron, who succeeded me in the presidency of the mission, was left to deal with affairs.

On July 4th, my sixty-fifth birthday, John Hawkins, one of my fellow-laborers of forty-two years before, who had apostatized and joined the Josephites, called, with others. He was particularly bitter towards the Church. That day little Tapura, between six and seven years old, brought me, of her own volition, a large and beautiful bouquet of flowers—an act of kindness scarcely to be expected in one so young. She is the daughter of Mr. Topaz, who was very kind to us.

The day previous to our going on board, the neighbors brought in bananas and cocoanuts for our use on the voyage, and we were treated well. We bade farewell to friends and associates, all being sorry at the parting, and on July 8th I sailed for the last time from the harbor of Papeete, island of Tahiti. The words of Apostle Lorenzo Snow, spoken to me before commencing my journey, had been fulfilled. Though this mission had not been so long as some of the others I had filled, it had been one of the greatest and best I had performed, so far as relates to the work I had been the means of accomplishing in reopening and establishing the Society Islands mission.

Our vessel this voyage was very different to those we often had to use in our travels from place to place, even in the same island. We also bade adieu to the native method of landing from boats, which always brought discomfort and often serious peril. For illustration, it was no uncommon thing, when approaching harbor, to have to pass through breakers across a coral reef where there was barely room for the boat to glide between the rocks. Sometimes the vessel would be run close to the opening, the occupants would spring out on to the rocks on each side of the passage, and seizing the boat, would hold it there till the large or "three-twin-sisters" wave came along; and then, by its aid, would drag or push the boat through in safety. In such times as these my lame condition was hindersome to the extent of being more than annoying; it was exasperating.   But I always got through, though it was hard work, and my companions gave the needed assistance with perfect willingness.

The voyage to San Francisco was without particular event more than is usual on such occasions, as was also the journey from San Francisco to Salt Lake City by rail.   We reached home about the middle of August, and were welcomed cordially.   I reported to the First Presidency the condition of affairs in the mission, the progress we had made, with the difficulties that were to be met with. Elando and I had been absent for sixteen months, and had worked with diligence to perform our part.

Our efforts had been blessed of the Lord, for many people who had been astray from the path of life were led to direct their footsteps in the straight and narrow path.   The Society Islands mission had been reopened successfully, and yet continues to prosper, the membership in the Church there being quite numerous.

CHAPTER LXVII.

AS my health was far from satisfactory, I was able to do but little after my return from the Society Islands in August, 1893. I gave my farm some attention, and traveled occasionally among the people. In February, 1894, I received an invitation from James H. Love, manager for the concession of the '49 mining camp at the Midwinter Fair, in Golden Gate Park, San Francisco, to be present there. The invitation came to me through Israel Evans, of Lehi, Utah, who had been with me in California in 1848. I accepted, and in company with Israel Evans and my son James T. Brown, went to California in the month named.

This visit to California extended about thirty days. We were treated with the greatest kindness. Our place of lodging at the miner's cabin on the fair grounds was comfortably fitted, and besides viewing the most excellent exhibits of this notable Midwinter Exposition, we also visited most of the places of interest in the locality. We were honored guests in every parade, and nothing more could be desired in the way of courtesies to make our stay pleasant.

While in California on this occasion I wrote my pamphlet, "Authentic History of the First Discovery of Gold in Sutter's Mill Race, California." This was the first accurate history of that event I had seen in print, all the other accounts having been gathered from hearsay and broken narratives, while I had the advantage of being an actual participant in the historic occurrence.

In March, 1894, I returned home, and continued my ordinary labors, my health being considerably improved. At this time I began preparing my journal for publication, having to rewrite it to place it in presentable form, as much of it had been noted down under very adverse circumstances; it was also necessary to condense it greatly, many items of real interest being abbreviated to a considerable extent.

I believe now that if I had realized at the outset what a great task it was, I should not have attempted it, notwithstanding the fact that I was fully aware that my life's experience had been filled with unusually interesting episodes. But I had not been accustomed to giving up a work once undertaken with a good aim; so I have continued to the present, and as I prepare this chapter, the earlier part of the work is in the hands of the printer. The only literary experience I have had previous to this work is writing a history of the first mission to the Pacific Islands and the subsequent progress of events in the Society Islands mission up to 1893, the manuscript of which history was filed with and is now a part of the records of the Church historian's office.

In July, 1897, Utah's Semi-Centennial Jubilee was celebrated, the occasion being the fiftieth anniversary of the entrance of the Mormon Pioneers into the valley of the Great Salt Lake, July 24, 1847. The chief ceremonies were in Salt Lake City, July 20th to 25th, and I had the honor and pleasure of being present. I had not the privilege of being classed as one of the pioneers, for these were limited in the celebration to those who reached Utah in 1847, and I did not arrive there from the west till 1848. With the Mormon Battalion members, however, I was a Mormon pioneer, in the memorable journey across the country to the Pacific; I was also a pioneer in California, and later in Utah and surrounding places. The committee on the semi-centennial celebration, however, noted the fact that the members of the Mormon Battalion were entitled to recognition in connection with the Utah pioneer band, for the work of both was intimately associated. In pursuance of this, there was sent to me under date of July 19th, a letter containing this announcement:

"Survivors of the Mormon Battalion. the Nauvoo Legion, Captain Ballo's Band, and the Martial Band, are requested to meet at Pioneer Square on Tuesday next, July 20th, at 9 o'clock a. m., sharp, for the purpose of marching in advance of the original band of Pioneers to witness the unveiling ceremonies upon that occasion. Those who are able to walk are earnestly requested to do so, but those who are too feeble to walk will join them at the Monument.

"Hoping to see you with us at the appointed time, I am,
"Yours respectfully,
"H. F. McGARVIE,
"Assistant Director-General."

I responded to this limited notice, in common with other members of the Mormon Battalion at hand. But the summary treatment was in such strong contrast to the consideration and courtesy extended at the Midwinter Fair, and subsequently at the California Golden Jubilee, that its effect was to enhance greatly, in the minds of those who participated in the California and the Utah celebrations, the admiration for the California managers in their broad and thorough comprehension of the amenities of such historic public events. But I must add here that the Mormon Battalion members, whose journey west was over another route than that followed by the companies which came direct to the Salt Lake Valley, were fitly honored in the hearts of Utah's people as of the pioneer band in the great west.

December 1, 1897, I received the following;

"1216 HYDE STREET, SAN FRANCISCO,
"November 29, 1897.

"*Mr. James S. Brown:*

"DEAR SIR: The celebration committee of the Society of California Pioneers, expect, though as yet no formal action has been taken, to invite yourself, Mr. J. Johnston, Mr. Azariah Smith, and Mr. Henry W.B igler, who were with Marshall at Coloma on the 24th of January, 1848, to come to San Francisco as honored guests of the Society, and at its expense, to participate in the semi-centennial celebration of that eventful day, on the 24th of January next.

"If we should send such an invitation to you, will you come and be with us? Letters from Mr. Bigler and Mr. Smith lead me to hope that they will accept the invitation.

"So soon as formal action is taken, you will be informed either by myself or by the secretary of our committee.

"Yours truly,

"JOHN S. HITTELL.

"A member of the Celebration Committee."

My response was that if my health would permit, and all things were satisfactory, I should be pleased to accept such an invitation. I received another letter from Mr. Hittell, under date of December 15th, in which he said:

"*Mr. James S. Brown:*

"DEAR SIR: This evening the celebration committee of the Pioneer Society adopted a resolution to invite you to attend the Golden Jubilee of California, as an honored guest of the Society, which will provide you with first class transportation from and to your home, and take charge of your hotel bill from the 22nd of January till the 31st of January, 1898, in this city.

"Mr. B. H. and Mr. H. B. Luther, brothers, say that they were at Coloma on the 24th of January, 1848, as boys, with their father and mother. Do you know them and remember when they reached Coloma? They say their mother, who was with them there, is still living."

Under date of December 25th, Mr. Hittell also wrote me:

"*Captain James S. Brown:*

"DEAR SIR: Please let me know the amount of the railroad fare from Salt Lake to Ogden, so that we may forward the sum to you by letter; we expect to send you a ticket from Ogden to this city, including a lower berth in a sleeping car.

"We hope that you, Bigler, Smith and Johnston will all come in the same car. I have addressed a similar letter to each of the other three.

"Thanks for your letter of December 20th. I was satisfied that Gregson and the Luthers were not at the sawmill on the 24th of January, 1848.

"I suppose the best train would be the one leaving Salt Lake City at 9:10 p. m., on January 20th, arriving at San Francisco January 22nd, at 9:45 a. m. Does that suit you?"

The next communication on the subject was as follows:

"EXECUTIVE DEPARTMENT, THE SOCIETY OF CALIFORNIA
PIONEERS, No. 5, PIONEER PLACE, SAN FRANCISCO,
CALIFORNIA,

"January 7, 1898.

"*James S. Brown, Esq., Salt Lake City:*

"DEAR SIR: The Society of California Pioneers invites you to attend the Golden Jubilee Celebration of our State, and to accept the hospitality of the Society in San Francisco, from the 22nd till the 31st of January, 1898. Enclosed find a pass from the S. P. R. R. Co., for your passage from Ogden to San Francisco and return. We send you today by Wells, Fargo & Co.'s Express, fifteen dollars in coin to pay for your sleeping berth and meals on the way. We have engaged a lower berth for you on the Pullman car which leaves Ogden on the night of Thursday, the 20th instant.

"The reception committee will meet you on the Oakland boat on the morning of Saturday, the 22nd, and will wear the badge of the Society. Should you miss seeing them you will go to the Russ House, where we have engaged rooms and board for you.

"Should you not be able to come, please return the enclosed railroad pass, and notify the ticket agent at Ogden that you will not use the sleeping berth.

"Yours truly,

"J. I. SPEAR, Secretary.

"P. S.—We have arranged to have your railroad pass extended for thirty days if you wish it.   S."

Like my Mormon Battalion companions who were with me on the memorable 24th of January, 1848, I could not but feel highly gratified at the courtesy extended, and look forward with pleasure to the commemoration, under so favorable circumstances and with such marvelous progress as California had made in civilization, of the fiftieth anni-

versary of a notable event, which at the time of its occurrence, came to us in the midst of hardships, fatigue and
almost exile from home and relatives, yet was a world-
wonder in the results which followed the announcement to
the world of California's great gold discovery.

CHAPTER LXVIII.

TRIP TO CALIFORNIA—MET BY THE COMMITTEE ON RECEPTION OF
THE SOCIETY OF CALIFORNIA PIONEERS—RECEIVED WITH GREAT
CORDIALITY—HONORED GUESTS AT CALIFORNIA'S GOLDEN JUBI-
LEE—THE CELEBRATION—COURTESIES EXTENDED TO MORMON
BATTALION MEMBERS PRESENT AT THE DISCOVERY OF GOLD—
RETURN HOME—RESOLUTIONS BY SOCIETY OF CALIFORNIA PIO-
NEERS — REPORT OF RECEPTION COMMITTEE OF CALIFORNIA
GOLDEN JUBILEE—SKETCH OF MARSHALL'S SURVIVING COMPAN-
IONS—COMPLETE MY AUTOBIOGRAPHY—MY SON HOMER ACCI-
DENTALLY KILLED—THE OLD FOLKS—PUBLICATION OF LIFE OF A
PIONEER—CONCLUSION.

IN response to the invitation from the Society of California Pioneers, I left Salt Lake City on January 20,
1898, in company with Henry W. Bigler, Azariah Smith
and Wm. J. Johnston, who, like myself, were guests of the
Society. We reached Oakland, California, January 22, and
were met by Mr. John H. Jewett, president of the society,
and a committee consisting of Messrs. John S. Hittell, Almarin B. Paul, General Wm. H. Pratt, and Misses Anna P.
Green and Mary M. Green. The ladies pinned badges of
the Society of California Pioneers on the lapels of our coats.
We were received with the greatest cordiality, and were
taken to the Russ House, San Francisco, where we were
comfortably lodged, being shown special consideration by
the proprietor and his amiable wife, and from that time on
we were given the best of attention. Nothing that could be

done was too good for us, and language fails to express our high appreciation of the courtesy and kindness bestowed.

Whenever we attended any of the functions of California's Golden Jubilee Celebration, or desired to visit a place, carriages were at our service.   January 24th was the fiftieth anniversary of the discovery of gold at Sutter's mill race, and there was a magnificent pageant in celebration of the event.   We occupied the post of distinction in the procession, our carriage bearing the legend, "Companions of Marshall."   We were the only survivors of that notable occasion, fifty years before.   The place of honor was also accorded to us at the celebration ceremonies in the evening at Wood's Pavilion, and on the 27th we were at a reception in Pioneer Hall, and greeted the multitudes, old and young, anxious to see and shake hands with us; and at the Mining Fair our treatment was characterized by the same cordial and distinguished welcome.   The celebration ceremonies lasted the entire week.   When at our hotel we were besieged by reporters, and hundreds of people called to see us, and get our autographs.   Our photographs also were taken for the Society of Pioneers.

Outside of the celebration proper, there was the same magnanimous kindness.   I could not name all the citizens who extended to us marked courtesies, but feel that I must specially mention Captain John T. McKenzie of the steamer *San Rafael*, who was very attentive, also Hon. Irving Scott, manager of the great Union Iron Works, at which place we had a particularly interesting visit and entertainment.

Two of my companions started home on January 31st, and the third on February 2nd.   I stayed a few days longer, visiting my brother at Petaluma.   I also went to many other places of interest, then returned home, all expenses of my journey being provided.   A few days later I received the following:

"EXECUTIVE DEPARTMENT, THE SOCIETY OF CALIFORNIA
  PIONEERS, NO. 5, PIONEER PLACE, SAN FRANCISCO,
  CALIFORNIA,

"February 9, 1898.

"*James S. Brown, Esq,, Salt Lake City, Utah:*

"DEAR SIR: I have the honor of advising you that at
the monthly meeting of the members of the Society held at
Pioneer Hall on Monday, February 7, 1898, the following
resolutions were unanimously adopted:

" *Whereas,* The Golden Jubilee just passed marks the
second grand event as connected with the first discovery of
gold in California, and as all pioneers feel gratified at the
universal desire of the people to pay tribute to the pioneer
days, now be it

"*Resolved,* That the Society of California Pioneers ten-
ders its thanks to the press generally; to the state and city
officials; to the military as a body; to the various mining
associations; to the Native Daughters and Native Sons of
the Golden West, and to the many other organizations that
participated in making the grand pageant of January 24th
a splendid success. And be it further

"*Resolved,* That the thanks of this society are also tendered to Henry W. Bigler, James S. Brown, Wm. J. Johnston and Azariah Smith, the companions of Marshall, in
lending their presence for the Jubilee; and especially do we
appreciate the efforts and labors of the executive committee
of the Golden Jubilee, and we also return thanks to the
Southern Pacific Company for complimentary passes to the
four companions of Marshall to and from San Francisco and
Ogden, also for its liberal contribution to the Golden Jubilee
held under auspices of the society; and also to Irving
M. Scott on part of the Union Iron Works, for the invitation to the companions of Marshall and members of this
Society to visit the works, and the placing at our disposal
their tug for the trip, and further for the many courtesies

extended to all by the several officers connected with the works while there.

"J. H. JEWETT, President.

On February 20th this note came:

"1316 HYDE STREET, SAN FRANCISCO,
"February 18, 1898.

"*Mr. James S. Brown:*

"DEAR SIR: Your letter of the 16th inst, with the news that you had arrived safely at home, has given me pleasure. I felt some responsibility for my part in bringing four old men so far away from home, but now that I know all have arrived in good health at Salt Lake, I congratulate myself that events have turned out so favorably. I have had no letter from Mr. Bigler or Mr. Smith, but they will write to me.

"I spoke promptly to Mr. Spear, the secretary, about sending fifteen dollars to pay for the expenses of your return trip, and I understood him to promise that the money would be transmitted to you by check.

"The Pioneer Society will long preserve a pleasant recollection of the participation of the four companions of Marshall in our Jubilee celebration, and personally I shall always be glad to hear of their welfare.

"Yours truly,
"JOHN S. HITTELL."

Here is the closing communication in relation to my latest visit to California and the occasion which caused it:

"SAN FRANCISCO, March 9, 1898.

"*Mr. James S. Brown, Salt Lake City:*

"DEAR SIR: Enclosed please find a copy of the report of the reception committee of the Golden Jubilee:

"*To John H. Jewett, President of the California Pioneers:*

"The reception committee appointed by the Society

to receive its guests attending the celebration of the Golden Jubilee on the 24th of January last, begs leave to report that its task has been completed.

"On the morning of January 22nd all the members of the committee received and welcomed the four companions of Marshall on the overland train at Oakland, and escorted them to the Russ House, where, under the direction of President John H. Jewett, they were provided with comfortable accommodations.

"These four men, the only survivors of those who were with Marshall at Coloma when he discovered gold there on Monday, the 24th of January, 1848, are:

"1. Henry W. Bigler, born in Harrison County, West Virginia, August 28th, 1815, who in his diary made the only written record of the gold discovery on the day of its occurrence. He is now a resident of St. George, Utah.

"2. Azariah Smith, born at Boylston, New York, on the 1st of August, 1828, who, on the first Sunday after the discovery, wrote in his diary that gold had been found in the preceding week.

"3. James S. Brown, born in Davison County, North Carolina, on the 4th of July, 1828, who recollects that on the evening of January 24th, 1848, H. W. Bigler said he would write in his diary that something like gold had been discovered, as it might be important some day. He resides in Salt Lake City.

"4. Wm. J. Johnston, born near New Baltimore, Ohio, on the 21st of August, 1824, and now resides in Ramah, New Mexico.

"These four men are all clear in mind, and for their years, strong and active in body.

"In the procession on the 24th they occupied a carriage marked 'Companions of Marshall.' On the evening of that day, they were entertained in our hall with special honor, and two days later they held a reception in the same place.

Various members of our Society, and especially Captain McKenzie, showed them much attention. They were guests of honor at the Mining Fair on the opening evening. Hon. Irving M. Scott, manager of the Union Iron Works, gave them a special entertainment at his shipyard; and other citizens contributed to make their stay in our city pleasant. The whole Jubilee week was a round of festivity for them.

"Messrs. Bigler and Smith were escorted to their returning train at Oakland on the 31st of January, Mr. Johnston two days later, and Mr. Brown in the next succeeding week. They all reached their homes safely, and all have written to members of the committee acknowledging the attention and honor shown to them by the Society of California Pioneers.

"As they are the only persons now living who saw gold in the days of its discovery, their attendance at our semi-centennial celebration connected our Jubilee in a highly interesting manner with the great event which it commemorated. We may add that personal acquaintance with these venerable men has been a source of pleasure to all members of this committee, as well as to many other Pioneers.

"Respectfully submitted,

"JOHN S. HITTELL, Chairman.
"ALMARIN B. PAUL,
"W. H. PRATT."

Upon my return home, I again gave attention to this autobiography, which proved no light task, as my health has been far from good.

On the 14th of December, 1899, a keen sorrow came to myself and family. My son Homer, in his twenty-sixth year, died on that date, as a result of injuries received at a cave-in at the Silver King mine, Park City, Utah, three weeks before. When war broke out between Spain and the United States in 1898, he enlisted in response to President McKinley's call for volunteers, and became a member of Troop C, Utah Volunteer Cavalry. After his return from California, where the cavalry was sent, he was married, the event occurring two months before the accident which cost him his life. On December 19, he was buried in Salt Lake City, the funeral services being held at. the Seventeenth Ward assembly rooms.

In the summer of 1898, I was added to the list of Utah's Old Folks, attending the excursion to Lagoon, Davis County, in July, 1898, to Geneva, Utah County, in July, 1899, and again at Lagoon on July 6, 1900. The Old Folks include all people over seventy years of age, independent of creed, race or color; these are accorded receptions, excursions, and similar happy courtesies, as marks of honor and respect to the aged. The central committee having this highly appreciated undertaking in charge has for its chairman the Presiding Bishop of the Church of Jesus Christ of Latter-day Saints.

By the close of 1899, I had completed the preparation of my life's history for publication in a neat volume, and soon thereafter arranged for the printing, which at this date, July, 1900, is accomplished. Now that I have reached the seventy-second annual milestone of my life, I realize that the period for especially notable or thrilling events in my mortal career is past; and in the publication of my autobiography, I sincerely trust that this humble final extended labor on my part will achieve the principle aim of its performance, that of doing good to those who live after me, in the witness its record bears of the mercy, power, and goodness of God, and the latter-day progress of His great and loving design for the blessing and salvation of His children. With this attairment, the influence of the record, LIFE OF A PIONEER, will be in accord with the sincere desire and earnest effort of my soul throughout life.